Sovereignty in Ruins

A POLITICS OF CRISIS

George Edmondson and Klaus Mladek, editors

DUKE UNIVERSITY PRESS *Durham and London* 2017

Typeset in Carter + Cone Galliard
by Copperline

Library of Congress Cataloging-in-
Publication Data
Names: Edmondson, George, [date] editor. |
Mladek, Klaus, editor.
Title: Sovereignty in ruins : a politics of crisis /
George Edmondson and Klaus Mladek, editors.
Description: Durham : Duke University Press,
2017. | Includes bibliographical references and
index.
Identifiers:
LCCN 2016041935 (print)
LCCN 2016043713 (ebook)
ISBN 9780822363026 (hardcover : alk. paper)
ISBN 9780822363170 (pbk. : alk. paper)
ISBN 9780822373391 (e-book)
Subjects: LCSH: Sovereignty. | World politics. |
Crisis management in government. | Biopolitics.
Classification: LCC JC327.S64445 2017 (print) |
LCC JC327 (ebook) | DDC 620.1/5—dc23
LC record available at https://lccn.loc.gov
/2016041935

Chapter 2, "Left and Right: Why They Still
Make Sense," by Carlo Galli, originally published in Italian as *Perché ancora destra e sinister*
(2013), is copyright Gius. Laterza & Figli and
republished with permission.

Cover art: Anselm Kiefer, *Pietà*, 2007.
Acrylic, oil, shellac, and dried branches in
metal frame under glass. 190 × 280 × 12 cm.
© Anselm Kiefer. Courtesy Gagosian.

CONTENTS

ACKNOWLEDGMENTS

A collection as wide-ranging as this one relies on the help and encouragement of many friends and colleagues. It gives us great pleasure to acknowledge those parties here and to thank them publicly for their support.

First and foremost, we would like to acknowledge the Leslie Center for the Humanities at Dartmouth College for funding Sovereignty, Security, and the State of Exception, the humanities institute that made this collection possible. In particular, we would like to thank Jonathan Crewe, the director of the center who approved the institute; Adrian Randolph, the director who facilitated it; and Isabel Weatherdon, the administrator who kept the whole thing on track.

A special thanks goes to the participants of the institute, who helped develop most of the ideas found in these pages. For their hard work and even harder thinking, we first acknowledge our colleagues from Dartmouth College: Amy Allen, Rebecca Biron, Colleen Boggs, Michelle Clarke, Mary K. Coffey, Jennifer Fluri, Andrew McCann, Klaus Milich, Donald Pease, and Dale Turner. For their extraordinary generosity and dedication to the project, we next thank the institute's external fellows: Kathleen Biddick, Adam Sitze, Jacqueline Stevens, and Carsten Strathausen. We owe a special debt of gratitude to Adam Sitze, who deserves credit as nothing less than our shadow coeditor. Adam gave us invaluable comments along the way, cotranslated Esposito's interview from the Italian, and secured the talents of Zakiya Hanafi, who translated Carlo Galli's essay so beautifully. Unquestionably, the countless conversations we held with Eric Santner, the institute's senior fellow, were, like the seminars he led, enormously important. Their formative influence on us continues to this day. We are grateful, finally, to the invited speakers and seminar leaders for the institute: Michael

Hardt, Albrecht Koschorke, Jörn Münkner, Andrew Norris, Martin Puchner, Elaine Scarry, Rei Terada, and Burkhardt Wolf.

We would like to acknowledge the two anonymous readers for Duke University Press, whose very helpful comments improved the manuscript in ways both great and small. Thanks are due as well to Liz Smith and Sandra Korn, of the press's editorial staff, and to Karen M. Fisher, who copyedited the manuscript with the keenest of eyes. Words can hardly express our gratitude to Courtney Berger, our editor, for her patience, her encouragement, and her guidance. We could not have asked for better ground control.

Finally, in good times and bad, we could always count on the unfaltering support of Hazel-Dawn Dumpert and Kristin O'Rourke.

Sovereignty Crises

George Edmondson and Klaus Mladek

We are fortunate to find ourselves living in interesting times: times not simply of change or transition but of universal crisis.[1] History is full of crises, of course. Yet compared to its predecessors, today's crisis feels more permanent and enveloping because it lacks the one certainty they shared: that it will, for better or worse, have an end. When the term *crisis* acquired its contemporary meaning (as a time of social upheaval and epochal transformation) in the late eighteenth century, "the only unknown quantity" was "when and how" the crisis in question would be resolved, and by what means.[2] Today, our ubiquitous crisis consciousness appears to have cast such assurance in doubt. Alain Badiou can usually be counted on to defend robust revolutionary solutions, yet even he contends that the promise of a remedy—an alternative political vision, a new praxis, or a compelling symbolic fiction—"is in a state of total crisis."[3] (Which is exactly why the search for such a fiction remains an urgent political project, as we argue here.) Meanwhile, as if confirming Arendt's observation that there is "no longer any 'uncivilized' spot on earth" and that "we have really started to live in One World," the symptoms of crisis have spread boundlessly to become, in a manner very different from what Carl Schmitt envisioned, the new *nomos* of the earth.[4] How far does crisis extend? Far enough that even the traditional concept of *krísis*, with its spatiotemporal limits and inherent faith in resolution, has itself been thrown into a crisis powerful enough to affect the category of the political as such: its ordering function, its concept of historical and organizing space, even, as the surging critical interest in bio- and zoopolitics attests, Aristotle's definition of the human as the only political animal. More than two millennia on, the very origins of the political are so thoroughly in crisis that the margins of the *apolis*, stalked by the beast and the god, have once again come into view.

To its credit, contemporary political theory has succumbed to neither resignation nor quietism in the face of crisis. On the contrary, a generation of scholars is right now mulling over an array of new political thoughts and forms of life—the outgrowth of a renewed inquiry into the origin and genealogy of political ideas and practices that might yet prove capable of reorienting our future, even in spite of their troubled histories.[5] Yet despite this enormous effort, nothing major seems to have changed in the global political order. The Western democracies have not been swept by a revolutionary tidal wave, while the riots and revolutions of the non-Western world are local and easily contained. Nor do we find many reasons for optimism. In a time of political stalemate and unfettered global capitalism—a time when even the smallest advances in legislation seem impossible and complicit parliamentary systems are dominated by often indistinguishable parties that join together to mouth the vacuous abstractions of an outmoded political vocabulary—there may be many new words and ideas, but there is little material change. Instead, a crisis mode, crouched and paralyzing, affects nearly every field in nearly every segment of life.

That is where the essays gathered together here come in. There was once a time, let us recall, when the sphere of crisis was "conceptually fused" with that of critique.[6] Etymologically, both terms derive from the Greek word κρίσις, or *krísis*, meaning to differentiate, to judge, to select, to decide, to separate; both capture the sense that a situation is at a crucial turning point—that a critical diagnosis needs to be made, a judgment rendered, and a course of action charted. What we now think of as the sharp distinction between crisis as objective event and critique as subjective engagement—between crisis as the concept of an occurrence and critique as an ad hoc practice, part intellectual, part moral, part material-interventionist—doesn't appear until the eighteenth century, when it emerges as a corollary to the development of our modern concepts of history and the subject. But in fact the two concepts had begun to separate long before then, with the result that, over time, krísis came to denote little more than administrative and legal judgments made in the interests of governmental crisis management: a decisionist consciousness focused on delimiting a more encompassing crisis.

This incremental fusion of crisis with the practical dimension of governing would not go unchallenged, however. In the eighteenth century there begins to grow a sense, imperceptible even to some of the radical thinkers who advance it, that the only practice capable of counteracting the drift toward managerial krísis, with its merely restorative forms of critique, was the neglected philological-philosophical form of critique, now given a new force by the epoch's transformative-revolutionary crisis. Rooted in the philological art of judging texts practiced by the *criticus* or *grammaticus*, this subjective dimension of crisis had long stayed in the shadows, a victim of its own potentiality. For even when not overtly political, both philology and philosophy assured the perpetual recurrence of crisis, in the sense that one form of crisis, critical judgment, held the potential to throw another form of crisis, the decision making called for by governing, into a third form of crisis, the turmoil brought about by potentially infinite division. Where the medical, theological, and legal forms of critique sought to rejuvenate an order in crisis by reforming it, improving it, and consolidating it, this other mode of self-encountering—or, better, enfolding—critique fell back upon itself in the furor of its own power: a critique forever in crisis. The practice of critique, to round it off to a formula, made it possible to arrest decisionist krísis through the divisive act of piling up crises.

To the extent that they share anything at all, the essays assembled here extend that practice of enfolding critique by violently forcing critique back into crisis, restoring both terms to their common etymology precisely by continuing the paradoxical tradition, begun in the eighteenth century, of dividing critique from crisis just enough to allow critique to put all forms of krísis, including its own, into permanent crisis. Simply stated, the essays in this collection model the different ways that critique might reinject crisis, understood as a time of tumult and upheaval brought about by a potentially infinite partitioning, into krísis, understood as a species of determinate decision and judgment. For only so violent a gesture is enough to separate—to put into crisis—the conjunction between the juridical dimension of crisis, with its tendency to couch lawmaking violence as managerial decision making, and the theological dimension, with its faith that all time is a crisis heading toward a resolution, a Last Judgment. In this regard the essays are especially timely, insofar as they remind us that the current time of transition in which we live is not an *eschaton*, not some sort of providential revelation. To believe as much would be to fall back into judgment time, as if today were only an interval in linear time, an interregnum. Our present moment is something else entirely. More than a simple transition from one mode of governing to another, ours is a time of nonsimultaneity. To actualize crisis is thus to extract our time—not the end of time toward which we march, but the time of the end, our intensely historical time, charged with an additional time that is genuine crisis time: a time out of joint, a noncoincidence with representations of time. All time—historical, salvific, evolutionary—is tinged with a more fundamental form of crisis, one that expresses how thoroughly humankind is out of sync with the horizon of a last judgment and world-historical *chronos*. And it is our crisis judgment, achieved through our political constructions, that conjures that additional crisis-time. As Hamlet says to Horatio, "It will be short. The interim's mine" (act 5, scene 2, line 78). Interim time partitions the time of crisis maintained by the allegiance between the juridical and the political.[7]

To carry out the work of that partitioning, our contributors turn to a variety of conceptual wedges: the impolitical; the impersonal; the category of flesh; the worst; an overturning of the idea of origin; a critique of ancient nomos; a pluralized subject; a theatrical dispersion of sovereignty; the rebirth of a different history. Countering the impulse to reduce politics to modes of management and activism, *Sovereignty in Ruins* insists on the necessity of a theoretical political act prior to what have traditionally been regarded as the practical ends of politics: a voiding in the midst of both nomos and politics in order to alter the very coordinates and vocabularies through which political action might take place.

The volume is divided into three parts, beginning with our own long essay, "Natural History: Toward a Politics of Crisis." Legible both as a freestanding meditation and as a considered response to the questions opened up by its ten companion chapters, this first essay constellates a group of thinkers—Kant, Marx, Foucault, Adorno, Kafka, and Paolo Virno—in order to theorize the central role that natural history plays, both as master category and driving force, in the development of a politics of crisis. For us, natural history is more than, or not only, the mutually negating dialectic it was for Adorno. Natural history indicates the movements of a *physionomos* detectable, for example, in the eternal perishing of groundlessness, in Kant's indestructible and unforgettable will to revolution, in the ungovernable form-of-life enacted by Foucault's "critical ontology of ourselves," in the laws of fermentation that, according to Marx, govern even the capitalist and his products, and in the enigmatic comings and goings of the creature Odradek and the fanatical accountings of the bureaucrat-god Poseidon.

The volume's second part, "Italian Affirmations," opens with an English translation of a short book from 2010 by the Italian historian of political thought Carlo Galli, *Left and Right: Why They Still Make Sense*. In his forceful intervention into contemporary politics, Galli explains that the designations *left* and *right* must be preserved, as they are names for different relations to the political origin. Whereas Noberto Bobbio's 1994 book *Left and Right: Signification of a Political Distinction* locates the source of the left-right indistinction in the crisis of parliamentary democracy after the collapse of communism, Galli detects a much deeper crisis. Drawing on Schmitt's genealogy of modern politics, Galli argues that the real source of the left-right distinction is the incomplete and accidental manner in which modern politics inherits the very premodern political forms it presumes to overturn and reject. Yet even though contemporary politics might remain bound up with an ambiguous political heritage, it nonetheless inhabits institutional architectures and political terminologies that point to a new chain of active subjectivities and conflictual political spaces outside state politics, ones in which the traditional distinctions begin to get crowded out by emerging questions of ecology, biopolitical potentialities, and new rebellious collectives.

Pitched somewhere between essay and conversation, the section's next piece, "Politics in the Present," records an exchange in which the voice of the Italian philosopher Roberto Esposito merges with that of his interlocutor, Roberto Ciccarelli, to create a "third person." The two figures, at once diverging and blending, present a succinct yet comprehensive account of many of the concepts, such as biopolitics, the impersonal, and the impolitical, that have begun to pervade our political terminology and that inform many of the essays assembled here. The result is more than just a précis of Esposito's work to date, however (although it is that). It is also an experiment in a common search for, and presentation of, the crisis in our theological, philosophical, and juridical tradition that will activate the philosophy of immanence and affirmative biopolitics lying dormant there, patiently awaiting its vindication in contemporary thought. At a time when political theory seeks an alternative to the juridical concept of the person that for too long sustained a practice of subordination and exclusion, it is no accident that Esposito's works should be increasingly studied in the Anglophone academy and his philosophy of immunity and life more widely received.

In his wide-ranging essay "*Cujusdam nigri & scabiosi Brasiliani*: Rancière and Derrida," Alberto Moreiras first addresses a blind spot in Hardt and Negri's concept of the multitude and in Marx's view of history and class struggle: the almost inextricable knot between war and production that underlies the question of revolution as well as much of contemporary leftist politics. Are revolutionary movements still part of what Foucault identified as the modern "ontology of war," making them a result of antagonisms inherent in the development of productive forces in the biopolitical economy of capitalism, or can we detect in them the silhouettes of an alternative political theory that could end politics as war—and as production and self-production? According to Moreiras, Rancière's critique of Derrida's democracy to come, that it advocates a messianic ethics at the expense of political practice and democratic eruption, overlooks (like much of post-Althusserian or neocommunist polemics against Derrida) the degree to which a politics of deconstruction has already destroyed pious visions of history and progress. Moreiras's essay arrives at a defense of Derrida's democratic politics and his ethics of hospitality, with its insistence on the perilous conflicts and potentials that arise with the entrance of the visitor, the friend, or the stranger.

Rounding off the section, Rei Terada's "Pasolini's Acceptance" confronts us with an almost unbearable thought: that politics as such, let alone leftist political activism and revolutionary transformation, is so thoroughly futile and such a farce that a certain posture of acceptance is all that is left to us. Analyzing Pasolini's film *Salò* alongside his essay "Repudiation" allows Terada to track the bewildering intensity of the demand made, and the incendiary effect created, when a deeply political thinker and artist begins to think the unthinkable and accept the unacceptable: that politics has irrevocably ceased to exist and what remains is nothing but the convergence of freedom and slavery, autonomy and control. Terada shows that Pasolini's complete repudiation of the nullity of Italian politics, the vacuity of its political parties, and the disappearance of the people in homogenized capitalist society is neither one more postpolitical reflection on the end of politics nor another search for alternative or impolitical areas of political struggle. In Terada's account, Pasolini's adaptation to the given constitutes a new relation to the damaged world, one carried out through a strangely provocative power of hostility toward the status quo. Pasolini's cinematic cruelty, like his unsparingly critical essay, offers Terada a point of departure for a thought of the worst that dwells outside politics after its utter catastrophe.

"The Endgames of Sovereignty," the volume's third part, revolves around certain lacunae in political philosophy that continue to obsess political thought even as they offer alternatives to its current configuration. Adam Sitze's "Reopening the Plato Question" goes right to the heart of the matter by revisiting political philosophy itself, that unprecedented genre of thought inaugurated by Plato's *Laws* under the auspices of that most imperial of institutions, the colony. Sitze's essay focuses on the conceptual aftershocks stemming from book 3 of *Laws*, where Clinias reveals to his interlocutors that he has been commissioned to settle a new colony. As Sitze shows, the philosophical activity of inventing a new political order—as if such a thing could be instituted entirely from scratch, as if philosophical lawgiving and wisdom could forgo the memory of past civil strife and the already existing arrangement of *oikos*—will silently shape the course of exploration in the *Laws* and in much of colonialist thought after Plato. Philosophical nomos suddenly acquires a paradigmatic and, if the accusations Badiou levels at the lawgiving apparatuses of late Plato are correct, disastrous name in the emerging discourse of political philosophy, a name born from the immunitarian logic of colonial thinking: to solve the war within the home by constructing the space of a home away from home. The essay focuses on two readings of the *Laws*, Strauss's and Badiou's, that appear to be pitted against one another but that are in fact, as Sitze shows, mutually implicated in a tradition where the relation between law and philosophy is understood as a nonrelation, "an unbridgeable distance between philosophy's open question ('what is?') and law's definitive declaration ('what is')."

Eric L. Santner's "The Royal Remains: The People's Two Bodies and the Endgames of Sovereignty" identifies one possible name for the crisis described in this introduction: flesh. Expanding upon Kantorowicz's study of political theology by tracing the dispersal of sovereignty in postmedieval Europe from the body of the king to the flesh of the people, Santner shows how the flesh that was once contained by sovereign krísis now floods the modern scene, overwhelming and deranging it. This, Santner concludes, constitutes the basic dilemma of our present moment: having rid ourselves of sovereignty's representational regime, we can no longer figure out what to do with the flesh bequeathed to us by the demise of krísis, leaving us with a crisis (an "investiture crisis," as Santner puts it) that the so-called sciences of immanence are no longer capable of managing.

Judith Butler's essay, "Arendt: Thinking Cohabitation and the Dispersion of Sovereignty," takes up Arendt's account of the Eichmann trial in order to derive, out of the text's rhetorical and theatrical dimensions, an imperative regarding the rights of cohabitation. In a dramatic turn of her court report, Arendt invents a scene in which she assumes the role of a judge to directly confront Eichmann in the second person with her own explanation for why he deserves to die. Arendt accuses Eichmann of having abrogated a fundamental principle of human rights that, to this day, no sovereign state has been able to articulate: no one has the right to choose with whom to cohabit the earth. Butler reads this right in terms of the right, grounded neither in natural nor in positive law, that Arendt elaborates in *The Origins of Totalitar-*

ianism: the "right to have rights." Arendt asserts this distinctly social right on the presupposition of a plural subject able to put pressure, through its inherent performative power, on the status of the sovereign exception. Could we even go so far as to rethink the performative more fundamentally, as a dispersion of sovereignty? The cohabitation on earth, and the internal company we keep, are for Butler the two forms of socializing plurality through which Arendt promotes a form of federalist democracy able to guide us beyond the sovereign exception as it is conceived in Schmitt and Agamben.

Andrew Norris begins "Beyond the State of Exception" with a critique of the tendency, common to Schmitt and Agamben (and their followers), to reduce the phenomenon of sovereignty to a largely unhistorical structural category. Opposing itself to the recent critical trend toward understanding sovereignty as the inevitable logical effect of conceptual conflict, Norris's essay advocates for a Hegelian analysis of the concrete universals and actual institutions that generate the moment of sovereign decision. Norris's reading of Hegel's *Philosophy of Right* not only explicates the universalizing ethical life of a modern society; it goes further by arguing that only a discussion of subjectivity, irony, and evil allows us to deduce the monarch's exceptional executive powers from Hegel's thought. Hegel deserves credit, Norris argues, for being the first to fully grasp the political potential of Socrates's destructive irony for our times. In a manner very different from the abstract self-determination of romantic irony, Socrates asserts his daemonic subjectivity as a substantive universality in excess of the ethical life of the Greek polis and as a true political art capable of radicalizing the truth of a Sophist project still pressing today: how to create discursive communities and other commons in an atheistic spiritual universe wherein man is the measure. By shifting back and forth between ancient Greece, nineteenth-century Prussia, and contemporary American politics, Norris's study mobilizes Socrates and Hegel as legal, political, and ethical resources for a dialectical alternative to the decisionist and logical concept of sovereignty.

Cary Wolfe's essay, "Humans and (Other) Animals in a Biopolitical Frame," works dialectically to put into crisis the central terms of postsovereignty: *subject, life, living, norm, value, equivalence*. Sifting through the work of Foucault, Esposito, Derrida, Levi Bryant, and Martin Hägglund in search of a nonexclusionary, nonimmunitarian *who* (neither human nor nonhuman) to whom things might matter, Wolfe ends by making a case for a paradoxically responsible decisionism, a decisionism that endlessly limits itself by closing off any recourse to a perspective outside the frame of biopolitics. By doing away with immunity and its reciprocal trappings, Wolfe suggests, we could arrive at an affirmative, and thus far more radical, vision of biopolitics and community, one predicated not on a strict economy of equilibrium but on an uneconomical apportionment of valuation, perspective, and responsibility.

Finally, Carsten Strathausen offers us, in "Thing-Politics and Science," one possible way of practicing a politics of crisis. Ranging widely (the essay touches upon epistemology, the continuing importance of the university as a privileged site of critical engagement, the limitations of Deleuzean singularity, the siren song of vitalism, and the challenges that science poses to the so-called new materialism), Strathausen makes good his point that concepts, too, are objects—and not just objects but objects in relation, objects in conflict. That point is essential, Strathausen argues, for counteracting the incoherence generated, in the first place, by thing-politics' overemphasis on the "cooperative potential of concepts" and, in the second, by its reduction of humans to things. Not only are humans irreducible to things, Strathausen concludes; we remain, as we were for the scientific materialism of the (old) Marxism, the agents of history—that is, the agents of crisis.

One premise of this collection is that a crisis has seized the inherited terms of politics, terms like *sovereignty*, *state*, *liberty*, *party system*, *territory*, and *national community*, to name but a few. That should not be taken to mean, however, that we endorse the view that we live in an age only of confusion, accelerated frenzy, and dread.[8] Our belief is that we live in an age of confusion, accelerated frenzy, and dread that is at the same time an age of delight. Admittedly, it is easy to be awed and dumbstruck by one's own feeling of impotence. But dread, submitting as it does to the confusion supposedly engendered by mobility and flux, only perpetuates the contemporary assumption of an existential struggle for scarce resources and places.[9] Meanwhile, thought incessantly moves, not only to think something new, but to think "the same things differently."[10] Thought itself—and what should a critic do but think and write?—is an agent of crisis, bringing with it both the small shifts and large ruptures that have begun to manifest (or, in some cases, reassert) themselves today, whether in the form of riots, as Badiou holds, or in more taciturn modes of withdrawal.[11] Crisis ought not to be misconstrued as an opportunity for innovation or as the ecstatic vision of an eschatological transition time. Nor should crisis be reduced to an essentially capitalist and bourgeois idea, an obstacle we must traverse in order to realize "the autonomy of biopolitical production" proper to the multitude.[12] To fully assume the consequences of crisis—to wield its positive modes of destruction—will require more than viewing it merely as a setback in progressive development or as a symptom of the impending collapse of so-called disaster capitalism. The "logic of crisis," as Paolo Virno has argued, both emerges from and affects the crisis of the underlying grammar that sustains the ineluctable background of our customary political thought and life.[13] That descriptive logic of crisis, designed to explore how moments of crisis dissolve the otherwise unexamined ties between what are habitually seen as facts of life and the grammar of norms, can help prepare the thinking of an affirmative mode of crisis, or what could be called a politics of crisis. In such a politics, crisis would be understood not simply as a perilous situation to be overcome but as the unleashing of a commonizing energy to be used. This understanding might then allow us to think the contemporary manifestation of the political with reference to the internal, implicit crisis from which it continues to emerge and whose changing grammar the essays collected in this volume set out, in the interest of enacting the politics of crisis inherent in critique, to explicate.

For just as Nietzsche feared that "we are not getting rid of God because we still believe in grammar," we cannot rid our politics of figures of domination and sovereignty if we continue to believe in a grammar that has sustained our obsession with them.[14] A situation of crisis irrevocably returns us to the fundamental questions and terms themselves: to their grammatical organization, the instances of their enunciation, the origins and scenes in which they emerge, the responses and judgments they compel. In short, crisis returns us to critique.[15] The very form of crisis demands the patient labor of a critique bereft of routine answers, recipes, robust affects, and actions — a critique, in short, mindful of the origin and genealogy it shares with crisis. There are precedents for this: Badiou reminding us of the force of declaration and appearance, Deleuze and Esposito challenging us to invent political terms worthy of the event, Agamben emphasizing the "poetic moment" in the terminology of every political thought. If Agamben is right that behind the "irrevocable exodus from any sovereignty" lies an accord between a power of speech or Marx's "general intellect" and political life—if indeed there can be found a "form-of-life" that does not sever *physis* and *bios* from nomos and *logos*[16]—then it is to be hoped that such acts of naming and thinking will force new practices and living contexts to emerge (and vice versa) until we reach the moment when a form of life converges with experience and the power of thought. Collectively making up a political poetry of thought, these thought acts hold the potential to move us beyond the false alternative between thought and action toward something truly novel: an active theoretical practice in which the power of speech and the expressiveness of the living and the dead join forces to seize the surrounding contexts devised to immunize against them.

At any rate, they bring us to the impetus for this collection. Critique and the sovereign function share a long and intimate history together, one born from their common root in crisis. The sovereign function has emerged repeatedly from crisis in order to quell crisis, including the crisis of the sovereign's own precarious nature as mortal creature. When Bodin and Hobbes ushered the modern sovereign onto the political stage in the sixteenth and seventeenth centuries, it was as a political crisis manager in times of civil war. But that rootedness in crisis also meant that the sovereign became answerable to critique, which is itself intimately linked to the diagnosis and management of crisis. Given their shared history, it is entirely fitting that critique and the sovereign function in its various guises (as state of exception, empire, the master's discourse, and so on) should also share a profound irony. Both have come to be regarded as, at best, vanishing forces and, at worst, obstacles still to be overcome; and yet both have been revived, even reanimated, by the efforts made to banish them once and for all.[17] The nature of this ironic resuscitation has added another twist to Foucault's famous pronouncement that "in political thought and analysis, we still have not cut off the head of the king."[18] Strictly speaking, Foucault meant by this that we continue to live under the sway of the repressive hypothesis and the idea of negative liberties, and a generation of theorists took up that line of interpretation by eschewing the sovereign and turning their critical attentions instead to the analysis of biopolitical or governmental power and disciplinary regimes. It is no longer enough to say, however, that our clamoring for liberty is itself an implicit recognition of the king's *caput*. For the fact remains that the dread and pleasure once associated with the sovereign have not just been transferred to governmentality; they have also been perfected there. Our continuous attempts to conjure ever more sinister and productive formations of power—the disciplinary, the biopolitical, the teletechnic, the technoscientific, the economic societies, or what Deleuze calls the "societies of control"—what are these if not an unmistakable index for how much we mourn the corpse of the traditional form of politics? It is as though we were in need of an even more dreadful and refined power, one that would finally remedy the insufficiencies of a crisis-ridden sovereign and fill the gap of his vacated throne (a frightening vision indeed if thought to its radical end: the throne itself missing from the place of lack) so that we might reconfirm our pleasure narrative of tragic struggle, failure, and overcoming. It is as though we wanted nothing more than to believe that we can still resist, subvert, strike blows, or invent counter-*dispositifs* as a form of crossed obedience or loyal disobedience to a superior force.

So let us propose another way of interpreting our failure to cut off the head of the king: rather than assuming that we have moved into a post-Westphalian age ushered in by the demise of the sovereign, let us recognize, as much of contemporary Italian philosophy has done, that the king, empire, and sovereign powers are all alive and well even in and as crisis—that politics remains sovereign so long as we remain enthralled by a repetition compulsion compelling us to redeem crisis. From its inception, politics has assumed different permutations of the sovereign function, from the point of command above the social field to widely dispersed apparatus, from premodern sovereignty to contemporary governmentality.[19] If it is not so easy, then, to throw off the sovereign function, it is precisely because the sovereign, like political economy, is infinitely protean; each one can quickly assume the guise of the other. There is a sovereignty effect at work in the economy, just as there is an administrative organization and providential, eschatological direction—an *oikonomia*—inherent in the sovereign function. To interrogate the one does not then mean evading the other. On the contrary, we are tempted to view the dispositif of sovereignty itself as a sovereign apparatus, one might even say the apparatus of apparatuses (the exceptional apparatus and the apparatus of exception)—that is, as the first, primordial, and generalized form of what Foucault circumscribed with the term *dispositif*.[20] Foucault is ordinarily hailed as the chief thinker of the transitions of power formations, the visionary critic of networks of social micropractices. Yet he early on detected the ways in which sovereignty has the capacity to morph, to adapt itself to any new political economy by appropriating emerging diagrams (the disciplinary, the biopolitical, political economy in general) and overcoding them once again with its concrete strategic demands and mechanisms. Not only is "the problem of sovereignty . . . more acute than ever," according to Foucault. The problem of sovereignty is "never posed with greater force" than once its premodern forms begin to wane: once it needs fresh general principles to function alongside the idea of the social contract and the general will, once it needs more room to maneuver within and above the "art of government."[21]

The enormous staying power of sovereignty is due, then, not simply to the fact that it has proved impossible to root out. It is due to the fact that sovereignty is continuously returning.[22] Sovereignty might well be regarded, in fact, as the figure of return, the creature of our repetition compulsion: "The king is dead, long live the king! The king is dead, long live the king!"[23] Sovereignty, invented as a secularized successor to divine representation, to its oikonomia and providence, at once compensates for the breakdown of those same medieval categories and also perpetuates them, through a tropological exportation, in modern contexts.[24] As sovereignty's seriality—that long living in continuous dying—suggests, however, there remains one more reason why we have yet to cut off the head of the king: because it is more consoling to maintain the illusion that we can leave behind an interrogation of sovereignty effects than to confront the possibility that the sovereign function might be constitutively ruined—that it might have always existed in a state of continuous perishing. The attraction of postsovereignty is that it means not having to face up to the ruination, the perpetual downfall, of the sovereign function. Following the example of Dario Gentili's anthology *La crisi del politico*, which assembles the most interesting contributions published between 1981 and 1986 in the journal *Il Centauro*, one aim of this collection is to reinvigorate the nexus of crisis and critique by inserting strife, continuous perishing, and a revolutionary reordering into the different permutations assumed by the sovereign function. This might take the form of intervening in the current moment of transition, when the stars seem to have aligned around a new manifestation of empire and sovereignty—of exposing that transition to the crisis out of which it emerged and that it is called upon to manage and heal. The goal here would be to deploy genuine crisis in order to thwart any smooth passage toward a new configuration of the triangle of governmentality, sovereignty, and discipline that, in Foucault's analysis, constitutes contemporary political economy. But the critic might also return to other moments of transition within sovereignty in order to disrupt them after the fact, thereby drawing out the permanence of crisis and the force of negation. Now, though, that permanence and force would constitute a politics of crisis and not simply a descriptive logic of crisis. The thought acts that make up *Sovereignty in Ruins* are intended, in part, to help facilitate that transition from descriptive logic to forceful politics, from an understanding of crisis to its affirmation.

Our interest in permanent crisis was inspired in part by Lacan's reaction to the events of May 1968. In a self-interview included in *Seminar XVII: The Other Side of Psychoanalysis*, Lacan breaks down his students' revolutionary outburst to a basic fallacy: any revolutionary aspiration rooted in or instigated by experience cannot break free from experience and is therefore destined to end in a master—that is to say, in an embodiment, a practitioner and beneficiary, of experience. If your aspirations are directed toward a master, Lacan warns, you will get one.[25] Ordinarily, this moment in *Seminar XVII* is invoked to emphasize the passage from S_1 to S_2, the master's discourse to the university discourse. But it might more accurately be read as a critique, not simply of activism or the university, but of the superficial way in which they are pitted against one another, as if they were not already mutually implicated. What matters in the passage is not the transition from S_1 to S_2; what matters is the transformation of the form of knowledge manifested in the university—the university you don't leave when you hit the street in protest. If it is structures that walk the streets, not people, then the aim must be to revolutionize those structures. Activists get so agitated by the enjoyment exhibited by S_1/S_2 that they in turn risk exhibiting the form of enjoyment, the form of a, necessary for their own way of suturing the master with knowledge. They risk becoming a spectacle of enjoyment, when what they need to be doing is making an exodus from the scene. In this, Lacan agrees with Foucault and Derrida (and Agamben, for that matter) that the traditional view of revolution, with its grand narratives and its particular modes of seizing power, must be dismantled in order to remain faithful to the idea of the revolution. What is needed is a revolution, be it philosophical, political, or poetic, of the revolution. What is needed, in short, is something along the lines of what Marx calls, against the drunken spectacle of the bourgeois revolution, the proletarian revolution: something critical, repetitious, self-encountering, accumulative until it reaches the point of no return: a true crisis.[26]

How is such an idea of revolution to be accomplished? It cannot be directed at the sovereign, the target of traditional revolution. But neither can it have as its aim the fantasy of a mastery without the master, a fantasy rooted in the belief that all we have to do to cut off the head of the king is abandon a dream of freedom and turn our critical attentions to the interrogation of disciplinary practices, governmental bureaucracies, and biopolitical dispositifs. Foucault makes a compelling case that "to govern means . . . to govern things" and that "the things . . . with which government is to be concerned are in fact men, but men in their relations, their links, their imbrication with those things" that surround and define them: wealth and resources, customs and habits, accidents and misfortunes.[27] If sovereignty is the administration of territory, government is the disposing of such things. But even a cursory glance at the woodcut of Hobbes's leviathan or a consideration of Foucault's own claim that the sovereign makes die will suggest that sovereignty, too, is not only a disposing and organizing of things, including people; it is a particular relation of forces and is itself inscribed into the microphysical diagram of things. Sovereignty is the habitation of those things of which government disposes. What governmentality and sovereignty share, then, is a rootedness in a realm of things. That such a realm is thought to require any form of disposing at all should alert us, however, to the way it threatens to stray from the codes and norms of an imposed economy. Sovereignty and governmentality are both engrossed in the life of things; but since the lives of those things are given over to an energy of passing, an energy of crisis, then it follows that both governmentality and sovereignty, each of which is dependent on the destiny of things, are in turn given over to the force that drives the passing of things (to the point that even prior forms of governmentality and sovereignty become things). Theorists of governmentality tell us to forget sovereignty. Theorists of sovereignty counter that government and sovereignty have always been fused. Our aim is to work through both of those categories in order to touch upon the realm of ungovernable things that persists in each. As we see it, the challenge for the critic is to push beyond twinned fantasies—the fantasy, on the one hand, of an efficacious sovereign who paradoxically ensures our freedom to critique him and, on the other, the fantasy that there could ever be mastery without a master—and instead restore to the position of sovereign function a ruined, eternally perishing sovereign, an impossible master. Critique must ground the sovereign in a particular form of crisis, one rooted in that continuous perishing of social formations and things through which otherwise imperceptible forces in history assert themselves. Those unseen forces—political, yet positively nonexistent in either time or space; neither a simple negating of politics nor a positive affirmation of it but a canceled trace within the political; taciturn and sedimentary, reverberating in politics without being fully acknowledged or articulated—go by various names in this collection: *apoikos*, flesh, the infrapolitical, the impolitical. Following Marx and the Frankfurt School, we choose to call the historical form of those transient forces *natural history*. For it is natural history that, as we shall go on to argue in our own contribution to *Sovereignty in Ruins*, dissolves not only the link cementing the political subject to S_1 and S_2 but also the link cementing sovereignty to the economy. Marx, contemplating the creative destruction practiced by the bourgeoisie, marveled at how "all that is solid melts into air."[28] Natural history does something similar, but in a different element. The solid bond between the juridical and economic rationalities held in place by the sovereign, natural history grinds into dust.

Notes

1 In the last paragraph of his "Postface" to the second edition of *Capital*, Marx alludes to just such a "universal" or "general crisis," a crisis measurable by the "universality of its field of action and the intensity of its impact." Marx, *Capital*, vol. 1, 103.

2 Koselleck, *Critique and Crisis*, 127: "The eventual solution is uncertain, but the end of the crisis, a change in the existing situation—threatening, feared and eagerly anticipated—is not. The question of the historical future is inherent in the crisis."

3 Badiou, *Philosophy for Militants*, 43.

4 Arendt, *The Origins of Totalitarianism*, 297.

5 Meta-, para-, imp-, infra-, bio-, ecopolitics, and so on.

6 Koselleck, "Crisis," 359.

7 Our thinking here is indebted to Giorgio Agamben, *The Time That Remains*, esp. 62–69.

8 Thinkers of biopolitics such as Nikolas Rose, Bruce Braun, Paolo Virno, and Antonio Negri proceed from the common assumption that the workings of a dark, fearful biopolitical capitalism necessarily generate its obverse, an affirmative potential in which the mobility and flux of molecular life are the direct expression of an enormous productive power inherent in capitalism and are also capable of overthrowing it. The limitation of such a premise, as we see it, is that it cannot do much more than recognize dread, albeit with the added hope that within that dread there lies the potential for recombination—that dread is "radically open, full of surprises and unexpected forms." Taking the world as it is, these thinkers try to turn it further, in the direction of something like communist capitalism. Dread, they seem to believe, can be turned to our advantage in the production of a biopolitical commons. Unfortunately, this full extension of the affective register does not fundamentality sever its connection to the productivity paradigm. The similarity between biocapitalism and an affirmative biopolitics remains too great; rather than working through the distinctions, these thinkers make those distinctions indistinguishable. See, for example, Braun's "Biopolitics and the Molecularization of Life," esp. 17–18, in which the author tries to work through the fear and dread that biocapitalist rhetoric exploits but that can also be used to articulate "the virtuality of molecular life" (18).

9 See Adorno's formula #34, "Johnny-Head-in-Air," in *Minima Moralia*: "The almost insoluble task is to let neither the power of others, nor your own powerlessness, stupefy us" (57).

10 Foucault, "For an Ethic of Discomfort," 444.

11 Foucault, "For an Ethic of Discomfort," 444.

12 Hardt and Negri, *Commonwealth*, 301. But see Negri, *Time for Revolution*, as well: "It is well established that the entire history of the bourgeoisie is nothing other than the permanent attempt to live through crisis, that crisis is linked to the definition of the bourgeoisie itself. Even to say 'the market' is, in a way, to say crisis. But it is also well known that the bourgeoisie makes crisis the key to the progress of capital, and so succeeds in its project to organize productive time and to exert its dominion over crisis" (54).

13 Virno, *Multitude*, 152–53.

14 Nietzsche, *Twilight of the Idols*, 48.

15 See Arendt, *Between Past and Future*, 171.

16 Agamben, "Form-of-Life," 155.

17 This is an irony neatly captured by Eve Sedgwick, who observes that the codification of Foucault's *History of Sexuality*, vol. 1, has only ended up "propagating the repressive hypothesis ever more broadly by means of displacement, multiplication and hypostatization," a situation that Sedgwick likens to a feedback loop wherein every attempt at stepping outside the repressive hypothesis necessarily leads to the continuing rigorous study of its protean inclusivity. Looking beyond a sovereign function that has become curiously attenuated and yet also all powerful and inescapable, Sedgwick allows us to see how ideology critique itself has lent a prosthetic afterlife not only to a concept of politics as necessarily activist and emancipatory—that is, as necessarily inseparable from the sovereign function whose workings it brings to light and whose place it might, in the interests of putting an end to itself, assume—but also to the sovereign function, which ideology critique repeatedly propped up for no other reason than to once again demystify it. Sedgwick, *Touching Feeling*, 9–12.

18 Foucault, *The History of Sexuality*, vol. 1, 88–89.

19 Hardt and Negri, *Empire*, 88.

20 For Foucault, a dispositif designates a dominant strategic function that intervenes into forces of relations in order to direct and stabilize them, to manipulate them so they can be assembled into an integrated apparatus or network that draws the most heterogeneous elements—institutions, statements, discourses—into its force field, supported by the power/knowledge nexus. Its networking power has the extraordinary capacity, Agamben adds, "to manage, govern, control, and orient—in a way that purports to be useful—the behaviors gestures, and thoughts of human beings." Agamben, "What Is an Apparatus?," 12, and Foucault, *Power/Knowledge*, 194–96. Roberto Esposito makes a similar point when he suggests that "sovereignty effectively proved to be the first and fundamental immunitarian dispositif, together with the categories, preventatively immunized, of property and liberty." See his "Community, Immunity, Biopolitics," 8.

21 Foucault, "Governmentality," 218.

22 This is true even with respect to what Pheng Cheah calls the "more universal, higher sovereignty" of the modern subject and its "inalienable rights." Whether the self-determining sovereign subject produces with other such sovereign subjects a government of popular sovereignty or collaborates for its image or protection with a premodern sovereign, that subject nevertheless makes a compact with sovereignty whereby the most diverse multiples can still speak "as if by one mind," as Spinoza puts it. This mutual interdependence of sovereign subject and state sovereignty demonstrates how thoroughly the individual subject remains primordially invested in the figure of the sovereign. See Pheng Cheah, "Second Generation Rights as Biopolitical Rights."

23 As Derrida says of the French Revolution's failure to revolutionize sovereignty: "It is not interrupted, and at the death of the king one can still say: 'The King is dead, long live the King!' One has simply changed sovereigns. The sovereignty of the people or of the nation merely inaugurates a new form of the same fundamental structure. The walls are destroyed, but the architectural model is not deconstructed—and will, as you will see, continue to serve as a model and even as an international model." Derrida, *The Beast and the Sovereign*, vol. 1, 282.

24 See Agamben, *The Kingdom and the Glory*, 276–82.

25 Lacan, *The Other Side of Psychoanalysis*, 207.

26 See Marx, "The Eighteenth Brumaire of Louis Bonaparte," 597.

27 Foucault, "Governmentality," 208–9.

28 Marx, "Manifesto of the Communist Party," 476.

PART I

Ruination and Revolution

CHAPTER I

Natural History:

Toward a Politics of Crisis

George Edmondson and Klaus Mladek

Virno

Beneath our built environment of cultural habits and rules, behind our "organization of work and solid communicative habits," between the furrows of every form of life, there persists a substratum of human uncertainty and groundlessness that constitutes a natural-historical invariant—or so Paolo Virno would have us believe.[1] As Virno sees it, we humans are disoriented animals, so thoroughly lacking an instinctual blueprint to guide us, even at moments of maximum danger, that we are always generalists, always adaptable, never constrained by a preordained set of rules.[2] Our instability and our language faculty, our anthropogenetic flexibility and mobility, our "dearth of specialized instincts," our permanent crisis: these qualities mean that we can adapt to any environment.[3] But they also condemn us to a Manichean existence in which, on the one hand, our flexibility and adaptability make us ideally suited to the demands of the contemporary capitalist labor process while, on the other hand, our natural historical invariance—or, to be more precise, our invariant and dangerous groundlessness—constitutes an indestructible opening that makes us capable of insubordination.[4]

Virno is clearly onto something important with his explication of the link between crisis, which he defines as "an emergency situation" wherein "a certain pseudo-environmental setup is subjected to violent transformative traction" and "the potentiality . . . of the human animal takes on the typical visibility of an empirical state of affairs," and natural history, which he defines as the inventory of "the multiple socio-political" representations (i.e., diagrams) of "the biological invariant that characterizes the existence of the human animal" as a "potential animal" in time.[5] We admit, in fact, that our position varies from his only by a matter of slight degrees. All the same, we find that his concept of "natural-historical diagrams," by which he means "the socio-political states of affairs which display, in changing and rival forms, some salient features of anthropogenesis," remains uncomfortably close to the harsh excesses of "biolinguistic capitalism" precisely because, like Negri and Hardt's "biopolitical productivity," it meets capitalism on essentially the same terrain: the same anthropocentric machine that separates political and linguistic human life from nonhuman and dumb apolitical life; the same fascination with original forms of productivity, innovation, and change arising from the dangers of an unruly state of nature; the same concept of an incontestable "metahistory" so basic as to determine the common behavior of humankind.[6] Rather than further historicizing and politicizing natural history, Virno, in a distinctly Heideggerian manner, tends instead to ontologize natural necessities and, in that way, risks repeating the classical gesture of political thought: to separate an objective, indisputable sphere—nature—from the subjective interventions of thought and praxis. That can only mean reducing the critical ferment inherent in natural historical crisis to an organizing principle for future political life, which for Virno means only those "institutions of the multitude" that rely exclusively on the human form.[7]

In Marx and the Frankfurt School, by contrast, natural historical crisis is permanent and pervasive, and it follows a specific dynamic of thought totality and dialectical decline in any given historical situation. Accordingly, it exposes even the assumption of capitalism's unfathomable complexity, the ungraspable character of its mobility and flux—in short, the ideology of permanent change that is said to be our fate—to the dynamics of transience. (One might even go so far as to say, in fact, that the permanent succession of crises on which capitalist circulation thrives is arrayed against precisely this insight into a more all-enveloping crisis.) For Marx, a real dialectics contains "the recognition of [the] negation" of every state, "its inevitable destruction; because it regards every historically developed form as being in a fluid state, in motion, and therefore grasps its transient aspect as well; and because it does not let itself be impressed by anything, being in its very essence critical and revolutionary."[8] A real dialectics is "critical and revolutionary" (always complementary terms for Marx) because it is not merely a dialectics of concept and logic but a dialectics of natural history that extracts the transient kernel and momentary existence from any "historically developed form." Not surprisingly, this critical and revolutionary dialectical procedure draws out all the resistances and anxieties of the bourgeois order. In Hegel, nature had merely behaved unreasonably, refusing to play along in the dialectical playbook except as negation and as an antithesis to be sublated. Natural historical dialectics in Marx expresses real relations determined in particular historical situations wherein the inherent laws of nature operate as fundamental principles in the real.[9] For Marx—and, following him, Adorno and Benjamin—the natural historical stratum identified by Virno is never *sub*, never an "invariant human nature" that suddenly erupts from underneath established cultural encrustations in times of crisis.[10] In Marx's idea of natural history, what Virno calls "species-specific prerogatives" are themselves profoundly historical and constructable, inseparable from the sphere of world history in which they are enmeshed.[11] Other than invariant, always part of a specific historical constellation with its own mode of expression and laws of transition, natural history persists as an indestructible layer in the midst of any cultural formation—there as infinite perishing and transience—even when that formation is thriving (because natural history elicits an immunitarian response that is coexistent with what is perceived as crisis). The persistent truth content of things, their still-living obstinacy, is not an authentic being; nor is it a constitutively dislocated and unsheltered "Being" in the Heideggerian vein. This is where Virno goes astray: drawing heavily on Heidegger's terminology, he gives natural history the status of a more authentic and generic layer in human life, an "as such" that, as in Heidegger, tends to become our irrevocable historical destiny. Naturalizing natural history, Virno removes it from analytical scrutiny, from the practice of intervention and presentation, and thereby repeats the concealment of the very natural historical layer that he advocates as the engine of revolutionary politics in times of crisis.[12] The result is that politics then gets cordoned off, as exclusively human history, from nonhuman forms of life, including things and animals, their techne, or the life of machines. To draw political philosophy out of its self-satisfied contemplation, political analysis must, as Marx and the Frankfurt School well knew, close off any recourse to metahistorical invariants grounded in the generic nature of man. Politics must instead be cognizant of the fact that truths, far from being permanently available for reflection, are to be seized in concrete, pressing situations and from fleeting, exigent objects—be they inorganic matter, ideas, or living beings—that can get irrevocably lost. Hence a natural history that manifests itself, both in health and in crisis, as an energy of passing away, an indestructible that is not an invariant groundlessness of humans alone but the continuous perishing, the total and infinite passing away, that encompasses concrete political formations, including all nonhuman and thingly life.

Natural history is thus to be understood not only as a perishing that befalls even the nothingness and groundlessness of the human but as a perishing that is itself a new ontology, realized in the task of critical intervention, of ourselves and of the present.[13] What this means, in the first place, is that there can be no stratagem of governance predicated on the separation between a wild thinking underneath and the social calcifications above. Subversion and containment, health and disease: these supposed dichotomies are in fact complicit, with wild, anarchic thinking and the pastoral power of law and order sharing the same topology, one figured in terms of regeneration, of a cyclical understanding of perishing and rejuvenation, like the ups and downs of markets. By contrast, natural history manifests, in specific historical sites, a perishing even of the system of a rhythmic, predictable, regular perishing. To understand natural history is to understand that there persists an incompatible order—transient, unstable, deeply historical, decaying, and therefore dialectical—which folds over and doubles a capitalist order that, like the sovereign, exploits crisis as its engine and foil. It is to understand, moreover, that the vision of the critic must be attuned to the difference between a mythological knowledge that props up the government/sovereign executive order and the scrutinizing, ruinous knowledge that, in its capacity to disarticulate this first order, allows critical knowledge to distinguish between the crises that give rise to police interventions and the crisis that is constitutive of critical ruination. In short, the critic must prompt a self-encounter of critique and crisis with the ambiguous genealogy they share.

Foucault/Kant

Perhaps the prime example of such critical prompting can be found in Foucault's sympathetic engagement with Kant. For Foucault, Kant's critique of reason constitutes an especially bold move because it manages to exceed the bounds of the Enlightenment—manages to become transhistorically imperative, universalizing, even revolutionary—by being a double of itself that, degenerative and self-ruining, dismantles not only the idea of governing crisis but the art of governing as such. When the late-period Foucault returns repeatedly to the question of critique, it is to apply the pivotal concern of the Enlightenment, "the relationships between power, truth and the subject," "to any moment in history" by staging a confrontation between the two arts that, according to Foucault, give rise to modern critique: the art of governing and the art of being "not quite so governed," "not *like that*," "not for that, not by them," or—Foucault flirts with anarchic defiance—"we do not want to be governed at all."[14] The art of critique begins with this primary decision, which is a *critical* decision in the original meaning of the term: one that reorients history around a new cause that never fails to be an efficacious power in the real. It expresses an individual and collective will, detectable throughout history, to revolt against government—and against modern governmentality, where the subject is piloted through life with the help of precise medical, legal, and theological techniques of self-governance, in particular. The incandescent traces of this will cut diagonally across history and return to modernity as primal scenes of critical dissent and insubordination. These include, for example, the strategy, common to Saint Paul and Kant, of disobeying the order as though one obeyed it or, as happens with many of Kafka's protagonists, disobeying it by being excruciatingly obedient. Or they appear in the past scenes of upheaval that Foucault invokes—the trial of Socrates and the revolts of mysticism and reformation against the pastoral powers of the church—scenes whose historical diagrams become legible only belatedly, once we encounter the question of Enlightenment reason.

It is one question in particular, however—Kant's question, "What is Enlightenment?"—that openly declares a bold, courageous exit from the discursive field, from the trappings of a "self-incurred immaturity" that indolently relies on the guidance of such self-proclaimed guardians as books, doctors, and priests. As an art of subtraction and separation from the discursive scene, Kant's manifesto for Enlightenment critique marks for Foucault the advent of a completely new self-conscious political attitude toward one's own contemporary reality. Kant's critical operation asserts itself as a principled, recalcitrant *gestus*, an act born of a philosophical ethos that both partakes in and parts with the master discourses of his own time—the art of governing and Enlightenment reason—by interrogating and finally reversing the conditions of their acceptance. It does so, moreover, by making critical use of the very faculty of reason, otherwise destined to validate the systems of knowledge (legal, medical, theological) that undergird mechanisms of coercion: deploying reason's inherent critical powers against its own power effects, endlessly applying its own universalizing truth procedures against it. Kant's reason critiques, and then critiques reason, in a self-limiting auto-dissolution, curtailing the force of knowledge it generates and, in so doing, delimiting knowledge's hold upon the subject. The end of critique is to make it impossible for us to accept naturalized forms of knowledge.

But critique as transformative truth procedure does more than just derail natures and legitimacies; it instills crisis in the core of those traditional legal, medical, and political forms of critique that seek to liberate us or merely reform our sociopolitical institutions. Such forms of critique remain, in their goal of liberation and reformation, profoundly wedded to the logic of the sovereign, who welcomes our critical care, impatience, and indignation. The conjoined tasks of liberation and reformation come at the steep price of resuscitating a sovereign just as he is about to expire. Foucault's patient form of critique, by contrast, advocates a critique that confers upon itself an insubordinate, intransigent right beyond juridical rights "to question truth on its effects of power and question power on its discourses of truth."[15] In this respect, critique—critique as an ungovernable right without legal rights—resonates with the twin concepts, Pauline on the one side and Kantian on the other, that neither what is covered by the law nor what is deemed to be outside the law is up to the self-appointed task of critique. Only a critique that folds back on itself, perpetually demarcating the limits of its power, expanding and contracting its reach, accelerating and stopping short, truly understands its revolutionary power as something more than reformational. It grasps its capacity to coin new terms, terms worthy of the event, and enduringly loosens the hold of the sovereign by tethering him to his crisis.

In this spirit, Foucault proposes to name his own historical-philosophical project of critique a "procedure of eventalization," the key strategy in the art of not being governed. Submitting pyramidal figures and principles of sovereignty (final authority, unitary origin, necessity) to an archaeological and genealogical examination designed to dissolve the links between elements of knowledge and procedures of coercion that induce governable behavior and discourse, the eventalizing operation injects crisis into the natural, necessary appearance of such established links so that their singular elements might be reconfigured for the construction of events.[16] Exposing a scientific or institutional system to its "essential fragility," following its "breaking points" until the full display of its arbitrary nature and violence makes it more and more difficult to accept, eventalization reverses the destination of knowledge and power as a prop for the art of governing by making the effects of power contained within a strategic field available for the presentation and creation of pure singularities and positivities.[17] Thus Foucault's rhetorical question: "How can the indivisibility of knowledge and power . . . induce both singularities, fixed according to their conditions of acceptability, and a field of possibles, of openings, indecisions, reversals, and possible dislocations which make them fragile, temporary, and which turn these effects into events, nothing more, nothing less than events?"[18] Eventalization is the archaeological and genealogical procedure of making crisis return in governmental orders, the aim being to ensure the power of reversibility and therefore of transformability as such. Accordingly, it forgoes historical veracity and necessity for the sake of transmitting expressive truths and singularizing events. Foucault's passion for the event, beginning "with this decision not to be governed," entails bringing about nothing, understood as the perishing of those seemingly irreversible powers that derive from masters, deep-rooted foundations, legitimizing laws, and unitary causes. The radical will not to be governed at all finds its counterpart in the will to relegate such sovereign figures to "disappearance" or, barring that, in the capacity at least to identify "by what and from what [such] disappearance is possible."[19]

This convergence of care of the self, virtue, and critique is the closest Foucault gets to an affirmative biopolitics; for not to be governed this way (or not at all) now concerns, as in the term *self-governance*, equally one's singular life and one's investment in a political form of life. To engage in critique means, according to Foucault, "to make available for the work that we can do on ourselves the largest possible share of what is presented to us as inaccessible."[20] To which we would add: what Foucault claims is "presented to us as inaccessible," occulted by any given regime of intelligibility, is what is in fact unforgettable, and thus indestructible, in history and our lives today. To recognize as much is to recognize that history is not tied to the boundaries of world history but instead touches, in affect and in thought, upon the critical powers that return to us from disavowed strands in our history and prehistory, or what we are attempting to name with the term *natural history*. "Understood in these terms, criticism (and radical criticism) is utterly indispensable for any transformation," according to Foucault, since it is now "a matter of making conflict more visible."[21] To make original modes of civil strife, or what the ancients called *stasis*, appear is to insert, by way of critique, crisis into politics and into the fantasy of the market economy—the realm of *homo œkonomicus*—in its deceptive guise as the new common. Foucault was the first to emphasize that modern governmental technology in general obeys the rationality of the workings of economy, loosely defined as the rule of equivalence and the processes of production and exchange that encompass both the economical and the juridical. Modern civil society is born from "a juridical structure (*economie juridique*) of a governmentality pegged to an economy understood as a process of production and exchange (*economie economique*)."[22] In other words, the dichotomy between sovereignty and governmentality is a false one. Agamben is right to extrapolate from Foucault's insight and turn *oikonomia* into an umbrella term, strangely permanent and operative in multiple contexts throughout history: the internal operations of the Trinity, divine providence, law, theological apparatuses, the governance of individuals, the sovereign exception, and so on. This allows Agamben to come to the surprising conclusion, given his previous work, that "the central mystery of politics is not sovereignty but government" or, better, "economy and its government."[23] The two terms are now interchangeable. World history, or the alternative term, universal history—essentially the parade of great men, empires, executive powers, and masters in our tradition—has thus been viewed exclusively as the ongoing refinement of governmental machines formed and supported by different permutations of oikonomia, a term that reaches back to the despotic management of a household (*oikos*). Indeed, Agamben has raised the question of whether the sovereign is not merely a fantastic supermanager with the power and legitimacy to suture together two otherwise incommensurable rationalities, the "political-juridical" and the "economic-governmental."[24] To push this further, we would suggest that an unacknowledged oikonomia knots together governmentality and sovereignty in a mutually reinforcing circle. In light of this, the twofold task of critique becomes much clearer. It is to disarticulate, by articulating the crisis in each, not only the links between the political-juridical and the economic-governmental rationalities but the permanence of oikonomia as such.

Foucault's essays on Kant are where we discover the critical mode by which that disarticulating articulation can be achieved and by which something ungovernable in history and in ourselves can be created aside from the economic paradigm. According to Foucault, Kant accomplishes this disarticulation through two related historical interrogations: "What is *Aufklärung?*," Kant's epochal question from 1784, and his follow-up question from 1798, raised in the wake of the French Revolution, "What to do with the will for revolution?"[25] Crucially, however, Kant does not treat these historical occurrences in historical or historiographical terms. He treats them as unforgettable, indestructible, transformative events that forever define, as affect (courage or enthusiasm) or prophetic sign, how we relate to and act within our present and how we actualize an origin, here and for a future politics. In order for an event to become real and active, in order to dissolve the economic-governmental-sovereign alliance, one must isolate that event in history and give it the value of an affect and a passionate sign. In this way, Kant ties the task of critique inexorably to the idea of revolution. In "The Contest of Faculties," for example, the constitutive strife among the theological, medical, and juridical branches of the *universitas* (again: the priest, the doctor, and the lawyer) barely veils its roots in a critique and crisis that culminates in the indestructible will to revolution. And when Kant discusses how history could be a priori, he in fact raises the possibility that crisis, understood as the exposure of apparently consequential events to historical transience, might coexist with an indestructible and unforgettable predisposition in human nature. The revolution thus becomes the transcendental condition for modern politics and for thinking through the fragility of history. Kant himself may speak of the prophet; but in doing so, he can also be heard to evoke the critic as a revolutionary, "the one who occasions and *produces* the events he predicts."[26] The prophetic critic predicts, by his actions in the present, the events that will take place in the future, since those events will result from his present actions. This confers an order to the crisis he puts in motion. Not only should the critic be aware of the unintended and unwitting ramifications of his declarative and diagnostic intervention, he must be, since what a prophetic critic does is to put a state into crisis by introducing something untenable and unbearable within it. What makes the act revolutionary and at the same time a question of crisis is that it introduces a memory of revolutionary will into whatever attenuated form the revolution might take after the fact, a memory that makes hope possible precisely because it introduces the inevitability of failure into the makeup of any political formation. The unredeemable becomes the precondition of the unforgettable. If the hopes of the actual political revolution of a people remain unfulfilled, they perpetuate themselves all the more powerfully and comprehensively, beyond the specific location and time of a revolution, in the aspiration and nature of universal humankind.

Thus the enduring existence of revolution as what Kant calls a "historical sign" in its rememorative, demonstrative, and prognostic temporal vectors gathers a given polity around a permanent cause of traumatic crisis and disjointedness—a permanent unrest—since all subsequent orders are then grounded in that instance of dissolution. Revolution introduces a politicizing tendency that takes every order out of itself, given that revolution is itself proof that there exists "a *tendency* within the human race as a *whole*."[27] This tendency introduces into the traditional concept of what Kant calls the natural history of man a moral history that confers upon the natural laws of the planetary orders a revolutionary truth content for universal human history. In this, Kant effectively reprograms the empirical laws of nature so that, suffused with a moral law of revolution tied to the permanence of crisis in human institutions, those laws attain a heightened political status that licenses us to envision a new mode of thinking about nature and history. Traditionally, politics needed nature to justify historical continuities; in Kant's critique, nature begins to work as the agent of profound historical and political breaks. Kant's critical and at times poetic procedure exhausts the full weight of the overdetermination with which the term *nature* is at once blessed and plagued (laws of nature, natural laws, the nature of man, the nature of the noumenal world, i.e., what Kant calls the "kingdom of nature," the state of nature, natural history, etc.). It is as if Kant's confusing deployment of the term *nature* were meant to name a crisis and revolution in nature itself, and so render all expressions of nature immediately historical and political. More to the point, his deployment of the term wrests control of revolution away from world history and resituates it in natural history. In "The Contest of Faculties," Kant refers (albeit with caution) to Blumenbach's concept of a *Naturrevolution* occurring before the advent of humans on the stage of history, while in "Perpetual Peace" he writes of a "complete revolution . . . brought about by nature alone."[28] Although Kant is always careful to interlace this idea of a revolution of and in nature with human history and the nature of man, with what in human history and human nature *"can never be forgotten,"* he nonetheless embraces the idea of natural, objective laws of motion in our unconscious history. Not only, then, does the phenomenon of revolution emerge as an irresistible natural historical event; it can now be understood as at once the irrevocable cause and promise in "the prophetic history of mankind."[29] And precisely because this nature proceeds behind the backs of acting humans, eluding our conscious grasp, the subject is primordially invested in natural historical time and must respond to what is unthinkable in it by subjectifying its revolutionary truth-content.

In this way, Kant invents a new grammar of revolutionary critique—"an aptitude and power" with new causes, signs, and affects guiding humanity throughout history—that introduces (or inserts) a permanent crisis mode into our concept of world history, commonly understood as the "path to progress."[30] This grammar, however, is now deeply historical, in that it moves through an essentially revolutionary form of time and space; and because of that movement it is forever diagrammatic, never resolving into a self-contained form and order. Fortified with this new grammar, the philosopher-critic now grants himself the right to activate a revolutionary will and proceeds, like an advocate, with proofs and public judgment to constitute a new *nomos* for a people and for nature. Kant's revolutionary is no anarchic firebrand. He is a disciplined organizer for a natural history that is now full of signs and internal laws capable of drawing humans out of their accustomed oikonomia. It is not enough for the revolution to have a "permanent virtuality," as Foucault puts it.[31] The revolution must be seen as the fundamental real effective in nature and history: in me, in the polis around me, and in the starry sky above me. After that, judging the true meaning of historical events becomes a matter of assuming the proper standpoint. As Kant insists in "The Contest of Faculties," the Copernican Revolution enables us to view both ourselves and human history from an entirely different perspective, one from which other, more expansive and enduring laws of movement—the *nomoi* of a revolutionary, albeit highly fragile, nature—come to light. Deprived of their central viewpoint, humans now see their objects and themselves as if they were spectators: spectators permanently revolving within a greater spatiotemporal reference system of astronomical forces whose underlying movements, propensities, and laws they must decipher in order to decipher their own. Insight into man's nature comes from the outside of man, from a blind spot that diverts his attention away from the active part he purportedly plays in the grand dramas of history. No longer strutting and fretting, we find ourselves standing on a very different stage, one where historical objects and dramatic scenes are newly constructed around transformative events, where unfamiliar players demand the articulation of a completely new historiography and politics.

By identifying an unforgettable revolutionary "predisposition in human nature," Kant effectively posits a quasi-natural eventual force that is stronger, albeit less perceptible, than any earth-shattering accomplishments generated in the course of world history.[32] To find a new certainty in a natural predisposition or sympathy for the revolution must remain strangely paradoxical. Revolution is in some sense impossible and uncertain, filling both its actors and its spectators not only with enthusiasm but also with the distress, anxiety, and disorientation that every fundamental crisis generates. In this case, however, certainty is guaranteed by a prophecy that can be envisioned vividly and yet remains completely untenable to any given order. The unforgettable and indestructible resides precisely in a cause that is continuously dissolving, being itself highly tenuous and forever on the brink of dissolution. In "The Contest of Faculties," Kant tarries with this permanent fragility of the revolution, which, like the moral law that in our daily lives is dismissed, watered down, compromised, evaded, and glossed over, is both indestructible and completely impossible. It can be infinitely destroyed and yet, for precisely that reason, remains indestructible. Like the revolution itself, the frailty of revolution is, by virtue of that very frailty and "in view of the frailty of human nature," to be taken as a prophetic "sign of history."[33] Crucially, however, this insight into an essential frailty eludes the monarchs, priests, and doctors who make it their business to heal crisis and promote narratives of improvement (to the point, Kant wryly notes, that a patient could not help but confess how much he is *"dying of sheer recovery!"*).[34] It thus falls to the Kants of this world to warn the masters of crisis that their antidotes, by mistaking critical frailty for a misery that is in need of their care and intervention, are in fact unprincipled and anarchic.

For Foucault, then, Kant's double critique of reason, always turning back upon itself in a gesture of autodissolution, introduces a model of genuinely revolutionary critical practice. And not only that: Kant's own isolation of the fragile revolution as a prophetic sign—a singular, affectively charged event—models how the critical modes of passion and prophecy can transform present reality by naming, and thus introducing, the unforgettable and indestructible will to revolution that manifests the moral history at work in man's natural history. Revolution in this sense makes no reference to transcendence or *telos*. Instead, it is driven by a critique that, itself being intimately tied to crisis, is in turn rooted in an unforgettable—and, in that sense, moral—prehistory. The singularity of an event such as the revolution derives from the fact that each one is a perishing, fragile instance of a prehistoric will. Thus critique, homing in on a symptomatic, critical point, intensified by its incisive, restricted concentration on a singular occurrence, aims to bring about an order of singulars. Heterogeneous, incommensurable to one another, such singularities dwell in an ever-expanding constellation of concrete, historically determined struggles, actualized for the present and made compossible by the critic in a manner akin to Kant's enthusiastic spectator of the French Revolution, who mobilizes his own situated standpoint from outside participatory action for a prognostic reversal of history.

The Foucault that emerges here is a different Foucault from the well-known prophet of bio-thanatopolitics, the Foucault whose conception of biopolitics has emerged as a new S_1/S_2 in which "life" looms so ominously as to once again elude critique. This is a Foucault who enlists Enlightenment critique in the search for a historical-philosophical analysis reminiscent of the dialectical truth procedure with which Benjamin and Adorno actualize distant pasts in the present (and vice versa) by constructing disturbing new origins and a priori objects of history. "Actually, in this historical-philosophical practice," as Foucault himself puts it, "one has to make one's own history, fabricate history as if through fiction."[35] Like Deleuze, who proposes giving Bergson's notion of fabulation a political meaning, and Derrida, who coins the term *affabulation* to define the strategies that render a political logic and knowledge meaningful by putting a fable to work in politics, Foucault sheds light on the commonality between political theory and poetic practice, on the fictions that politics and art share. What Foucault has in mind, however, is the invention of politically efficacious fictions that are in accordance with the art of not being governed. Every relation of forces, every complex network of powers and truths must traverse through a fiction in order to become effective as a historically determined real. Within every fictional artifice resides an unarticulated strength of fiction, just as any given nexus of power-knowledge contains a strength of power and knowledge whose energy can be redeployed for the construction of events. At this instance, the critical procedure of eventalization and the poetic practice of fabricating "history as if through fiction" converge. Both examine and dissolve the intimate and necessary relays between structures of knowledge and the mechanisms of coercion; both dismantle the intimate links joining real historical objects to established representations designed to mask or legitimize the violence of elementary power struggles and to dissipate or neutralize the efficacy of ungovernable singularities. Most important, such fictioning critique creates events; for "one 'fictions' history on the basis of a political reality that makes it true, one 'fictions' a politics not yet in existence on the basis of a historical truth."[36] Foucault himself fictions the very power of fiction, using the reality effects of fictions to exhibit the complex poetic, scenic, and diagrammatic—and also material, factual, and microphysical—procedures that make historical truths real and acceptable.[37] Foucault's fictions thus tend to widen the same gap between imaginary semblances and real struggles that dominant discourses attempt to both represent and conceal. In this sense, Foucault's fictions are counterfictions, diagrams that employ the power of fiction to intrude into fictions of naturalized, legitimized power. They also are counterscenes that rearrange concrete systems of power-knowledge by infusing them with crisis and the *gestus* of critique. A fiction of this sort—the diagram of a power struggle, the scene of a moment of crisis, the particular attitude of critique—intervenes in historical moments at the point of their greatest symptomatic tension. And in so doing, it confronts a specific political reality with the history of the will, with a real that derives its force from the art of making lives ungovernable. Conjoining historical scenes with the rigor of thought, Foucault's exemplary scenes begin to think, while, conversely, thoughts themselves become scenic or a central part of a scenic arrangement. One must only paraphrase Foucault's paraphrase of Kant to crystallize this critical operation into a single imperative: "One must isolate an event in history that will take on the value of a *scene*."[38]

Foucault himself models just such a scene—models, we should say, the critical practice of fictional actualization, eventalization, and compossibility—in his reading of the fateful collision, circa 1800, between psychiatric power and the sovereign recounted in Pinel's case history of George III's treatment at the hands of a certain Dr. Willis (in essence a reordering of an ordering of events). Foucault characterizes the scene of George III's madness not simply as a deposition but as a "total inversion of sovereignty": not the triumph of psychiatric power over the sovereign but the profanation of both forms of transcendent sovereignty, sovereign power and governmentality.[39] Before turning to the scene itself, Foucault reminds his audience of the classical iconography associated with sovereign power, a tableau organized around oppositions and the asymmetrical submission of subjects beneath the king, who towers over all with his ermine, scepter, and globe. It is exactly those insignia that psychiatric power sets out to rearrange. Confined now to a padded cell, cut off from his relations, the mad king falls upon himself and into the hands of the two brutish, "magnificent," "Herculean" pages who were once members of his household, but who have now assumed the wordless task of subduing him.[40] George III's world has turned to shit, and not just metaphorically. Before he would have ordered the suppression of the filth and excrement thrown at his carriage by the poorest of the poor. Now he is reduced to using his own ordure as a weapon of last resort, daubing it on the old doctor who comes to visit him. At the moment when "the crisis intervenes"— intervenes not only into the midst of sovereign splendor but into the critical act of decision itself, throwing established ways of judging and deciding into crisis—what had been the stratified and oppositional structure of the royal scene gives way to a new scene, one in which a host of miniature tyrants (doctors, helpers, and bureaucrats) enter the stage at the very site of royal decomposition, filling the vacuum left by the demise of the royal function and converting the symbols of royal power into meaningless, dumb matter.[41]

But it is not until Willis, the doctor who has appointed himself both director and protagonist of this new scene, enters into the midst of the ceremonial of sovereign power—not until the microphysics of psychiatric power have overwhelmed the political field with their elemental mode of operation—that we begin to detect the microphysical underside that was always at work within the premodern sovereign diagram. For embedded within this primal scene of a total inversion of sovereignty and of the advent of psychiatric microphysical power is the truth content of another scene, one that erases any distinction between a microphysics of dejected, excremental things of crisis and humans as they are rearranged by variable power relations. It is true, of course, that George III would recover from his madness enough to reassume the throne. But from the moment he enters his cell, he is irrevocably the subject of microphysical power—one actant in a wider microphysical diagram of power, no better or worse than his brutish pages or the poorest of the poor, who once threw filth at his carriage. This does not mean, however, that Willis is suddenly in charge. One gets the sense at first that Foucault, in staging the scene as he does, has set up the doctor as the modern crisis manager par excellence and psychiatric power as the emblem for the managerial, policing approach to crisis per se. The doctor, in seizing hold of the course of crisis, and thus making abnormal life a new political object, believes that he has the power to foster life where the sovereign used to take it. But the richer, more active manifestations of microphysical life that his analysis and crisis management have brought to light, a life embodied in the imposing pages and the other tenacious, masterless things that crowd the royal cell, exceed the control of the doctor as silent crisis manager to an even greater degree than they did the asymmetrical form inscribed in the ostentatious insignia of sovereign power. Crisis, in fact, more than exceeds the doctor's control, for the crisis that he has induced, manipulated, and healed returns to him as the inverted truth of his own discourse. Forced to confront the melancholic, the paranoiac, or the psychotic on their own turf, the doctor has little choice but to devise a fiction of cure that is "exactly patterned on the delirium itself, homogeneous with the erroneous idea" produced by the patients he treats. Yet that can only mean that the stratagems of his truth are from the outset entangled in the same delirious forces, in the same real and fictional causes of madness, that he at once authenticates and works to suppress.[42] Like all crisis managers, doctors of psychiatry are mimetic geniuses who closely model the verifying strategies and truth procedures of their *dispositif* on the capillary diagram of forces at play in the crisis of a disease. But precisely in that way, they unwittingly incorporate the incomplete, delirious logic of those forces, the uncontrollable rhythms of their return. After all, to eagerly bring about an event within a delirium only in order to then forcefully discipline individuals on the grounds of this fictional event is also a way of taking something on, of contracting the powers of deviant life the doctor meant to regulate. Foucault is too subtle a thinker to settle for a simple dichotomy between transgression and containment or undifferentiated abyss and rigid systematicity. On the contrary, his masterless, tenacious things, like his isolated scenes, would murmur the two correlating psychiatric declarations drummed into every mad patient—"You are not king" and "Your body is not made of glass"—to both sovereign powers, king and doctor. For the very fact that no one is ever a king, not even the king himself, is exactly what releases indestructible tenacious powers, powers that can be stifled neither by the power of kings nor, conversely, by the sense of one's own powerlessness.

So much for the doctor. What of his counterpart in crisis, the critic? The doctor's form of treating crisis must, in more ways than one, elicit the scrutiny of the critic, whose task it is to return crisis to its critical core by once again fictionalizing the "labyrinth of fictional verification" fabricated by the doctor in his pursuit of the cure.[43] Following the lead of Foucault, then, the critic is to act as a counterdoctor, reverting psychiatric domination (in all its forms) back to microphysical powers and forces. Pinel's small tyrants—the pages who apply brute psychiatric force to quell the obstinacy of unacceptable crisis things and crisis bodies, the doctors who submit the sovereign's fragile, transient body to a regimented framework of psychiatric discipline meant to tie sovereignty to the economy of a proper, reasonable government—have one chief objective: to knot together the two different rationalities of sovereignty and government, politics and economy, power and knowledge, the juridical and the disciplinary as though they were indivisible, mutually legitimizing, reasonable only in their union. The archaeological-microphysical critic, by contrast, recounts and then reverses this institutionalized fusion, embodied in sovereign government or governmental executive power, back to its heterogeneous, microphysical scene of ruination.

But the other, divisive scene that Foucault stages within the psychiatric scene does something else as well: it disarticulates, critically, the fiction that there exists an inevitable, epochal struggle among sovereignty, disciplinary power, and governmentality. Intimately bonded, this triumvirate in fact shares a common will—to perfect the art of governing—and the same root: a common oikonomia of mastering a crisis as a despot manages his household. Against the anomic principle that dwells in the midst of the triangular disciplinary-governmental-sovereign oikonomia (the despotic administration of a household not being bound by a system of rules), the critic thinks an *"ungovernable,"* as Agamben writes, *"something that could never assume the form of an* oikonomia."[44] Thus the task of the critic: to create ungovernabilities that remain heteronomous to the disciplinary, governmental, and sovereign permutations of oikonomia even as they insist upon their own inherent nomical organization.

Yet one might push this further still and say that Foucault's "critical ontology of ourselves," the historical-philosophical form-of-life that critique at once denotes and embodies, itself constitutes just such an ungovernable life, a life that articulates a self-legislating nomos incommensurable with oikonomia.[45] What would this life of critique consist of? How would it do justice not only to the "ourselves" of a new critical ontology but to the nomos of things? From the time that Pindar's sovereign law (*nomos basileus*), conjured to justify violence "with the strongest hand," joined forces with the Sophists' fantasy of a "right of the strongest," political philosophy has stumbled over the egregious conflation of might with right, of violence (*bia*) with justice (*dike*), that constitutes the inner workings of both sovereignty and government.[46] One way that politics has tried to counteract that conflation of might with right is by drawing sovereignty itself within the ambit of the law. But while the generality of the law purports to have forever constrained the whimsical nature of sovereign rule, effectively ending the crisis behind that rule, critique reminds us that the authorized recourse to legal force might be a continuation of Pindar's nomos basileus by other means. Political philosophy, meanwhile, has itself long been suspected of aspiring to the role of master or of creating a system of knowledge that is in service to the master. But at the same time—and here we see its intimate connection to critique—political philosophy has never ceased to dream about a noncoercive nomos and an immemorial *physis* able to elude the grasp of sovereignty and government while being highly active in them. Consider the idea of *chora* (space) in the *Timaeus*, Plato's dramatized theorizing of cosmogony and natural history. Plato's reflections, "as in a dream," on the unsettled and yet indestructible chora seem to be driven by a single-minded pursuit of a third, bastard nature capable of breaking open the dichotomy between a changeless sphere of commanding, lawful being (a "source" and a "father," 50d) and an anomic nature of becoming and semblance apprehended by changeable opinion (*doxa*).[47] Here and elsewhere in his political philosophy Plato, very much like Kant, tends to multiply the terms nature (physis) and law (nomos) in order to avoid the false alternative between a sovereign nomos that becomes one with nature, as in Pindar's poem, and the Sophistic notion of an anomic, brute nature anterior to nomos. For this notion of a lawless nature only serves to justify the violence of the strongest and, in Hobbes, the intervention of the sovereign into the state of nature. Meanwhile, Plato's chora, this nearly incomprehensible space, formless and yet capable of receiving and giving form, compels us to think a nomic kind of nature suspended between the hypernomic order of unchanging forms and the anomic sphere of visible nature. A "choratic" *physionomos* would make appear a singular life—its specific materiality, its metabolic processes, the rhythms of its appearance, its peculiar ways of being and perishing— that is inseparable from its form. It is as the Athenian remarks in Plato's *Laws*: such physionomos would replace and displace Pindar's "decree of nature . . . that the stronger should rule and the weaker should obey" (690c). The Platonic pursuit of physionomos effectively derails the operative fantasy of the Sophists that a physis can be severed from its nomos—that underneath law and logos roam the unfettered forces of a wild state of nature in need of despotic rule.

It is this tradition, in which thought devises a cohesive physionomos able to retain a disposition toward justice and the event for each singular being, that informs both Kant's critique and Foucault's microphysical diagram of ungovernable forces. Foucault's procedure of eventalization is not only an integral part of the art of not being governed; it is also, as in Plato and Kant, a novel form of self-governance (or of not governing oneself at all) among masterless, transient things and common powers unwilling to play their part in the economy of sovereignty and government. The task of the critic is then to shed light on the uneconomical fold in the living—to tease out a different economy of powers, an economy at once heteronomous to the governmental economy but dwelling as a disintegrating kernel in its midst. It is our recourse to the power of crisis and critique that opens the horizon for a different politics. Sovereignty and government may both be preoccupied with apprehending things and lives, yet they are apprehended in turn by what they cannot avow in themselves: the growing power of their perishing, which is at once a downfall and an elevation. What sutures the juridical rationality to the governmental economic rationality and the theological-political paradigm to the economic-providential paradigm is not, as Agamben holds, the fiction of sovereignty. It is the ordering and disposing of lives and things, either as fostering life or as making die, within a circumscribed territory meant to hem in the relatively autonomous physionomos of things and lives.

Marx

In the figure of the psychiatrist, Foucault was able to identify a particular type of conjurer, a sorcerer of providential economic governance. But it was Marx who gave that figure his proper name: the capitalist. And it was Marx who put his finger on an effective critical practice in response. Marx's materialist critic intervenes at the precise juncture where the capitalist conjoins mystery to economy in the form of nature and in the processes of naturalization. Where Foucault's critic unleashes microphysical powers in the midst of microphysical institutions, the Marxist materialist critic intensifies a double already at work within the "naturalized" capitalist economy. This Marxian counterpart to Foucault's diagrammatic microphysical force goes by the name of natural history. Natural history is the critical fold of a physiocratic economic nature.

Hegel, to give the man his due, had at least found it tragic that history necessitated the subjugation of first nature in our constitution of second nature. He could recognize how ironic it was: the fact that we had no choice but to overcome the very nature whose laws we nonetheless assimilated in our development of the ethical/historical world. Yet beyond that he had dismissed nature and natural history as nothing more than an unreasonable antithesis, a roadblock of thought. Nature had therefore remained for him the disavowed outside of history. Marx, for the first time, thinks nature as the outside inside man: his history, his inorganic body, his techne, his machines, his unconscious life activity. In the *Economic and Philosophical Manuscripts of 1844*, this concept of nature remains largely anthropocentric and even anthropomorphic: that which drives the life activity of human beings. It is not until *Capital* that natural history becomes even more externalized and outside, even more alien and nonhuman, than it had been for Hegel. But now, in a crucial overturning of Hegel, this radical nonhuman outside at work in natural history is understood to constitute the truth content of world history, determining the unconscious evolution of history and "of the economic formation of society, [which] is viewed as a process of natural history."[48] Human actors are not individuals, but "personifications of economic categories, the bearers of particular class-relations and interests," and an individual can therefore not be made "responsible for relations whose creature he remains, socially speaking" (92). Contrary to the naive anthropology behind traditional world history, Marx presents things, realities, materials, animals, machines, and men within relations of production, within differential structures that define and distribute places and functions. At every turn, Marx inscribes things, human actors, raw materials, objects, and instruments of production into relations and structures of a natural historical diagram.

In *Capital*'s brief chapter on the production of absolute surplus, for example, Marx exemplifies his dialectics of nature and the metabolism carried out by humans as itself a natural power. His point is not so much that the givenness of earth history—of nature independent of human beings—has become indistinguishable from our transformation of nature and, through that process, of our own nature. His point is that nothing exists apart from the continuous transformation and perishing at work in the dialectic of natural history. In Hegel's master-slave dialectic, the liberation or self-consciousness of the slave stems from his transformation of the world of things. All the same, the master and the slave remain lead actors in an exclusively human drama where the overthrow of the existing order assumes an almost heroic cast. In Marx's natural-historical dialectics, that same master and slave are reduced to props on a side stage: given over to a natural-historical return, a natural-historical rotation or revolution, in which nature furnishes the materials through which ideas, and governing ideas in particular, are built up. It is like Marx's image of the architect who, in a supposed departure from the bee, "builds the cell in his mind before he constructs it in wax" (284). That image may seem like an affirmation of humankind's radical difference from nature—of the putative gulf between the "worst architect" and the "best of bees"—but it remains embedded in a larger drama of man's loss of mastery (284). Here man does more, but also less, than transform nature; he also realizes himself in nature, traverses nature, to such an extent that he subordinates his will, however indirectly, to that which he has transformed. The more the laborer becomes impersonal, the more he gives himself over to the traversal of natural history and its laws, the more capable he becomes of realizing life as metabolized with and through a nature that has also produced his own actions and organs. Marx may want to insist that "an immense interval of time separates the state of things in a which a man brings his labour-power to market for sale as a commodity from the situation when human labour had not yet cast off its first instinctive form." "We are not dealing here," he writes, "with those first instinctive forms of labour which remain on the animal level" (283). But by extending his critical, political history into time immemorial, collapsing epochs until prehistorical states are found to be still pulsating in our organs and modes of production, Marx himself draws even modern labor processes into another history altogether, one in which humankind's metabolism with the earth continues to guarantee our capacity for genuine, revolutionary transformation.

For what truly interests Marx is not the historical development of labor as such. What interests him is the idea of a symptom-like return detectable in the moment that man becomes an object in the same process by which he subjectivizes nature and by which nature itself becomes a subject. But if natural history operates through a dialectics of return, what is it that returns? Marx is unequivocal: what returns is a "complex of things," things characterized by their transformative agency, their transience, and their torment, which continues to pulsate in the processes of production (285–86). What returns, to put the matter another way, are the relics of past means of labor in which we can discern the outlines of lost forms of social organization. One only has to shift perspective from the product of labor to the process extinguished in it and that "form of unrest" reveals the traces of torment left behind by past lives and labor (287). In a crowded universe of things, perished forms of life reappear. Past labor is only ever evident or objectified in decaying things. Like symptoms, which only manifest themselves at the point where psychical operations fail, this "form of unrest" becomes our matter of concern when it manifests itself in products falling into disrepair. We only ever become aware of the past labor objectified in a commodity— that is, we only ever become aware of the form of unrest extinguished in a product—when that commodity breaks down and reveals its inherent dysfunctionality and inoperativity. "Past labor," as Marx calls it, having once produced these now idle objects, returns to conjure the revitalizing sparks inherent in living labor. Living labor may thus be understood as seizing the dead corpus that makes up the humus of accumulated dead labor and decaying things. And by the same token, the process of decay—a process that encompasses things, machines, forms of life—insofar as it is a metabolic process full of its own force, calls living labor to it and, in so doing, calls living labor to itself. Such decaying and passing things "are therefore not only results of labour, but also its essential conditions" (287). Generated by the labor process, entered into it, they also cause that process to realize its revitalizing force and to carry out its redemptive work. The destructive power of natural processes—a power to which machines fall prey, that rots wood and rusts iron, that turns unwoven yarn into cotton wasted—is itself the engine for living labor. It is decay that confers life on living labor (289). The contact point between living labor and such things, at the deepest root of their uneconomical deadness, makes it possible that things might not only become real use-values but also effective ones. The dialectics are thus, that while dead objects give rise to living labor, seizing it and reanimating it, living labor in turn must revitalize dead objects by consuming them further. In that sense, living labor furthers and instills the force of transience already at work in perishing things and idle machines.

In this respect, Marx is a critical thinker who takes literally the labor of the term *Stoffwechsel*, metabolism. This term translates as "change of stuff" or "change of materials"; and it is to such continuous change that the active theoretical practice of the materialist dialectic is attuned. Such an active theoretical practice says not only that every production of theory is also a practice, defying the opposition between pure theory and applied practice; it says that every production of theory is also an injection, into political economy, of differentials such as metabolism. This goes beyond the mere historicization of political economy. The critical historian of metabolism ties ends to new beginnings and, in the process, becomes a montage artist who amalgamates different states, temporalities, and collectives. But Marx does not stop there. He reinserts those conjoined states, recomposed things, and collectives into the very digestive apparatus of consumption that once dissolved their original, innate ties, his aim being to produce a different type of consummation: a consuming that, in the form of a devouring (*verzehren*) of the "living means" (*Lebensmittel*) in the process of (critical) labor, creates a novel product "distinct from the consumer" (290). Marx metabolizes those objects to such a degree that he composes a new body, prosthetic and monstrous, made up of relics, including economies that have fallen out of history and dropped from view: a prehistory that disappears even from the natural sciences. "Nature becomes one of the organs of [man's] activity," writes Marx, "which he annexes to his own bodily organs, adding stature to himself in spite of the Bible." He then continues:

> As soon as the labour process has undergone the slightest development, it requires specially prepared instruments. Thus we find stone implements and weapons in the oldest caves. In the earliest period of human history,

domesticated animals, i.e. animals that have undergone modification by means of labour, that have been bred specially, play the chief part as instruments of labour along with stones, wood, bones and shells, which have also had work done to them. . . . Relics of bygone instruments of labour possess the same importance for the investigation of extinct economic formations of society as do fossil bones for the determination of extinct species of animals. It is not what is made but how, and by what instruments of labour, that distinguishes different economic epochs. . . . Among the instruments of labour, those of a mechanical kind, which, taken as a whole, we may call the bones and muscles of production, offer much more decisive evidence of the character of a given social epoch of production than those which, like pipes, tubs, baskets, jars etc., serve only to hold the materials for labor, and may be given the general denotation of the vascular system of production. (285–86)

Marx, we see, quite dramatically reuses objects whose lack becomes obstinate, including machines that drop out of circulation and lose their use-value, in order to display how thoroughly objects must traverse a process of near complete extinction and consumption before their true power, the power to call living labor into action, can be unleashed. Once past labor loses its sense, its mediating purpose, along with the objects and forms of life activity that sustained it, only then can it return to us; only then can the objects of labor encounter themselves apart from the drudgery of a specific usefulness or the life context that once animated them.

And more: it is only through the power of decay that the critical historian can fully assume the mandate of reanimating things that were once extinguished. The power of such passing awakens the critical activity of the historian who, in the midst of persistent crisis, distills and hastens the downfall of objects and forms of life so that they can then be reabsorbed and recycled for a process of revolutionary germination. Labor rests on the unrest of objects that are released from the productivity of past labor. Mindful of his own critical activity, an activity that is, after all, part of the natural historical dialectics, Marx's natural historian incessantly returns to objects that return, no matter how deadened they are, in order to consume them and mediate them further in the process of living labor activity. As the laborer and the materialist allegorician continue to wear away, to mortify, the material elements of objects and products of past labor, they in fact realize the truth content of those things: the efficacy of their downfall and return, "the destructive power of natural processes" (289). Living labor is a mighty power because it is a deadening process. In its midst dwell forms of unrest: the ruins of past labor and once useful things. Together, idle objects and the "trace[s] of past labor" manifest the power of a most efficacious destruction and return, particularly and paradoxically when they are consumed or when they fail, decay, and become the dead matter for a different, common use. Perceiving as much, Marx emphatically conjoins the redemptive core of living labor with what he posits as a commonality beyond all traditional forms and manifestations of the common: "the universal condition for the metabolic interaction between man and nature" (290).

It is thus a peculiar natural-historical dialectic that drives the passage from an economy of domination ruled over alternatively by the slave driver, the anxious capitalist, the stone-wielding savage, and the managerial Cincinnatus—ultimately a world-historical economy—to Marx's metabolic nomos.[49] We don't use nomos lightly here. "True history," the history of living labor, is by no means anarchistic or undifferentiated simply because it cannot be said to abide by the natural law of the physiocrats: the natural law that predetermines the economy of nature (*oeconomia natura*) and so sustains the political economy characterized by the ordered rise and fall of managers and masters. Marx, at the height of his critical fervor, no longer describes the nomos basileus of physical laws that support the political world. Rather, he encircles the physis of a nomos radically different from a political economy that is simply a social rationalization of the providential *œconomia* at the root of modern liberalism and government.

Marx's own, implicit metaphor for this natural-historical physionomos is that of the laws of fermentation by which the capitalist and all his products unwittingly abide (292). Fermentation, apart from becoming the matter for any specific user, let alone master, is a process of controlled rot or natural-historical decay that is at once a form of petrified unrest and a politicized apprehension of metabolic germination: that which is apparently most dead, utterly extinguished, most actively works through the living. "By the purchase of labor-power, the capitalist incorporates labor, as a living agent of fermentation, into the lifeless constituents of the product, which also belong to him. . . . The labor process is a process between things the capitalist has purchased, things which belong to him. Thus the product of this process belongs to him just as much as the wine which is the product of the process of fermentation going on in his cellar" (292). What Marx grasps here is that, on the molecular level, seemingly nonliving agents such as yeast and bacteria produce convivial luxuries through the energy generated by the process of dissolution that happens when things, nature, and human labor come into contact. Marx thus concludes the section on the natural history of the labor process with a thought image about a form of life and a life activity that is firmly in touch with the advances in microbiology and fermentation technology of the 1850s. The discovery of the power of bacteria and microorganic life in the work of Pasteur, Swann, and others—life activity below the threshold of recognized agents, or what Pasteur calls "life without air"—germinates, like the concentrated medium of high-yielding, fast-growing microorganisms itself, in Marx's critical analysis. Indeed, such microorganisms act as the unrecognized engine of Marx's materialist dialectics, wherein something idle and inoperative turns out to be the most fecund, where what had been dismissed as "unorganized ferments" according to the physiocratic diagram reveals itself, through a slight rearrangement of those diagrammatic coordinates, to be highly organized, even politically potent. Suddenly the inorganic, or that which was thought to be dead, manifests itself as filled with dialectical unrest: a possible model for communal living and the actual overthrow of the physiocratic economy at the heart of the capitalist economy. The distributed networks of, and the quorum sensing among, microbiological forms of life not only cannot be owned or possessed (however much they might be subjected to the seal of copyright and patent law); their silently persistent physionomos is incessantly bubbling up within the products and commodities that the capitalist claims as his own. And indeed they are his own, but not just in the way that he believes or that Marx implies. They belong to him in a way that he cannot own up to, for he cannot get rid of all that life, or even recoil from it, simply by transmuting its excessive activity into surplus value, for he has literally incorporated its surplus life. Standing at the present end of a long history, the capitalist, the only human figure that Marx allows into the concluding paragraphs of this section, is the heir and proprietor of a vast cellar filled not only with the elements, both living and dead, of production but with the relics of past labor activity, superseded economic formations, and the accumulated unrest of things. In the deepest chambers of those cellars (which are themselves natural-historical, built in the caves of prehistoric peoples), there is a life that persists without air. And that life continues to boil in barrels filled not with wine alone but with the accumulated unrest of its making and consumption: a common good of conviviality, luxurious excess, and sociability. This stuff that, according to Marx's contemporary Nietzsche, flows through Dionysian tragedy and through the sacraments of Christian communion, has now been privatized and turned into profit. Out of the cellars of the capitalist flows a stream of commodities meant not to intoxicate us but to narcotize us, capture us in the stupefying aura of world-historical gravity and progress. But fermentation continues. It is the task of the materialist historian to venture into the darkest recesses of those cellars and put her hand to the labor that is already under way there, that is always under way there—that is under way in the countless barrels belonging to the capitalist—in the process of fermentation.

Marx thus describes the capitalist as a latecomer who, having traversed through a thingly technical history, is subjected to a metabolism of which he is an integral part and by which he will finally be consumed. This is how Marx understands crisis: not as a detrimental process demanding management and resolution but as in itself redemptive. It is as though Marx works through and then beyond that which, etymologically, crisis concerns: the symptomatic analysis and resuscitation of a diseased body or—why not?—body politic. Marx's critic is not concerned with bodies. Contrary to the capitalist, whose sole care is for the effective administration and distribution of bodies— bodies to consume and to be consumed in the process of labor, bodies to be used up or cast aside, inexhaustible bodies, elite bodies to be disciplined and perfected—the critic is obsessed with the incorporation of alien elements and histories as they gut corporations, turning the organs of their operation inside out. What preoccupies him are the technical prostheses that expand the habituated corporeal confines, the power of exfoliating cadavers, the energy of decaying things and forms of life: all the things that a privileging of the body encourages us to dismiss as pathogenic or parasitical. In short, Marx's critic turns traditional political-economical criticism inside out because he eviscerates the thinking that takes place in and through bodies. The Marxian critic is a nonimmunological thinker. Like the capitalist, that quintessential figure of the undead—adding nothing to the metabolic interaction between labor and nature but instead vampirically sucking out the life activity of labor—the materialist critic manipulates and measures organic undead matter, including the capitalist himself, but with this crucial difference: unlike that of the capitalist, the critic's symptomatic reading functions not by seizing upon the recombinatory potential of undead materials but by dissolving even the treasure of the symptom that can be turned into a surplus. In a nutshell, he makes that which belongs to the capitalist befall the capitalist, and to such a commonizing extent that the capitalist becomes yet another agent—yet another critical agent—of physionomos.

Let us finally understand what Marx is up to here. Marx describes, and in so doing effects, the infinite expansion of the objects of labor and the means and materials of production until "the distinction between principle subject and accessory vanishes," alongside the "original composition" of all substances and products (288). That means that Marx systematically dehierarchizes the metaphysical taxonomies of substance and accidents that continue to reverberate in the capitalist distinction between the finished product, which interests the capitalist only insofar as it is a commodity, and the raw materials, means of production, and labor processes that went into it. Whereas the capitalist turns all means, things, and processes into substances, the critic liquefies those substances, transforming them into accidentals by reentering them into natural-historical circulation. Being a materialist natural historian means transferring the transient and transformative force of things, regardless of the position, be it raw materials, products, or means of labor, that they happen to take in a given labor constellation, to the world of political economy. In this way, the classical natural order of the physiocrats, with its hierarchies and distributions, its overall properness, is dissolved and rendered uneconomical. So profoundly natural historical is Marx's structuralist and functionalist thought that this uneconomy can be best described as a physionomos in which semimanufactured things—cotton, thread, and yarn—are "submitted to whole series of different processes, changing their shape, their specific function by the position [they] occup[y], as [their] position changes" in a given moment, losing and attaining characteristics, becoming imperfect, failing, dying, until they achieve their complete extinction, at which point they release their destructive powers and also call out living labor (289). Marx thus invents a completely new, ever-expanding universe of infinite means and things: a physionomical logic in which everything is unsettled by the unrest extinguished in it. In the process, he reveals himself to be not only a profoundly structuralist thinker, a thinker for whom structures and constellations, and not subjects and people, determine the political arena. He reveals himself to be a universalizing revolutionary thinker of minute things—bacteria, stones, dye, rust—as they come into contact with the grandest accomplishments of mankind—canals and so on—both past and present.

Far from being extinguished, Marx's idea of natural history would continue to return—and, in returning, call living labor to itself—long after Marx himself was dead and buried. Arguably the most fruitful of those returns can be found in the correspondence between Benjamin and Adorno, whose exchange on the commodity draws attention to the enigmatic comings and goings of one particular denizen of the natural historical realm, Kafka's creature Odradek. For both Benjamin and Adorno, Odradek lends a face to the natural historical dimension of the commodity. But for Adorno especially, Odradek embodies nothing less than the promise for a future politics, a politics defined by the end of the oikos and the advent of postcommodified life. Does Odradek "not anticipate precisely the overcoming of the creaturely state of guilt," asks Adorno,

> and is not this concern—truly a case of Heidegger put right side up—the secret key, indeed the most indubitable promise of *hope*, precisely through the overcoming of the house itself? Certainly, as the other face of the world of things, Odradek is a sign of distortion—but precisely as such he is also a motif of transcendence, namely of the ultimate limit and of the reconciliation of the organic and the inorganic, or of the overcoming of death: Odradek "lives on." Expressed in another way, it is only to a life that is perverted in thingly form that an escape from the overall context of nature is promised. . . . No, Odradek is indeed so dialectical that it can also properly be said of him that "almost nothing has made everything well again."[50]

How is it that Adorno can arrive, from out of distortion, the dregs of the commodity, and the crisis of the patriarchal form of life, at the "promise of *hope*"? What Adorno perceives here is that crisis, first and foremost, exposes the precariousness of the world of things and their names. When a social form of life that had contained the thingly world through an order of naming founders: that is when we apprehend the thingly world in all its obstinacy. At such moments, the critic must recognize himself, in Benjamin's formulation, as a physiognomist of the world of things and their names in crisis: as the one who knows how to read crisis into the constellation of things. At such moments, it is the task of the critic to act as an agent of natural history, seizing upon crisis lest crisis be seized upon as the pretext for its resolution.

The beginning of Kafka's text epitomizes this operation of critique.[51]

What starts off as an etymological critique of Odradek the name soon becomes an ontological critique of Odradek the being, until finally critique expands to become a generalized crisis of knowledge and language: the fruitless investigation of a creature without discernible origin that no existing language can claim as its own. Not only then is Odradek a name for crisis; it speaks the very crisis of naming and being. The etymological critique introduced by the mere existence of Odradek intensifies the crisis of an existing form of life, a crisis that only becomes palpable through a program of interminable study and irresolvable concern. The neologism Odradek intimates the formation of a logic yet to come and a critique that pledges fidelity to that logic. This critique yet to come drains *krísis* from crisis by divesting a modern understanding of crisis of its etymology. For once we divest crisis of its etymological roots—once we drain krísis from crisis—we simultaneously deprive ourselves of the resolution and overcoming associated with crisis. What remains is then a form of critique that, like Odradek's name and existence, will live on beyond the house, inflicting crisis upon the nomos of the oikos in perpetuity. This is not to imply that either the house or its father will themselves exist in perpetuity or that the aim of critique is to bring down the house. Odradek cannot be given a political purpose or get enlisted in a political project that would provide him with a permanent abode. That would be to misunderstand the ongoing, still unfolding, not altogether dreadful delight at work in the Odradekian form of crisis.

If the new, all-consuming object of epistemological and political critique goes by the name of Odradek, its new, deranged temporality first announces itself with *sometimes*, as in "sometimes he is not to be seen for months . . . but then he invariably comes back to our house again. Sometimes when one comes out of one's room" (176). The intervals between Odradek's returns are as unpredictable as where he will appear—the attic, the staircase, the corridor, the hallway—for Odradek is "exceptionally mobile and refuses to be caught" (176). What happens to a subject—the father of the family, in this case—when his affective attachment (in the mood of worry) to the outside world, the world of objects, comes via an elusive, mobile object whose location and time remain uncertain? At the very least, it means that what Heidegger calls the "Age of the World Picture," wherein a subject makes the representation of an object dependent on how he places himself firmly in the scene—that is, the way humans position themselves "to beings as the objective"—has come to an end.[52] With the arrival of furtive and nomadic objects like Odradek, we are no longer at home in the age of the world picture, where a stable subject-object opposition licenses man to subjectivize himself through the world of objects, while objects themselves are subjected to the fixed positioning and measurements of man. Now dwelling in a world populated by whimsical, ill-disciplined, and vaguely impish Odradeks, the father and his world picture are unsettled by the obstinacy of things that withdraw from us, only to return on their own time and in their own manner. The moment when Odradek derails the oikos is the moment when the ennobling care (*Sorge*) that had defined oikonomia, the care for things and bodies, turns into an all-consuming concern and worry (Sorge).

If the appearance of Odradek should worry anyone, then, it is the father of the family; but even he, as Judith Butler observes, finds it *"almost* painful" that Odradek will outlive him.[53] How are we to read that *almost?* The father of the family, as Marx, Freud, Lacan, and Foucault (for starters) well knew, stands at the gateway to modern economic and political thought. The Roman paterfamilias, with his right over the life and death of his children and his right to enjoy the usufruct of the products of their labor, is the archetype for the modern sovereign, capitalist, manager, and master. As Foucault notes, the family, although sovereign in origin and grounded in the *patria potestas* of Roman law, constitutes the cell of the disciplinary archipelago.[54] "In Rome," writes Foucault, quoting Montesquieu, "after fathers were no longer permitted to put their children to death, the magistrates inflicted the punishment that the father would have prescribed."[55] Juridical and disciplinary power radiates outward from the family bond to the government and the state. It is not only that the Roman magistrates are the first figures to occupy the threshold between sovereign, disciplinary, and biopolitical regimes; it is that the doctrine of the *parens patriae* establishes, once and for all, the obligation of the state to care for the legally incompetent and the infirm—a doctrine built on the paternal and familial model. But if the father acts as the fulcrum for three diagrams of governmental power—the juridical, the disciplinarian, and the biopolitical—it is because he embodies the origin of our primordial investment in the social and political spheres. The paterfamilias of Rome amasses legal and moral obligations, establishes a regime of permanent relations and loyalty, and consolidates, among his sons and heirs, a regime of contractual and personal indebtedness to him, in the process creating a guilt history tied to the past and to a future genealogy. In the family structure, as Foucault reads it, the flat, isotopic politics of contiguity associated with discipline joins the hierarchical, asymmetrical politics of verticality associated with the sovereign. The care and welfare of the *parens patriae* characteristic of modern societies simply adds the biopolitical dimension to the "double role," at once sovereign and disciplinary, already performed by the family man.[56] But if the care and welfare of the father of the family primarily concerns the production of docile and efficient offspring, he also, in the end, becomes responsible for those who fall outside of the home: "the uneducable, undisciplinable, unusable and unwanted human waste" produced by and yet anathema to biopolitics.[57] The father, in other words, becomes the caretaker of Odradek, while his home becomes the repository in which the *homo œconomicus* meets the *creatura physionomicus*.

And so the father of the family finds it "*almost* painful" that Odradek will outlive him. Because if, on the one hand, the father harbors the secret worry that his reign will replicate itself without him, on the other hand he betrays the not-so-secret hope that nothing of his reign will be reproduced at all—that a completely new progeny will emerge, one with no connection to his genealogy. Just as the superego ambivalently wishes that the child would accede to its demands while forever failing to become like it, so the father of the family invites his children to eventually supersede his rule and become Odradek's playmates. The mercilessly perpetual feast days that celebrate the cult of capitalism—a cult grounded, as Marx well knew, in the paternal oikos and the *homo œconomicus* in general—are transformed into playdates with Odradek.[58] Once the state of the father (the literal sense of *patrimonium*) is dissolved, not only will his children be freed from a regime of worry and care, but the father too will be unburdened of the immunity that he is expected not only to dispense but to protect. For we flatter ourselves if we assume that the problem the father faces is that of protecting us; the problem he faces is that of protecting the immunitarian paradigm of protection. And it is a problem of which he would just as soon be relieved. So it is that while the father initially worries about protecting the rule of the paternal home, he ends up worrying that Odradek, in outliving him, will fail in his appointed task and not unmake the patrimony whose dissolution will absolve the father of his worry. If the father's new concern is also the source of his hope, his new worry is that he will lose that hope.

The father has no choice, then, but to learn to live in the midst of the worst, encapsulated in Kafka's text by the *einstmals* (once, erstwhile, one day) of Odradek's perpetual reappearance. "Can it be," the father asks himself, "that he [Odradek] might one day [einstmals] still be rolling down the stairs, with ends of thread trailing after him, before the feet of [our] children and children's children?" (177). Einstmals denotes an event in the past that, in Kafka's peculiar handling of the term, stretches into the most distant future, thereby challenging the frame of origin and last judgment that delimits the perimeters of our patrilineal mode of history. With the arrival of Odradek, we find ourselves in the realm of the almost: a middle where all acts, either the ones that run precipitously forward to the *telos* of history or those that run nostalgically back to a pure origin, are spliced. But even in this acting and being in the middle, which is the act our time demands, the father of the family does not give up on a remnant of last judgment. For every present spent with Odradek or wondering about his absence is an opportunity for more than the mutually beneficial exchange that the father seems to have in mind when he first meets the living spool. Every such present holds out the potential for a true last judgment of the present, one that paradoxically declares fidelity to the ruination of the father's oikos and to the end of all paternal judgment. Odradek's existence in the einstmals, indexed by the impossibility of determining the precise date of his appearance, detemporalizes chronometric time so utterly that it derails an epoch and a logic of decisionism.

Read from the perspective of the capitalist cult, in fact, Odradek's crooked calendar traverses generations and confuses cause and effect, before and after, in a manner akin to the metaleptic temporal reversal of the Trinitarian father-son incest that Marx detected in the capitalist production of surplus (256). Only in the debris of capitalist production, at once its cause and effect, will we encounter a new type of infinity, one that departs from the immortal regime of fathers and sons rolling out quietly and solemnly before us. In a kind of infinite finitude—old, torn, knotted, and discontinuous—or infinite decompletion of the surplus value produced and enjoyed by the father, we find the prospect of a newly anxious type of care. The very idea of Odradek being ground down by purpose so worries the father that his anxiety becomes a care; and that new care relocates him and his household to a dominion where the only master is the laughter, "like the rustling of fallen leaves," at our creaturely stupefaction (177). Simply by relating to Odradek, the father of the family and his children so thoroughly contract the creature's discontinuous temporal and indefinite ontological status that they can no longer establish the distinct moments, delimited by a determinate before and after, when the trauma of concern began and might end. Odradek's einstmals, about which "it is not possible to state anything more definite . . . since Odradek is exceptionally mobile and refuses to be caught," renders impossible the retroactive constitution, in a second encounter, of the first time he vexed, concerned, and traumatized the father. Not even the psychoanalytic narrative of subjectivity, in which we relate to the impudent impossibility of our existence by returning to the past trauma through which we become subjects, is available to the father; for his nightmare has yet to arrive and never will have arrived since it has not even begun and therefore cannot end. Odradek, who moves into and, by moving into, voids the very position of the master, turns the father into a creature-object unable to subjectivize himself and thus to become a Being. Yet in that conundrum, the father discerns the outlines of an immanent transcendence, reachable only by traversing the figure of Odradek and the natural-historical rhythm of his reappearance.

The father of the family is not alone in catching a glimpse of that traversal, however. He has an important counterpart in another of Kafka's sovereign-cum-managerial figures: Poseidon, from the parable of the same name.[59] Poseidon, one might say, is a more developed, because more paralyzed, version of the father of the family. Poseidon has a crisis of naming of his own. Everyone seems to think that he is a god. Worse, everyone seems to think that he is a Homeric god. This is almost more than Poseidon can bear. Not only is he not an idle, indolent god out cruising the waves, as everyone seems to believe. On the contrary, "the administration of all the waters gave him endless work" (85). Cruising around the waves, trident in hand. As if he had time for such nonsense! The only opportunity he ever gets to act like the Homeric god people wrongly conceive him as being is when he goes up "now and then" to meet with Jupiter. (And when had his own brother, Zeus, become Jupiter, figure of the imperium? Had he been so immersed in the management of the seas that he had missed the passing of the old order? Was he the last holdout of a form of life that had already faded away? If so, why had no one informed him?) At such times, he gets to pass fleetingly through his realm, but the meetings with Jupiter are invariably petty and humiliating, and he ends up returning to his office in a rage. Hardly the all-powerful god of the oceans he is made out to be.

Instead, Poseidon dwells where the father of the family dwells: in the midst of the worst, the realm of the perpetual almost. As he himself well understands, Poseidon is neither a god nor a bureaucrat. Rather, he inserts the bureaucrat into the god and, in so doing, occupies an origin different— neither coming to be nor passing away, neither divine nor profane—from the one imposed upon him by Homeric myth. In that sense, Kafka's parable can be understood as a restaging and, in turn, an exit from the anarchy at the heart of Olympian management. His trident now propped up in a corner of his office, Poseidon's image (as a god) and his nature (as a bureaucrat) cancel one another out, leaving him nowhere other than in a natural-historical middle. To judge by his complaints, one would think that Poseidon finds this situation intolerable. "In fact, he had already filed many petitions for—as he put it—more cheerful work" (85). But the few times he is given an opportunity to be something other than he is—appointed to a new post, given new responsibilities—Poseidon panics, his divine breathing becoming troubled and his bronze chest beginning to tremble (85). The office of ocean management could not function without him. That, at least, is what he tells himself. But underneath his conflicted emotions, underneath the complaints and frustrations, Poseidon understands that there is no other, or no better, place for him than in the mutually canceling middle. He panics because, were he to leave his present position, he would cease to be the natural-historical figure he is; and it is only insofar as he retains his natural-historical position, only insofar as he continues to occupy his origin, that he has any hope or chance at happiness.

Poseidon, then, could be said to occupy—occupy voluntarily-unconsciously, as it were—the place that the father of the family comes to occupy only when forced to do so by the arrival of Odradek. Odradek draws the father into a different calendar and a different constellation. But from time immemorial, Poseidon has been immersed in that same calendar, that same constellation, by virtue of his bureaucratic task administering the creaturely life found in the depths of the sea. Poseidon is not simply an accountant. He is stuck in a state of perpetual accounting, of forever taking inventory. Is that not the ideal position for the figure, now understood to be one and the same, of the sovereign-cum-governmental manager? As an activity, accounting negates both poles of the spectrum that runs (in place) from sovereignty to biopolitics. The sovereign, to use Foucault's elegant formulation, lets live and makes die, while biopolitics fosters life and lets die. But accounting, thorough accounting, accounting performed to its fanatical extreme, follows neither of those patterns. It lets nothing die; and yet it makes nothing live. Accounting, moreover, cannot be said either to enliven or to deaden its practitioners. It simply repeats without end. It therefore removes the accountant from the realm of care (which still promises a kind of grandeur) and relocates him, along with the father of the family, to the realm of concern: a realm where he is utterly absorbed, rendered harmless and distracted, no longer interested in aspirational or managerial redemption—a realm where he sits "in the depths of the world-ocean, doing figures uninterruptedly" (87).

As we have known since Derrida's *Archive Fever*, however, there is at the same time no historical or critical world apart from the archive. Were the accounts and inventories of the archive to disappear, so too would the historical and critical worlds. And given the precariousness of every archive, this means that the historical world is forever on the verge of apocalypse. Already, then, Poseidon looks ahead, in his very occupation, to the end of world history. In fact, "he was in the habit of saying that what he was waiting for was the fall of the world" (87). But insofar as he takes perpetual inventory, insofar as he is caught in the endless repetitive task that has been his "from the beginning" (85), the end of the world is held in abeyance even as it continues to unfold. The archive continues, albeit without resolution (there being no resolution to the taking of inventory). In that way, Poseidon can look ahead to an end that is always on the verge of arriving, or that arrives perpetually in its imagined anticipation. On that last day, Poseidon will finally be able to "to make a quick little tour" around the oceans that he administers but has never properly seen (87). But before doing so, he will look through (*Durchsicht*) his accounts one last time. Then, in a moment of transparency (*Durchblick*), he will realize that, all along, his rows were empty but for the figures, the "destructive characters" as Benjamin might call them, that it had been his job to enter there. In that moment of looking through, he will grasp that, behind the clamor of the historical world, there was a nullification even of the nothingness that stirs the drama of the world-historical stage: that the historical world was filled, not with itself, but with the figures of natural history that he had spent his time "doing uninterruptedly." Then he will be released from the burden of guilt that sustains all managerial care. His hope in the worst will have been confirmed.

Notes

1 Virno, "Natural-Historical Diagrams," 138.
2 Virno, *Multitude*, 41.
3 Virno, "Natural-Historical Diagrams," 142.
4 Virno, "Natural-Historical Diagrams," 146.
5 Virno, "Natural-Historical Diagrams," 138, 139, 135.
6 Virno, "Natural-Historical Diagrams," 133–34, 135–44.
7 Virno, *Multitude*, 42.
8 Marx, "Postface to the Second Edition," in *Capital*, vol. 1, 103. Subsequent references to this edition appear in the text.
9 It was Bataille who pointed out the extent to which nature in Marx and Engels

is antithetically developing not as a movement in thought and spirit but in the real, in politics and the class struggle themselves. See Bataille, "The Critique of the Foundations of the Hegelian Dialectic," 106–9.

10 Virno, "Natural-Historical Diagrams," 138.

11 Virno, "Natural-Historical Diagrams," 132.

12 Virno, "Natural-Historical Diagrams," 141–44.

13 Foucault summarizes this link between the transient existence of human order and what he calls the labor of "constant criticism" thus: "Thought does exist, both beyond and before systems and edifices of discourse. . . . There is always a little thought occurring even in the most stupid institutions . . . even in silent habits. Criticism consists in uncovering that thought and trying to change it. . . . So many things can be changed, being as fragile as they are, tied more to contingencies than to necessities . . . , more to complex transitory historical contingencies than to inevitable anthropological constants." Foucault, "So Is It Important to Think?," 456–58.

14 Foucault, *The Politics of Truth*, 44, 57.

15 Foucault, *The Politics of Truth*, 57.

16 Foucault, *The Politics of Truth*, 63.

17 Foucault, *The Politics of Truth*, 65, 62.

18 Foucault, *The Politics of Truth*, 66.

19 Foucault, *The Politics of Truth*, 65.

20 Foucault, "So Is It Important to Think?," 458.

21 Foucault, "So Is It Important to Think?," 457.

22 Foucault, *The Birth of Biopolitics*, 296.

23 Agamben, *The Kingdom and the Glory*, 276.

24 Agamben, *Democracy in What State?*, 4.

25 Foucault, *The Politics of Truth*, 94.

26 Kant, "The Contest of Faculties," in *Political Writings*, 177.

27 Kant, "The Contest of Faculties," 181.

28 Kant, "Perpetual Peace," in *Political Writings*, 119.

29 Kant, "The Contest of Faculties," 184.

30 Foucault, *The Politics of Truth*, 88.

31 Foucault, *The Politics of Truth*, 93.

32 Foucault never quite brings himself to say that Kant makes our and humankind's history natural or that he turns human history into something natural. It is nonetheless clear that what Foucault calls the transformative ontology of us and our present, Kant calls nature.

33 Kant, "The Contest of Faculties," 189.

34 Kant, "The Contest of Faculties."

35 Foucault, *The Politics of Truth*, 56.

36 Foucault states in an interview, "I am well aware that I have never written anything but fictions. I do not mean to say, however, that truth is therefore absent. It seems to me that the possibility exists for fiction to function in truth. One

'fictions' history on the basis of a political reality that makes it true, one 'fictions' a politics not yet in existence on the basis of a historical truth." Foucault, *Power/ Knowledge*, 193.

37 While most political theorists seem to be interested in the question "What is a dispositif?," the pivotal question might be "What is a diagram?" It is clear that the use of the term *diagram* in Foucault, Deleuze, or Virno goes beyond describing a mere visualization technique or graphic tool for illustrating relations of power and networks of forces in a new cartography (in maps, graphs, lines, arrows, visual links, etc.). The construction of a diagram gauges the mode of its presence in its effects. The effects generated by the way a diagram orders its specific phenomena or combines its elements demonstrate that diagrams do not intervene into a real from the outside, as if it were a preexisting object. Rather, a diagram is immanent to the phenomena in its effects like a grammar is to the norms and thoughts it expresses. A diagram is a condensed graph or map that, like a monad or a microcosm, sketches and measures in miniature—often coarsely and abstractly—the coordinates and internal proportions of a discursive field. Diagrams are always on the verge of becoming one with the networks and relations that they actualize. In fact, diagrams produce those things by touching their nerve center and designating their symptomatic charge. A diagram places and displaces the phenomena and forces in which functions; it is at once outside and inside the field it affects. Diagrams in this sense distill the transcendental structure for the demarcations of a specific region, ensuring that it appears in a specific way and that it appears as such. In this way, diagrams enable modes of experience; they demonstrate that it is not enough to explain a constellation, but that the diagrammatic act of enunciation is an integral part of its emergence and structuration. "Diagrammitization" is then a deforming truth procedure that restores phenomena to their true disfigured state and excavates the inherent crisis and instability of a system. This procedure is a praxis, for it makes the experience of an effective political constellation possible, thereby realizing historical objects that either did not exist or that lie dormant in a dross of impassive *Geschichten* (stories/histories). *Mise-en-scène* is one form of diagrammitization.

38 Foucault, *The Politics of Truth*, 88.

39 Foucault speaks of the "inversion," as opposed to the overcoming or abolition, of S_1, and with good reason. In doing so, he confronts us with the trembling contours of a literally inverted S_1, one whose body surface, whose whole spirit and body politic, is turned inside out: that becomes flesh, exposing its decomposing organs and intestines. From then onward, once we track the afterlife of subsequent manifestations of S_1 (the small despots and tyrants, the governmental and administrative graph, or contemporary biocapitalism), our politics can never forget this horrifying vision of a divided and decomposing sovereign. Even when Foucault calls "civil society," including our high-flying ideas of democracy and popular sovereignty, our new master signifier, the triangulation sovereignty-discipline-biopolitical governmentality remains fundamentally

fragile, saddled with contradictory rationalities and permeated with a host of countervailing microphysical forces and diagrams (Foucault, *The Birth of Bio-politics*, 295). In this sense Jacques-Alain Miller is right to call our very idea of democracy "the master-signifier which says that there is no master-signifier" (Miller, *Le Neveu de Lacan*, 270). That the three rationalities sovereignty-discipline-biopolitical governmentality often appear nefariously conjoined in our democracies means that the very gaps and inconsistencies between them provide the points of entry for devising a novel, albeit still tremulous, political microphysics grounded in positive rights (without juridical rights) for ungovernable subjects and people.

40 Foucault, *The Politics of Truth*, 20.

41 Foucault, *The Politics of Truth*, 32.

42 Foucault, *Psychiatric Power*, 34.

43 Foucault, *Psychiatric Power*.

44 Agamben, *The Kingdom and the Glory*, 65.

45 Foucault, *The Politics of Truth*, 115.

46 Agamben, *Homo Sacer*, 31–32. Agamben would go so far as to claim, in fact, that "the hidden paradigm guiding every successive definition of sovereignty" is precisely Pindar's sovereign nomos, which works by melding the principle of superior force with a force of law said to have originated from a natural source.

47 We have used the edition found in Plato, *Complete Works*.

48 Marx, "Preface to the First Edition," in *Capital*, vol. 1, 92. Subsequent references to this edition appear in the text.

49 Marx provides an intriguing footnote to this event that suggests how much he wished to emphasize the prehistorical origin of capitalism: the primal fall or, better, primal cast of capitalism. Marx cites Colonel Torrens: "In the first stone which the savage flings at the wild animal he pursues, in the first stick that he seizes to strike down the fruit which hangs above his reach, we see the appropriation of one article for the purpose of aiding in the acquisition of another, and thus discover the origin of capital." Marx then proceeds to speculate whether this "*Stock*" (stick) is not the reason why in English *stock* is synonymous with capital (291).

50 Adorno and Benjamin, *The Complete Correspondence*, 69.

51 Kafka, "A Problem for the Father of the Family," 176–77. Subsequent references to this edition appear in the text.

52 Heidegger, *Off the Beaten Track*, 69.

53 Butler, "Who Owns Kafka?"

54 Foucault, *Psychiatric Power*, 82.

55 Foucault, *La volonté de savoir. Histoire de la sexualité 1*, 177, cited by Minkkinen, "Michel Foucault on Sovereignty and Law," 9n21.

56 Foucault views the family as essentially a linchpin of disciplinary apparatuses. As he says in *Psychiatric Power*: "The family, then, has this double role: the pinning down of individuals on disciplinary systems, and the joining and circula-

tion of individuals from one disciplinary system to another" (83). We are reintroducing the father as a player in that double role and, in so doing, distilling the biopolitical content of the family insofar as it represents an intersection between the sovereign and discipline.

57 Minkkinen, "Michel Foucault on Sovereignty and Law," 10.

58 See Benjamin, "Capitalism as Religion," 288–91.

59 Kafka, "Poseidon," 85–87. Subsequent references to this edition appear in the text.

PART II

Italian Affirmations

_____

CHAPTER 2

Left and Right:

Why They Still Make Sense

Carlo Galli

Translated by Zakia Hanafi

The issue of left and right still warrants reflection. Although widely debated, the topic has yet to be exhausted: the distinction between left and right, displaced from its original political space, and even from the somehow classic opposition between capital and labor, still remains effective and meaningful.

The thesis of this work is that although there have been, and continue to be, many lefts and rights, two broad categories can be identified within this plurality that are general, useful, and meaningful. The goal, therefore, is to simplify through synthesis, not to classify through analysis. We aim to arrive at a radical level of understanding, but not through the politological clarity of ideal types—models constructed according to the needs of the researcher—or through the historical variety of concrete forms. Nor will we proceed through essences or ontologically stable ideal clusters (such as liberty and equality, risk and security, preservation and revolution), or even through transepochal, psychological, or anthropological attitudes. Left and right will be treated rather as different modes, separate but inseparable, opposing but complementary, for accessing the original energy of the modern, through which—in the history, institutions, political ideas, and common feeling of public opinion—modern Western politics is articulated. This means that left and right can be radically thought only through a genealogical procedure that goes back to the ground zero of modern political institutions. This thesis also includes the observation that the categories of left and right do not survive today because of the persistence of the modern political space, with which they came into existence, or because they represent a fundamental dichotomy of society, one that is far more divided and fragmented today. The reason these categories have survived is because through them is expressed a force and a problem, namely, subjectivity—in the modes we will be describing—which may very well be something more than simply an echo of an original big bang, the fossil radiation that pervades the universe of politics. Rather, subjectivity is one of the contributions of the modern period to the historical continuity of Western civilization, as were the Greek *areté* or the Roman *ius* or Christianity. Of course, if the distinction between left and right is not yet vestigial, it can still become so: in the same way the legacy of the ancient can be evacuated, the West can also lose all the driving force of its institutional ideals. This may well happen, although the major powers that have sprung from it—science, technology, the capitalist mode of production—have extended themselves (of course, in superficial and varying degrees) throughout most of the world. At play in the categories of left and right are specific political, historical, and cultural institutions of the West—secular humanism and democracy to begin with—which, although implicated in them, are not coextensive with the planetary expansion of Western practical skills.

A caveat I would do well to include, then, is that the arguments presented in this work—stemming from an interest in deciphering the intellectual and political forms of the right that currently governs Italy, and which is leaving its mark on the country, although one of uncertain duration—are primarily relevant to Western democracies, where the question of left and right first arose. There is a further caveat to be issued: this is not just another piece on the incidental fates of the left or right, an analysis of their ills, advice (unsolicited at that) on the issues to be addressed by their policies, and in answer to the question whether a moderate or aggressive, institutional or radical praxis is called for. There is no normative intent to this inquiry; if anything, normativity is the object of its reflection. In any case, there is no intention to hand out badges of authenticity to any true left or true right. The purpose of this work is to recognize two cardinal modes in the past, and in the present as well (meaning, even in the rudimentary politics of today). Both are interpretations of original, unavoidable aspects of modernity, so that we cannot say that one is false politics and the other authentic politics. The indeterminacy of politics, its constitutive contingency, makes this impossible.

An Obsolete Dichotomy?

The heuristic, theoretical, and practical obsolescence of the political distinction between left and right has been proclaimed since the 1980s, and with even greater intensity in the wake of globalization following the fall of

Soviet communism. While in the 1980s criticism of the distinction was suspected of being essentially right wing, beginning in the 1990s it was viewed instead as a sign of epochal, structural crisis. In the age of electronics and the consumer society, immaterial labor, and the disappearance of traditional classes, the left-right opposition—an archaic legacy of contrasting ideological arguments played out around the centrality of factory labor—was declared to be a mere lexical holdover, blamed on the incapacity or laziness of the political and intellectual class (the same result comes from reversing the signs, in other words, if you express nostalgia for a world polarized by strong ideologies).[1]

In reality, the difference between left and right was determined in the nineteenth century in reference to factory production: it identified the dialectic, at times a harsh one, between those who advocated a prudent slowing down of the inclusive dynamics hardwired into capitalism, and those who advocated their advanced, progressive acceleration (in terms of citizenship, equality, and access to health and education) until its final, eventual overturning or fulfillment. At the beginning of the twentieth century, transformed into the opposition between the liberal logics of the individual and the democratic logics of mass societies—both of which, as Tocqueville saw, had been inherent to modernity—the categorical pairing nonetheless seemed inadequate and stifling to many, like an intellectual and political cage to be broken out of by taking a leap forward, so as to go beyond right and left.[2] The fascists who held this stance to the bitter end attracted a great deal of the most evolved intellectual adherents in Europe, who at least in the early years were deluded precisely by this position.[3] In reality, fascism had actually constructed another right, more radical than the traditional conservative one, by constructing something new, the totalitarian regime; or, if you will, it had realized its plan to go beyond left and right. This was a new political experience, but one that negated the reasons for the very problem leading to its creation (and even if the truth of Western modernity were to be found in this negation, left and right nonetheless lose all meaning in it).

In any case, with the disastrous loss of the war, fascism delegitimized the right in Europe and legitimized the left in all its forms, both communist and (broadly speaking) social-democratic. These seemed to occupy the political space of the left after the Second World War, while the right was forced to present itself as the center (and in many ways to also converge on it). Similarly, forty-five years later, the defeat of real communism would mark not only the end of the extreme left but also the weakening of the social-democratic left. More generally, the real democracies had indeed won a historic victory over real communism, weakening it, precisely thanks to their profound internal economic and political transformations. But they had come to triumph so full of insuperable contradictions that at the time of their victory, the whole conceptual apparatus of modern politics was almost unusable: the almost complete disappearance from mass democracy of the individual subject, the heart of modernity—made now into the object rather than the subject of new, pervasive powers—was fundamental to this process. The postmodern era of globalization thus witnessed the crisis of socialism as well as the crisis of conservativism, made extremist and populist after the disappearance of its adversary, while witnessing at the same time an internal critique of neoliberalism itself, which was unable to lend a stable form to society.[4]

In short, the end of modernity and the fluidity of the present were supposed to lead to the recognition that both left and right had lost their purpose just as much as they had lost the chain of subjectivities and means to fulfill them. The present and the future were also supposed to have demanded going beyond modern political alternatives, so as to position themselves under the banner of the new: the new left and new right, if the same terminology really had to be used. But, in reality, the new was, obviously, substantially the same, and it differed only by subtle tonalities, by only (slightly) different interpretations of the same political divide. There was the unquestioned centrality of the capitalist mode of production, but of consumption instead of labor, of pluralist parliamentary democracy effectively emptied of its meaning, and of the middle classes, to whose cultural and social mediateness politics was supposed to adapt as a structural and strategic factor, becoming a politics of the center. The cultural and political news over the last twenty years has indeed been full of convergences to the center, of right and left being surpassed, and also of social democracy and environmentalism, proceeding along new third paths, despite all the differences in the various Western political worlds (but also the acceptance of capitalism by the Chinese communist regime, which is no small theoretical and interpretive challenge).

True, there were those who refused to embrace the changes, rejecting the dilution of their power, and who spoke, from the far left, about two rights: the real right and the one the new left was turning into.[5] Conversely, from the opposite bank, the Italian and French New Right pursued a different way of overcoming the traditional dichotomy: in metapolitical terms, meaning, radically categorical ones, rather than from a merely factual convergence; although not devoid of historical and theoretical awareness, it nonetheless held little practical effectiveness (the new right that has emerged in Italian politics has nothing in common with the New Right). In any case, the mainstream interpreters were nevertheless oriented toward perceiving the blurring of the boundaries and of the contrapositions, and toward the resulting shift of politics into an elsewhere—in which, at best, issues that involved neither the left nor the right should have been able to take on shape and importance, such as environmental issues—challenged if anything by the relics of the old extremisms and, much more, by the emergence of new populist forces, the vehicle of new extremisms, whether ethnic, cultural, or religious in character.

All this is partly true, especially in the obvious perception of the changed geopolitical and also conceptual landscape, but in other important respects it is simply inaccurate. In fact, in the West, the political space continues to be polarized around the left and the right—just think, for example, of the history of the last fifteen years in Italy, Spain, Poland, France, and the United States. This contraposition is no longer fueled by the complex ideological constructs of the nineteenth century or even purely from the positioning of individuals in the industrial space, in the material sphere of relations of production. In any case, the global economic crisis is showing that there is an attempt in politics to regain a central role through a new capacity to regulate the economy, or in general by providing post-laissez-faire regulatory solutions that involve social politics as much as the symbolic and cultural realm. There is no doubt that in this new phase distinctions of left and right are meaningful, from the standpoint of the political forces and their way of presenting themselves as well as from that of the voters' response: in the European Parliament elections held in June 2009, for example, voters were clearly successful in distinguishing between left and right, rewarding the first and punishing the second.

In short, left and right are categories that belong to the politics of the modern era but somehow they continue to make sense in the largely postmodern politics of the global age, which means that something of the modern tradition is also at work in a context that is very different from the one in which they came into existence. This is exactly the problem that calls for an explanation.

Formal Schemas and the Complexity of History

The left-right cleavage only makes sense starting from modernity; in other words, it cannot be used to characterize all the conflicts of power and knowledge that have marked Western history, to explain the struggle between Caesar and Pompey, or the conflict between the Guelphs and Ghibellines. In terms of political history, this means that the opponents engaged in the struggle between church and state, and those who later faced each other down in the space of political economy, are lined up across its divide.

In the first case, the oppositional association between left and right describes the bourgeois, rationalist, and individualist fight against the authorities—as much against the pontiff as against the traditional monarch—on an intellectual path that runs from Hobbes and Locke to the Enlightenment, and from Rousseau to Kant. Politically, it has its high points in the revolutions that affected both sides of the Atlantic, in France and the United States, during the late eighteenth century. The goal was to make politics the space in which human beings are self-governing, where power only responds to human reason and not to other, dogmatic pleas.

In the second case, this opposition describes the change of front, after which the bourgeois world would give itself the goal of preserving the workings of capitalism, with its associated organization of the individualistic, representative-based public sphere—the rule of law—while the socialist world sought, using various strategies, to go beyond this economic and political organization. From this point of view, too, the new front that opened up with Babeuf already participated in the dynamics of the French Revolution and was destined to refine itself with the maturing of the Industrial Revolution and the emergence of Blanc, Blanqui, Proudhon, and Marx. A formal schema can be put together out of this showing the difference between left and right based on the parameters of value (difference or equality between people), politics (authority or liberation, hierarchy or autonomy, state or individual removed from bourgeois alienation), and time (preservation or progress).[6] In reality, this diagrammatic approach requires far more nuances. The political traditions of left and right are contradictory and anything but unambiguous in their historical reality. In other words, they are not determined by any specific contents (but—this is my thesis—neither are they empty containers that get randomly filled up from one occasion to the next).

It has been observed that the matrixes of the many possible versions of the right appeared on the political scene between 1789 and 1848.[7] First, the counterrevolutionary Catholics (Maistre, Bonald, the early Lamennais), the kind of right that supports the embedding of politics within an inaccessible foundation which precedes it (tradition, religion, nature, or for the romantics, the nation, and history) and which must be preserved without being criticized by human reason lest the political order suffer a catastrophic collapse. This was a radical right, consistently anti-individualist and anticapitalist, which strictly speaking did not even seek to be right wing: what it wanted was to abolish the modern political space of left and right altogether (without success, of course, actually ending up trapped in it).

With the July Revolution, this right was flanked by another one, that of the Orleanists, in some ways its opposite, which, along with François Guizot, took for granted that the revolution was definitively over and that social and political democracy was a problem to be brought under control. It represented individual initiative capable of creating wealth for individuals and for society, while also selecting the winners and the losers, the fit and the unfit, according to the objective laws of the market and success, guaranteed by the legal apparatus of the state. This was a conservative right. What followed as a development of and reaction to the revolutionary events of 1848 was the Bonapartism of Napoleon III, or the revolutionary right of political leadership from on high, of the plebiscitary head who, by his decision, reorganized the whole body politic of the nation by extralegal and extrainstitutional means. In this particular right, Karl Marx (in "The Eighteenth Brumaire of Louis Bonaparte") saw a constant of bourgeois politics, namely, that the bourgeoisie, fearing the power of the proletariat, may give up its own liberal, parliamentary, and democratic political forms.

What we have here are different forms of the right: some are confronted with modernity from its outset, while others are formed within it; some are economic and others political; some are moderate and others extreme. But they are the germs of many subsequent versions of the right: ones that have been and are conservative, traditionalist, and reactionary, but also avant-garde, revolutionary, modernist, and futurist; authoritarian, totalitarian, but also anarchic; statist, but also laissez-faire; equally organismic and individualistic. The extreme variety of the different rights, both intellectual and political, in the nineteenth and twentieth centuries—which were often allied with each other in different power relations, but which also fought bitterly against one another—shows that for them the political space was sometimes fixed, sometimes only slowly evolving, and sometimes even completely unstable, while at other times instead it was dynamic and dizzyingly in motion.

At times the political space was strictly unitary, nationalist, and imperialist, while at others it was broken up into small, xenophobic countries. Just to name a few, the right embraced such disparate figures as Maistre and Scruton, Burke and Maurras, Marinetti and Lorenz, Evola and Schmitt, Stahl and Spann, Malinsky and Guénon, Jünger and Gentile, Céline and Sironi, Eliade and Bishop Lefebvre; and politicians as far apart as Solaro della Margherita and Hitler, Franco and Mosley, Mussolini and Churchill, Rattazzi and Degrelle.

The right has taken every possible position on the main problems and categorical notions of modern politics: the relationship between religion and politics has taken the form, at different times, of politics being founded in religion (the counterrevolutionaries), of the depoliticized internalization of religion (the liberal-conservatives), of the authoritarian instrumentalization of religion by politics, and of the political religions of totalitarianisms. The various right-wing attitudes toward the state are equally far apart, ranging from out-and-out worship (what was called statolatry) to suspicion at its inherent secularism, which had to be balanced by the authority of the church, from the respect for its laws which were viewed as bringing unity and order to the intolerance toward those that hindered or slowed down economic dynamism. Right-wing attitudes to the state have also included a decisionistic overthrowing of its institutional and legal logic (so that the state remains a structure of mere domination) and, finally, open rebellion against its unitary and equalizing pretensions, in the name of territorial differences and regional roots, but also of heroic and exceptional subjectivities.

For the culture of the right, the individual was also sometimes a wolf to keep in check with harsh repressive laws, and sometimes a helpless sheep that had to be protected from the dangers of treacherous enemies; at other times, the individual was the lone hero who, entirely on his own strength, was capable of taking on his destiny. The swings on the part of the right when it comes to the economy are dramatic: at times, with a disdainful, aristocratic-warrior attitude, they have rejected the logics and ethos of capital, an opposition that can also take the form of a nationalistic rejection of the internationalism of capital, attributed to cosmopolitan classes or races (whence anti-Semitism, the socialism of idiots). At other times, they have given unquestioning support to the market as the new earthly Providence; and at other times again, they exercise a watchful and suspicious political governance (sometimes corporate) over its dynamics. With regard to the people, finally, the different rights have manifested their intrinsic plurality by sometimes abhorring the people as an unclean revolutionary beast, and sometimes coaxing the masses like a docile herd of consumers; now idolizing them as the nation—the source of historical tradition or race, in biological terms—that legitimates any politics of power; now presenting them with the fate of being ruled by wealthy or superior elites, or perhaps by charismatic leaders. Or yet again, they may hold up the people (this is right-wing populism) in contrast to the legal institutions and professional politicians, as the bearers of an essential legitimacy and spontaneous morality.

Between 1789 and 1848, the three basic forms of the left also appeared: the liberals who sparked the revolution, through the theoretical armory of rationalism and the Enlightenment, secularism, and individual rights; the radical democrats, with their egalitarian and moralistic republicanism (that of the Jacobins but also the Mazzinians); and the socialists in their various and often opposing groups: those that would be defined by Marx as utopians, Proudhon above all; the Marxists (destined to be internally divided between revolutionaries and reformists); and the anarchists.[8] Statist and individualistic, libertarian and authoritarian, even totalitarian, focused on spontaneity or discipline, pauperist or productivist; industrialist or ecologist, bellicose or pacificist, universalist and differentialist, utopian and scientific, from a historical standpoint, the left also seems to constitute a pluralistic universe. The world of the left is one of infinite variety and extraordinary polyvalency, one that on the historical and practical planes has had and continues to have more of a taste for separation than union, more drawn toward fratricidal war than collaboration. The conflicts between Marx and Bakunin, between Lenin and Luxemburg, between Stalin and Trotsky, between socialists and communists, are just a few of the exemplary peak, bloody moments in a political and ideological history marked by division.

Once again, a few conceptual indicators may help to illustrate how deeply divided the polymorphous universe of the lefts really is. On the question of subjectivity, the various lefts can be split into two large camps: those who consider the subject to have precedence over politics, and to be bestowed with an originary autonomy (individual rights); and the other, made up of those who view the subject as engendering itself in the process of historical struggle for emancipation (the collective subjectivity of the proletariat). The first position is liberal-democratic, while the second is the kind of dialectical thought that already at the time of Hegel (considered here not because he can be ascribed to the left but because he is the founder of a tradition of thought) united an enormous value assigned to subjectivity (the phenomenological theory of the substance-subject that constructs itself through history) with a critique of the abstractness and superficiality of liberalism, thus opening the way to the critique of Marx and Marxisms toward liberal individualism (for not being humanistic enough, since it focuses on the image of the alienated man), with the prospect of developing a fully liberated subjectivity (through the collective subject of the proletarian class, and beyond in the multiform humanity of communism). The issue is clearly rights, which have an a priori status for the democratic left. In the dialectical tradition, on the contrary, human rights cannot escape being historicized (as bourgeois), being made dialectical (as contradictory), and finally sent back—no longer as rights but as the height of practical and concrete being—to the dimension of the realized communism. With all the consequences we are only too familiar with.

The state is viewed with equally strong ambivalence: some on the left interpret the state as an instrument of class oppression, to be fought with a nonalienated, collective force, such as the party. Others, instead of considering it a Leviathan to be struck down, see it as a means to bring a bit of justice into society. Even the universal dimension of the political space—which in theory unites all the left, from liberals to proponents of antiglobalization, passing through the various forms of socialism—has many powerful exceptions: there has often been a country, a nation, a state that has incorporated the idea, and whose mission it has been to propagate the idea throughout the world, the USSR, obviously, being the most extreme example.

In addition, just to make any diagrammatic approach even more impractical and every history even more confused, we must recall the many overlapping critiques from the left and right that have been directed against the concepts and institutions that form the political structure of capitalism, in the forms of both liberal democracy and social democracy. Although their intents and logics may have been different, the convergence has been remarkable, leading to the common use of entire sets of arguments. The ease, for example, with which Lamennais passed from his counterrevolutionary phase to his democratic phase is thus explained by the persistence in him of a constant antibourgeois polemic. Although from opposite political sides and from very different cultural matrixes, we may also recall the assonance between the critiques of parliamentarism issuing from left and right: it is no coincidence that some antiparliamentarian motifs from the Frankfurt School were believed to be influenced by Carl Schmitt, with an antiliberal slant. Or the more or less successful syntheses (Conservative Revolution, national Bolshevism, to say nothing of National Socialism); or the convergence of left and right, in the first half of the twentieth century, for the purpose of organizational solutions, like planning, to overcome the individualist-based capitalist economy.

Finally, the same political force (for example, liberalism) can play a right-wing or left-wing role from one time to the next according to historical contingencies. The same goes for concepts (for example, the nation) and thinkers (the most renowned example being Sorel). Conversely, seemingly deciding oppositions such as individualism and statism traverse and intersect with the right as much as they do the left. However, despite the inadequacy of formal schemas and the ambiguity of historical content, the left-right binary opposition seems to persist even on the contemporary political scene. What is needed, therefore, is a radical deciphering of the political categories of modernity, not to explain the concrete political choices of individuals or collective subjects or various political forces—largely contingent choices— but to understand how the categories of left and right came into existence and why they are so long-lived. Without resorting to essentialisms, to definitions that apply to all periods, what we require is a genealogy of the concepts of right and left, performed using the tools and categories of a philosophy that is not limited to merely recognizing that the left-right cleavage makes sense in a modern political topology, but which goes back to the roots of a vast, contradictory phenomenology of lefts and rights.

The Origin of Modern Politics, and Its Consequences

The existence of the left-right binary opposition is an expression of the fact that modern politics is originarily indeterminate, meaning that its unity does not consist in exhibiting shared structures or foundations. Its unity consists rather in a problem that takes the form of a structural duality. The conceptual building blocks of thought that innervate modern politics, seeing as it had to give up on the traditional idea of Justice—the idea, that is, of an order of being that, if it were not for human sinfulness, directs even the political order—consists in the centrality of the link between disorder as a given and order as a requirement. On the one hand, there is an ominous and unstable reality, the state of nature; and on the other, it is essential to construct a contrivance that gives shape and stability to politics. These are the two, inseparable sides in the modern way of regarding politics.

When interpellated down to its roots, the history of modern political ideas—in its mainstream form of political rationalism—can be interpreted as a political cosmology, as a series of texts on the construction of order. The element of novelty does not only reside in the epochal compulsion to create order, but also in the fact that its actor, center, and star is the individual subject—rational, free, and equal.

In Hobbes, Locke, Pufendorf, Rousseau, and Kant—in spite of their differences, at times becoming oppositions—the same conceptual structure, the same view of the world, can be found: there is a primary experience (either natural or historical) of disorder, scarcity, and aggression. But at the same time there is also a need for the individual subject to be freed from anxieties and shortcomings. As senseless as it may seem, reality has a seed in itself of rationality and equal human dignity that can be made to flourish within the political contrivance.

There is thus a rationalistic program encoded in the DNA of the modern period. It can be interpreted in a triumphalistic or more skeptical key; seen as a glorification of humanity, or as a lowering of the ends traditionally assigned to politics (to achieve the summum bonum, replaced by the *conatus sese conservandi*), a program that can be said to be always belied, in the historical and geographically reality, by the many forms of unequal citizenship or hierarchical inclusion or internal exclusion—the phenomenon of slavery, consubstantial with the birth of modernity, the formation of colonial empires, and the racist construction of domination over indigenous people, the struggle of (and against) dissidents, rebels, the subordination of women—in which the modern political project of Europe was substantiated. And even in Europe (in the West), where modernity unfolded in all its fullness and power, the subject was in fact placed inside forms of a material universal—the capitalist economy—that created powerful forms of inclusion, but in contradictory and hierarchizing ways. All this could lead to the modern project being interpreted as a *dispositif* of domination rather than one of liberation. In effect, what we want to emphasize is that among the effects of this apparatus—and indeed at the origin of the conceptual structure that characterizes the modern era—there is included, and there must necessarily be the possibility, indeed the necessity, for the right as much as for the left.

The most radical critics will say that precisely because they are modern neither one of them is a bearer of liberation; rather, they are both forms of domination. My intention here, however, is simply to show their common roots, their diversity, and their permanence: indeed, the horizon on which the modern is surpassed has so far appeared in spurious forms, in which left and right continue to exist.

In any case, the originary modernity of the right and left, their difference and, at the same time, their sharing of the same origin, their being the two ways in which the modern necessarily manifests itself, has to do with the different radicalism with which they participate in one and the other of the two sides of the originary, structural duality of modern political discourse. A genealogical look at the origin of modern politics (of the modern way of conceiving the origin of politics)—rather than a reference to this or that specific event—is what allows us to establish the criterion of their difference. It is a criterion for recognizing political and ideological positions that were articulated during late modern and contemporary history, even without it being clearly present and made explicit in them or by them. It is a criterion, however, that does not seek to judge the intentions, whether overt or hidden, of the political proposals and forces, but which examines their deep logical, categorical, and reasoning structures.

That said, it is quite easy to see that the lefts, despite their historic variety, have proclaimed themselves the heirs of rationalism and the Enlightenment. They share the greatest attention to the side of the modern consisting in an intrinsic element that is normative but not directly ordering, namely, human nature in its seminal form. Because of the innate qualities that are inherent to human nature—translated, according to the semantics and syntax of modern political discourse, into rights, a more politically spendable and less demanding term than *essence*—it is taken a priori as a value to be affirmed equally for all. The historical development of modernity toward democracy has led the goals of the lefts to consist in conceptions of politics aimed at actively ensuring the freedom of the flourishing of the subject—singular or collective (in freely chosen communities)—in equal dignity. A liberal of the left like John Stuart Mill, when writing his *Autobiography*, could magnify "the importance, to man and society of a large variety in types of character, and of giving full freedom to human nature to expand itself in innumerable and conflicting directions." Following the same logic, albeit with very different conceptual tools, the young Marx spoke of communism as the dimension that achieves the newly found correspondence between liberated man, society, and nature ("the naturalism of man and humanism of nature both brought to fulfillment"), and which enables work to be a "free manifestation of life, hence an enjoyment of life."[9] In short, the norm (which does not necessarily imply normativism) here is the idea that it is good that the seeds of human rationality develop freely, in subjectivities characterized by equality of dignity and autonomy, while renouncing violence, discrimination, and domination. Here, too, is the idea that Justice is not the order of being, but a project on the part of the subjectivities to emancipate themselves, through politics, from obstacles and constraints. This is a goal, anything but generic and obvious, that brings together liberal politics and radical politics, and which is anything but moderate, because it implies difficult choices in all circumstances. If it is true, as Rousseau expressed it, that man is born free but everywhere is in chains, then politics—which at this point reveals its modern character of being at once instrument and destiny—is assigned the task of concretely realizing humanity.

Therefore, it is thanks to politics that this normativity to be found in the natural world takes shape: human nature is not a given, but an impulse; it is not predetermined but is only a seed of immediacy, which makes the mediation of institutions essential. It should be emphasized that the left does not coincide with the hypothesis of the rationality of the real, but only of its rationalizability with regard to the subject, in terms of equal dignity. Hence the image of flourishing may be misleading: if taken literally, it implies spontaneity, a kind of unidirectional necessity, the same way that starting from a seed inevitably leads to a flower (and only to a flower) and to only one fruit. On the contrary, despite the appearance of essentialism and naturalism that pertains to modern rationalism, the truth of its image of humanity—a truth that was made manifest in twentieth-century thought (in Rawls as much as in Habermas, for example, albeit in different languages)—is indeterminate: rights are in reality a way to name that which is only truly essential; in other words, the free expression of a Self that has the right to be whoever he or she wants to be from one time to the next, or who is not an essence bound to actualize himself or herself according to obligatory schemas, or suitable configurations. This desire of the subject to live according to that which, in each person's interpretation, represents fulfillment is the deep logic of modernism viewed from the left: it is the impulse toward humanist democracy; it is the way we now talk about the pursuit of happiness. This logic contains in itself, by necessity, the equal dignity of the different wills and different projects, with the consequent exclusion of domination and violence (both incidental and structural: from the domination of class to the domination of gender).

In the world of the lefts, this ideal of free development can also be conceived as divine in origin, like a command or grace or an exhortation of God to humankind. The important thing is that human nature must not be interpreted monistically, since it is indeed intrinsically plural and dedicated to the complete autonomy of the multiple subjectivities, or coercively: it is not legitimate institutions or agencies of meaning—parties, churches, or other—that provide a binding (and thus exclusionary) version of the flourishing of the seeds of humanity, which argue in terms of true human nature, of individual disorder with respect to an objective and imperative order, legitimized by a transcendence that is not accessible to human reason and its critical capacity. The reason for civil and political existence and its legitimation does not reside in anything that transcends individuals.

Normalization and discipline are, of course, well represented in the intellectual world and historical practice of the lefts, as means to achieve the end: their special relationship with the dual origins of the modern can inspire, politically, government control aimed at spontaneity, coarctation aimed at liberation (as well as a rejection of any authoritarian means that contradicts the liberating end). The lefts are split on the question of the natural qualities of man (and woman), on the obstacles that impede them, and on the means for emancipating them: but democrats, socialists, communists, anarchists, libertarians, revolutionaries and reformists, and maximalists and gradualists, sectarians or national populists, the militants and the left-wing parties—even in the most bitter, fratricidal conflicts—have in common the idea that all human beings naturally have the right to a human destiny, one that comes through their inclusion in a rational and equal political space that is constructed free from violence and from any arbitrary rule, and whose purpose is the flourishing of multiple life programs, all of which have equal dignity. In this principle of equality lies the risk of abstract universalism that in actuality, but not necessarily, pertains to the left: the risk, that is, of losing the determinacy and concreteness of politics, of ignoring its constitutive contingency, or of overlooking the fact that to politics belongs not only the goal of humankind's free flourishing, but also our grouping together into identity-making collectivities that mutually estrange each other and are potentially hostile. This risk is closely akin to that of constructing a necessity effect, that is, to interpret one's liberating purpose as if it were sustained by an intrinsic providentiality, guided by an immanent teleology, by a philosophy of history to which any contingency can be sacrificed (including the lives of the men and women to be liberated).[10] This is an argument unfailingly reintroduced by the right, in polemics with the perfectionism of the left and its perverse outcomes (according to Hirschman's rhetoric). However, it must be said, the left is not necessarily biased or naive, and it may very well be aware of human limitations, of the very contingency of subjectivity and politics, of the fact, in short, that the objective spirit is not absolute and is necessarily tinged with contradiction. The distinguishing trait is not that the expressive development of the subjects is perfectly achievable, in equal dignity, but the fact that this constitutes the primary objective of politics. The left can even accept that the subject is not the origin of modern politics; but in any case it cannot help but consider the subject, in its equal dignity, as the end in itself: if not what is, then what ought to be.

The right, for its part, cannot reject—even if it tries to at times—the space of the political game, the originary mode of interpretation of the real that constitutes modernity. But it entertains a different relationship with it. The right puts the natural seeds of universal subjective rationality in the background, and is defined primarily by the perception of the instability of the real, of its anomie, its incapacity to be ever completely ordered: a contingency, a disorder that can take on the appearance of a threat but also of an opportunity, of a nihilism to be confronted, but also to be used to indefinitely shape reality. The given that the right accepts as insurmountable is not a system of values but the ontological inconsistency of reality: one of the two originating sides of the modern.[11]

This perception explains many themes that are typical of the right, which does indeed often draw on forms of organismic thought, or appeal to a transcendent order, to an inexorable law that is inaccessible to the emancipatory action of humanity. These sorts of foundations, however—and this is the deciding factor—are not only threatening (because they are not in the measure of man), they are also threatened. The rocky, unyielding, substantialistic foundationism of many of the intellectual expressions of the right— which would like to have politics firmly guaranteed by (and dependent on) God, nature, history, tradition, values, nation, race, destiny, the market—is always accompanied by the theme of permanent aggression against order, the true source from which the right really derives its political energy. Order, therefore, is neither natural nor necessary; the primary experience is that nature is not anthropomorphic but rather unstable, and therefore order must be achieved, certainly, but not so much by means of a rational contrivance as through a relentless fight against anyone who threatens it. The acceptance of disorder—the fact that in nature there are no seeds of anthropomorphic rationality as an original given—holds even where political order is a real dogma: it does not escape a radical thinker like Maistre that every dynastic legitimacy has a mystery at its origin, the illegitimate moment of its inception.

But acceptance of disorder is not only a defensive stance: disorder, evil, is not just the problem; it can also be seen as the solution, as the main re-source that politics has at its disposal. The right is not, in fact, synonymous with preservation or quietism. The continuous thread running through it, the more or less obsessive perception of the instability of the real, since it is devoid of even a seminal normative element in the measure of man, and therefore of its precarious prehuman randomness or of its necessary destiny beyond humanity (which is not the same as Machiavellian contingency, be-cause Machiavelli is located in an early modernity that lies on the other side of, and looks beyond, the dualistic disorder/order device of the modern fully developed into rationalism), is the deep logic of a complex phenomenology. This leads the right to pursue the grim, authoritarian armor plating of polit-ical order against its internal and external enemies; to openly accept the risk of instability with the individualism of the economic subject, which relies on the logics of the market (whose presumed objectivity, which in reality is ever changing, is also a model of an unstable foundation of politics), eventually to be mitigated by an order that cannot fail to carry within itself the memory of the natural reality of disorder and to seek, at most, to transform it into the hierarchy (compassionate or not, as the case may be) of the strong over the weak, the victors over the defeated, those who are successful over those who fail; or finally, to resort to nihilism, that radical model of instability by which the right affirms the inconsistency of the real, exhibiting itself in a tough, tragic, extralegal decisionism, but also in imaginative futuristic creativity, or in manipulative illusionism—and this, too, in its festive artificial irre-sponsibility, is nothing but a sophisticated strategy for addressing an ever-present disorder, for preserving it in reality and sublimating it in fiction. It should be noted that the malleability of reality, its anomic being, is certainly modern: it is the result of the idea that reality has so little objectivity that it is at the disposal of the subject. But it is not a constructivist idea, because this term refers to a particular action on the real that takes place when the desire is to develop the seminal reasons of subjectivity, already present in nature, into a rational political contrivance. Whether they claim to arrive back at the most archaic origin or project themselves into the most visionary future, which they perceive as an opening to a destiny of power or as a tool for administering the existent and its natural logics; whether they make use of technology to consolidate the world or reject it because it manipulates the world too radically; whether they profess the most close-minded, solid values or practice the most unconventional nihilism; whether they manifest themselves in the conservative, middle-class pursuit of security or in the fascist cult of death; whether they entrust themselves to the market or to the state, the individual or the corporation; whether they compare 1789 to 1914, merchants to heroes, or give themselves over to the most unbridled laissez-faire; in every case, right-wing policies are marked by the conviction, more or less explicitly declared and rationalized, that the goal of politics is not to realize the natural norm of humanity by artificial means. Compared to the flourishing of subjectivity in equal dignity, there is always a more important task to accomplish, a more stringent compatibility to be recognized, a more cogent context to be respected, a higher interest to be served, a more realistic goal to be pursued, a more exciting narrative to be staged, a deadly anomie to be averted, a contingency (or conversely, a law) that cannot be overcome.

Thus, when the right makes its theme order, substance, stability, weight, uniformity, and also when it proffers the entertainment of fictional drama or the audacity of the imagination, it always develops the unstable side of the real as its main leitmotif: the harsh underscoring of the need for nonhuman law makes sense because disorder is either undoubtedly a law of nature to be accepted, or it constantly threatens human law. The species of concreteness of which the right is a bearer is to be understood not as ontological solidity, but as immediate acceptance of the disorder of the world and the contingency of politics: the transcendence it appeals to is another name for immanence, for the nonhumanity of reality, unilluminated by any seminal anthropocentric reason.[12]

In short, the dominant given, for the right, is the need for exception, namely, the intrinsic randomness and nothingness of reality: the recurrent polemic against the relativism that would become typical of the left conceals and reveals a deep connection to the relativity of the real, viewed as the primary given, and which is never completely surmountable. This is not the idea (of the left) that free subjectivity is threatened by the disorder of the context, but rather, the idea (of the right) that it is preferable (or at least inevitable) to submit to the context that transcends it: for example, abortion or divorce should be banned because society, to exist, requires the nonfreedom of its subjects; or, at most, abortion or divorce should be tolerated as a lesser evil, but never welcomed and claimed as rights. And conversely, when the left is pursuing change, the continuous struggle against injustice—the revolution, but also progressive reforms—what it has in mind is the intrinsic normativity of human nature: its movement, its continuous transcendence with respect to the given, in reality its telos (as the ultimate horizon of meaning) is peace, as stability, finally achieved through justice. The left is thus characterized by transcendence, not in the strict sense, but rather as critique, as going beyond, as what ought to be; in other words, by the negation of the world as it is, and by the effort to create another, better world, which is already a possibility (although negated at the moment) immanent to the present.

So it is the politics of the left that is guided by the idea that security and stability are possible, even ultimately as the result of emancipatory policies that are far from peaceful and even highly dynamic and conflictual: polemical policies for the political achievement of the natural seeds of human rationality. For the right, instead, despite the emphasis placed on order and tradition, disorder is politically paramount.[13] At the most—but without falling into simplistic dualisms—on one side, there is hope for peace, while on the other, endless fear or conflict (also diluted in the form of competition); on one side, there is analogy (the possibility that the subject can inhabit a world in his or her own image), and on the other, anomaly (permanent disconnection from the world): on one side, subjectivity (understood as ideal), and on the other, objectivity (defined as the nothing that reality is at bottom); on one side, there is the personal, and on the other, the impersonal (as an active denial of the centrality of the subject); on one side, culture (the *regnum hominis*) and on the other, nature (resistant to any anthropomorphic configuration).

The real is conceived to be extremely malleable by the left, but not entirely so; in other words, only as a possibility to emancipate and educate humankind: the left has in mind a political contrivance (a party, a state, a revolution) that, at least in theory, assists in allowing human nature to flourish, in restoring its autonomy, in dealienating it. In principle, for the left, not everything is possible, since—regardless of how problematically—there is a purpose in the world, a normative grain of reason (and dignity), or at least we can and should behave as if there were. Its restlessness has a peaceful end; its politics (with its hard edges) has a liberating end. When Bruno Bauer wrote that "nothing is impossible for man," he meant it in an emancipatory sense: we can liberate ourselves from all chains.[14]

To the right, however, everything really is possible (and this is good, for the postmodern and futuristic right, and bad for the traditional right), because there is no universally and egalitarian human norm in nature, no matter how implicit, to be developed explicitly in the political order. Because the real is infinitely anomic, unstable, and therefore also, temporarily, malleable, for the right, groundlessness—disorder, conflict, indeterminacy, radical contingency—is the ultimate, untranscendable dimension of politics.

Both left and right can develop these logics in a partial and limited fashion, or with no limits: extreme coercion (pedagogical, the Soviet model; or hierarchical, racial domination) has been carried out as a result of both as well as the paranoid fight against the enemy, whether historical or natural (a conflict that the left also participated in, not only under totalitarianism but also under democracy, in the fight against communism no less, during the Cold War). Permissiveness, prohibition, control, spontaneity, and violence may be as much a part of the right as they are of the left, depending on the circumstances.

Two forms of thought, therefore, both modern, though very divergent (one based ultimately on the exception, the other on the norm), both open, but in different ways, to contingency (the multiple forms of human flourishing, not reducible to a single figure, in one case; the radical senselessness of the world, on the other), and both tempted by the necessity effect (by the effect of the teleological development of history, or by the objective acceptance of nonhuman logics). Some clarification is needed on a few historical and intellectual experiences that seemingly diverge from the general outline we have sketched out thus far.

First, the position of liberalism needs to be defined. Its historical, philosophical, modern, rationalistic origins (practically speaking, beginning with Locke) are the indispensable first step, which consists in making subjectivity and its rights the core of politics. Once this has been established, liberalism can mix itself up with thinking and practices both from the right—where individual freedom can be interpreted in aggressive, derogatory, or hierarchical ways—or from the left, as long as the idea prevails that individual self-determination should be accompanied by the idea of the equal dignity of individuals, and of the political struggle to free them from the constraints that inhibit or prevent their flourishing. In any event, even in its right-wing formations, liberalism has comported itself nobly.

The sober realism of the historic Italian right, the Christian and national patriotism of de Gaulle, the English resistance to the Nazis under the leadership of Churchill, were great human and intellectual experiences, but also transitional forms, the result of specific historical emergencies, of provisional political and economic equilibriums, in which the perception of public duty or extreme threat turned into a real legitimate hegemony of the right. Personages who can be ascribed to this category do exist: Cavour and Einaudi, to provide other examples, despite their different places in history, and the distance that separates the impelling role of Cavour in the construction of the unitary state from the more defensive position of Einaudi with regard to what is wrong with fascism and to the naïveté that can be found in socialist and democratic projects. They stand on a sort of crest, in an intellectual and political balance, which makes them wonderful and precarious characters whose excellence and political effectiveness have something exceptional, random, and unrepeatable about them—making them anything but paradigms, then.

The political thought of English constitutionalism and then of Scottish skepticism and Enlightenment, which is not historically attributable to the genealogy of the modern outlined here, is actually drawn into the logic of the left-right opposition. On the one hand, there is (for example, in Burke, Hayek, and Scruton) a sort of methodological individualism, but that always transcends the individual and his or her equality in dignity in the name of some logic superior to it (history, the market, tradition, success). On the other hand, there are cases of market governance by the state in terms of social justice (think of the laborism and, in some respects, the Democrats in the United States; the ideology of the American Republicans, though, even with all its individualism, does not accede to the equality of dignity or to the dynamics of liberation, and remains in various ways inscribed within the idea of always threatened orders that transcend the individual, such as the market or religious foundations of politics).

The anticonstructivist polemics that this right engages in against the left hits the mark, but only up to a point and with severe limitations. Taken seriously, the argument should not only apply to the left but also be extended to the historical and conceptual sphere that seeks the existence of a left and right, that is, at the very origins of the modern. For anticonstructivism to cease being ideological, it would have to become truly deconstructionist, in other words, shaped by traditions of thought—from Nietzsche to Heidegger, and from Foucault to Derrida—that in themselves are neither left nor right, because they are capable of revealing the devices originating in modern political discourse from the outside, and of displacing them. A similar, radical goal of arriving at an understanding of the modern beyond its own principles, but in somewhat constructive terms and, in any event, opposed to this one, inasmuch as it was substance-subject oriented, was shared by Hegel, who indeed, as to the intrinsic quality of his thought, transcended left and right. This is shown by his antiliberal polemics but also by his attacks against a reactionary Catholic like Haller and a Germanist like Savigny.

These deconstructionist authors certainly do go about annihilating (or at least radically historicizing) the more or less naive beliefs of the left and right, attacking faith in the order to be opposed by disorder as much as they attack faith in the subject to be liberated. Yet, despite the fact that they locate themselves, from an intellectual point of view, outside and beyond the left and right, even these thinkers were fatally sucked back into these categories when it came to their individual positions, or the ideological twist their thinking assumed in their lives. While not wanting to do any wrong to Nietzsche and certainly recognizing his ultrahuman effort to be truly impolitic, that is, to remain outside the categories of modern politics, the susceptibility to take sides brought Heidegger's life history—and some of his intellectual traits, transformed into ideology—back into the categories of left and right. Heidegger was certainly capable of positioning himself before the origins of modernity and of brilliantly interpreting it as the fulfillment of Western metaphysics. He was also, therefore, able to predict the fate of subjugation and technical destruction of the selfsame subject who sought via technique to make himself master of the world (which was reduced to an image, to be sure, but not of man). But this superior philosophical vision also led him to overlook every mortal offense humanity has to undergo before recovering from the malady of metaphysics and radically changing its relationship with being (the *Verwindung*). His was a path of fierce intellectual lucidity and political and human blindness.

A kindred thinker, although not part of the same line of thought, and more easily ascribable to the right, is Carl Schmitt. His deconstructionism is powerful and invaluable in revealing the original dynamics of modern politics, its groundlessness (which he defines as "exception" or "political"). In this respect, his work is a great intellectual contribution, and can be welcomed by the left as well (which indeed it was in Italy in the 1970s), as (antidialectical) awareness of the absolute contingency of subjectivity, that is to say, the fact that the subject and action, even those of the left, are determined rather than necessary. But Schmitt is right wing because the source of politics—the original aporia of the modern, by which a politics whose end is the subject cannot have the subject as its beginning, because the beginning is indeterminacy—is interpreted positively, still on (and not beyond) the horizon of modern politics, as a politics of origin, or as a political project that repeats indefinitely the undetermined origin of the modern, which absolutizes and perpetuates the constitutively nonrational traits of rationalism, and which therefore excludes the possibility of the subject as builder of the political order (which in any case is destined to always contain disorder inside itself, to never free itself from the state of nature) from ever being an individual (if anything, it is the constituent power of the people, or the party). In short, Schmitt not only criticizes liberalism and humanism in their naive forms, he also sweeps away any obstacle to extreme political cynicism, because he delivers himself over to a nihilism that negates the subject in its fulfillment, and even any politics that envisages the subject as an end in itself. For him, anything truly is possible (a relativism that he tried to curb with his frightening *völkisch* roots), precisely because politics is that originary indeterminate negative that makes useless any specific contradiction that revolves around a subjectivity, and which can be surpassed in further freedom.

For every two examples of deconstructionism that ended in the right (however accidental this characterization may be for Heidegger), we can cite many that finished in the left—Foucault and Derrida, of course, but also Deleuze and Rorty, and others (for example, a thinker on a path that runs distant from these but converges with them in a critique of modern subjectivity still in its metaphysical, necessary form as well as in a reassessment of contingency is Adorno). While taking for granted the obsolescence of the concept of a subjectivity that is to be liberated, even discerning the trap of liberation (the discipline, coercion, the continued construction of dispositifs of truth), they acted on the political scene, as if the subject they themselves had deconstructed and desubstantialized (a figure in the sand erased by an ocean wave . . .) enjoyed a sort of fantasy or larval survival, a residual internal force that is less powerful with respect to the tradition of progressive rationalism; as if, in short, in the name of decency and compassion, if not in the name of reason or natural rights, subjectivity still guided the political discourse, at least in dictating concrete options, contingent stances, against violence, cruelty, domination, discrimination, and racism. Deconstructionist radicalism also ends up adopting stances that, if not close to liberal ones, are not contrary to them either. Even if it does not naively embrace the theories of rights and considers them one discourse among others, and no more true than the others, one cannot go against the impulse for the free flourishing of subjectivity. This shows that even if we can think, in theory, beyond left and right, praxis—which is obviously central to the world of politics—prevents it; and it is precisely the presence or absence of the political centrality of the subject and its equal dignity that makes the difference. This is the case regardless of the awareness of the epistemological crisis of subjectivity (which can be narrated through psychoanalysis as well, and the discovery of the original cleaved and desiring structure of the subject), and regardless even of the historic setbacks of humanism. So strong is the field of attraction emanating from the modern opposition between left and right that even the Catholic Church—which obviously stands outside it, and which was in some respects its original polemical target—is involved in it, although only in historical contingency. It was led to modify its action and theory of the person, which are supposed to stand outside the left-right opposition, sometimes in one direction, and sometimes in another (from Pax Christi to Bishop Fisichella, to give just two examples that are familiar to Italians, or from the theologians of revolution to Lefebvre). Even if the faith and hope taught by Catholic doctrine transcend history, not even the church's authority has escaped the dilemmas that lie on the modern horizon.

It remains for us to analyze how the genealogical criterion we have advanced here interacts with some important parameters in political theory and practice.

As far as the relationship between risk and security is concerned—two categories that in themselves, in the abstract, cannot be ascribed exclusively to either the left or the right, because there are so many highly contradictory examples of them—the categorical explanation provides the reasons for a chiasm, or intersection, that can be experienced in everyday politics as well. The right is in favor of security, in the police sense of public order, a sphere dominated by a perception of threat (especially focused these days on immigrants, viewed as a font of disorder, and whose presence has sparked the conflict between equal dignity and hierarchical inclusion, as the security package of July 2009 showed, resolved more in the direction of the latter). And yet the right supports risk in the economy (a number of aspects make risk inherent to capitalism, even if it does not take the form of a purely competitive market, as shown by the crisis starting in 2008). The right is sometimes for risk in politics, too, when the ontological disorder is expressed in nihilistic, heroic terms (the fascist theme of beautiful death and the heroic theme of adventure and challenge). The left, on the other hand, is in favor of facing the risk of the new and different (immigrants) with an open mind, as an enriching human experience, while it is a tenacious champion of social security, of safety at work and in the workplace, because it views human dignity as at stake in this issue.

As for individualism, by no means does the left adopt it directly: the free flourishing of subjectivities (whether individuals or free associations) is not the same thing as spontaneous flourishing, since in situations of injustice and alienation the latter is actually a synonym for survival of the fittest or passive adaptation to the context. Hayek, despite the claims he makes for himself, belongs to the right (in his lexicon, a conservative) although he is an individualist (in the past one might have said precisely because he is an individualist, since bourgeois individualism was considered right wing and collectivism was considered left wing). His almost total exclusion of the issue of justice on a human scale (which he discredited as *taxis* and juxtaposed to spontaneous order, to *kosmos*) from politics in reality compromises equal dignity, something that is always connected to free flourishing (also positioning a figure such as Jünger's Anarch, no matter how impressive, outside the left). There is no need, in short, to theorize inequality in order to be right wing: it suffices to practice inequality—which need not be only social and economic but also political, in forms of open hierarchy or exclusionary separateness (under which the friend-enemy relation also falls)—and accept it as inevitable, irremediable, and insurmountable, and to make it the main premise of political order.

Thus, Norberto Bobbio's idea of inequality as the discriminating factor between left and right is empirically true, and constitutes a fairly safe criterion for judging between the two: except that it should be interpreted as the result of a more fundamental difference between left and right, one which lies in the relationship to the two sides at the origin of modern politics.[15] Apart from the fact that equality is an indeterminate concept that should be expressed more precisely as equal dignity, it is true that equality in the normative sense is excluded from the world of the rights. Their power is to be found more in variously combining the inherent instability and fragmentation of the real, accepted as natural and legitimate and temporarily stabilized, through legal ways (so that the order of the right is actually a permanent conflict, resolved only temporarily and randomly by politically reinforced social hierarchies or individual adventures). And it is also true that the pole star of leftist politics is not to be found in a unification that levels out social and political differences, but at least in their delegitimization—allied with promoting the value of existential and individual differences.

As far as the link between subjectivity and context is concerned, finally, it is clear that the left may well know that it is essential to the free flourishing of subjectivity (that is to say, that cosmopolitanism and nomadism are not the only practical option for subjectification): in other words, the left may well be aware of the determinacy and contingency of politics. But for the left, context is never an insurmountable given, nor is it a roothold, because the full expression of the subject—the free, differentiated flourishing of the individual, in freely chosen collectivities—is a primary duty. Even in the best of cases, however, the right will view this flourishing as determined by (and subordinate to) context: this is what is imposed on the individual as value. And it is a value that is continually threatened, rather than being peacefully foundational, a context that is always potentially chaos: the rootedness of the individual is a duty; it serves to prevent the disorder that stems from rootlessness, the risk of anomie always present and imminent (in reality, it is immanent in the sense that disorder is the only true reality, which transcends the subject). The defective structure of being is responsible for this risk, but even subjectivity itself—a solution for the lefts—is in reality part of the problem of disorder, and certainly not central to the political order. So, ultimately, democracy without adjectives—in line with its modern essence—is the goal of forces variously oriented toward the left (which hardly means that all lefts are democratic in their actual practice); nor does this imply that all rights are antidemocratic, only that their democracy is always qualified as an expression of something else (which can be quite varied: market democracy, authoritarian democracy, national democracy, protected democracy, Christian democracy).

Based on these observations, because the notion of society is the concrete, real ground adopted as the field of investigation and struggle by the left, we can see that the theme of community (in its standard meaning) is basically foreign to the left, which projects it if anything into the future, as communism, or as a regulative ideal of its praxis, and that, in its democratic forms, the left prefers solidarity (a sort of synthesis between altruism and brotherhood). Community is instead a leitmotif of the right, which situates it in the past or in the present—and can also provide it with a robust, natural ontological consistency, but in one way or another, always sees it as threatened by something or someone. Similarly, for the left, the social bond is a dialectical and historical given (the context) that must be overcome and transformed into an act of free will: the social contract, solidarity, cultivated relationality. The common good does not transcend individuals, but is desired by each person as a condition for the flourishing of the all. For the right, instead, the social bond (the common good) is a given to be accepted as natural (God, the nation, race, market, history, civilization), and therefore it makes individuals passive, rendering them vulnerable to all sorts of manipulation and isolation, despite the emphasis that is placed on community.

Our genealogical criterion thus also identifies the underlying reason for the superficial but often well-founded observation that the right is the bearer of a negative anthropology (namely, political thought in which the subject, in its condition of equal dignity, cannot be central) while the left carries with it a view of human beings that is at least potentially positive. It also explains the closely related fact that political realism is more suited to the right, since it assumes as its principle the nonanthropomorphic side of nature, its total contingency, and from this develops a discourse on man in general, on the necessary limitedness of human expectations (although a school of thought that traverses multiple ages, originating with Thucydides and Tacitus, passing through Machiavelli and Hobbes, and culminating in Schmitt, is nothing but an anachronistic optical illusion, constructed entirely within the chamber of mirrors of modernity, to which the right inherently belongs).

The Global Age and the Italian Case

The global age is distinguished by numerous crises involving the normativity of the subject, its rights, the importance of work, and the state. The decline of the Fordist factory and the social-democratic compromise; the new importance of consumption (the linguistic turn in politics) and of its ensuingly weak, polymorphic, narcissistic, and malleable subjectivity; the collapse of communism, that hyperregulatory model: all these events inaugurated what in many respects is a postmodern era, the iron age of global war, in which the validity of the politically vital categorical distinctions of modernity—interior-exterior, public-private, norm-exception, peace-war— has become highly problematic.

It is an epoch of blurred, uncertain political spaces in which different scales—local, national, postnational, regional, universal, and global—coexist and confront each other. It is a liquid, fluid, unstable, fragmented, insecure world traversed by conflicts, fears, and uncertainties. In this context, politics does not appear in the egalitarian contours originating in rationalism and the Enlightenment, accompanied by the inclusionary institutions of the welfare state; rather, it is structured according to multiple, continuously changing contrapositions and exclusions (de facto or in principle): the difference between friend and enemy, between the West and Islam, between civilization and terrorism, between citizens and migrants, between rich and poor, between educated and uneducated, and between whites, blacks, and colored people. In addition, the public space tends to appear random, as an assemblage of social powers founded on exception and anomaly. The transition from modernity to contemporaneity is the transition from growth to risk, from progress to labyrinth; it is the crisis of the normative capacity of politics and law (centered on subjectivity), and the triumph of the unstable and ultrahuman normativity of technology and the economy.

In these crisis conditions affecting modern and late-modern neutralizations (the state, in the form of the welfare state), the political forces (public opinion) seem to position themselves with new intensity around the left-right cleavage. In this amorphous, anomic political space, the right was the first to recover its strength and avail itself of this momentous historical opportunity that stretched across a good part of Europe, the first since 1945 (true, there had been Thatcher in the 1980s, but her considerable political weight was exercised mainly in the transatlantic English-speaking world). Entirely immune from nostalgia and wanting anything but to restore past world orders, the postmodern rights—all at work today to a greater or lesser degree depending on the various national political contexts: charismatic and technocratic, foundationistic and nihilistic, personalistic and racist (or biopolitical), nationalistic and localistic—act without prejudice from within the internal diversity and complexity of contemporary societies. They intervene with policies pandering to corporate divisions and alarmist fears, to social resentments and cultural fragmentation, to closures and exclusions (or subordination) of the nonintegrated, and to xenophobias, both overt and concealed. Organizing temporary, hierarchical combinations of social differences; putting forward contradictory policies of freedom of the market (neoliberalism with its savage mobilizing powers) and freedom from the market (state neointerventionism, with its force of stabilization); bringing together fear of competition and fear of the enemy in hopes of winning the struggle for existence, or carving out a protected niche; engaging in egoistic individualism while cultivating collective identities in imagined communities, with folklore and volunteer patrols to create the illusion of being able to recover lost territories and social spaces; inventing a threatening other onto which all tensions are discharged, without offering any rational response to them: all this means that the image of society promoted by the right does not have a project of emancipation at its heart whose norm consists in the equal dignity of all citizens. For the rights, society should remain divided in its different interests and in the variegated drives that traverse it and break it apart; it must find precarious equilibriums based on hierarchy and exclusion (or better yet, based on unequal inclusion): a revolution to keep everything from changing, to ensure that differences remain.

This strategy—expressed with varying intensity—is possible thanks to the fact that the right interprets reality as ontologically unstable and anomic. Unifying and stabilizing identity-making forms (the nation, religion, life, the local community) that are offered at the symbolic level are actually mobilizing, polemical, and organized around conflict with an enemy, around the exorcism of a communist, Islamic, terrorist specter (although they are also rounded up by traditional agents of meaning, like the Catholic Church, who, by taking some of these propaganda issues seriously, are given the opportunity to intervene in politics, in society, and in individuals).

The Italian case is in some ways paradigmatic of the new opportunities and new forms available to the postmodern rights, and of their ability to shape the real, without being constructivist in the strict sense. The end of the double *conventio ad excludendum* created between 1943 and 1948 (the founding moment of the Republic, initially antifascist and later anticommunist), which was slow to come about, has already led, for fifteen years now, after the destruction of the political system due to the action of the judiciary, to a government in which the regulatory element of the republican political subjectivity—expressed by the association between the parties of the Italian National Liberation Committee and the social-democratic state—was no longer the politically driving factor. In the by-now advanced consummation of the defining traits of modernity—in social anomie and in the obsolescence of the difference between public and private (a difference that in itself is neither left nor right, but which traverses both, just as the alternation of the primacy given at any time to one or the other is not the defining difference, since only the political purpose to which it is directed is a deciding factor)— today the right successfully (in elections, at least) implements a policy managed according to the logics of exception and anomaly, taking the utmost malleability of the world as achieved and for granted. The world is broken down and put back together according to multiple possible combinations that enable the coexistence of symbolic unity and real fragmentation, passive populism and hierarchizing oligarchy, tradition and postmodernity, racism and rhetorics of solidarity, real flexibility and imaginary communitary rootedness, tough political leadership and mass-media dissolution of reality. This *complexio oppositorum* is made possible, in intellectual terms, by the most profound adherence on the part of the rights to the instability of the real, to its radical contingency and, therefore, to the relations of power that actually occur in society. In truth, this is very close to a state of nature (the individualism of the right is egoistic and anomic; it is the private that seeks immediately to be public), while the political state understood as a rational contrivance is reduced to pure power (not all that powerful in actuality), and almost dissolved in effect by the systematic bypassing of constitutional balances and the very principle of legality.

The immanence that characterizes the right resides equally in its adherence to the world as it really is, and in its compensatory illusion—continuously nurtured—of a dream of individual and group power, of fantasized community, of prosperity and happiness that could come true, if only a few obstacles were removed (the communists, terrorists, migrants, magistrates, corruption bashers, journalists, and many others). And Italians largely share the perception of the world as devoid of rules, other than those that sanction success no matter how pursued, the subordination of the less able, and the exclusion of those who are different. The very centrality of the security issue passes off as obvious what is in fact a hierarchical construction of society, by which the second-last to arrive find partial relief from their subordinate status by means of laws that sanction hardline policies against noncitizens, the last to arrive: what matters is that rather than equality guaranteed by the state, the political guideline now guarantees exception. At most, the idea may be acceded to that it is a good, uplifting thing to soften the hard law of inequality, when possible, with the balm of compassion (but as charity, not as rights). Sentimentality is the surrogate of humanism.

But if the success of the right in Italy is ensured by its ability to tap unscrupulously into state power beyond the horizon of stateness, if the form of Italian politics is an example of the revolutionary force of the right, one cannot fail to mention that its success is mainly due to its leader, Silvio Berlusconi, a singular example of a charismatic storyline of biopower, minidramas, performance, and television populism. Berlusconi's political proposal is that his own person, his own body—transfigured by the virtual apotheosis of the mass media—creates the fusion of the one with the many, and of the many with the one, through love. This is a curious reversal of the Sun King's motto "the state is me." Indeed, Louis XIV defined himself as the personal beginning of the impersonal public machine, while Berlusconi makes his person and his private interests law, just as he renders his own body identical to the all. This is dramatic representation, not political representation, the fruit of an emotional contract lying somewhere between religious mysticism and theatricality: the mystical body of the head—which is simultaneously king and people—is the living and concrete figure of a multitude that sees itself in him, and which in loving him loves itself, boosted but not overwhelmed by feelings of inferiority: the head is simultaneously everyone and each individual; he is a common man, easy to understand, and someone we can identify with. Thus is established a radical separation between being citizens and being members of the mystical body, and strong competition between dramatic representation and political representation (the parliament). The latter is destined to an increasingly marginal political role, because being a citizen is tedious and difficult, alienating and sometimes depressing; while being part of the mystical body is not as tiring, and it offers joy and happiness: the fusion-transfiguration of the one into the many and the many into the one is vital, optimistic, and expansive (not by chance, the militants of Berlusconi's People of Freedom party have been defined missionaries of freedom, since they are expected to carry its image "into the lands of the unbelievers" [*in partibus infidelium*]). Moreover—and this is true hegemony, combined with real illusionism—the head succeeds in making people believe that defending his interests (and interests of those like him) is in the interest of working people, who reward him heavily in elections. Hence, Berlusconi is doing politics in the strongest sense precisely when he conveys the illusion of going beyond politics in the fullness of the life of the nation, thanks to a daily media plebiscite, thereby incorporating in himself the antipolitical, the prepolitical, and the (allegedly) postpolitical.

More than anything, this political presentation has a deresponsibilizing effect. Political transfiguration has the effect of making what is real coincide, in full immanence, with what is represented: the difference—which was the starting point of modern politics—between what is and what ought to be, between an actual situation and a project, between natural and artificial is abolished; what is real has been transfigured, but left essentially how it is. Rather than criticism, an effort of the imagination and optimism accompanied by individual initiative make problems surmountable; in the event they are not, the fault is to be attributed to scapegoats, to the forces of evil, who are opposed to the forces of good, and who love neither the head nor the people.

Of course, the ends of these policies are those of any right-wing revolution: to change everything so that everything remains as it is. Which today means a design, a rather effective one, to go beyond parliamentary democracy toward an executive made strong and legitimized by the charisma and power of the head, so as to stop the project of democratic equality, and of emancipation, of the republican constitution, so that the current contradictions of society are blocked, so that the increasing gap in power and wealth between the citizens is not bridged, and is not even noticed, suffocated and transfigured as it is in the new fated community embodied in the body of the head: and since in a community there is no thinking in terms of rights, it is to his compassion that we are obliged if no one is left behind. In concrete terms: this revolution, in these forms, serves to safeguard the person and interests of the head, so that the economic crisis is not managed in the interest of progress and development, and so that its effects are endured by the people as happily (or distractedly) as possible.

From the practical, empirical point of view, the success of these politics structured like a *Gefolgschaft* who is unheroic, but winking in complicity— in which the thaumaturge king encounters the satrap, and unleashes the futuristic power of a populist fantasy that makes the people the political protagonist (but only in words, because in reality, they are increasingly passive)— is made possible by the almost total control of television broadcasting and most of the print media: the right has always been at ease making innovative use of technologies.

We are spared from having to say that the whole world is on the right now: Obama's victory in 2008 in the United States, even though essentially determined by the economic crisis that American public opinion viewed as having been caused by the right-wing government, is proof to the contrary. Yet based on the Italian experience—unusual, to be sure, but significant—it is clear that the right is more at home in a postmodern world because it can energetically play with the modern perception of the profound instability of the real: this is the reason why, in effect, it is able to achieve political, social, and cultural hegemony. Its thinking, hastily put together in the 1980s through the criticism of modern philosophy, but much more through the minidramas of commercial television, intercepts common sense, manipulates it, and, without transcending it, molds and validates it.

The left, on the contrary, is disoriented because every one of its statements is counterfactual, referring to the world not as it is, but as it should be, and at the same time lacking many of the theoretical and political tools necessary for its praxis. Only when it knows what it really wants from politics can it credibly seek to realize, in the circumstances of any given moment, the only goal it really can have: the creation of a form of politics guided by the intrinsic normativity of the flourishing, in equal dignity, of individuals and groups in their concrete differences. Its appeal to conscious subjectivity, to rights, and to what remains of the welfare state, to the public-governmental sphere, can sound behind the times and ineffectual: although in some contexts and in some circumstances it has seemed more realistic and reasonable than the fantasies of the right, the 2009 European elections showed that the left does exist, that it is different from the right, but unlike the right it is having difficulty evolving adaptively to the new ecological environment and feeling at home and sufficiently flexible and protean in the new, profoundly anomic context of economic crisis. This slowness is confronted, moreover, by the quickness of the right (which, however, is highly unstable in its solutions).

The Present and the Future: Provisional Conclusion

The transition to the postmodern (or global) age has thus transformed the left and the right, causing both to lose their traditional identity and political forms. But even though they both derive their reason for being from the origins of modernity, this does not make them obsolete as political categories. And the past has not been surpassed, not because left and right are permanent acquisitions, but (only) because the modern structural duality of politics—suspended between natural anomie and norm implicit in its subjectivities—has indeed lost its subjects, forms, and horizons, but it has not been replaced by any solid ground, by any new justice, or by a functional equivalent that can act as a yardstick, as a measure, for new political categories, or even by a new polemical front line capable of creating a new horizon of political meaning. In short, while the original duality of the modern has persisted, the structures of its political and institutional architecture have not. Consequently, both pundits and public opinion can still tell from one instance to the next if a position and policy are from the right or left, if they privilege exception or context, or—on the contrary—the latest normativity to enable the subject to flourish. The world interpreted by politics oscillates today between the nothingness of the order of human things (or defending a continuously threatened order to the bitter end) and the perception of a seminal norm that, as a (remote) possibility, consists in subjectivities—if not in their rational essence, then at least in their capacity to suffer and their willingness to live and flourish. Thus, although the world has changed, although the problems vary and solutions are lacking, if politics remains structurally undetermined, if these remain the lenses through which we view politics, if subjectivity as an end in itself can still be the defining trait, at least in political discourse—then left and right continue to determine the political space and to oppose each other.

The agenda of the challenges to be tackled, the new political guidelines to be thought out, is staggering. We are confronted with new forms of relationship between the universal and the particular, with the dialectic implicit in the connection between humanity and cultures as they present themselves within the political space of the state, which today is called upon to accommodate differences that are far more heterogeneous (although communicating and comprehensible) than the antithesis between capital and labor.[16] We must deal with biotechnologies and their ambiguous biopolitical potential—just one of the multiple powers that enter into the naked flesh of living beings, molding it and shaping it to the point of subjugation—and new options for the possible expression and liberation of subjectivity. It is not a matter of fighting biopower because it distorts the supposed true essence of human nature, but because it may violate the freedom and dignity of the real subject; but then, the prospect of humanity hybridized with technology is in itself neither new nor scary, provided this marriage takes place in the prospect of freedom and maximization of the expressiveness of subjectivity. The challenges also involve managing the refragmentation of the global economy and governing globalization, in a new world order in which the West is no longer the center, and in a plurality of large economic areas. Democracy must be revitalized: by enabling it to address conflicts; by seeking, through the state, to work with the change in scale (apparently required by the denationalization of politics) that (at least in part) places politics beyond the state, in the direction of federation or empire; by interpreting the agents of fluidity and disintegration of international relations (from the power of corporations to migrations to terrorism) using realistic thinking and creative imagination; by deciding between growth and restraint; by overcoming the conflict between nomadic and sedentary peoples that seems to have hypnotized the popular European consciousness.

All the points of this agenda target the subject, capitalism, technique, biopolitics, the environment, and cultures as strategic centers of real contradictions generated at the global level, but which we perceive critically as inside—and as breaching—the local space of the state and the vestiges of its ordering capacity. And if the possible answers to our current challenges still involve the contraposition of anomaly versus norm, exception versus legality, domination versus autonomy, rumormongering or propagandizing versus responsibly speaking out, and inequality versus equality; if, in these new scenarios, the alternative continues to be framed in terms of whether civil and political life should be something normatively different from a jumble of unequal relations, or whether, on the contrary, it can only oscillate between chance and necessity; if it still makes sense to ask whether the last word should be given to the capitalist economy, which presents itself as a series of bubbles and crises, as an independent entity that shapes itself and demands the sacrifice of people, forms, and orders in order to function, or to the centrality and dignity of subjectivities, affirmed by politics; if the subject, no longer transcendental, of course, but no longer simply deconstructed by critical theorists or turned into an ideological larva, a purely sentimental entity or a consumer or a spectator—in its life, its reproduction, its way of loving, its illnesses, suffering, and death—is still the battlefield between threatening and threatened authority versus freedom, this means that left and right will have a life beyond the modern age, surviving into the global age.

It is by no means to be taken for granted that they will retain their current forms. There is nothing preventing the left—it would actually be desirable if it did—from expressing a humanism that is not naive: a transparent hope, entirely free from the coerciveness of all its old necessity effects, one that is also attentive, however, to real contradictions as they authentically come to exist in bodies and spaces. Similarly, there is nothing preventing the right from putting itself forward as the bearer of a grave seriousness, of a realism that is not cynical, of a nonhumanism that is not also antihuman, of a sense of contingency that is neither ruthless nor ephemeral. Both left and right, if capable of it, should relaunch the normativity of politics and law against the deviations of the economy and technology. The strategic task of the right will continue to consist in coming up with continually new solutions for order—all of which they believe to be foundational and transcendental, but which in reality are transient, conflictual, and anomalous—for problems and threats they know they cannot (and will not) solve at their roots. The left has the task of taking on the existence and value of individuals as they ought to be, and of firmly articulating the rights of the subjectivities, but not in an essentialistic, identity-making way; in other words, not to turn the individual into a weapon against the other, but rather to arrive at it in all its concreteness. And in general, not to just wait until the imaginative bubble of the right bursts, but to actively pursue a new hegemony, that is, to outline a new chain of active subjectivities and effective political means; and to offer a new vision of the world, a framework within which individual and collective energies can find their space, working toward an emancipation that may be conflictual, but not unequal. If it comes down to it, the left must dynamically incite the power of populism, respond to unanswered political questions by establishing a new subject people at the heart of the political, beyond state neutralization.[17] What this means to the left, having abandoned any pretense of necessity, is to discover a *kairòs*, an opportunity that legitimates another shared undertaking to be pursued, beyond the last creation of the left (or center-left), the welfare state; but, equally, to reinvent the institutional and intellectual tools that will allow us, without making a utopian leap out of it, to pass from the world as it is to the world as it ought to be. Struggle and contingency, mobility and escape, but also a new era for rights, freedoms, and responsibilities, of individuals and collectives, singular and plural: these are the many options that open the way from here to a praxis, with the natural divergences between moderate and radical lefts; and perhaps the clash between unstructured, rebellious subjectivity and institutions is the new name for the traditional dilemma of reform versus revolution.

If and when the original modern structure of politics, balanced between nature and contrivance, is consumed and inconceivable; if and when the ground of politics is radically changed, because subjectivity is no longer a category that holds strategic value for forming the political space, and its flourishing is no longer the key political question; if and when politics is organized around other conceptual axes (for example, polluters against environmentalists, and the ecological crisis is in itself capable of crowding out the left-right cleavage, and of creating a front that unites humanity against nature gone mad, or, more radically, unites man and nature, meaning, all nonhuman living beings, in a new alliance based on restraining growth), then left and right will no longer mean anything, which was how it was for almost the entire historical and political experience of the West. But until then, left and right will continue to say, in a feeble whisper or perhaps out loud, something modern about our postmodern political fortunes.

Notes

This chapter was originally published in Italian as *Perché ancora destra e sinister* (2013). Copyright Gius. Laterza & Figli; republished with permission.

1 De Benoist, "End of the Left-Right Dichotomy," 73–90.
2 Sternhell, *Neither Right nor Left*.
3 Hamilton, *The Appeal of Fascism*.
4 Giddens, *Beyond Left and Right*.
5 Revelli, *Le due destre*.
6 Revelli, *Sinistra Destra*.
7 Rémond, *Les Droites en France*.

8 Lefranc, *Les gauches en France*.

9 Mill, *Autobiography*, 259; Marx, "Economic and Philosophic Manuscripts of 1844," 85; Marx, "From the Paris Notebooks," 95.

10 Galli, *Contingenza e necessità nella ragione politica moderna*.

11 Santambrogio, *Destra e sinistra*.

12 Mannheim, *Conservatism*.

13 Cofrancesco, *Destra e sinistra*.

14 Bauer, "The Capacity of the Present-Day Jews and Christians to Become Free," 149.

15 Bobbio, *Left and Right*.

16 Galli, *L'umanità multiculturale*.

17 Laclau, *On Populist Reason*.

CHAPTER 3

Politics in the Present

Roberto Esposito

─────────────────

*Translated by Margaret Adams
Groesbeck and Adam Sitze*

Explaining oneself in an interview, a dialogue, or a conversation is
so difficult.[1] The questions, like their answers, are faked. They're
constructed, only to be rewritten in new combinations that take off from
the problems they're supposed to confront and that, mysteriously, they
cleverly manage to evade. What counts therefore is the problem. And the
problem directly interrogates the present as well as the interlocutors who
live in the present. As such, we've decided to renounce the binary form
that privileges the exchange between two but excludes other eventual
addressees, preferring instead what has been defined in philosophy as
the art of constructing problems. We take as our point of departure the
unwinding of the thread of Roberto Esposito's thirty-year meditation
on philosophy and on politics. But this starting point is more convention
than dialogic standard. Whether undertaken alone, shared with one other
or many others, this reflection is necessary but not entirely satisfying
when what's in play is a politics that has declined to the present. We must
instead restore to this reflection the movement that carries us to the
problem, a movement in which past and future become contemporary
with respect to the position reality has assumed. Here we deal with
a convention—one we've respected—that mirrors footnotes at the
bottom of a page and, more generally, the literary form of an intellectual
biography written in the first person. This convention itself is revealed
to be useful as a genealogical lens focused on the present. This same
form, after all, is born in the moment suspended between the actual
questioning and the virtual present in which we live. The conventional
schema of this essay is based on four categories: the impolitical,

immunitas/communitas, biopolitics, and the impersonal. This schema will develop itself in the style of free indirect discourse, which will not shut off the flow of the reflection by preexisting stylistic modalities. And if the flow were about to be curtailed, it would show up right away: free indirect discourse aims to restore thought from its start in the immanence between language and the problem it confronts, that it intends to express and that it wants to delimit and reintroduce. This style constitutes a heterogeneous approach to interrogation, a meditation precisely on the present, its development and its state of permanent imbalance, its continual variation, open to the outside. In literature, free indirect style has created an alliance among the writer, the protagonist, and the reader. In philosophy, this style intends to carry the multiplicity of the problem, the plurality of voices, into the logocentric heart of the thought. It's as if you're jumping up on a trampoline, hanging suspended up in the air, before you flip and plunge back down.

—R. E., R. C.

Impolitical

Reflection on the impolitical was born in a phase in which the crisis of political action was one with a renewed vitality of thought on politics. Throughout the West, the crisis of the political apparatus, the crisis of the social state, combined to transform the historical meaning of the concept of government. I'd like to reflect on why, at the beginning of the 1980s, one political cycle that lasted for at least thirty years appeared to end, while another cycle of reflection on politics opened, one that still continues to this day. Between 1981 and 1986, with various thinkers such as Biagio de Giovanni, Bruno Accarino, Remo Bodei, Massimo Cacciari, Umberto Curi, Giuseppe Duso, Giacomo Marramao, Roberto Racinaro, and Maurizio Zanardi, I took part in the publication of *Centauro*, a significant journal for so many reasons. In those years, in Italy, there emerged a consciousness of the radical crisis of one of the *topoi* of the political culture of the left and, more generally, of the modern conception of politics.[2] By then the dialectic, based on contradiction and on its recomposition in a higher unity, that joined class to party, movement to state, was shattered. Against this background of this new consciousness emerged an irreducible distance that separated a new reality from subjects of politics who were inspired by modern categories of sovereignty, state, population, and nation. That new reality no longer enjoyed the transcendental guarantee of political order. The prerogative of an international equilibrium described by Carl Schmitt in *The Nomos of the Earth* as having been in place in Europe since the peace of Westphalia failed—and failed forever.

The intellectuals who took part in the experience of *Centauro* demonstrated a keen awareness of this change. They interpreted it in terms of a crisis of modernity and positioned themselves at its very limit. On one hand, this formula echoed the emerging debate about the end of the great modern narratives about politics, history, and philosophy launched in 1979 by Jean-François Lyotard in *The Postmodern Condition*. This debate, soon expanded to a dimension unforeseen by even its promoter, extended the so-called end of history and the unrepresentability of social conflict. A model of rationality in interpretation of the modernization of politics and economics was no longer credible. On the other hand, the crisis of modernity radically placed in dispute modern politics' capacity to represent a reality whose own exclusively national consistency had been undermined and whose subjects had difficulty recognizing the unique and irreplaceable role of the sovereign. The sphere of the political could no longer be separated from the social, anthropological, and ontological forms it had tried to dominate, transform—even create from nothing—during the long adventure of modernity. Drawing my inspiration from the pages of Machiavelli's *Prince*, I proposed the concept-symbol of a centaur as the title of the journal, in order to take up once again this tragic coexistence of contraries. Politics could no longer trust itself to general subjects capable of mediating conflict, given that conflict was inscribed in politics' very reason for being. To politics fell the unfortunate assignment of holding together force and order, Machiavelli's fox and lion, life and forms. But so much indicated that this last attempt at recomposition would have to be the last.

The philosophical juncture at which this reflection occurred was characterized by a *koinè* that permitted diverse groups of intellectuals to come together to shape a horizon of common research. Since then, it has no longer been possible to create a collective journal with a sense comparable to *Centauro* in Italy because there is no longer a stable relationship between life and political forms, between theory and practice, between philosophy and politics, no matter how relocated and instrumental the relationship may be. And because of this, the philosophical alternatives present in *Centauro* split apart and have offered up radically different perspectives in the course of the last twenty years. It is with this awareness that I would reread the texts and opinions of those who, in various ways, anticipated the passage we were living through at the beginning of the 1980s. While the journal *Mondoperaio* advanced a fiery revisionist polemic against the Marxist tradition and Lucio Colletti had confirmed the crisis of Marxism (even Italian Marxism) with his *Intervista politico-filosofica*, space for a renewal of themes and authors was opened up in the postmarxist *Intellighenzia*. In *Krisis* there was the thought of Massimo Cacciari, who first formulated the concept of the impolitical, by means of which the categories of sovereignty, representation, party, and power were more and more depoliticized. This concept tore open the theological-political fold that had kept these categories pinched together up to that moment and incorporated a technical modality destined to render meaningless the representative assumptions about modern politics. In relation to this entropic fate of politics, the only possible discourse seemed to be expressed by an impolitical decision.[3] For some time, in an attempt to find a dialectical solution capable of giving form to conflicts, authors like Massimo Marramao and Angelo Bolaffi had reflected on the "Weimar laboratory," expanding on the debate in Germany of the 1920s between Carl Schmitt and the social-democratic jurists Kirchheimer, Neumann, Fraenkel, and Heller.[4]

It would be impossible to describe with just a few strokes the theoretical richness of Italian thought on this crisis.

I'll confine myself to pointing out in schematic terms the alternatives in play in those years. The first was negative thought, variously interpreted by Cacciari and Tronti. It engaged crisis as an originary dimension of the political, from which the political, in turn, drew the ability to create new forms of order through the force of its own decision-making power. A second interpretive line accepted the extinction of the subject to which negative thought still attributed representability, even though this representability was no longer based on work as traditional Marxism had held. In this way there emerged various and even diverging geopolitical trajectories: while one reassessed the authors of the so-called conservative revolution, Carl Schmitt, and then Nietzsche, Heidegger, and Wittgenstein, the second—the one in which I mostly see myself today—docked on the French shore where Derrida, but above all Michel Foucault and Gilles Deleuze, understood the crisis of the modern political subject as resistance to the pretension of imposing a sovereign form on the life of individuals. What these trajectories had in common then was the consciousness of the failure of the autonomy of politics and therefore the necessity of articulating a different response to the crisis. But where to start? And where did criticism find a place? We can say that there were three different hypotheses in place, even though they were not entirely disconnected from one another. For some, like de Giovanni, the crisis still positioned us in the modern, even if in a problematic way. Others like Bodei and Marramao landed on its margin, in a sort of hypermodern drawing out of modernity.[5] Finally for others—first for Cacciari and for me as well—that point cast us outside, to the impolitical reversal. In one area, even among thinkers who were far from the experience of *Centauro*, one discussion acquired real importance. It focused on the three principal authors of early modernity: Descartes, Hobbes, and Spinoza. In this debate, hypotheses that were not only philosophical but also political came into play. On one side was Mario Tronti, who worked on the autonomy of the political—in a theoretical frame in which the reflection on Hobbes took precedence. On the other side stood Toni Negri, who insisted instead on the break between Hobbes and Spinoza, in light of the revolutionary rupture with modern political theology.[6] Last but not least, de Giovanni chose a line of problematization that held Hobbes and Spinoza together against Descartes. He wanted to differentiate, within the modern tradition, the Cartesian perspective centered on the conscious subject from another, espoused by Spinoza and Vico, that ties life to forms in a new hypothesis of restoring the vitality of politics.[7]

We can't say that, in general, this debate was made up of political referents around which that varied philosophical *koinè* turned. Looking back, I consider it the most evident proof of the rupture of the bond between theory and practice, between reflection on politics and politics itself. In Italy this link had been embodied in an organic intellectual—that is, an intellectual specialist in the humanities or social sciences who interpreted his own role as a political leader, especially in the Communist Party. I am not surprised by the conclusion de Giovanni, who was editor of *Centauro*, drew later on.[8] The Communist Party did not understand the meaning of questioning ourselves about the crisis of modernity. Leaders like Gerardo Chiaromonte, Alfred Reichlin, and Giorgio Napolitano stepped in to keep the *Centauro* group from allying itself with the group coordinated by Mario Tronti, who edited *Laboratorio politico* in those years. A whole season of Italian intellectual life drew to a close—and with it the idea that journals about philosophical-political culture constituted, in a certain sense, the laboratory in which categories were created that politics would put into practice. Those first years of the 1980s were culturally lively despite recurring signs of the end of a political cycle. Then there started to assert itself a style of analysis stamped with the extreme personalization of theoretical apparatus and with the sophisticated, conceptual articulation that radically changed the rapport between philosophy and politics. Let me note that the years in which *Centauro* ended witnessed the birth of a new journal, *Filosofia politica*, founded by Nicola Matteucci, whose editorship I shared with Carlo Galli and Giuseppe Duso. Both of them were engaged in significant interpretation of modern political categories that constitute for me a site of continual confrontation. But here we deal with an academic journal—in the best sense of the word—no longer one that represents a tendency. *Filosofia politica* is entirely separate from politics in action.

The fact that the rapport between philosophy and politics has never been mended, not even within the paradigm of the "crisis of the political," proves that one stage has given way to another. In *Categorie dell'impolitico* I intended to distance myself from this paradigm, on one hand converging with, and on the other detaching myself from Cacciari's interpretation of the impolitical.[9] As I later understood, at that time, despite any precautions, I ran the risk of providing a somewhat gnostic—that is, constitutively negative—reading of the impolitical. Despite my having refused to talk about any other or different view of the political—but rather about its limits and its reversal—the category of the impolitical could be understood in an implicitly dualistic key. In reality the impolitical is the unforeseen margin, the silent heart, the empty point—certainly not a feasible alternative—of politics. It's not a political philosophy precisely because it refuses to establish an instrumental relation between philosophy and politics; it's not a political theology because it excludes any representation of good, any dialectical relationship between politics and good; and it isn't even a political ideology because it deconstructs the traditional bipolarities, starting with the one between right and left. In a strict sense, the impolitical is nothing but the determination of the political, in that the impolitical is that which defines the limits of the political. It's the political imagined departing from its confines—without which there's nothing but the conflict of power and interests. But insisting on the inevitability of conflict, that category wanted to sanction even failure, or the constitutive antinomy, of modern political philosophy that is always, no matter how, a thought about order. From the moment that political philosophy resists thinking about a conflict neither ordered nor representable, the impolitical is exactly what bursts forth from its representation as well as what by its very being annuls it. Political philosophy, understood as the foundation of modern political science, was born with this dramatically neutralizing meaning.

Machiavelli shows us the reason why Italian philosophy today seems to have a different fate from that of other European philosophies. Machiavelli alone maintains not only the impossibility of canceling out conflict but even its productivity. His problem lies in being able to imagine a conflict that heads neither toward civil war nor toward total incorporation within order. We can say that in modernity this theoretical possibility has never been realized historically. It has remained silent, imprisoned in the impolitical heart of politics, even though it has maintained within itself the unexpressed possibility of nonneutralizable conflict.

The impolitical therefore falls within a genealogical work on the modern political *episteme*, which cannot be considered as a single block but rather as a set of tensions in which, at least theoretically, more than one possibility in relationship to actual history opens up. Essays in *Centauro* had already established the modern as a horizon from which lines may diverge—or at least project—from that dominant one that runs from Hobbes to Hegel. In this sense, we must rethink cues and problems such as the antagonism between order and conflict in Machiavelli, the thought of immanence in Spinoza, the theme of plasticity of humankind in Pico, Giordano Bruno's opening on the infinity of worlds, Vico's idea of catastrophic cycles of history. From this point of view, my work on the impolitical has an element in common with my earlier reading of humanism.[10] Within this frame, at their extremes, the categories of the impolitical and of conflict tend toward each other. We're dealing with the same overall meaning viewed from different angles. Their symmetry, or contiguity, springs from a common laterality in relationship to the prevalent tradition of the modern based on the agreed-upon neutralization of conflict springing from the constitutive relationship between the individual and sovereign order.

Communitas/Immunitas

In relation to the impolitical, the diptych *Communitas: Origine e destino della comunità* and *Immunitas: Protezione e negazione della vita* is no longer projected against the backdrop of the crisis of modernity or the crisis of the political. Starting in the mid-1990s, I turned to what Michel Foucault defined as the "ontology of the present."[11] I ascribe a special importance to this definition since it reverses the general significance of the interrogation of the crisis of modernity up to that moment. I'd given an interpretation of certain historical-conceptual meanings of that crisis. I'd singled out a field—

impolitical, conflict—that couldn't reenter the modern semantic, either as a negative implication or as a presupposition of its concepts. The interrogation of the current moment, on the other hand, freely permits a genealogical gaze at not only the history of concepts but also all knowledge that cast the present in its current form—as this present appears to one who questions it and lives in it as well.[12]

This saggital gaze on the present allows assessment not only of its genealogical depth but also of the political and epistemic alternatives it contains. Within this frame the (nondialectical) relation between *communitas* and *immunitas* represents the first modality of a reflection that carried me from interrogating the impolitical to examining the biopolitical. The impolitical was an analytic of finitude declined in negative terms—in this sense, something not very far from a transcendental category of a Kantian type. When I wrote the introduction for the new edition of *Categorie dell'impolitico* in 1998, I already felt myself within the horizon of ontology. It was the beginning of a new laboratory that retained some elements of the impolitical perspective but pushed the analytic of finitude in the direction of an ontology of relation and change. Though rejecting every reference to values, every subjectivist presupposition, the impolitical still had an ethical imprint, attitude, tonality. The theorization of community, by contrast, has a clear ontological inclination. During this transition, I realized that the philosophy of the impolitical was perhaps the last pledge paid out to the idea of a crisis of modernity that tries to overcome itself, but, for this very reason, remains all the same. This feeling, this possible interpretation, left me at least partially dissatisfied. The impolitical was a reactive and dissenting category that remained entangled in the crisis of modernity. Still, the impolitical posed an important question: what is the structural, constitutive reason for the defective being of modernity, of this impossibility of filling its initial void? At a certain point I started to answer that modernity may have immunized itself against this originary deficiency. To be exact, we can talk about modernity as a determined, historical-categorical apparatus, when a politics directly concentrating on the survival and reproduction of life was invented.

In the transition from an ethical interrogation to an ontological one, we see determined a repositioning of the historical-political reading of modernity as well: modernity doesn't simply start with the institution of a sovereign power, as Hobbes posited, one with the intention of neutralizing—or immunizing—a conflict identified with a state of civil war that precedes politics. Rather, that very modernity, understood as affirmation of sovereignty, is the product of this conflict. The relation between community and immunity gives voice to this inversion of perspective. When individuals in a community submit to sovereign power because they realize they can no longer sustain the threats that community poses to itself, we can say that such a community has been immunized. Of course such immunization is hardly definitive because, given the equality of strengths and weaknesses, the conflict starts up again soon enough. This is the fundamental condition for instituting the sovereign pact—but also the principal cause of its destabilization. This conflict is inscribed on the dark heart of the community: it reflects back to a gift—the *munus*—that continually passes from one person to another and belongs to no one permanently. The foundation of *communitas* starts with the ontological debt that constitutes the originary defect, the lack of being, of those who are part of it. The members of the community are all equally at fault. They fail themselves—in the sense that they commit a crime—as all the foundational stories start their narratives with a murder, often between brothers. Under these conditions, the community identity of whoever receives the gift is destabilized and fractured from its origin. Now the sovereign immunizes the community from its own community excess, but he is also the principal actor in this excess.

Community and immunity therefore cannot be considered in two opposing and alternative semantic structures but rather in an ontology of co-involvement and change. Immunization is always relative to community. Like everything else an individual takes part in, community is always immunized in various ways. This involvement between the two concepts isn't a kind of dialectic, because it can't be understood as a relation between two different poles. Therefore it never reaches a definitive synthesis. Immunity and community are the same thing seen from two opposing sides, as a double possibility that is also—always—a double necessity. If community is at least partially immunized in all its historical forms, immunity also has a community side, or tangency. Autoimmunity—that is, the destructive force in the face of an organism that means to protect itself—is only one of the latent possibilities in immunitary practice. In fact, on a biological plane, the immunitary system does not have only a defensive or aggressive capacity. It is also that filter that permits organ transplants as well as birth itself through so-called immune tolerance. Just as one can infer from the sphere of biology the possibility that life, understood in its singularity, may not be exclusively a product of either defense or offense in relation to external agents, so one can also see that life may be the result of self-regulation established by the immanent norms that govern its development. Still, it would be an error to fix on a symmetry that immediately associates the biological and political horizons in a single plane: politics can't be reduced to the biological measure of life, for fear of its transformation into a thanatopolitical form. In the same way, life can't be completely incorporated into politics to avoid falling into a form of totalitarianism. I would rather consider the coinvolvement of this process in their constitutive asymmetry, oriented toward the constitution of life—whether individual or common—that tries to escape from autoimmunitary logic.

To question modernity genealogically beginning from the ties between community and immunity means, in the end, to bring to light that fundamental ambiguity or aporia, established as fundamental in the rapport between power and life, between biology and politics, that Foucault has described as "the acquisition of power over man insofar as man is a living being," his claim "that the biological came under State control, that there was at least a certain tendency that leads to what might be termed State control of the biological."[13] As I showed in the last section of *Immunitas* and more completely in *Bíos*, Foucault never succeeds in integrating these two perspectives—you see it in the never well-defined rapport between sovereignty and biopolitics. We're in the center of the antinomy of modernity, which I had already identified—albeit in a different way—in my book on the impolitical. My thesis is that in Foucault exists an irresolvable contradiction, because Foucault tends to view the rapport between politics and life as one between two entities already constituted in themselves. He does not interpret it instead as a relation of reciprocal immanence in which one is constitutive of the other. When you think of biopolitics as a relation between two preconstituted entities, you end up overlaying one on the other relation in which one is necessarily the subject and the other subjugated. Here necessity dictates that one leads to a sort of thanatopolitics or in what we might define very nearly as totalitarianism. I think that looking through a genealogical lens, biopolitics may be considered older than the modern, dating back to a coincidence with the birth of the political understood in its valence marked by conflict. But biopolitics finds in the modern paradigm of immunization a fundamental shift that gives it something more and different from Foucault's formulation. Immunity is the power to conserve life. With this paradigm, there is finally a full articulation of the two elements. From this point of view, in modernity biopolitics experiences an intensification—and also a semantic mutation—that renders it radically different from ancient biopolitics. In Greek sanitary politics and Roman agrarian politics, for example, biopolitics has a partially community structure, turned toward the ties between polis and *civitas*. The modern epoch, by contrast, determines an immunitary impulse that first passes through Hobbes's project of individual salvation but that, following a dramatically discontinuous course, reaches an obsessive syndrome of a thanatopolitical type. This stage provides that the life of one group seems protected by the violent elimination of another, as generally happens with racism or, in an infinitely more violent way, with Nazism. Here I don't want to give the impression that thanatopolitics casts its shadow over the entire spectrum of modernity—as if it were possible to reconceive modernity in a nonhistoricizable ontology in which, from its very beginning, life gets caught up in the mesh of power and crushed. On the contrary, when I speak of the ontological shift from the perspective of the impolitical to that of the biopolitical, I do intend to historicize the political, juridical, and anthropological dispositif of the mutual entanglement of life and politics in the face of very precise historical conditions—even including ruptures between them. In the light of these ruptures, one can argue the differences between the concepts of life and politics in modernity and those of antiquity. But differences also exist within modernity itself, and so we can avoid characterizing all of biopolitics in necessarily negative or thanatopolitical terms. In fact, what interests me is to bring to light the dispositif of coinvolvement and reciprocal change between *communitas* and *immunitas* that is at the foundation of biopolitics. The ontology I'm talking about is a historical ontology, which Foucault defined as "the ontology of the present," an ontology that doesn't get considered in traditional terms of history of being. It's cast instead in terms of history of the present—or, in other words, of genealogy.

Jacques Derrida's interpretation of the terrorist attacks of September 11, 2001, on New York is one example of the ontology of the present. This event created a crisis—really an explosion—of immunitary defenses of Western political systems. I share the presupposition of this analysis, even though indulging in it may draw out the equivocation of assuming inevitable immunization of a body in relation to autoimmunization, with which, under certain circumstances, this same body might experiment with destructive results. In the analysis of September 11, we run the risk of assigning features of autoimmunization to an entire political regime—in this case, democracy. In this way we would fall into an antinomy analogous to Foucault's analysis of biopolitics, when he superimposes politics on its possible—but never discounted—thanatopolitical outcomes. In New York, and in London in 2005, liberal democracies recognized a new, tremendous problem: the terrorists aren't aliens; they're citizens educated in Western schools; they speak the same language; they share the same culture, carrying to its extreme the death drive that passes through the community in an excessive, self-sacrificial suicide. In turn, this autoimmunitary crisis of democracy has produced political decisions, such as the preventive war against terrorism and a series of exceptional juridical dispositifs that have partially deprived democratic laws of any national or international authority. Derrida has related this autoimmune disorder of contemporary democracy to a fate that seems to impose suicide on democracy, keeping it from realizing its potential. But if democracy has been autoimmunitary from its beginning, then it is impossible to discount any form that, from time to time, democracy may assume.

Now this shift from ontology to politics conflates a political and juridical dispositif with a thanatopolitical fate of democracy. This consolidation has been going on for centuries but has its own significance in the present. Clearly, we can explain the actual autoimmunitary crisis by citing the weakening of national sovereignties and the spectral return of religion to the heart of political decisions. These decisions deny the life of some while protecting the life of others. But this doesn't demonstrate that the process of autoimmunization always degenerates into an autoimmunitary, suicidal crisis. What counts, even more than analogies, are distinctions. For example, always following Foucault's line of reasoning, we certainly can say that today we live in liberal biopolitical regimes that no longer fit into the frame of what's traditionally understood to be democracy. That is, if we understand democracy as something like equality of subjects—or at least as a theory of subjectivity based on equality—then today we can no longer say that such a regime is real. Whether in a negative or positive sense, contemporary biopolitics is centered more on difference than on equality—as always happens when we deal with live bodies and not abstract subjects of the law.

In a certain sense, this outcome had already been established—even though for other aims—by Carl Schmitt in his important essay about democracy and parliamentarianism in the 1920s.[14] Today we live in liberal regimes of various natures that have little to do with democracy—far removed, at least, from Rousseau's original concept. Even before September 11, we could recognize that immunitary democracy no longer resembled that concept. Naturally I'm not thinking of a totally community regime as an alternative, if we imagine as the alternative the concept of *communitas* in its radical form of global contamination; in that case it would necessarily be given over to self-destruction. But democracy cannot even be a totally immunized regime, because then the excess of security would lead to a total block and therefore implosion. If, on a conceptual plane, the two alternatives counter one another in their differential clarity, on a historical plane we've always had some form of commingling of the two. We can imagine a democracy with a low immunitary intensity that may offer absolute safety from the risk of the *munus*. And, in the reverse, we could have a democracy of low community intensity that may give protection from the risk of a suicidal autoimmunization. Securitized—or liberal—democracy functions in just this way: it produces one liberty, destroying another; it protects one part of life, abandoning another to whatever fate. Foucault theorized all this, even though he didn't succeed in pointing out the various paths to this short circuit that brings biopolitics back to its originary antinomy.

Biopolitics

To talk about biopolitics, I'll start from its most complex apex, from what I've defined as affirmative biopolitics. And I'll lay it out in relation to the problem of democracy. To understand the meaning of an expression like "affirmative biopolitics," we must start out from an alternative paradigm that clarifies the philosophical matrix in which it ripened. The affirmative qualities of biopolitics can be understood only by departing from the divergence experienced—not only in the sphere of political philosophy—between an interpretation of processes based on a transcendent approach and another interpretation focusing on immanence. The transcendent—or even the transcendental—perspective always makes reference to an external and superior point of view vis-à-vis the constitution of subjectivity—whether it be of sovereign, state, or party. The division between government and governed remains irreducible in this view. On the other hand, there opens up the possibility of an immanent reading—one that does not accept the idea of a sovereign power that regulates life from the outside. This reading is the only one that conceives the political according to a modality that does not consider philosophy a mere support of practice. Reconsidering the perspective of the impolitical today, I draw a double conclusion. The first is that philosophy can—and should—no longer have a metaphorical and instrumental rapport with politics. Second, today the space of political action falls outside its traditional confines—and lies precisely in the terrain that has been defined impolitical in various ways. When at last we overcome the barrier that modernity has created between philosophy and politics, and thought recognizes itself radically immersed within a biopolitical horizon, then philosophical reflection acquires a weighty political significance that it did not have before.

I consider this double evaluation the ultimate landing site of my reflection started twenty years ago. At that time, I tended to give the impolitical a predominantly negative representation—as the reverse of modern politics. In the meantime, it became clearer and clearer that the negative of the impolitical had been filled with that object apparently alien to politics—life. The impolitical had been from the beginning a paradigm critical of power—never apologetic or legitimating. But that discourse, justifiably critical of what exists, assumed a potentially affirmative modality when it turned to interrogate the importance assumed today by the dimension of biological life.

By now we've determined a relation of reciprocal immanence and coinvolvement between politics and life that's no longer subject to interpretation by the transcendental philosophy that runs, in various forms, from Kant to Heidegger; instead the line, even though sometimes discontinuous, in its own way, must join Spinoza to Nietzsche. This shift in the axis of categories responds to the clearly visible circumstance that all great questions that have opened up from the 1980s to today arose within the crisis of the state form—questions about sexual difference, immigration, new forms of war, terrorism, and biotechnologies. These questions demonstrate that politics no longer depends on the transcendence of an order governed from above or from outside; rather, they directly address every person's life in its immanent measure. Now that state politics and its principal paradigm—sovereignty—have been placed in serious discussion, the immanence of life is the only dimension in which contemporary politics finds its most essential meaning.

We can understand in this sense Foucault's assertion that politics is always a form of government in confrontation with life. It shouldn't make us think exclusively about power's decisions about life but also about a possible form of self-governing of individuals' own lives. Certainly politics can do nothing but stay within life—this is what *immanence* means.[15] It isn't possible to think of politics and life outside their rapport with one another. That great transformation I have been describing has been generated by the yielding of dialectic categories of mediation and recomposition that have structured politics since the dawn of modernity. Government, organization, and form are nothing but articulations of the plane of immanence, along which life enters into rapport with politics. In this sense, philosophy itself becomes a form of the political, a practice. If the impolitical inaugurated a season in which philosophy took on itself the task of making politics, albeit in a negative sense, biopolitics affirms that there exists a politics of philosophy. To make politics of—or in—philosophy is exactly the contrary of vindicating the role of political philosophy.

When I proposed the definition of affirmative biopolitics in *Bíos*, I intended to point out a possible way of overcoming Foucault's antinomy between politics of life and thanatopolitics; I turned toward another horizon of thought at whose center was an idea of porous democracy, facing its external limits. This would be a democracy with low immunitary intensity, whose forms might always be objects of innovation and self-control. I am thinking about institutional modalities that not only support but may actually be produced by politics *of* life rather than politics *on* life. With this formula I intended to root Foucault's conflict between biopower and biopolitics within life—that is, within that immanent horizon in which *communitas* and *immunitas* are always intertwined. In the category of affirmative biopolitics this coinvolvement gets read from another angle: that of the relation between life and norm, individuality and community, institutions and liberty—paying strict attention to avoid considering these terms as opposing polarities but as elements that interact in the same immanent process with political forms.

When we speak of the affirmative qualities of biopolitics, we situate politics in a horizon of innovation and production—not different from what Machiavelli did in his own way. From this point of view, I maintain we may imagine an immunity—one labeled positive—that would, on one hand, deliver life from the mortal dangers that lie in wait for it and, on the other, push it in a direction different from destructive results toward which its own autoimmunitary tendencies—and temptation—drag it. It's not a given that conflict, which is at the basis of every definition of politics, may be assimilated into a generalized state of war, into a state of permanent exception, and may, on its own account, impede the realization of democracy. Conflict can also be productive of new possibilities and horizons for democracy. To theorize this possibility, we must enter into the logic of the conflict itself—in the sense that we must deconstruct the thanatopolitical dispositifs in action, pointing out their genealogical relations with the structure they derive from. But we cannot delude ourselves that a dialectic reversal from negative to positive immunity can resolve the problems. In the ontology of the present

I'm trying to think, the dimension of conflict is not canceled out; rather it's transported to a productive, not self-destructive, ground.

In *Communitas* and *Immunitas* the discourse was still focused on an idea of community understood to depart from its constitutive deficiency. It was the final outcome of a deconstruction of modern concepts that tried to determine an outside of politics, representing this outside as a kind of line, or even an empty center, understood as individual—or even collective—nonbeing in the relation. With *Bíos*, by contrast, my objective was to demonstrate that this emptiness, this outside of politics, is not necessarily subject to the thanatopolitical outcomes of immunization. It's instead rich in affirmative possibilities; it's rooted in life according to the immanent declension that first Nietzsche and then, in other ways, Foucault and Deleuze gave it. The background against which this last transition took place was the interrogation of thanatopolitics—especially the Nazi version, which was the most radically negative expression of immunization. My intention was to open up a series of passages into the historical dispositifs that had pushed biopolitics to such lethal results until I could think of *bios* as form of life in common, knowing that meant rethinking democracy itself in the end.

In *Bíos* I articulated this form of common life in terms of birth, individuation, and constituent power. The category of birth should be understood not only as the origin of a living being but also as the capacity of life itself to continually start over from itself, producing new forms—whether in individuals or in multiplicity. As first formulated by Georges Canguilhem and then by Gilbert Simondon, the theory of individuation can be tied to that theory of event that links Bergson to Deleuze in the sphere of thought on immanence. The question of constituent power must ultimately be considered in light of the fact that today—in contrast to what happened in the epoch of modern politics—we're not dealing with establishing states or peoples. Today what politics constitutes—being in its turn constituted out of it—is life, in the sense that life is what produces conflicts and institutions. Its field of action is political, economic, and technical individuation on an individual or collective level. From a strictly philosophical point of view, this idea of form of life in common breaks with the paradigm of historicality or destiny, established by Heidegger with the second part of *Being and Time*. I will limit the term *destiny* (*Geschick*) to *Being and Time*, even though in succeeding works, *Geschick* and *Schicksal*, destiny takes on a wider meaning. Heidegger designates destiny as "*Dasein*'s primordial historizing, which lies in authentic resoluteness."[16] This decision permits *Dasein* to historicize itself in the sense that it rejoins its destiny—death—and, in this way, it *"hands itself down to itself, free for death, in a possibility which it has inherited and yet has chosen."*[17] This complicated game of destination of being-toward-death and of repetition, or transmission of death in the moment when *Dasein* decides for its own existence, imposes a paradigm of presupposition according to which every opening to the future can exist as such only if it roots itself in a form of inheritance of the past. In this way, the future is made possible only by a hereditary transmission of what is contained in the origin—even if this transmission is subsequently thought about in the form of absence or withdrawal. What stays unchanged is the political declension of this paradigm of the presupposition by which the paradigm is thought—whether it be individual destiny or common destiny of the German people. In this case, life takes the form of repetition of an origin that signals in advance the destiny of a community of people. So the glorious future of Germany is conditioned by an elaboration of an inheritance—originally descended from Greece—passed down from an immemorial past.

In contrast to this philosophical declension of life in common in whatever common destiny or community of people, I believe that affirmative biopolitics goes in exactly the opposite direction: one that breaks the historicizing chain whose premise dictates that the future is shaped by beginning from its originary supposition. Repetition does not realize a common destiny for a people but rather the singularity of everyone's life. That implies that life in common must be thought of outside the modern presupposition of its origin, just as democracy must renounce the idea of bringing up to date a transcendental order. Placing the problem of order before democracy means reaffirming the Hobbesian canon according to which politics is only conceivable from the starting point of security. So to pose the problem of origin to singularity of life means to reaffirm that what comes first—and remains the same forever—is the common destiny of a people with respect to who lives in the present and for the present. This reasoning has an immediate effect on politics: the overturning of the historical plane on which Heidegger constructed the immanence of life permits us to think about a democracy that's not presupposed but rather opened up to continual innovation. There could be a democracy imagined on the basis of the affirmation of birth and not the repetition of death. Life is no longer what repeats the destiny of man, which is death, but instead what affirms the event of birth in its singularity.

Here stands the difference between affirmative biopolitics and thanatopolitics: the latter is constructed around the obsessive requirement to safeguard life from the death to which it is promised. Thinking about politics starting from the idea of birth means not going back to origin; on the contrary, it establishes a dimension of event renewed from time to time, uprooted from every presupposed antecedent. In the same way, thinking about conflict and democracy together signifies freeing the dimension of conflict from the modern supposition about order. If anything, it's order that is realized as the basis of the emergencies that crop up in life from time to time.

The reference to the element of birth and individuation—to life's capacity to be reborn and renewed—can't be carried through to a new theory of human or subjective rights. Rather the perspective of affirmative biopolitics involves a deconstruction of the idea of a subject of law and even of law as such. The juridical dispositif is always a dispositif of parts—partial—so law is always in a certain sense private—and privative—even if we are dealing with what we call public law. It inevitably implies a dividing and excluding line between who has rights and who, instead, is deprived of them. We deal with an essentially separating dispositif. This is much more so with respect to individual rights. The theory of individuation, on the other hand, is not reconcilable with the concept of individual as predefined entity. Simondon, Canguilhem, and Deleuze have quarreled with the idea of an individual closed in himself and ontologically separated from others. That attitude opens a compelling interrogative of the category of individual rights as they are thought about in the liberal tradition. Luhmann defines these rights as the immunitary system of social systems. These rights must be rethought beginning with a philosophy of justice in whose center stands the idea of relation. This idea allows us to imagine the coinvolvement of birth, individuation, and constitutive power of life within the form of the common. The theory of individuation is what ultimately characterizes biopolitics in an affirmative light and places the political forms of democracy in relation to the living being, to the immunitary apparatus, and to the community. In other words, affirmative biopolitics turns to a form of life that places in tension—even in conflict—these diverse dimensions of individuation of life in its communal force. Here conflict is not synonymous with violence—but instead with the production of structural transformations.

Impersonal

All I've discussed requires a radical rethinking of the political categories that we have at our disposal. Through this lens, another, analogous concept— sovereignty—should be subjected to the same critical inquiry to which I subjected the concept of person in *Terza persona*. And the same discourse should be applied to the category of representation. In short, to maintain that the entire political lexicon of modernity must be rethought is no formula like any other. Instead it responds to an exigency hidden from the twentieth century up to now—which, from Schmitt to Heidegger on, has seen technology as the ultimate dimension of politics, as the very thing that has caught up modernity in a horizon of catastrophe. Unlike the philosophy of immanence, this philosophy does not understand that, beyond technology, there is the exigency of life, which becomes the new central reference point that includes technology. Today, from a political point of view, there is no discussion of the distribution and balance of power—in other words, the idea of representation. The dialectic between liberty and authority is not even in play. What's in play is the definition of what life is on an individual or collective plane. The same ruling groups who have organized the politics of what we call empire have understood this well. Even leaving out the often thanatopolitical modes with which these groups express this exigency, the principal question remains for them the survival of life and the security of the population. Today what strikes me as completely out of the game is continuing to press politics on the question of representation. All that is truly over.

On a not merely categorical plane, affirmative biopolitics necessarily passes through a deconstruction of biopolitical categories in action. In its most radical meaning, deconstruction is politics of philosophy, or philosophical practice, that serves to define the genealogy of the present. In this case, it passes through a reversal of thanatopolitical categories carried to their extreme by Nazism. In *Bíos*, this hypernegative referent served to give me a necessary point of contrast because Nazism, unlike liberal-democratic regimes, had thought through the rapport between life and politics. Fifty years after Nietzsche, Nazism had theorized that politics isn't thinkable, and operable, outside of life. Today this element is being taken up again and overturned. In *Bíos*, affirmative biopolitics must be thought within the reversal of three major political paradigms of Nazism: the enclosure of life in the organic body is opposed by the postphenomenological—but also post-Christian—

concept of flesh; the reduction of life under the domination of a single transcendent norm opposed by an immanent normativization of life that dates back to Spinoza; the anticipated suppression of birth by means of negative eugenics opposed by a politics of birth already foreshadowed in some ways by Hannah Arendt.

The discourse on the impersonal that, for now, brings to a close the journey of my reflection implicitly reenters this horizon. From its origin, negative biopolitics is founded on the separation between life and body. The notion of person expresses this separation to the degree that it distinguishes juridical subjectivity from the body, thus dividing within *bios* one privileged zone from the other, subjugated zone of life. The critique of the idea of person that moves in the direction of the impersonal is one of the most powerful openings for discourse on affirmative biopolitics; it places in discussion the paradigmatic axis on which modern politics is founded, starting from its deepest classical roots. This does not mean that the impersonal may show in a normative way what affirmative biopolitics is. We're dealing here with an open horizon. Moreover, if I were to provide a normative version of affirmative biopolitics, I'd return to situating biopolitics in a transcendental dimension. That politics inscribes itself into a genealogy of immanence means that it can no longer be normative in the abstract. Immanence does in fact reveal itself from time to time—and always in a different way—departing from the situation in which it's realized, never from norms that apply. For example, saying that the immunitary system isn't always—and only—negative, even if it often ends up that way, means that we undo the presumed superimposition of biopolitics and thanatopolitics.

All this, anticipated in *Immunitas*, stands at the center of *Bíos*. In relation to them, *Terza persona* positions itself within the same problematic orbit. *Terza persona* manages a double step ahead, or to one side: on one hand, in relation to the question of subjectivity—or, better still, the processes of subjectivization—and, on the other hand, to the problem of historicity and, especially, to the antinomic relationship between continuity and discontinuity. The first point has to do with seeing the performative concept of dispositif. The dispositif of *person* is neither a concept nor even a category; it's a dispositif that produces real effects. The first of these is to hide its effects in the personalistic rhetoric that today is reaching its apex. Let's be clear: my book does not contest the various discourses focusing on emancipation that have brought back the value, dignity, and individuality of the human person since the Second World War—and today more than ever. But it does contest this semantic connection between person and man. In reality, I go back to the double genealogy of the term *person*—the Roman juridical model and the Christian of a theological brand. I've tried to prove that its dispositif unifies the subject furnished with personal quality and the living being in which it's installed—but always within the form of their presupposed separation. And that the original performance—whether theological or juridical—of the dispositif of person lies exactly in the capacity to define the threshold of division and exclusion within *bios* between the fully human life—endowed with rational and moral signs of the person—and a life of bestial nature subjugated to it.

Despite their enormous historical, categorical, and semantic distance from one another, Roman and even modern law give, consciously or unconsciously, meaning to the notion of person with this result of separation—a result that renders the practice of something like human rights unthinkable today because it is structurally aporetic. Moreover, the Christian conception of the Incarnation, Christianity's most extraordinary legacy, implies the simultaneous presence in Christ of two natures—one divine, the other human. These two natures aren't only structurally different but also furnished with different value. Within each human being, the immortal soul and the mortal body subjected and subordinated to it are similarly different and given disparate value. If we return to the insoluble relation between subjectification and subjugation as theorized by Foucault during the 1970s, we recognize the exact role played by the dispositif of the person: it's to create subjectivity—even juridical subjectivity—through a practice of subjectification, or objectification, of one zone against the other within each living being, and therefore also between men capable of governing their own bodies, on the one hand, and, on the other, those considered incapable of doing so, and who thus are cast into the sphere of animals.

This double, intersecting process of subjectification and animalization is reconstructed through the contamination of various languages—from philosophy to anthropology to linguistics and finally, naturally, to law and politics. That calls into question the way in which the apparatus of the humanities performs. These fields themselves can't be understood as neutral disciplines. Rather, they're sites for the production of a concept of humanity that's tied to specific logics of power and, better still, biopower, along the naturally broken line that runs from the great biologist Bichat to contemporary bioethics. Naturally, the construction of discourse runs not only on a diverse disciplinary course but also along a quite profound diachronic axis; it imposes a fine-tuning of a so-called methodological character, relative to the question of continuity and discontinuity. My effort has been to superimpose them—placing them in tension with one another—within a single gaze capable of taking in each within the other. That implies a conception of history of a stratified type that may see within itself the simultaneous presence of different times. Without forgetting the "future past" Reinhardt Koselleck talks about, this reference turns above all to the genealogy of Nietzsche and to the archaeological method of Benjamin when, especially in *The Arcades Project*, he goes researching the originary fragments fixed in the heart of modernity.[18] Naturally the antinomic connection singled out by Freud between *familiar* and *foreign* lies in this constellation of thought. It's especially important in relation to the circumstance in which the past—especially a denied or repressed past—returns in the present with a phantasmic or spectral force that carries us back to Foucault's connection between bio- and thanatopolitics. It's precisely in this anachronic and anachronistic way the archaic dispositif of the person returns to the center of contemporary experience with power to separate and exclude. Naturally, if we want to pick up on its exigency, we have to cast an oblique, sagittal gaze capable of singling out, from time to time, the nonhistorical, or hyperhistorical, elements that run through and unhinge history.

And so it is that I come to the latest part of my work, which is still being fully developed: in opposition to the categorical and hierarchical effect of the dispositif of the person, I've proposed a philosophy of the impersonal, as much as it is possible to draw out the impersonal from the most advanced experiences of contemporary reflection (but of art as well). I've substantially created it along three paths, within three semantic horizons. These are themselves anything but internally homogeneous, but all refer in some way to that third person which Émile Benveniste already defines as the nonpersonal—exactly impersonal—of the person. The first leads off with the idea of justice. Already in his *Outline of a Phenomenology of Right*, Alexandre Kojève alludes to justice as the only sphere in which the third— understood as an exteriority that cuts off every personal interest—won't be only the judge, but so will anyone else who casts a glance toward a posthistorical condition in which humankind will rediscover its original, animal dimension. But it's Simone Weil who makes the impersonal a sacred point of view that, through radical deconstruction, recognizes the separating power of the person. It's further testimony to the intrahistorical connection between the ancient and the contemporary, as well as to the violent resurgence of the original in modern times, that Weil singles out, with absolute lucidity, Roman juridical culture at the beginning of that excluding dispositif implicit in the personalistic declension of modern law. From this point of view, I find a thread of discourse that, starting from *Categorie dell'impolitico*, runs through the intersection of *communitas* and *immunitas* and arrives at my most recent texts: for her to support the primacy of justice over the law means not only to look at the modern political from its impolitical side; it also proposes a communial (*communiale*)—because neither immunitary nor immunizing—conception of the relation among men.

The second vector of meaning in the philosophy of the impersonal came to me from a series of authors—from Robert Musil on—who had practiced a neutral approach to writing, as it delves into that dialogic word which, in current speech, ties the first and second person in a rapport of interlocution. In twentieth-century philosophy, Maurice Blanchot cast himself as witness to such a lateral passage that decentered the narrative voice, espousing literary work continually in exile from itself. With Blanchot, we're by now far from the mystical result of Weil's experiment; we're instead handed over to a movement of depersonalization that, before any consideration of community, looks at language in its constitutive relationship with silence— not only with the end of the identification of the subjects of action with themselves but also with the aphony of narrative voice covered over by the anonymous murmuring of events. In political interventions of the 1950s and 1960s, Blanchot practiced within his work collective an anonymous form of protest in which all individuals' voices were inextricably mixed with the voices of all others up to the point of losing all proper names. In political action, as in writing, what counts is the impersonality of an event shared by all but belonging to no one. This happens when "it rains" (*piove*) or "one dies" (*si muore*).

Above all, Blanchot thinks about the impersonal from the point of view of death, in a form that lies in some ways within the Heideggerian horizon. Foucault and Deleuze bring the impersonal back to the form of life. The reverse of "one dies," thought from the perspective of whatever transcends us in whatever way, is "one lives" (*si vive*), the central—but also decentered— place from which we'd taken off. This is the ultimate and definitive deviation in relation from the thought of ontological difference still present in authors, like Derrida, who have still thought after Heidegger. We've already seen what may be the role of life within the conception of Foucault—even in life's rapport with politics. It's simultaneously the site of the exercise of sovereign power—but also the site of ultimate resistance to it. It's precisely where we may recognize the impersonal dimension as opposed to the juridical form, which, at the origin of the modern, Hobbes had tied to the sovereign person capable of representing all who transferred their own rights to him in exchange for his protection. How clearly, then, can we say to Deleuze that his essential service to philosophy may be exactly in the deconstruction of the category, or dispositif, of the person in every sphere—psychoanalytic, literary, political. His call to "become animal" constitutes the most intense way to cut the knot that inextricably ties the figure of the person to the practice of subordination and exclusion of those who place themselves, or get placed, outside its limits. In a theological, philosophical, and juridical tradition that has always thrust one part of humanity into the dimension of bestiality, the revindication of animal nature as the most intimate nature of every man shatters the interdiction that has always governed us. Such a vindication of the impersonal in, or of, the person may be the point at which the philosophy of immanence becomes one with the shift from philosophy meditating on death to philosophy reflecting on life already under way with Spinoza and followed by Nietzsche. But how the impersonal may be able to see itself in a new form of biopolitical democracy—or of affirmative biopolitics—is a question that concerns not only my future work but all contemporary thought.

Notes

This text is a translation of a 2008 conversation between Roberto Esposito and Robert Ciccarelli, published as "La Politica al Presente," edited by Robert Ciccarelli, in *Impersonale: In dialogo con Roberto Esposito*, edited by Laura Bazzicalupo, 13–37 (Milan: Mimesis Edizioni, 2008). Although the opening note was coinitialed by both Esposito and Ciccarelli, the text's opening page designates Esposito as its author and Ciccarelli as its editor. The text's original closing page, meanwhile, is initialed by Laura Bazzicalupo.—Trans.

1 Deleuze and Parnet, *Dialogues*.
2 See Gentili, *La crisi del politico*.
3 Cacciari, *Krisis*; Cacciari, *Pensiero negativo e razionalizzazione*. See also Cacciari, *Sull'autonomia del politico*; and Cacciari, "Law and Justice," 173–98.
4 See Fraenkel, Arrigo, and Vardaro, *Laboratorio Weimar*; Marramao, "Teoria della crisi e problema dello Stato"; Marramao, "'Technica sociale'"; Marramao, *Tecnologia e potere nelle società post-liberali*; Duso, *La politica oltre lo stato*; Galli, *Genealogia della politica*; Bolaffi, *Il crepuscolo della sovranità*.

5 See Bodei, Borso, and Tronti, *Società politica e Stato in Hegel, Marx e Gramsci*; Duso, *Weber*; and Bodei, *Geometria delle passioni*.

6 See Negri, *Spinoza*; Negri, *Subversive Spinoza*; and Negri, *The Savage Anomaly*.

7 See De Giovanni, Esposito, and Zarone, *Divenire della ragione moderna*; and De Giovanni, "'Politica' dopo Cartesio," in Gentili, *La crisi del politico*.

8 See Biagio De Giovanni, "Al tempo de 'il Centauro,'" in Gentili, *La crisi del politico*.

9 Esposito, *Categorie dell'impolitico*.

10 See Esposito, *La politica e la storia*; and Esposito, *Ordine e conflitto*.

11 Foucault, *The Politics of Truth*, 95.

12 Foucault has defined philosophy as "the problematization of a present [*attualità*], and as the questioning by the philosopher of this present to which he belongs and in relation to which he has to situate himself." In this "ontology of the present [*attualità*]," or of "the present," philosophy is "the discourse of modernity on modernity." See Foucault, "The Art of Telling the Truth," 88. The first Italian translation of this important intervention was published, under the editorship of Giacomo Marramao, with the title "Che cos'è l'illuminismo? Che cos'è la rivoluzione?" On the relation between the ontology of the present, on the one hand, and, on the other, the exercise of the critique of the governance of our life in the present, see Foucault, "The Subject and Power." See also Foucault, "Illuminismo e critica."

13 Foucault, *"Society Must Be Defended,"* 239–40.

14 Schmitt, *The Crisis of Parliamentary Democracy*.

15 See Deleuze, "Immanence: A Life." On the genealogy of immanence, see Ciccarelli, *Immanenza*.

16 Heidegger, *Being and Time*, 435.

17 Heidegger, *Being and Time*, emphasis in original.

18 Koselleck, *Futures Past*; Benjamin, *The Arcades Project*.

CHAPTER 4

Cujusdam nigri & scabiosi Brasiliani:
Rancière and Derrida

Alberto Moreiras

War or Production?

In *Commonwealth*, Antonio Negri and Michael Hardt discuss two different forms of understanding antimodern forces. Both of them refer back to Max Horkheimer and Theodor Adorno's analyses in *Dialectic of Enlightenment*. For them, while it is obvious that freedom in society is inseparable from Enlightenment thought, enlightened societies keep within themselves the germ of their regression toward despotic barbarism. Horkheimer and Adorno's examples are Nazi Germany and the Soviet Union under Stalin, which causes the authors of *Commonwealth* some moral consternation. According to the latter, there is a need to posit two opposite types of antimodern reaction: the despotic type, which aims to enslave the multitude, and the reaction of those who "do not stand in a specular, negative relation to modernity but rather adopt a diagonal stance, not simply opposing all that is modern and rational but inventing new rationalities and new forms of liberation."[1]

The dialectical assimilation of antimodernity to the dark forces of regression ends up closing a vicious circle unable to understand "how the positive, productive monsters of antimodernity, the monsters of liberation, always exceed the domination of modernity and point toward an alternative."[2] The posited alternative, of course, is one with the communist or neocommunist revolution of the multitude that Hardt and Negri seek or, rather, confidently expect. It is simple: the problem of total or absolute democracy is a mere matter of letting the forces of total or absolute democracy triumph. Foregone conclusion: it is enough to keep the other ones from triumphing. The other ones are those whose antimodern polemical orientation consists of liberating the sovereign from his obligation toward his subordinates, as Juan

Donoso Cortés or Carl Schmitt would have suggested, not to mention the Nazis, the Ku Klux Klan, the proposers of ethnic cleansing, or the American neoconservatives dreaming of world domination.[3] There are two positive tasks, say Negri and Hardt: "The first is to pose a clear distinction between reactionary antimodern notions of power that seek to break the relationship by freeing the sovereign and liberatory antimodernities that challenge and subvert hierarchies by affirming the resistance and expanding the freedom of the subordinated. The second task, then, is to recognize how this resistance and freedom always exceed the relationship of domination and thus cannot be recuperated in any dialectic with modern power. These monsters possess the key to release new creative powers that move beyond the opposition between modernity and hierarchy."[4]

War or production? Is the revolutionary question today a matter of war, antimodern war, reactionary war, or war that seeks the liberation of the dominator, as could be the case were the revolution a populist revolution led by the hordes of the U.S. tea party or by the Islamic fundamentalists? Or is revolution simply the foreseeable result of a development of productive forces in the biopolitical economy, at the time of the total subsumption of life into capital? The question is not new. To read Karl Marx and Friedrich Engels's "Communist Manifesto" is already to ask that question, where a lot more than a possible response to the conditions of constitution and overcoming of modernity lies. That the "Communist Manifesto" may itself presuppose a productionist or polemological primary orientation is important only to the extent one considers the previous question regarding an exit from capitalism important. But—do we know whether capitalism is primarily a question of production or a question of war?

In his seminar "Society Must Be Defended," Michel Foucault says that the end of the politico-juridical dispositif of sovereignty theory marks the beginning of modernity in the transition toward a historical conception that privileges an ontology of war. It is not easy to determine how far Foucault wanted to go—things are rather tentative in those seminars that he was not thinking of publishing directly. Foucault analyzes the notion of war in modernity against sovereignty theory, and we know that he finds in the responses to the political situation of seventeenth-century Britain, not just the most remarkable and exhaustive formulation of sovereignty theory (in Thomas Hobbes's *Leviathan*), but also the practical beginnings of an ontologico-political alternative based on war as the real engine of political existence. This ontologico-political development, Foucault thinks, will become central for the constitution of modernity, that is, of the second modernity, the modernity whose conventional beginning dates back to the second half of the eighteenth century. Although Foucault makes no explicit reference to the "Communist Manifesto," it is obvious that its initial sentence (after the famous exordium about ghosts and Europe), that is, "The history of all society up to now is the history of class struggles," marks the seminar.[5] The sentence resounds through it, and it is a sentence that cannot be made compatible with sovereignty theory. It is the sentence that would make the 1848 Marx-Engels text one of the central texts of political modernity. The "Manifesto" has a performative dimension insofar as it does what it says, that is, as it participates in the struggle it announces, and in that sense it is within the region of experience that Marx's 1845 eleventh thesis "On Feuerbach" opens up: "The philosophers have only *interpreted* the world in different ways; the point is to *change* it."[6]

All history is the history of class struggle: "Freeman and slave, patrician and plebeian, lord and serf, guildmaster and journeyman, in short, oppressor and oppressed stood in continual conflict with one another, conducting an unbroken, now hidden, now open struggle, a struggle that finished each time with a revolutionary transformation of society as a whole, or with the common ruin of the contending classes."[7] There has always been war. Sometimes the real situation is hidden, and there is an appearance of peace; sometimes the situation is open, and what is apparent is war. But open or hidden war, not peace, defines the state of things, and that is so not now or yesterday but through history. Or at least through history "up to now," as Marx and Engels say.

If war is, in modernity, the name of being, then politics is effectively a continuation of war, in the Foucauldian phrase that inverts von Clausewitz, and the end of politics is either to win the war or to keep on winning it, that is, to hold on to the benefits of victory. That means above all to keep the situation of domination of the enemy open as a situation of domination. When one says, "the history of all hitherto existing society up to now is the history of class struggles" from a militant position such as that of the "Manifesto," one would seem to seek the place of victory, to occupy the position of the victor. But Marx and Engels never say that the proletariat must permanently assume a position as the oppressing class—that the proletariat must aim to keep a situation of endless domination open. "Let us win the war" means "let us make the enemy lose it." To have the enemy lose means that the enemy will be made to pay the consequences of having lost. Or not?

Can Marx and Engels be saying that the proletariat as the universal class, as the class whose historical function is to rush and accomplish the end of class division, must win the last of the wars, that is, the war whose real result will be the very end of war, and the end of the paradigm of war? "Up to now" we have only had war, my friends, but if we win this war, then we will be in a position to promise that there will be no further wars. My friends, there will be no enemies anymore. Or at least there will be no internal enemies, until the time when we take victory in the war to its properly universal and interplanetary stage.

But the promise of the end of war by the winner of the war is always everywhere the announcement of the eternity of victory, hence inevitably the announcement of the eternity of war. The obligation—a war obligation, or better, an obligation of defeat, the price of defeat—to consider the eternal enemy an eternal friend is a heavy one. Perhaps there is no worse slavery: it is the inquisitorial obligation par excellence. What is at stake here? Can we rescue real meaning from this apparent contradiction? In Foucault's terms, to insist that the winner must be a winner forever, must become the unconditional sovereign and lord of all discourse, would seem to be a relapse into sovereignty theory. But Negri and Hardt call that a false problem, to the very extent that biopolitical economy will win, not through war, rather through the unconditional liberation of life from the chains of an inoperative and inefficient capitalism, from the ruins of capital. Class struggle will always have been a mirage, or rather: if there was struggle, it ended when one of the parts defeated itself, so now we only have to welcome the orphaned and exhausted soldiers that are surrendering. The resolution of war will not have been bellic. Could it be understood as an exception to war? Strange tropology.

Foucault says that war is, in modernity, that is, for instance, for Marxism, the very name of being, that war is ontological ground, and that politics is only the continuation of war. But if war is ontological ground, then politics cannot stop war, since politics could not transcend its own ontological conditions. Is the "Communist Manifesto," as Foucault would seem to indicate, a polemology? Is there an identification of war and being in Marxist philosophy? Is there one in the Hegelian philosophy from which Marxism derives? If the "Communist Manifesto" posited the identification of war and being, then it would have to account for its own claim that communism is an exception to war:

> Political power in its true sense is the organised power of one class for oppressing another. If the proletariat necessarily unites as a class in its

struggle against the bourgeoisie, makes itself into a ruling class through revolution, and as a ruling class forcibly transforms the old relations of production, then it will transform, along with these relations of production, the underlying conditions for class conflict and for classes in general, hence its own supremacy as a class. In place of the old bourgeois society with its classes and class conflicts there will be an association in which the free development of each is the condition for the free development of all.[8]

"A world to win" implies "the end of class conflict," and that is the direct consequence of proletariat domination, it is claimed.[9] It would be a domination that looks for its self-annihilation as such, for the termination of its character as domination. To bring the class conflict to an end is to accomplish the eternity of the ontological exception. If all social history is the history of class struggle, then the history that initiates the triumph of the proletariat revolution is the history of an exception—the ontological exception of communist peace. But all exception is exceptional and cannot affect the rule it interrupts. Is it possible that communism or, now, neocommunism may confirm, rather than belie, as an exception to it, the thesis of the ontological priority of war?

One could say that this kind of reasoning was rejected by Marx avant la lettre a few years before writing the "Manifesto," that is, in 1845, at the time of his study of Feuerbach, when he was trying to establish his own notion of materialism against the Hegelian left. I will quote three of the other theses on Feuerbach. In the second thesis we read, "The question whether human thinking attains objective truth is not a question of theory but a practical question. It is in practice that man must prove the truth, the actuality and power, the subjective aspect and validity of his thinking. Argument about the actuality or non-actuality of thinking, where thinking is taken in isolation from practice, is a purely scholastic question." In the eighth thesis: "All social life is essentially practical. All mysteries which lead theory in the direction of mysticism find their rational solution in human practice and in the comprehension of this practice." And in the tenth: "The standpoint of the old materialism is bourgeois society; the standpoint of the new is human society or social humanity."[10]

They are fighting words, and they break with the philosophical tradition, not just with its Hegelian avatar. The young Marx wants to change the world, because only practice is a measure of truth. There is nothing beyond practice; there is no truth but practical truth when one abandons the bourgeois position and embraces the perspective of general human society or social humanity, which is, as the sixth thesis reminds us, the perspective of the essence of man himself, not dependent upon "isolated individuals" but rather upon "the ensemble of social relations."[11] The abandonment of the bourgeois position and the adoption of a new materialism, a materialism not of matter but of practice, is the inversion of Hegelian philosophy, the affirmation of a new metaphysical or postmetaphysical perspective, in philosophy and against philosophy. It may also be the site from where it becomes possible to say "all history up to now . . ." In other words, there is a before and an after. "Up to now" does not mean always up to now; that is, it is not up to now for us. Rather, Marx and Engels want to indicate the time of writing, which is the now of the political performativity of the "Manifesto." The "Manifesto," upon being published, had to open a "from now on" where history would no longer be measured by theoretical mysticisms. The hour of practice was upon us.

The contradiction referred to above—how is it possible to affirm the ontological priority of war, the condition of reality of war, and at the same time affirm the suspension of war in the time to come, as if the time to come could only be understood through the figure of the exception, of interruption, of an absolute *novum*?—could therefore be kept apart from the theses on the new practical materialism. If only practice is a condition of truth, then there is no ontological priority of war: there is only the historical knowledge that there has always been war up to now, and the imaginary projection of a new structure of the human, where the point of view of totality would impose a permanent end of the conflict. No more war, once the proletariat triumphs as the universal class; or the biopolitical multitude; or Alain Badiou's philosophical Idea, since for Badiou "communism is the only Idea worthy of a philosopher."[12]

The "Manifesto" includes a formulation that would be almost literally repeated in the preface to "A Contribution to the Critique of Political Economy," which gives it somehow a special status. The "Manifesto" says, "At a certain level of development of these means of production and trade, the relations in which feudal society produced and exchanged, the feudal organization of agriculture and small-scale manufacture, in a word feudal property relations, no longer corresponded to the forces of production already developed. They impeded production instead of advancing it. They became just so many fetters. They had to be sprung open, and they were sprung open"; and the "Contribution," "At a certain level of their development the material

productive forces of society come into contradiction with the already existing relations of production, or in what is merely a legal expression for this,
with the property relations within which they had previously functioned.
From forms of development of the productive forces these relations turn into
their fetters. Then an epoch of social revolution commences."[13]

No doubt these paragraphs are at the basis of contemporary neocommunist theorizations, from Negri and Hardt to Slavoj Žižek and Badiou.[14] They
initiate a possible alternative to the postulation of the ontological priority
of war. They do not say "there is war, and within it there is production" but
rather "there is production, and therefore there is war." War is a product of
the development of productive forces at a point when the old relations of
production have become fetters. There is war not because there can be war
but because there must be war—because practice imposes a movement, and
that movement imposes the revolutionary transformation of society and permanent change in the class structure. Marx repeatedly affirms the priority
of production (see the *Grundrisse*, and of course *Capital*), but we have not
yet properly understood the relation between production and war. Is class
struggle a mere historical derivation from production and the relations of
production? Or is it the case, as Foucault would seem to propose, that production is already the image and manifestation of war?

The preface to "A Contribution to the Critique of Political Economy"
continues with another famous passage:

> Humanity only sets itself such problems as it can solve, for on careful con-
> sideration one always finds that the problems themselves only arise where
> the material conditions of their solution are known to be on hand or at
> least in the process of development. In broad outline Asiatic, ancient,
> feudal, and modern bourgeois modes of production can be designated
> as progressive epochs in the economic development of society. Bourgeois
> relations of production are the last antagonistic form of the social process
> of production, antagonistic not in the sense of individual antagonism,
> rather of an antagonism growing out of the conditions of life in society
> for individuals, but at the same time the productive forces developing
> in the womb of bourgeois society create the material conditions for the
> resolution of this antagonism. With that social formation the pre-history
> of human society draws to a close.[15]

Social antagonism, says Marx in 1859 but in a way that I would consider
consistent with his position in 1848, belongs to the prehistory of that so-

cial humanity that constitutes the very essence of man according to "On Feuerbach." But if war belongs to prehistory, then there is no ontological priority of war. The social antagonism that pervades the known history of the modes of production is not foundational. It rather belongs to the avatars of production itself, and it constitutes in the last instance something like a ruse of practical reason. From the perspective of the inversion of Hegelian philosophy, of the new materialism, of the new practice, it is possible to affirm that the dictatorship of the proletariat, insofar as it would make it impossible that "labor can . . . be turned into capital, money, rent, in short, into a monopolizable power in society, i.e. from the moment that personal property can no longer be turned into bourgeois property," would accomplish the suppression of "power to subjugate the labour of others."[16] The history of production, in other words, will impose a political development whose final result will be the end of politics as war. If communism begins the history of social humanity or human society properly so called, that is so precisely to the extent that communism operates a break with society up to now in its character as class conflict, war. Communism is an exception to war, but not an exception that maintains the rule of war; rather an exception that liquidates its character as grounding and opens another history: "history." For communism, war is no longer part of history, but production is. And it is also production that has always already organized the war economy in communist prehistory.

What then about Foucault's thesis regarding the modern substitution of an ontology of war for the politico-juridical dispositif of sovereignty? Is Foucault simply wrong? Or does it remain possible to read Hegelian-Marxist dialectics in the light of an ontology of war after all? We can invoke a passage from a very late seminar (1973) taught by Martin Heidegger in Zähringen. Heidegger tells a few students that Marxian thought is part and parcel of the technological *Ge-Stell* precisely because it never leaves the horizon of production, or because it accepts production as the very horizon of the human. The transcribed notes say,

> Heidegger opens the volume of Marx's *Early Writings* and reads the following sentence, taken from the "Contribution to the Critique of Hegel's Philosophy of Right": "To be radical is to grasp the root of the matter. But for man man is the root himself." Marxism as a whole rests upon this thesis, Heidegger explains. Indeed, Marxism thinks on the basis of production: social production of society (society produces itself) and

the self-production of the human being as a social being. Thinking in this manner, Marxism is indeed the thought of today, where the self-production of man and society plainly prevails.[17]

Heidegger contra Foucault perhaps, regarding Marx and Marxism.

Foucault says: war. And Heidegger says: production. The self-production of the multitude is of course the only prevailing idea in the Negri-Hardt trilogy—a trilogy set against Heidegger, who obsessively appears as the real theoretical enemy or as the common denominator of all real theoretical enemies. This is perhaps so. In any case, Negri and Hardt, from the immanent productionism and self-productionism of the biopolitical forces of real and total subsumption, never stop making war, not so much on the empire, but certainly on Heidegger and the Heideggerian left. From the latter perspective, can self-productionism exist? Is production not essentially heteroproduction? This is the question I would like to rehearse by focusing on Jacques Rancière's meditation on the work of Jacques Derrida. It is a question about the ground of political practice today. The two main answers we seem to have are: yes, politics is the celebration and administration of the forces of production, and everything depends on understanding production in the right way and anticipating its future; or, politics is precisely always already an interruption of production, a refusal to recognize the priority of production, and a restitution of the priority of conflict. It would seem that there is a choice to be made, although the choice may well be to undo the alternative.

The Demotic Principle

Rancière understands very well that the problem of total or absolute democracy is far from being a matter of allowing the forces of total or absolute democracy to triumph. For him politics is always a polemical field, without stability, where every accomplishment can be reversed and every defeat is temporal. Politics is always at the mercy of the police, although the police can indeed suffer political defeat.

In his essay "Should Democracy Come? Ethics and Politics in Derrida," Rancière points out that the very concept of democracy lives in radical instability, not because those who govern are scoundrels, although that too, but rather because there is a difference inherent to democracy itself that makes it constitutively incapable of self-accomplishment as a form of government. So, insofar as democracy must be understood as "an excess with respect to any form of government," the postulation of democracy as absolute, as *imperium absolutum* in the Spinozian formulation, would make no sense.[18] But such nonsense of democracy should not take us toward its abandonment in the name of any kind of ethical purity. The ethicization of democracy is Rancière's old warhorse, and the source of almost every one of his theoretical critiques. For Rancière democracy, as a political term, must come under a strictly political rationality, even if such a rationality is far from being simple. Giving up democratic politicality in the name of ethical reason, of any ethical reason, is not just philosophically objectionable but, more importantly, it is politically objectionable. And such a problem is what seems to be at stake, for Rancière himself, in his confrontation with the thought of Jacques Derrida. The fundamental question Rancière asks is whether deconstruction can define a political thought, understood as "a thinking of the specificity of politics."[19]

For Rancière, the very possibility of democracy implies giving up any principle of legitimation, that is, any form of *arche*. The citizen in an ostensibly democratic regime, to the extent that she can indifferently participate in governing or in being governed, cancels beforehand any governmental *arche*. *Demos* is fundamentally and primarily the a-principial principle of indifferentiation—an an-archic principle that dis-joints, that is, joins disjunctively, the notions of power and *demos*.[20] There is no political community without such a disjunction: there can be politics only if there is indifferentiation in the principle of power, which means that the only qualification to exercise power is not to have any qualification. And it goes without saying then that only democratic politics is politics as opposed to principial domination. The part of those who have no part, to use the famous formulation of *Disagreements*, is not the subaltern remainder, it is not the oppressed or the victim, and it is not, primarily, any identitarian position whatsoever, but it is rather the very indifferentiation regarding any principle of calculation or count. The problem is that, in virtue of its indifferentiation regarding calculation, the part of no part always tends to be left outside the count, to be discounted. The discounting agent is of course what Rancière calls the police. Against the police, in every case, there is the indifferentiating affirmation, the negation of police negation—and such an affirmation in double negation is politics itself in its constituent character. It is always a source of dissensus, and it always therefore breaks apart and rends asunder the calculus of the police. Hence its always productively aesthetic character: it opens new sensoriums and it establishes new regimes of the visible.

For Rancière, however, there would be nothing in Derrida that might allow us to suppose he thinks of politics as power of the *demos*, as the power of the an-archic principle of indifferentiation. Rancière says, "[Derrida's] democracy is a democracy without demos. What is absent in his perspective on politics is the idea of the political subject, of political capacity."[21] Rancière thinks that, if democracy in Derrida is a democracy minus the *demos*, it is because Derrida refuses or is incapable of thematizing the idea of a subject of the political. That there is no full subject of the political means that no one can, according to Rancière on Derrida, take the demotic role upon herself and say, "I speak and act as if I, qualified by my unqualifications, were the very name of the people, the very name of the constitutive principle of democratic action." This hinders the process of counterhegemonic convergence.

There is no subject of politics in Derrida, Rancière says, because there is a fundamental ethicization of the political in their work according to which the sovereign is always the other, the host that, upon unconditionally imposing the law of otherness, excludes the demand of reciprocity from the realm of the possible, the demand of substitutability, and thus destroys the perspective of indifferentiation that is essential to a democratic politics. Derrida would substitute aporia for dissensus, where "aporia means that there can be no possibility of agreement in the practice of disagreement . . . that there can be no substitution of the whole by the part, that no subject can perform the equivalency between sameness and otherness."[22] Finally, for Rancière, it is not just that Derrida has no concept of the specificity of the political: it is rather that he is guilty of evacuating the very possibility of a political practice in democracy. Derrida may very well sustain the notion of a radical priority of war over production in politics, as Rancière himself does. But, for Rancière, Derrida would have made it impossible to win any political war on the side of democracy: the forces of democracy mire themselves, or are mired by deconstruction, in aporia, while the work of the police continues unperturbed.

Such is the heart of Rancière's argument against Derrida. From there he extracts consequences that I believe are contaminated by a basic misunderstanding regarding deconstruction—and one from which Derrida tried to take some distance every time he spoke about the thought of Emmanuel Levinas.[23] But the ghost of Levinas persistently haunts Derrida's work for Rancière, for Badiou, for Žižek, and for all contemporary neo- or post-Althusserianism. It does not allow Derrida's work to speak in its own name. It is peculiar that for a certain segment of the contemporary theoretical left, which accuses Derrida of opposing demotic or communist substitutability, Levinas and Derrida are perfectly substitutable. But there is a certain intention in this misunderstanding. Before going into it I will attempt to tell another story that will prepare a bridge between the two main parts of this essay. Spinoza's dream, as we shall see, tells a story of production and war that might mediate a thought of political democracy beyond Rancière's critique of Derrida, through the presentation of heteroproduction as the basis of political practice.

The Black and Scabby Brazilian

In a letter dated July 20, 1664, Baruch Spinoza replies to his friend Peter Balling—a man traumatized by the recent death of his young son. Spinoza lives in Rhynsburg at the time, and Balling is one of his contacts with the quasi-communist community of mutual friends in Amsterdam. Balling has apparently told Spinoza in some previous letter or conversation that he heard or thought he heard strange lamentations and wailing before the death of his son, coming from nowhere visible, and that they seemed to portend the death of his son, which occurred shortly thereafter. Spinoza tries to offer some consolation, but he does it in an awkward and apparently illogical manner. Spinoza says that it is perfectly possible that some dreams caused by the imagination can be portents of some proximate event, particularly if there is some previous intimate relation between the two subjects of the dream, in this case father and son. They were of course close, since "the soul of the father must . . . participate in the ideal essence of his son, and in its affections and in what it follows therefrom."[24] Spinoza also tells Balling, and this is what might be a little grating vis-à-vis the rest, that he himself had a disturbing dream where a "black and scabby Brazilian whom I had never seen before" showed up. Spinoza says that such a dream might have had purely physical causes, but that it represented just a kind of unconsequential delirium, with no foretelling power: "Your case was an omen while mine was not." Spinoza's was merely caused by his indisposition: "We find by experience that . . . those whose blood is thick imagine nothing but quarrels, troubles, murders and things of that sort."[25] But there is no prediction there—only, we understand Spinoza to say, although he does not say it, more of the same; I am that way, always dealing with those things.

Spinoza does not interpret his own dream; he merely tells of it. He gives it to his friend, to my mind carried away by the generous desire to comfort, to compensate with his own acknowledgment of private trauma for his friend's trauma. In 1957 Lewis Feuer published an interesting essay where he attempted to psychoanalyze Spinoza's dream. For Feuer, I summarize, the "black and scabby Brazilian" was no other than Henrique Diaz, a slave of the Dutch in Pernambuco who successfully led an insurrection of the Portuguese and Brazilian population of the colony that ended in the departure of the Dutch in 1654. One of those forced to leave Pernambuco was Rabbi Isaac de Fonseca Aboab, who would soon become rabbi in the Amsterdam synagogue and who, as such, would have direct responsibility for the process and then the decree of excommunication against the young Spinoza issued on July 25, 1656. For Feuer we should not fool ourselves: in spite of Spinoza's lifelong dissimulation, the event of excommunication was traumatic and provoked a long-lasting political passion having to do with hatred and resentment, perhaps involuntary but nevertheless no less real. One of the examples Feuer quotes: Johannes Colerus, Spinoza's early biographer, recounts how Spinoza took pleasure in drawing portraits, and among them, insistently, the portrait of the anti-Spanish Neapolitan revolutionary leader Massaniello. But Colerus adds that, in the drawing, Massaniello's face was really Spinoza's. Spinoza fantasized through his portraits about becoming the leader of a popular insurrection, about being the courageous avenger.

In my opinion Feuer destroys his own fascinating story when he finally interprets the presence of the black and scabby Brazilian in the following manner: "The figure of the Negro terrorist, the spectre which Rabbi Aboab had described to the Amsterdam Jews, came to menace Spinoza in his dream. He was the symbol of all the hostile forces that await a Jew in the external world, all the forces of hatred, and Spinoza, excommunicate, would have to deal with them alone. The Negro Terrorist was the embodiment of all the curses of the world's powers which Rabbi Aboab had summoned up against him."[26] In my opinion—there is some personal experience here as well—if Henrique Diaz was truly the historical figure conjured up by Spinoza's oneiric delirium, it was not because Diaz embodied the evils of the world. Rather, Diaz came up because he could have been the exterminator of Aboab, the excommunicating and sovereign rabbi—sovereign because excommunicating—that harmed Spinoza's life. That black and scabby fellow, a Brazilian, came through as an exterminating angel, alas only potential, an explosion of desire, not the devil that frightens.

Hence Spinoza's letter, in its short phenomenology of trauma, tells a story of production and war. His friend Balling's trauma was a trauma of production, compensated or symptomatized by the productive effort of an imagination that was captured by the love of a father for his son, as a father always already involved in the essence of his son, in helping him continue on his *conatus essendi*, all too prematurely interrupted. But Spinoza's own trauma is an improductive trauma, a trauma involving "quarrels, troubles, murder," which is the retrospective expression of a proleptic desire for revenge and extermination that must have a lot to do with the death of the sovereign, with the destruction of the figure of the sovereign, thus with the separation of the sovereign from the subordinate. Both are plausible traumas; both are figures of the human. The political problem has to do with the arbitrary, perhaps always already hypocritical denial of the massive facticity of the second. If Spinoza's thought and personality are fully oriented toward gaining the right to joy, it is because they fight a previous melancholy injury, not a natural one, but rather one caused by an act of war between men. From this perspective, Spinoza's philosophy is not self-production, but fundamentally heteroproduction. Not even the subject of the *conatus* self-constitutes— perseverance is always compensatory and retrospective.

This is why Negri and Hardt are much mistaken when, in the same pages of *Commonwealth* quoted earlier, they bring up Spinoza's Brazilian as a monster of modern racism, a Caliban that can in his representational inversion be offered as the emblem of the joyful body of a liberated humanity—fully nondialectical, fully productive. But if Spinoza's Brazilian is a true monster of imagination, his liberating benevolence is at the service of Spinoza's posttraumatic hatred, and in no way can it be read in the pious key that Negri and Hardt systematically privilege throughout their book. Spinoza's Brazilian is not a Caliban whose ugliness must be tolerated in virtue of the many benefits he procures for his master, and still less the figure of a self-liberating exodus: it is simply the embodiment of the desired promise of a will to take revenge, hence the heteroproductive dimension of political practice as a struggle for freedom. But revenge will bring no resolution: nothing political will have been gained at the end of it.

Radical Atheism

In the last instance that is what is at stake, in my opinion, in the post-Althusserian or neocommunist conspiracy against Derrida. Derrida destroys the pious key for a reading of history, not from the side of ethics; rather from a radical atheism, in Martin Hägglund's expression, that will allow for no resolution. But that does not amount to a negation of politics. It is rather the denial of the negation of politics that occurs through the pretension that, once the subject of democracy—whether demotic or despotic, democratic or communist, subaltern or hegemonic—speaks or performs her Idea, her word is good once and for all and must be unconditionally respected, as if the new regime of the visible, the new aesthetic sensorium were written in stone as a net gain and an uncontrovertible improvement for all future. It is not like that. One could say that it never is, but then one can't be certain. The demotic subject irrupts, and she can be good or not, for a time or for no time, but not eternally. Keeping that knowledge in permanent reserve is the atheist and undecidable force (atheist because undecidable, against all false fidelities and hypocritical infinities) that destabilizes the very possibility of a permanent state of democratic redemption and forces democracy to sub-sist and to insist always at the mercy of its heteroaffection. If the object of demotic irruption is always unstable, even suspect, certainly unreliable for Derrida, politics is therefore not foreclosed: that is where politics effectively begins, *pace* Rancière, for whom self-production is still the primary enabler of class war.

They misunderstand the meaning of unconditional hospitality, and they misunderstand the notion that the other or otherness must arrive and can-not not arrive. If there is unconditional hospitality it is because it cannot be helped, given our mortal opening to time and the world, which impose their own laws. The otherness of the other is not received through unconditional hospitality with open arms; rather it is received with fear and trembling, with doubt and reticence, if also with curiosity and anticipation. The oth-erness of the other very much includes the possibility that the other may be a scoundrel—but we can't close ourselves off beforehand to that danger and that risk any more than we can afford to ignore it. Indeed, that the other is a scoundrel is the very condition of political action as well as of political counteraction.

That hospitality is unconditional reflects that double difficulty, which is also an awareness of unpredictability, hence a call to political prudence. We cannot but be unconditionally open to the word or the presence of the other, because it is a condition of life even though it is also a condition of death. In other words, there is no truth of the political, there is nothing assured beforehand, there is only a decision in every case, and that decision is al-ways necessarily a partially passive decision.[27] Its conditions of possibility—temporality, mortal desire, affect—are of course also conditions of impossibility, because if the decision seeks justice, the guarantees that justice can happen are merely aleatory, always uncertain, and are not given beforehand, or even after the fact, since posteriority is endless. Nobody ever knows anything (except perhaps for the neocommunists). But, on the other hand, the decision may seek justice, even though it can be mistaken in and through its very will to justice. Some decisions in the name of uncertain justice open up the space of politics. Their ground is an excess regarding any form of government, as Rancière suggests, and that excess, also for Derrida, is, not the name, rather the effective confirmation that there is a power of anyone, an option for an-archic irruption, groundless and without guarantees, which is the very heart of democracy.

That is why democracy is always to come: because it can never be captured into presence. The subject, or whatever may represent it, is not responsible out of itself, does not self-produce, which of course does not exempt it from responsibility, and the other, or otherness, does not come from any responsible position (it is not itself exempted from responsibility, but saying so is ethics not politics). Any visitation can always turn into an undesirable one: any visit can be a bad visit—hence Spinoza not knowing what to do with his Brazilian exterminating angel and preferring to distract him away from his delirium. And this is also why it is absurd to posit a political horizon beyond conflict if not war, as if the total subsumption of life into production, that is, the identification of life and productive capacity, could itself liberate us from the unconditional: this is an anthropotechnic dream. In self-production, the human produces the finally human like a carpenter produces a table, liberating it from its unproductive imperfections. But that idea is pure productionism—in the beginning was production, says Marx, and that perhaps authorizes us to think that production is also at the end. Positing that production, radicalized into a self-constituting self-production, without heteronomic residue, saves and liberates is messianic theology, not democracy. Granted, it is not Rancière who does that: for him production is simply another life context, and it opens, here and there, and given certain conditions, a new sensorial regime, and it widens the quality of the visible.

Why, then, does Rancière accuse Derrida of proposing a messianic theology? He ends his essay with a rhetorical question: "Would it thus not be the case that Derrida, in order to oppose an alleged dependency of politics on theology, has to make it dependent on another theology?"[28] The analysis that precedes the question has tried to show that, for Derrida, democracy "cannot be presented, even in the dissensual figure of the *demos*," because the supplement to democracy that Derrida calls for condemns it to a heteronomy without relief or respite.[29] Justice in Derrida would be purely heteronomous. As in Levinas. It is here that Rancière establishes a differentiation between a first "ethical turn" that would be proper to Levinas and the later Jean-François Lyotard, whose essential gesture would be, according to Rancière, to subordinate democracy to divinity and thus destroy it, and a "second turn in the conceptualization of otherness," the properly Derridean one, derived from a Levinasian tropology but able to resend the thought of God to a heterogeneous whatever, and to go from the otherness of God to the otherness of whatever other.[30]

Rancière's question about Derrida's theology must be answered negatively. No, Derrida does not make politics dependent on theology any more than he makes politics dependent on any law of mortal otherness. The fundamental problem of deconstruction is the impossibility of setting stable horizons for the grounding of life, beyond all ethics and beyond all politics. But deconstruction does not create such a problem: it only sees that it exists, and thinks from it. Politics is generated, in its constitutive specificity, in the conflict between a hospitality of invitation and a hospitality of visitation, which Derrida discusses in several texts.[31] The visitor, the friend or the stranger, does not impose his law, only his presence, but one never knows where trouble will appear. The guest, stranger or friend, simply enters. Without an invitation or a visit nothing would ever happen—there would be no contact among human monads. Because there is contact there is conflict and there is the inevitability of conflict. Unconditional hospitality is what Hägglund calls the "nonethical opening of ethics," and I would like to call the indifferentiated condition of political conflict, that is, of politics, of democratic politics, not only demotic irruption, as in Rancière, but rather also the conflictive and conflicting reception of demotic irruption.[32] There is no prescriptive normativity to know how to deal with bad visits, or with good ones. For Hägglund, "the law of unconditional hospitality does not provide a rule or a norm for how one should act in relation to the other, but requires one to make precarious decisions from time to time."[33]

No doubt Rancière's conception of the political is not limited to understanding demotic irruption. The demotic subject that wants to be counted can also be understood as a good or a bad visit, in the same way that the police may always come into the home, for good and for evil. When suddenly the uncounted one counts, a new guest, or when one declares, since it is the time, that one will come to visit, it is then that we must decide, and when others decide for us without permission, like Spinoza did with his uncanny guest, *cujusdam nigri atque brasiliani*, to erase him or us from the visible or to demand or offer shelter in negotiation. That is the class struggle, even today, and the mortal opening of politics. We can understand it ethically or religiously if we so choose; we can call it biopolitics or communism; we can relate in any of those manners with the passive need for action, but it is not necessary. The decision to do it is itself an ethical or merely opportunistic decision, and even so it carries certain risks, but not to do it carries risks as well. Nothing is necessary except for the facticity of a situation that equalizes every one and by so doing makes democracy precarious but inevitable. At the end Rancière is not as distant from Derrida as he would ostensibly want to be.

Notes

1 Hardt and Negri, *Commonwealth*, 97.
2 Hardt and Negri, *Commonwealth*.
3 Hardt and Negri, *Commonwealth*, 97–98.
4 Hardt and Negri, *Commonwealth*, 100.
5 Marx and Engels, "Manifesto of the Communist Party," 1.
6 Marx, "On Feuerbach," 118.
7 Marx and Engels, "Manifesto of the Communist Party," 1–2.
8 Marx and Engels, "Manifesto of the Communist Party," 20.
9 Marx and Engels, "Manifesto of the Communist Party," 30, 28.
10 Marx, "On Feuerbach," 117–18.
11 Marx, "On Feuerbach," 117.
12 Douzinas and Žižek, *The Idea of Communism*, ix. Badiou has developed a strong notion of Idea as central to political practice in his *Second Manifesto for Philosophy*.
13 Marx and Engels, "Manifesto of the Communist Party," 6; Marx, preface to "A Contribution to the Critique of Political Economy," 160.
14 On neocommunism, see Douzinhas and Žižek, *The Idea of Communism*; see in particular Badiou's contribution to Agamben's volume *Democracy*, where communism is explicitly set up against democracy (Badiou, "The Democratic Emblem"); the most succinct version of Žižek's neocommunism is to be found in his *First as Tragedy*.
15 Marx, preface, 160–61.
16 Marx and Engels, "Manifesto of the Communist Party," 15.
17 Heidegger, *Four Seminars*, 73.
18 Rancière, "Should Democracy Come?," 275.
19 Rancière, "Should Democracy Come?," 274.
20 The notion of an-archic principle is given a particularly fascinating treatment

in Schürmann, *Heidegger on Being and Acting*, in ways whose connection with the Rancièrian use remain to be determined. Compare also Schürmann's *Broken Hegemonies*; and Gerard Granel's commentary on Schürmann, "Untameable Singularities."

21 Rancière, "Should Democracy Come?," 274.

22 Rancière, "Should Democracy Come?," 282.

23 The two most significant engagements are Derrida, "Violence and Metaphysics," and *Adieu to Emmanuel Levinas*, but there are others.

24 Spinoza, "The Letters," 804.

25 Spinoza, "The Letters," 803.

26 Feuer, "The Dream of Benedict de Spinoza," 240.

27 A theorization of the Derridean passive decision is given in Derrida's *Rogues*, 152. But see Derrida, *Adieu to Emmanuel Levinas*, for its genesis in the Derridean oeuvre.

28 Rancière, "Should Democracy Come?," 288.

29 Rancière, "Should Democracy Come?," 282.

30 Rancière, "Should Democracy Come?," 284–85. It is even doubtful that Levinas's politics can be derived from a theology. See in particular Levinas, "Au-delà de l'etat dans l'état," for a radical defense of democracy as hatred of tyranny quite independent of any theological connotations.

31 On this see Hägglund, *Radical Atheism*, 222n26. Hägglund's book is an essential reference for these topics, and I have borrowed extensively from his reading.

32 Hägglund, *Radical Atheism*, 105.

33 Hägglund, *Radical Atheism*, 105.

CHAPTER 5

Pasolini's Acceptance

Rei Terada

———————————

Writing "on June 15, 1975"—"an election day," he observes—Pier Paolo Pasolini composed a terse text of three or four pages, "Repudiation [Abiura],"
to preface an edition of the film scripts of his *Trilogy of Life*. *Trilogy of Life* is
what Pasolini called his films *Decameron* (1971), *Canterbury Tales* (1972), and
Arabian Nights (1974), and the films are discussed, by others and most of all
by Pasolini himself, as sensuous presentations of the vitality of the poor.[1] In
"Repudiation" Pasolini claims to abjure his erstwhile goals of celebrating the
innocence of the body and the political potential of "the youths and boys of
the Roman subproletariat."[2] Further, he asserts that the potential must never
have existed as he imagined it (xviii), or else the youth would never have
been able to participate so fully, as he thinks they do, in the degraded condition of Italian society: "If those who were *then* thus and so, have been able
to become *now* thus and so, it means that they were potentially such already
then; therefore, also their way of being *then* is devalued by the present. . . .
The collapse of the present implies the collapse of the past" (xviii–xix). In
light of the lives of the youth, Pasolini decides that he can no longer believe
in the political and moral benefits of what was called in the 1970s "sexual
liberalization" (xix). Although Pasolini's motives and concepts are necessarily unclear in a text so short, what he is negating in existential terms, as we'll
see, includes both parliamentary politics (election day) and the early 1970s
social movements that cast themselves as alternatives to it. And he does not
fail to ask the obvious next question: "Where will the repudiation of the
Trilogy lead me?"

Pasolini negates his personal and public projects simultaneously, assuming their psychological inextricability.[3] He ceases to believe in people he
knows—the "beloved faces of yesterday" (xx), "private sexual lives" (xviii)—

and also in the potential of a class, a belief on which his work and activities had thoroughly depended. What interests me initially in Pasolini's account is its separation of particularities that count as lost, and which he must bury and mourn, from a political life that he considers nonexistent and not possibly existent, and which he refuses to treat with a similar respect. It would confer too much tangibility on political Italy to treat it as extinct. Yet the period in which Pasolini lives extinguishes many forms of social being, and a tenuousness about one's very sense of existence is a common problem. The difference between these things must somehow be registered, his essay suggests. In what follows, I would like to ask what function Pasolini's insistence on existential terms—what he and others were, their way of being or not—may have, and how it is related to what he calls "acceptance," or confronting how one would continue without hoping for a real political Italy.

One feature of Pasolini's perspective in "Abiura" is the scale of it: the condition he describes is without horizon, an agoraphobic leveling of the present and past that leaves him without reference points for a future. He grapples with the nonexistence of a world. We might recall Hannah Arendt's conviction that the "world" is an artifact of work that is not an inevitable condition or outcome of human life, or Giorgio Agamben's thought of a state of exception that "coincides with reality itself."[4] Without endorsing Agamben's entire theorization of exception, we can admire his resonant evocation of the phenomenology of the totality he imagines, in which walking down the street or any everyday action may either transgress or carry out the messianic law that has superseded ordinary law: "The law, inasmuch as it simply coincides with reality, is absolutely unobservable."[5] Agamben's description is useful for thinking about a range of ways of life in which the apparent absence of the political appears as a characteristic of "reality itself."

Pasolini answers his own question, "Where will the repudiation of the *Trilogy* lead me?," in this way: "I am adapting myself to the degradation and I am accepting the unacceptable. I am maneuvering to rearrange my life [Dunque io mi sto adattando alla degradazione e sto accettando l' inaccettabile. Manovro per risistemare la mia vita]" (xx). This answer is even more enigmatic than the question. What counts as "accepting the unacceptable," and what would be the point of it? How should we understand a mental state whose obscurity, even impossibility, is indicated by the linguistic contradiction with which Pasolini names it? The strangeness of the text's "acceptance" signals the profound unfamiliarity of its psychic territory. For all that we condescend to disavowal and melancholy as aberrant states of mind—

assuming that they are failures to recognize and accept recognizable and acceptable conditions—it is their absence here that startles the reader. Five minutes of acceptance from Pasolini and we are stopped in our tracks; we no longer know what it means. Further, acceptance by Pasolini in particular carries special weight, since he had no general disposition to value positivity. Pasolini once wrote the sentence, "I cannot accept anything of the world in which I live"; he was so vocal in his protests that he was harassed with petty prosecutions (mostly for obscenity) all of his life, "roughly 365" times.[6] We might guess, then, that his standard for acceptability would be fairly high. "Repudiation" doesn't explain what makes the unacceptable acceptable; rather, it gives clues, mostly by specifying what is unacceptable. In reading Pasolini, then, I consider the question "What is the value of accepting the unacceptable?" as a philosophical question, as well as its pertinence to his object, the nonexistence of Italian politics (and perhaps even the historical formation of European politics per se).

Although others have addressed similar issues in Pasolini's generation and in our own, Pasolini's attempt is distinct in its suggestion that even the potential for the political does not and has never existed: to say this is to suggest that the conditions for modern political life have been wholly misconstrued. By following Pasolini's associations, I hope to indicate some ways in which that may be the case. First, however, I'd like to look closely at Pasolini's text for suggestions about what acceptance of the unacceptable is for him in 1975.

Repudiation

"Repudiation" and an article often known as "The Disappearance of the Fireflies," which appeared in February 1975, address the periodization of modernity as a matter of finality that can be verified as a coroner might verify a death. Both essays use vitalist and anthropological figures, and Pasolini's thought is more or less ethnically essentialist and troubling in that regard. But the vitalist figures do the work of allowing one to wrap one's mind around what Pasolini wants to call "extinction." For him, extinction pertains to particularities and attachments that can be killed and mourned; registering extinction is part of the exercise of sorting the dead from the nonexistent.

"Repudiation" is written mostly in very short paragraphs of a few sentences each. In the middle of the text some paragraphs are clustered into sections sequenced (a), (b), and (c). Pasolini calls parts (a), (b), and (c) "delaying elements [elementi ritardanti]" of his discussion (xviii). The unmarked segment of the essay that precedes (a) ends:

> Private sexual lives (such as mine) have undergone the trauma of false tolerance and physical degradation, and that which in sexual fantasies was pain and joy, has become suicidal disappointment, shapeless sloth.
>
> However, those who, annoyed or scornful, criticized the *Trilogy of Life*, should not think that my repudiation leads to their "duties [doveri]."
>
> My repudiation leads to something else. I am terrified of saying it; before saying it, as is my real "duty," I search for delaying elements. (xviii)

Sections (a), (b), and (c) follow, which correspond to circles of expanding circumference and to reflections on the past, present, and future. They reflect on the disappointing objects of Pasolini's affection, his critics and the condition of contemporary society, and the demise of politicized "people[s] [populi]" outside Italy: "Outside of Italy, in the 'developed' countries—especially in France—the die has long been cast; long ago, the people have ceased to exist anthropologically" (xix).

Pasolini confides that his repudiation leads him to something he is afraid to name, and he has still not named it as long as he remains in part (c), the last delaying passage. Now, these delaying sections render a world that is dead interpersonally, sexually, and anthropologically. Deadness, of course, is a trope of vitalism that projects the organic nature of such things as languages and peoples, and Pasolini's analysis never departs from this uncomfortably vitalist assumption. In the closing paragraphs of "Repudiation," Pasolini returns still more explicitly to the figure of the dead body of Italy: "I know that, even if—as is very probable—there will be a victory of the left [in the 1976 election], the nominal value of the vote will be one thing, the real value something else. The first will demonstrate the unification of modernized Italy, in a positive sense; the second will demonstrate that Italy—except, naturally, for the traditional communists—is by now, as a whole, a depoliticized country, a dead body whose reflexes are purely mechanical" (xx).[7] Tracking the social form of Italian unification, the contemporary world is most of all a depopulated one. Although he complains that ethnicizing the problems of political groups misses the point, he makes an even stronger ontological claim, that the extinction of Italy is an anthropological issue. This claim references Pasolini's lasting concern for the disappearance of historical cultural forms that cannot be maintained, replaced in kind, or revived artificially. The function of this anthropological move is to close off any idea of cultural revival.[8] Thus Pasolini attributes to his critics the hope that the various difficulties are "an unpleasant circumstance that will certainly resolve itself," and replies, "as if an anthropological change were reversible" (xix). At just the moment when the point of entropy is reached in his description of the contemporary scene—when "both the intellectuals on the right and the intellectuals on the left think, in exactly the same way"—the essay's own delaying also comes to an end. The intellectual discourse in Italy comes to be identified with a delaying tactic; it is itself a delaying tactic. Pasolini both participates in it and works through his participation in it by absorbing anthropological extinction.

Now, Pasolini implies that the extinction of the people and hence the impossibility of politics, the perception of which is being evaded, is easy to miss because it is just the same thing as the consolidation of the nation-state that supposedly makes the modern political process possible. In other words, Pasolini is suggesting that abstract citizenship is a contradiction in terms. "The Disappearance of the Fireflies" associates industrialization with the fading of fireflies from the Italian evening and uses the phases of this disappearance as a principle of periodization: before, during, and after the disappearance of the fireflies. Here Pasolini asserts that early 1960s industrialization

> involved the first true unification of our country. In other countries this unification was superimposed logically over monarchic or bourgeois and industrial revolution-imposed unifications. Perhaps the only precedent to the Italian trauma produced by the clash between pluralist archaism and industrial equalization was pre-Hitler Germany. In that country also, the values of different specific cultures were destroyed by the violent recognition process of industrialization, with the consequence of producing those gigantic hordes who had neither the ancient peasant or artisan roots or not even a modern bourgeois background, and who made up the savage, abnormal and unpredictable bodies of Nazi troops.[9]

The unification that, according to Pasolini, Italian regions had long ignored is here achieved suddenly through the dispositif of modernization. Like Foucault, or for that matter Weber, Pasolini assumes that radical changes to culture may occur in stealth forms when they can be mistaken for "a simple modernization of techniques."[10] Pasolini recurs to the vitalist figure of extinction, this time that of the firefly, to render the irrevocability of the processes he describes. Although the strong periodization he proposes here may seem to contradict his claim in "Repudiation" that the potential for politics never existed, attending to modernization in Pasolini's thinking helps to show in what sense that could be. The people, the political category of the universalizing modern nation-state, cannot exist because before the technologies of that state are introduced, there are only specific, plural peoples; after, the same technologies that call forth the abstract category of the people systematically eliminate the peoples whose differences would lend value to the European political system construed as a working through of differences. The people could exist only if peoples with actual distinctions worth debating still survived; but the peoples were destroyed so that the abstract universalized citizenry, the people, could take their place. Most modern political theory would instead see the construction of the people as the always shifting work in progress of specific peoples to create a common space. Alternatively, this space itself may be seen as a transcendental form unattached to any specific substance. Pasolini sees the dissolution of the specific peoples instead as the aporetic precondition of modern political life, which ensures the nonexistence of what it claims to bring into being. Modernizing homogenization offers a discursive and representational system in exchange for the handing over of anything one might have talked about or represented; the concept of the people is created by what makes its fulfillment impossible. The disappearance of peoples and the nonexistence of the political thus develop along with the nineteenth-century nation-state. Roberto Esposito writes of Hannah Arendt's awareness of this phenomenon: the aporetic inability of representation to represent multiplicity rather than unity; I return to this later on.[11]

To actively repudiate these categories would be to realize that they never were nor could be what they were supposed to be. Recently, Georges Didi-Huberman has used Pasolini's "Fireflies" essay to typify a despair of resistance that he finds continued in Agamben. Attentive to the resonance that the idea of organic light must have had to Pasolini as a filmmaker (and to himself as an art historian), he argues that images continue to offer openings for resistance.[12] Didi-Huberman's is the position I would call late modern— one that wants to say that the fireflies are potentially alive and the political a possibility to be recovered. This point of view and the historical framework of the political whose possibility it continues to assume, however, causes certain acts to appear as mere resistance (and indeed as mere existentialized survival), as in the title of Didi-Huberman's book, *The Survival of the Fireflies*. Pasolini's rejection of political possibility, on the other hand, rejects an entire order of thinking in which the political is preserved as a remnant or potential as compared to the given of capitalism, whose existence is never presented as similarly attenuated. For Pasolini, the cost of relying on the idea that political life is preserved as an unactualized, resistant potentiality is the reinforcement of capitalist givens as setting the terms for presentness and actuality.

Pasolini refers to people in the two distinct senses above: local peoples with particular cultures and languages and to the people who would be the pan-Italian citizenry. Although Pasolini's shift from poetry in Friulian to Roman writing and cinema is often read as a shift from regional to class-based thought, and late in his career Pasolini states in the most definitive way that dialects are moribund, "Repudiation" still assumes the significance of the very disappearance of ethnographic diversity.[13] Linguistic diversity is now connected to the political through their existential distinction— languages are dying out like the firefly while Italian political existence is a contradiction in terms.[14] The dead need to be sorted from the nonexistent, but the actual things that have been killed have been killed in the service of nonexistent entities that should not be grieved.

We can see such a line of distinction being drawn in one of the keynotes of Pasolini's late work, the song "Sul Ponti di Perati": "On the Perati Bridge, a black flag is flying." It is sung by the whole company in *Salò*, where it is taken by the characters to pertain to present as well as past circumstances. A World War I song, anthologized by Pasolini in his collection of Italian poetry, "Sul Ponti di Perati" was repurposed for World War II to commemorate the doomed Alpine division Julia, which suffered massive casualties in Albania. In *Salò* it is sung by torturers and victims together, and so also seems to describe the pointless doom of the youth in the film. "Che son partiti, non son tornati [those who left have not come back]," it goes; "La meglio gioventù va soto tera [the best of youth goes underground]."[15] The notion of resistance does not capture the tonality of this song, which is sung while a victim is being raped in the background. It is sung with feeling by the fascists. Although people could be singing simultaneously for opposite reasons, the possibility is nonetheless suggested that even from within fascism one can recognize the loss within the song. In this way fascism is given a background from which it emerges and which it has not even entirely left behind, in which it is fascism and yet still partly something else. In this case, fascism can be understood as a violent and distorted response to something even more violent that is referenced by the song. This is how Pasolini reads the bodies of the Nazi troops in "Fireflies," as well—they're monstrous and abnormal, but at the same time are reflections of the violence of modernization. Pasolini's camera dwells on the face of one of the youths as he seems to decide to join in the song. The expression and affirmative decision of this youth suggests that the song is a space in which the sources of violence can be acknowledged and lamented. What goes on in the finding of this space is not resistance; it's the registration of an ongoing catastrophe. The scene is not about saying yes or saying no to the matrix of violence, but rather asserting one's presence before it: "Yes, this disaster is my disaster: I exist now within this disaster, even as it is trying to extinguish my existence."

It is just when the illusion of the political, whose existence is predicated on the ability of public thoughts to be different, disappears from "Repudiation" that Pasolini writes, "It is time to confront the problem: where will the repudiation of the *Trilogy* lead me? It leads me to adaptation" (xx). If we had not been tipped off earlier, this would come as a surprise: the nonexistence of the political in Italy is not the problem? But it's true: that is not the problem of "Repudiation," but the premise of it. Even Pasolini's rejection of his former goals is not the problem of the essay, but another premise of it; the problem, the question to be answered now according to Pasolini, is where it leads. Pasolini answers first by reflecting on where it does not lead. The critics of the *Trilogy of Life*, he writes, "should not think that my repudiation leads to their 'duties.'" He explains that the duties prescribed to him "[concern] the fight for progress, improvement, liberalization, tolerance, collectivism, etc., etc." (xix). These prescriptions have undergone a collapse similar to that of his love objects covered in part (a). They have participated in, provided the terms for, the production of what Pasolini sees as a "degeneration [that] occurred precisely through a falsification of their values" (xix). Rather, saying that he is led to acceptance and adaptation is Pasolini's "real 'duty' [reale 'dovere']" (xviii), and this "real 'duty'" is something different from working with a corpse and, further, different from merely saying that the political does not exist in Italy (which has been the burden of the "delaying elements"). Pasolini is discriminating between the difficult things he can say and do, that indeed he is in the habit of saying and doing and getting arrested for, and the terrifying thing he can't at first name, terrifying because it lies outside their orbit. In other words, it's relatively unremarkable, in Pasolini's view, for him to say that Italy, along with the other developed countries, is a dead body. What is terrifying to say is that his realization of this worst-case scenario leads him to adaptation and acceptance. It's the acceptance and not the deadness that is terrifying—an acceptance that still remains undefined.

In the last phrases of the essay, Pasolini replaces "duties" ("'doveri,'" always in quotation marks) with "commitment" ("impegno"; no quotation marks): "I am maneuvering to rearrange my life. I am forgetting how things were *before*. The beloved faces of yesterday are beginning to yellow. Before me—little by little, slowly, without further alternatives—looms the present. I readjust my commitment to a greater legibility (*Salò?*) [Riadatto il mio impegno ad una maggiore leggibilità (*Salò?*)]" (xx). Acceptance is now approached through tentative figures of perception in which a featureless present looms into view through the reluctant fading of memories and alternatives. The figure is the cinematic one of focus, film development, or even film direction in the sense captured by the French word for direction, *realisation*. The introduction of "legibility [leggibilità]" shifts subtly from what Pasolini himself sees to what Pasolini may give to be seen—from remembering or looking at a represented image (on yellowing paper), to a different kind of perception of what is hard to see because it is present, and finally to a visuality that may be read like language (in keeping with Pasolini's ideas as a film semiotician). In the context of filmmaking, legibility hints at a recalibrated neorealism that may, this time, succeed in bringing into view a present that has been singularly repellent to the eye. At the end, in the form of a question, Pasolini offers *Salò*, one of the more upsetting films ever made, as the fruit of acceptance and legibility. It's no contradiction, however, that *Salò* is both Pasolini's example of acceptance and a nearly unwatchable film—maybe the single film, until very recently, that viewers are most likely to refuse to watch.[16] Whatever acceptance of the unacceptable was to Pasolini, if he had lived longer he would have been arrested for it, too. For he describes an acceptance that looks like protest, a giving up that we experience as a demand, an adaptation that appears as a provocation.

From the Trilogy of Life to Salò

To understand the subtlety of the psychic process he is demonstrating, it's worth understanding how "Repudiation" emerges from a line of cinematic thought that was under way before the texts of 1975 were written. Through a kind of latency, Pasolini's awareness of the nonexistence of the political actually precedes his passage from *Trilogy of Life* to *Salò*. "Repudiation" marks, not the absolutely new emergence of that hypothesis, but Pasolini's loss of his former proposed solution to it—the creation of an invigorating sexual culture—and hence a heightening of its urgency as a problem. Pasolini promises to "readjust" his commitment to the legible, to focus on the nothing that is there instead of the something that ought to be. Not a first but a second response to a perception of political nonexistence at the present time and place, repudiation is an active mode of realization, a going beyond of the perception that the political does not exist to realize that it could and should not. Recognizing the development of the repudiation of the political in Pasolini involves reading tensions within the *Trilogy of Life* itself; for the *Trilogy*—which confines itself to historically or geographically distant times and places—is in practice as much about the nonexistence of a political Italy (which never appears) as it is an imagination of how people might live differently.[17] As Pasolini later realizes, the potential, the otherwise, the elsewhere that he depicts both assumes and evades contact with the nonexistence of the political now.

Such a reading especially suits the last film in the *Trilogy of Life*, *Arabian Nights* (*Il fiore delle Mille et una notte*, 1974), in which mostly Italian actors, speaking Italian while playing Arabian characters, try to suggest how one might live as a slave and still possess sexual pleasure and personal integrity. One of the protagonists is a young female slave, Zummurud, whose last owner has given her the ability to choose her next owner. She uses this opportunity to select a barely adolescent boy whom she educates into the sexual arts. Their subsequent separation is resolved at the end of the film when Zummurud, who has been living as a boy king as the result of a misrecognition— enjoying her word become command, even taking the opportunity to crucify one of her former abusers—happily sheds her mask of sovereignty and exclaims, "Don't you recognize me? I am your slave!" With this the lovers fall back into one another's arms, having won from each other all the recognition they need for their fulfillment. *Arabian Nights'* contempt for power takes for granted a world in which the property relation of human beings excludes most of the population from any form of political expression, and asks how one would then strategize a life. Gender, economics, social status, and theology all contribute to the enslavement of the protagonists, while their response is to prefer eroticized and personalized slavery to false sovereignty. Although *Arabian Nights* is an unusually florid exoticist fantasy— outlandishly so—the thought experiment that it conducts remains a common scenario for transnational art films today. In more palatable guises, they often concur that the phenomenology of societies in the aftermath of global

Screen shots from *Arabian Nights* (Pier Paolo Pasolini, 1974), the last film in the *Trilogy of Life*.

capitalism consists in a constant exposure to violence, interrupted by idylls that allow one to recuperate temporarily.[18] In this light, "Repudiation" invites us to a new phase of Pasolini's already low political expectations in *The Trilogy of Life*. In the new phase, the interpersonal and sexual opportunities are no longer seen as modeling a future or a past.

It is as part of this project, then, that Pasolini comes to consider the Republic of Salò (Italian Social Republic), a puppet or remnant state that possessed no constitution and no economic funding independent of Germany. *Salò*'s opening scenes of administrative establishment stress that the events are supported by a substantively false governmental structure. But rather than "shed[ding] light on the historical phenomenon of fascism,"[19] Pasolini explains fascism as a still ongoing process that uses the illusion of a political Italy. *Salò* is a meditation on the various historical repetitions of this nullity that compose the history of modern Europe.[20] Through its reference to the revolutionary-era text by Sade which it repeats,[21] *Salò* places the possibility of history as farce as far back as revolutionary Europe—in other words, at the same time as the inception of liberalization and supposedly universalized political representation. A history that is already farce for Marx in *The Eighteenth Brumaire of Louis Bonaparte* becomes pornography for Pasolini. Once as tragedy; twice as farce; again and again as pornography.

Sexual liberation is only one of the possibilities *Salò* rules out, although the spectacular quality of its inclusion can make that hard to see.[22] In fact, the film shows almost no dissident sexuality whatsoever: almost all of the sexuality in the film is official and normative according to the laws we hear read out. What counts as anomaly is created by official code.[23] The professional madams responsible for introducing and contextualizing the orchestrated sex acts of each day maintain a carefully matter-of-course tone (along the way, they reveal that they have been coercively educated into their current tastes and opinions—circumstances that they divulge with the same coolness, as though they were also part of the inevitable course of the world). What is not tolerated is any autonomous organization of one's sexual life. Thus *Salò* becomes in part a pedagogical film for straight citizens; by identifying with the victims, they can see what it would be like to try to survive in a sexually prescriptive world—a world in which you could be tortured to death ostensibly for refusing to perform one kind of act rather than another.[24] If what counts is subjugation to code, there are only two acts of sexual dissidence in the film: an affair between two female inmates and another between a maid and a guard who are promptly executed. In an aggression against the *Trilogy of Life*, Pasolini goes out of his way to refute the idea that these private arrangements could suggest a way of inhabiting slavery: the executed maid is played by Ines Pellegrini, who plays Zummurud in *Arabian Nights*; Franco Merli, her lover Aziz in *Arabian Nights*, plays another victim whose tongue is removed.

In "Fireflies" Pasolini sketches several phases of fascism that parallel the years before, during, and after the extinction of the fireflies: these are fascist fascism, postwar Christian Democratic fascism, and late Christian-Democratic fascism. "Before the extinction of the fireflies" (i.e., around 1965), "Christian-Democrat fascism is a total and absolute extension of fascist fascism"; after, "fascist" values (family, church, order, etc.) are "falsified" and playacted, while others are actually substituted; and by 1975, Pasolini writes, there has been a further "decisive mutation compar[able] to that in Germany fifty years ago" that begins "a new era in human history" and exposes a "dramatic power void." Pasolini declines to refer contemporary fascism back to Italian wartime fascism because in Italy, according to him, "The fascist models were only masks that were donned and removed in turn [We might think here of Zumurrud's mask of sovereignty—RT]. When the fascist fascism movement fell, everything returned to its previous order." The previous order, fascist fascism, and postwar Christian-Democrat fascism fall in line, for better and for worse. All former phases, however, differ from the 1975 version of Christian-Democratic fascism, in which "all these things [the language and gestures of contemporary officials, their ostensibly fascist values] *actually are masks*" (my emphasis). Pasolini's oxymoron, "*actually* are masks," conveys that only now are things—not merely pretenses—empty in actuality, so advanced is the modernizing process of homogenization that calls the people into being as a void. He reserves apocalyptic language for this actualized power void. For "in history the void cannot remain in existence" as void, he argues, but will give way to positive disaster. The *Eighteenth Brumaire* echoes in this passage as well, but in reverse: the collapse of available positions does not prepare a place for the people but contributes to the violence-attracting void the extinction of regional peoples has created. The disaster, finally, will connect contemporary Italy to German Nazi fascism in a way that dwarfs its heretofore indirect connection through Italian wartime fascism. In other words, Pasolini distances himself from the notion of continuity between Italian wartime fascism and the "Christian-Democrat fascism" of 1975 only because continuity underestimates how fascistic the present is: fascistic not because it continues a past fascism, but because the conditions have been prepared for an even more robust fascism. These conditions are the processes of unification and neutralization that, according to Pasolini, weren't strong enough to produce "nationalized and therefore falsified" values in Italy in the 1940s. If, for Pasolini, the culprit is the nation-state, that is not because of the particularism of the idea of ethnicized nation, but just the opposite, because the universalization of modernist abstraction makes it impossible for groups to maintain their political differences.

What should provoke us further is that the villa in *Salò* recalls the classical prototype of the nation-state: the distinctly bounded *polis* in which thinkers like Arendt and Schmitt still believe earlier in the twentieth century.

The city-state of *Salò* is Pasolini's riposte to Rossellini's *Paisà*—the title of which is Neapolitan for "little town" while also containing the idea of *pais*, state. In *Porcile* (1969) Pasolini portrays such a medieval city-state and the outlaws who wander and terrorize the desert beyond it: we travel with the beautiful criminals, from which position we can understand the thinness of the city's legality. In *Salò*, we enter the villa and never leave it. The opening scene that introduces its plenipotentiaries also depicts its geographical location, its distinction from other cities, and the codification and distribution of its written laws: for example, anyone who mentions God in any way is condemned to die. When the torturers explain the laws to the victims, they emphasize, as camp administrators are reported to have done, that no one knows what happens there and that there are no longer any other possible modes of existence. The inmates are "beyond the reach of any legality," they proclaim, before going on, "Here are the laws." Reflecting the operation of late Christian-Democratic fascism, people(s) disappear within the walls and are never seen again.

The officials' proclamation is at once tendentious and true: in a way, the question of legitimacy is more prominent the less a realm, or a law, interacts with an outside (either external or internal to itself). Deleuze points out that while Pasolini's *Teorema* (1968) works out a problem introduced into a society from an agent (Terence Stamp) outside it, "in *Salò*, on the contrary, there is no longer a problem because there is no outside: Pasolini presents, not even fascism *in vivo*, but fascism at bay, shut away in the little town, reduced to a pure interiority, coinciding with the conditions of closure in which Sade's demonstrations took place."[25] For Deleuze, the nullity of everything portrayed is its most important characteristic. In *Salò* even fascism and perversion are being playacted—with real weapons and bodies—as much as sovereignty and normativity are. Pasolini's "fireflies article" and other writings put an ominous spin on what such emptiness is and means. In these writings the nullity brought by unification and the destructive liveness of "fascism *in vivo*" are related causally and a hair's breadth apart. Pasolini's perception in "Fireflies"—that at the time of production, playacting goes all the way down, so that underneath is not even "a heap of bones and ashes. There would be nothing, just emptiness"—imagines a paradoxical "nothing" *in vivo* that is the support of living fascism. In the terms of the regnant neutralization of 1975, more and more of the denizens of Italy are gathered inside.

Deleuze describes the difficulty that *Salò* explores in formal terms, noting that Pasolini's visual style in *Teorema* and *Salò* shifts from an emphasis on cuts, and thus the creative consciousness of montage, to a kind of "sequence" (*c2* 174) to which Pasolini earlier professed an aversion and whose projected consciousness dovetails with the position of the camera.[26] In an unrelated passage of *Cinema 1*, Deleuze calls this position "the anonymous viewpoint of someone unidentified amongst the characters" (*ci* 72).[27] The position corresponding to that of the camera is that of the narrator in the list of possible social roles Pasolini specifies in the credits of *Salò*: "Gentlemen [Signori]," "Narrators," "Victims," "Servants," and "Guards."[28] Celeste Langan has connected neutralization to "mediatization" in the context of European political theory, pointing out that the term "mediatization" is invented around 1800 as part of the pursuit of "a permanent neutrality, beyond or in the middle of the war of all against all." Schmitt objects to the neutralization of "politics" through media in "The Age of Neutralization and Depoliticizations" (1929), Langan reminds us.[29] "Media" in the contemporary sense, in other words, came to prominence along with rationalization's attention to neutral and exchangeable spaces. Further, mediatization is itself built upon a more general notion of mediation invented at around the same time. Hegel's articulation of mediation in the Napoleonic and post-Napoleonic period furnishes the dominant philosophical vocabulary for the unification of the nation-state whose neutralization Pasolini specifically deplores.[30] In *Salò*, if the neutral perspective is that of a camera that makes much of its own passivity, it is literally ever present because we're watching the film that the camera has made possible by preselecting what counts as there. Pasolini's *Salò* is an image of totality and an image of the false, a totality that is fraudulent to the same degree that it produces what counts as everywhere.

Deleuze remarks (in 1985) that the great political cinema of the twentieth century "know[s] how to show how the people are what is missing": the Spanish people in Resnais's *La Guerre est finie*, "the German people in the Straubs' *Unreconciled*" (*c2* 215–16). Instead of "addressing a people, which is presupposed already there," Deleuze continues (*c2* 217), filmmakers may bring "the consciousness that there were no people, but always several peoples, an infinity of peoples, who remained to be united, or should not be united, in order for the problem to change" (*c2* 220). These nonunited people—for Deleuze as for Pasolini, paradigmatically ethnic or linguistic minorities within their milieu—begin with "communication of the world and the I in a fragmented world and in a fragmented I which are constantly being exchanged" (*c2* 221). But Deleuze argues that filmmakers call a new people to come into being by filing these missing-peoples reports: that is exactly not what *Salò* is arguing against. Embedding the nonexistence of the political in the history of modern Europe since Sade, it neither assumes that the people should exist, nor assimilates the given reality in the hope of getting through mediation to a better or at least necessary world. Rather, Pasolini asks us to look at nullity in order to see modern political citizens as contradictions in terms.

Pasolini and the Political Horizon

What we might call the science fiction features of "Repudiation"—its figures of degeneration, ruin, and anthropological extinction—insist on the contradiction: the unthinkable is the case, and we are thinking it. The post-Auschwitz tropes of *survivre* and "damaged life," more recent psychoanalytic trauma theory, modern and postmodern "end of history" figures, and Agamben's development of messianic time and limbo are related ways of dealing with related paradoxes.[31] Pasolini's version raises the possibility that the nonexistence of the political has been considered unthinkable in the same way that trauma is thought to be unthinkable. This apparent unthinkability in turn, however, can be understood as an illusion of modernity.

Roberto Esposito's *Concepts of the Impolitical* (1988) is the most sustained and philosophically ambitious work that responds to the Italian parliamentary crises of the 1970s. Esposito takes another tack in describing a constitutive aporia, considering historical examples that have imagined the limits of the political—chief among them works of Arendt, Hermann Broch, Canetti, Weil, and Bataille—in order to argue that the impolitical is not opposed to the political but "is the political considered from outside."[32] In Arendt, the impolitical is the aporetic inability of representation to represent multiplicity rather than unity; in Broch, it is an inexpressible "alterity . . . presupposed outside the (idea of) the political"; and in Canetti, it is the dominance of a drive to unity in which life itself participates. The privileged point of reference for Esposito's argument is the ruin of Weimar, the same context that gives rise to Schmitt's *Crisis of Parliamentary Democracy* and *Concept of the Political.* Esposito replies to Schmitt by giving the impolitical a formative and yet self-dividing function within the political:

> The identification between freedom and slavery, autonomy and control, which marks contemporary politics (but is latent [présent en germe] in *all* politics) marks the "zero point" (*Nullpunkt*), the "negative pole," "which

our epoch has reached." Adopting a positive anthropology once again means not taking into account "that the desire of an absolute and unrestrained liberty for play . . . presses ceaselessly toward the control of one's neighbor": this occurs "thanks to the infernal interchangeability of masochism and sadism; a mechanism with which the slave himself is familiar"; like all political regimes, the democratic regime includes it, for all that it is preferable to the other regimes, when it can only break control into a chain of local micro-servitudes; it even—here the great Arendtian impolitical theme returns—penetrates to the dynamic of revolutions, as we will see further on.[33]

The "zero point" of the impolitical is the "identification between freedom and slavery" (the identification that Pasolini explores in *Arabian Nights*). Adorno calls this "unfreedom"—the internal ability to mistake slavery for freedom and vice versa. For Esposito, the impolitical is a transhistorical, logical necessity that all politics must reckon with. He therefore insists that there can be nothing apolitical or antipolitical about the impolitical, since the impolitical is the blind spot within the political.

The concept of the impolitical may function as a way to cope with the loss of horizon, encrypting that loss by rendering it structural and internal to a politics that continues to be taken for granted as another structural necessity. Pasolini rather suggests that what has happened is not a structural problem but a deception. Instead of following subtle traces of the proto- and postpolitical (e.g., underlining the nonhegemonic quality of power in *Salò*), Pasolini stresses that the fact that conditions are never hegemonic does not mean that politics is by definition not nonexistent, that the political is either immortal or undead and, either way, transhistorical. Similarly, a strict construction of the worst, like Derrida's in "No Apocalypse, Not Now," prevents a hegemonic model (of, for instance, totalitarianism) from being asserted, but the counterdanger of the strict construction is that it stores "the worst" permanently in the future and uses the possibility that something can always be worse to deflect past and present catastrophes that may be utter even if they are not absolute.[34]

When I mentioned that the loss of a political horizon is often treated as trauma, I meant that it is handled as though it could never register in experience. A correct Kantian understanding of the impossibility of experiencing the zero degree of anything is mobilized to conserve the value of whatever there is at the time, because it is by definition not nothing. However small that value is acknowledged to be, because it's never nothing it is also maximal, like the difference between life and death (hence the prevalence of the organic figure in the texts I have been reading). The premise of biopower, the irreducible value of life, is a subset of the conflation of value and fact, the conserving of value in whatever existence is available. According to Pasolini, such an attitude encourages faithfulness to politics although "it is by now, as a whole . . . depoliticized . . . a dead body whose reflexes are purely mechanical" ("Repudiation," xx).

The impulse to credit the smallest twitch of the proto- or postpolitical is well and deeply grounded in the post-structuralist critique of presence and hegemony, and in rightful suspicion about where the ability would come from to say when a potential is defunct. No one occupies a vantage from which to pronounce the end of history. The temporal logics of surviving and remaining complicate the picture by allowing that the present may be a continuation of a past catastrophe. In these logics, the questionable nature of the power to say when the worst has occurred is balanced by the equally questionable nature of the power to say when the worst has stopped occurring. This second logic, as mobilized, for instance, by Lanzmann's *Shoah*, implies that there is no after in the sense that the boundary of the catastrophe cannot be fixed; rather, there is open-ended catastrophe to which neither presentness nor pastness can be denied. Thus Didi-Huberman criticizes Lanzmann from a historicist perspective for acting as though Auschwitz is not over.[35] I've rehearsed Pasolini's rather elaborate argument for why he is not doing the same thing. To see his project as identical with those is to set aside his emphasis on arriving at acceptance and adaptation (to which we have still attributed no content), the results to which his recognition, he writes, leads him.[36]

Pasolini, similarly, writes in "Repudiation" that Italy "is by now, *as a whole*, a depoliticized country" (xx). As we've seen, Pasolini is indeed pointing out that it is "as a whole," as the false unity into which it has been made, that a country has no political dimension. This does not mean that there is no struggle; Pasolini writes, and dies, toward the beginning of the so-called Years of Lead, and in the "fireflies" article guesses at some of the turmoil ahead. So by what right does Pasolini eliminate the possibility of other, perhaps as yet unseen ways to channel political energies? Autonomian writings published around the time of Pasolini's death also understand their society as postpolitical. They claim that this very understanding, however, enables their activities to be political in an expanded sense: "if 'the end of politics' means the search for new dimensions of antagonism on levels other than the one defined by concrete needs (wage struggles, the 'attack on income' as a refusal of poverty, etc.) then with the Italian movement the 'end of politics' has a different meaning, not at all psychologistic, literary or philosophic. For there the 'end of politics' involves a search for new *political* areas of struggle."[37] For Pasolini this struggle is best thought of as something other than the political, rather than a rejuvenation of the political energies in a nonrepresentational form. For him, those nonrepresentational forms have died with the fireflies, and didn't the very notion of what it means to be political in modernity arise along with those forms, from which it may be inseparable?

If Marazzi and Lotringer envision a corrigible society that needs to refind the political in new areas, isn't that possibility of renewing the political the danger that haunts their writings and threatens to return it to the inside of Italy? My point is not that social and cultural phenomena contain no potential to create justice, nor that nothing could replace parliamentary politics, but that Pasolini's insistence that the political is nonexistent and not about to be remade applies to social movements as well as to formal politics, to the potential for Italian politics as well as its current state. In this way it may be further toward conceptualizing something different for the very reason that it abjures political possibility.

"Acceptance"

After delaying, acceptance. Pasolini's acceptance is strange because it furnishes an account of something of which there could seem to be no account—acceptance of the unacceptable. To get at the function of Pasolini's repudiation of his former strategies—the outcomes it carries of acceptance and adaptation—I'd like to make one final comparison between Pasolini's "Repudiation" and a culturally adjacent text that is its mirror image in nihilistic acceptance: Primo Levi's essay "Stereotypes," from *The Drowned and the Saved*, which was published in the same year as Esposito's *Concepts of the Impolitical*, 1988.[38] This is where Levi criticizes the "schematic image of prison and escape" that "bears little resemblance to the situation in the concentration camps" but is part of an idealized before, during, and after that appears only in retrospect.[39] Levi makes this criticism as he answers a question from the floor, so to speak, about why so many European Jews (and other persecuted segments of the population) did not more actively flee their elimination. His most radical point comes in the sentences restricted to those who, indeed, chose not to flee, since obviously many others did emigrate, and many could not, as Levi also makes clear. Levi nonetheless suggests that the phenomenon, in any crisis, of there being many people who choose to stay must be accepted—that it cannot be expected to be otherwise. Levi's considerable acknowledgment of all the people who were not in denial would seem to indicate that things could have been different. Yet finally his argument for acceptance is not historically or culturally contingent: "Many Europeans of that time—and not only Europeans, and not only of that time . . . [were] denying the existence of things that ought not to exist."[40] He ends the essay by comparing the state of mind of those who stayed behind with that of Europeans vulnerable to destruction by the Cold War powers, and invokes the threat that nuclear warfare poses "to the entire human species, indeed to all life on earth, with the exception perhaps of the insects":

> The threat is different from that of the 1930s: less close but vaster; linked, in the opinion of some, to a demonism of history, new, still undecipherable, but not linked (until now) to human demonism. It is aimed at everyone, and therefore especially "useless."
>
> So then? Are today's fears more or less founded than the fears of that time? When it comes to the future, we are just as blind as our fathers. . . . There are Polynesia, New Zealand, Tierra del Fuego, the Antarctic: perhaps they will remain unharmed. Obtaining a passport and entry visa is much easier than it was then, so why aren't we going? Why aren't we leaving our country? Why aren't we fleeing "before"?[41]

Levi's question is largely rhetorical: its unanswerability is turned toward the reader in order to suggest that the question is wrong. The quotation marks around the word "before" indicate what Levi argues elsewhere, that "before" is an illusion created by history. The conclusion that there is no "before" in which to flee is central to Levi's project of doing what he can to tear the public imagination of Auschwitz from hindsight fantasies; its refusal of pathos distinguishes Levi from many contemporaries.[42] Nonetheless, as Levi accepts that many will persist in storing catastrophe in the future, Levi himself assumes that the time of catastrophe is the future when he writes, "When it comes to the future, we are just as blind as our fathers." Levi's critique of the idea of "before" deflects criticism of the tendency to be blind to the present, a tendency Pasolini attacks when he includes a long list of the ongoing degradations his critics "don't notice" in 1975 ("Repudiation," xix).

Like Levi, who points out that "we" do not seem to be going anywhere,

Pasolini does not exempt himself from historical pressure. Rather, it is noticing this pressure upon himself—in the terms above, "the damage"—that opens his eyes, as he would have it, to the distinction of the present moment:

> Everyone has adapted either by refusing to notice anything or by inertly rendering the news less dramatic.
>
> But I have to admit that also having noticed, or having dramatized, does not protect at all from adaptation or acceptance.
>
> Therefore I am adapting myself to the degradation and I am accepting the unacceptable. I am maneuvering to rearrange my life. (xx)

Reading with Levi suggests another way to interpret the ending of "Repudiation" in an unimaginable acceptance. One thing that Pasolini is doing is noticing what he is already doing; his assertion of adaptation and acceptance is as descriptive as it is prescriptive. It's almost a syllogism: no one is protected from degradation; therefore Pasolini is not protected, and must be found among the people who are adapting to and accepting it. This acceptance is no more or less extreme than Levi's observation that it may well not be possible to protect most of the people on earth.

Yet Pasolini is able to do what Levi implies is not to be expected, and gives up on his object—the people, the political of Italy—in the present, in fact concludes that he has already done so, even though that nonexistent object had supported his identity, his work, and his idea both of the state and of its alternatives. With other late work by Pasolini, "Repudiation" shows how one does—how sometimes people do—act before, although it means turning away from everything that has previously been thought meaningful and instituting an unknown self.[43] We might adapt Derrida's thesis that forgiveness is paradigmatically of the unforgivable and suggest that acceptance is paradigmatically of the unacceptable. Levi adduces the poem by Christian Morgenstern in which the good German citizen (of 1910, before both wars) cannot fathom that he has been hit by a car because it happens on "a street where traffic is forbidden."[44] Pasolini's introduction of paradoxical language—acceptance of the unacceptable—points out that thinking the unthinkable can become caught in a similar categorial cul-de-sac: it can be seen to have occurred only at the end of time, and this is not the end of time: therefore, it could be worse; therefore, it's not yet necessary to change. For things to be different, the unthinkable must already have happened, "without further alternatives" ("Abiura," xx). To act before, it must be understood to be too late—in this case, too late to begin with.

That's why for Pasolini it's not just a matter of noticing the political nullity of Italy, but of including the idea of political possibility within it, leaving only acceptance and adaptation—but an acceptance and adaptation that are hostile to the given—as conceptual spaces in which to start filming *Salò*. The poetic analogue to the late prose texts is Pasolini's meticulous negation of his first book of poetry, *Poesie a Casarsa*, in his last, *Le nuova gioventù* (1975; called after the phrase in "Sul Ponte di Perati," as I mentioned). Repudiation here takes the form of the strikethrough. For example, Pasolini rewrites "Fountain of water in my country. / There is no fresher water than in my country. / Fountain of rustic love" as "Fountain of water in a country not mine. / There is no staler water than in this village. / Fountain of love for nobody."[45] Both poems are in dialect, although by the time of the latter Pasolini has declared categorically that "dialect and the world that expressed it no longer exist."[46] No longer conceivably nostalgic, Pasolini now writes dialect poetry that places neither nostalgia nor hope in dialect.

Similarly, the acceptance and adaptation of "Repudiation" build a language for alternatives to the present that does not assume that the political will be born from its impossibility. In an interview on the day before he died, Pasolini is asked whether he would do it if, with "magic thought," he could make disappear all that he detests, even though this would include the industries, institutions, and audiences that support his own work. When Pasolini replies that that is what he is trying to do, the interviewer, Furio Colombo, asks, "If you remove all this . . . what's left?" Pasolini responds, "Everything. I am what is left, being alive, being in the world, a place to see, work and understand."[47] The title Pasolini gives to this last interview is "We Are All in Danger." There is no basis on which he can deliver this message if he is still invested in potential.

Notes

1 See, for example, Moravia, "Dall'Oriente a Salò," 93–95, quoted by biographer Enzo Siciliano in *Pasolini*, 342–43.

2 Pasolini, "Abiura," in *Trilogia della vita*; Pasolini, "Repudiation of the Trilogy of Life," in *Heretical Empiricism*, xviii. Subsequent references to these editions appear in the text.

3 Generalizing a personal disaster, or personalizing a social one, is a style of magical thinking that seems, and may be, paranoic. Yet this magical thinking informs accounts of disaster per se, suggesting that the personalization of disaster is a mark of its reach. A quasi-canonical example would be Mary Shelley's

conflation, in *The Last Man*, of political disillusion and reflection on the deaths of most of her own family in an image of civilization's dissolution.

4 Arendt, *The Human Condition*, 134–35; Agamben, *The Time That Remains*, 105.

5 Agamben, *The Time That Remains*, 105.

6 Pasolini, "Civil War" (1966), in *Heretical Empiricism*, 148; Lawton, introduction to *Heretical Empiricism* by Pasolini, xl n3.

7 In the event, in the 1976 national elections the left parties failed to consolidate and the Christian Democratic Party remained the largest in Parliament. This situation framed the intensification of violence—the Years of Lead—that Pasolini did not live to witness. See Potter, "The Italian Election," 7–8.

8 Compare Pasolini's argument elsewhere that the contemporary working class is not the same as in Marx's time and so in need of a different theory. See Pasolini, "The PCI to the Young!! (Notes in Verse for a Prose Poem Followed by an 'Apology')" (1968), in *Heretical Empiricism*, 155–56.

9 Pasolini, "La scomparsa delle lucciole," originally published as "The Power Void in Italy," *Corriere della sera*, February 1, 1975. Also in *Ecrits corsaires*, 184–95. Christopher Mott's English translation of this text is available on the blog *Diagonal Thoughts*, http://www.diagonalthoughts.com/?p=2107. For commentary, see Consolo, "The Disappearance of the Fireflies."

10 Pasolini, "La scomparsa delle lucciole."

11 Esposito, *Categorie dell impolitico*.

12 Didi-Huberman, *Survivance des lucioles*.

13 For the idea that dialects are moribund, Siciliano, *Pasolini*, 364.

14 Pasolini's lack of control over anthropological figures punctuates his motif of "undevelopment"—for instance, in his statement that "for Italy it is all over. But Yemen can be saved entirely" (lines from Pasolini's short documentary *Le mura di Sana'a*, quoted in Rhodes, *Stupendous, Miserable City*, 151).

15 In the film, as in life, the song is sung with feeling as a recognition of the sorrow of its end, in the very place where that end is being accomplished, as well as by (as it were) believing fascists. Pasolini takes the phrase "La meglio gioventù" as the title of his last book of poetry (also 1975). On this scene in *Salò*, see Maggi, *The Resurrection of the Body*, 311–12. Maggi points out that Pasolini anthologizes this song in his collection of Italian poetry, and explains there that it is a World War II song based on a World War I song. According to Pasolini, "World War I saw 'a vast production of war songs' because of the static character of this world conflict" (Maggi, *The Resurrection of the Body*, 311). The translatability of songs from conflict to conflict reinforces the impression of stasis.

16 Technological developments have made instances of extreme violence more easily representable and more common, and directors such as Lars von Trier and Chan-Wook Park have explored their cinematic and philosophical possibilities. A part of von Trier's production company, Zentropa, made pornographic films for a time. Von Trier's *Antichrist* (2009) and Srdjan Spasojevic's *A Serbian Film*

(2010)—a film about a snuff film—may have gotten past *Salò* on the most-avoided list.

17 For a critical analysis of Pasolini's fantasies of ethnicity, see Bongie, *Exotic Memories*. Patrick Rumble reads the linguistic dissonance of *Arabian Nights*, discussing mostly visual languages but relating these to dialect, in "Stylistic Contamination in the *Trilogia della Vita*," in Rumble and Testa, *Pier Paolo Pasolini*, esp. 223.

18 A great deal of work along these lines is being done in East Asian cinema. See especially Tsai Ming-Liang, *I Don't Want to Sleep Alone* (2007).

19 Viano, *A Certain Realism*, 299.

20 The film's bidirectional anachronisms (backward to Sade, forward to its citations from Barthes, Beauvoir, Blanchot, Klossowski, and Sollers) indicate Pasolini's interest in periodization and intensely revisionary investment in modern history, as Cesare Casarino has shown in "Oedipus Exploded."

21 Pasolini notes in a brief written introduction to the film that Sade's characters "are clearly SS men in civilian dress." Bachmann, "Pasolini on de Sade."

22 It may seem that in associating Nazism with sexual dissidence *Salò* participates in a phenomenon brought to attention at the time by Foucault, and later by Andrew Hewitt: the false and retroactive "construction of homo-fascism" (Hewitt, *Political Inversions*). *Salò*'s thesis is that revisions to sexual norms do not herald a new political life, however, rather than that there is any cause and effect between dissident sexuality and Nazism.

23 Joan Copjec's interpretation of *Salò* preserves a distinction between "perversion" and "transgression" that allows her to maintain that the official sexuality depicted in the film is both conformist and perverse (and indeed that perversion is conformism, that it is characterized by fixity); see Copjec, *Imagine There's No Woman*, 224–25. At the same time, she proceeds as though perversion is characterized by specific, logically motivated fixities, for example, preferring the back to the front of a woman because, as in Freud's theory of fetishism, the front shows difference and so "this perception is disavowed" (222). The tension is inherited from Freud, but it isn't Freud who makes it an issue that "perversion is so often confused with transgression" (224). Copjec's insistence that the confusion is only on one side indicates that what she sees as a permanent difference appears as historical to others; and her use of forms of "confuse" throughout the book indexes her policing of various categories that need to remain static.

24 Pasolini suggests that the violations of law discovered inside the villa are only examples and that if we knew enough, we would perhaps see that everyone is out of conformity: the torturers discover the violations in a chain, when each culprit in turn tries to save herself by denouncing another, who denounces yet another.

25 Deleuze, *Cinema 2*, 175. Subsequent references to *Cinema 1* and *Cinema 2* appear in the text.

26 Pasolini, "Reflections on the Long Take," in *Heretical Empiricism*. See Deleuze, *Cinema 1*, 27.

27 I agree with Jacques Rancière that there's usually nothing necessary about the mimetic logic with which Deleuze, and film scholars generally, makes the formal and visual features of films allegorize their themes (*Film Fables*). Yet Pasolini was often this kind of film scholar, and the camera position of *Salò* may well have mimed the stance of neutralization for him.

28 Robert Meister notes that in their recognition of perpetrators, victims, and bystanders, liberal theories of transitional justice tellingly omit the category of the beneficiary. See Meister, *After Evil*. The anonymous viewpoint is noncommittal, neutralized, but sometimes implicitly charged with tension to the degree that neutrality would seem to be impossible in the situation.

29 Langan, "Romantic Neutrality," 3–4.

30 Pasolini "hate[s]" Hegel, whom he holds responsible for "hope," in his interview with Sergio Arecco. See Arecco, *Pier Paolo Pasolini / Sergio Arecco*. *Hope* here means expecting a better future from the synthesis of history; Pasolini claims definitively to lack the capacity for this.

31 Of end-of-history figures, Bataille's assumption of "unemployed negativity" is especially germane ("The Critique of the Foundations of the Hegelian Dialectic"). The postpolitical aspect is particularly stark in Agamben, who writes of "the inhabitants of limbo, in contrast to the damned": "Like the freed convict in Kafka's *Penal Colony*, who has survived the destruction of the machine that was to have executed him, these beings have left the world of guilt and justice behind them: The light that rains down on them is that irreparable light of the dawn following the *novissima dies* of judgment. But the life that begins on earth after the last day is simply human life" (*The Coming Community*, 5, 6–7). For comprehensive comparison between Pasolini's work and adjacent political theory, see Viano, "The Left According to the Ashes of Gramsci," 51–60; Ricciardi, "Rethinking *Salò* after Abu Ghraib"; and Righi, *Biopolitics and Social Change in Italy*, 73–102.

32 Esposito, *Categorie dell'impolitico*, 18.

33 Esposito, *Categorie dell'impolitico*, 102–3. In the quotation marks Esposito is citing Hermann Broch's *Politik: Ein Kondensat*.

34 This point is made by Derrida, and the complementary point—that thinking the worst could be self-fulfilling in the era of nuclear deterrence—is also made. Derrida, "No Apocalypse, Not Now."

35 Didi-Huberman, *Images in Spite of All*.

36 Other examples include Louis Malle's *Elevator to the Gallows* and Fassbinder's GDR *Trilogy*.

37 Lotringer and Marazzi, "The Return of Politics," 12.

38 The larger philosophical frame for the question of nihilistic acceptance is the Eternal Return, especially its twentieth-century versions.

39 Levi, "Stereotypes," 152.

40 Levi, "Stereotypes," 165.

41 Levi, "Stereotypes," 165–66.

42 Elements of acceptance in Levi were too much for Jean Améry, for example, who complains that Levi's attitude amounts to forgiveness for genocide, while Levi remarks that Améry's refusal of acceptance is suicidal. Each sees the other as nihilistic: Améry seems to Levi to reject the world as is, while Levi seems to Améry to describe a world not worth living in. See Améry, "Resentments," in *At the Mind's Limits*, 62–81.

43 Repudiation was a strategy Pasolini found repeatable: "Repudiation" was not the only break letter he ever wrote. Another notorious and interesting one is the mixed-mode text "The PCI to the Young!! (Notes in Verse for a Prose Poem Followed by an 'Apology')" (1968), in *Heretical Empiricism*, 150–58.

44 Levi, "Stereotypes," 164–65.

45 "Fontana di aga dal me país. / A no è aga pi frescia che tal me país. / Fontana di rustic amòur"; "Fontana di aga di un país no me / A no è aga pí vecia che ta che país. / Fontana di amòur par nissún." Pasolini, *Poesie a Casarsa*; Pasolini, *Le nuova gioventù*, 167.

46 Siciliano, *Pasolini*, 364.

47 Colombo, "We Are All in Danger."

PART III

The Endgames of Sovereignty

CHAPTER 6

Reopening the Plato Question

Adam Sitze

I

Contemporary philosophy, Alain Badiou has argued, is considerably more unified than its polemically opposed factions would lead us to believe. Despite the many and great differences between its constitutive schools—on the one side, continental thought stemming from Heideggerian hermeneutics, on the other, the analytic tradition growing out of Wittgensteinian logical positivism[1]—the strife that divides these camps is underwritten by a consensus that is all the more binding for remaining almost completely unstated. Both schools of contemporary philosophy, Badiou observes, define themselves in "violent opposition to the Platonic foundation to metaphysics."[2] Whereas Platonism remains loyal to the operations required by the category of Truth, contemporary philosophy suspends direct reference to the category of Truth. Whereas Platonism accepts the priority of the Idea in excess of any and all of its presentations, contemporary philosophy assumes language as the ultimate horizon of thought, converting philosophy into little more than the study of meaning (whether through the interpretation of texts or through the analysis of utterances). Above all, whereas Platonism holds that philosophy itself is at once possible, desirable, and necessary, contemporary philosophy puts itself on trial, subjecting itself to melancholic self-accusations regarding philosophy's impossibility, its complicity with evil, its interminable internal crisis, and the philosophic need for an end to philosophy.[3]

In Badiou's view, the task of philosophy today is to emancipate philosophy from the anti-Platonic consensus that silently unites its otherwise bitterly opposed schools. In place of the death sentence that anti-Platonism seems to require contemporary philosophers to pass upon contemporary philosophy, Badiou proposes a new and different task: to "reopen the Plato question," which is to say, to return to Plato's texts so as to seize there a new and different beginning for philosophy, and in so doing to revivify the desire, even the "imperative," to philosophize.[4] Commentary on Badiou certainly is not lacking in names for the position Badiou generates through this return (which, often following Badiou himself, has been called everything from "neo-Platonism," "ultra-Platonism," and "citra-Platonism," to a "modern Platonism," a "Platonism of the multiple," a "renaissance of the use of Plato," and a "materialist Platonism"[5]). Oddly, however, despite Badiou's own call for a return to Plato, few of his many recent commentators have heeded that call and followed him in that return.[6] Emerging from his seminars of 1989–90, which focused on Plato's *Republic* and *Laws*, Badiou's reading of Plato rests upon a very precise claim about the inner structure of the Platonic corpus.[7] For Badiou, Plato's writings assume the form of a gradual but decisive reversal. Whereas Plato's first work, *The Apology of Socrates*, seems to affirm Socrates's reckless, fearless, and subversive relation to the Athenian polis, his final work, the *Laws*, seems to imply the exact opposite: the justice and even necessity of the counts on which the Athenian polis sentenced Socrates to death.[8] On Badiou's reading, subsequent philosophic institutions even would seem to have internalized, under the very mask to which they assign the name "Plato," the criminal laws that express the antiphilosophic voice and gaze par excellence. If it should seem that philosophy today is incapable of proceeding in any other mode except melancholic self-accusation, permitting itself to philosophize only after first putting itself on trial for impiety toward this or that declension of the polis, this is perhaps because philosophy has not fully thought through what we might call the juridical forms that govern its relation to its own history. Philosophy today would seem to judge its own voice and gaze with reference to a conscience (or, in psychoanalytic terms, an introjected superego) whose injunctions are harshly, even mercilessly, antiphilosophic. Philosophy, it would seem, has not yet become fully self-conscious about the mode in which it becomes self-conscious of its own relation to politics.

2

That so few commentators have sought to question Badiou's reading of the *Laws* is all the more curious for the fact that it is with respect to this reading that Badiou's return to Plato is perhaps most discernible from another twentieth-century return to Plato, one whose relation to emancipatory politics is diametrically opposed to Badiou's, yet whose philosophic aims nevertheless remain remarkably close to, even symmetrical with, his own.[9] Beginning as early as 1924, Leo Strauss initiated a rereading of Plato that also may be summarized, without excessive injustice, as a "re-opening of the Plato Question." Strauss's rereading of Plato emerged from a desire to break with the "radical historicism" (Heideggerian and otherwise) and neo-Kantianism that dominated the political philosophy of his day.[10] To give shape and form to this desire, Strauss retraced the steps of Nietzsche's incomplete overturning of Platonism, fixing on what Strauss understood to be the clearest virtue of that overturning ("probity").[11] Along the way, Strauss rediscovered a politicized form of address internal to philosophic rhetoric ("esoteric writing") that he redeployed as a hermeneutic guide for a rereading of the entire history of political philosophy.[12] The keystone of that rereading was a long account of Plato's *Republic*, in which Strauss subtly but methodically demonstrated that Plato's text anticipates and refutes in advance all of the ostensibly anti-Platonic concepts symptomatically adopted by modern political philosophers.[13] Perhaps above all, Strauss sought to underline the ironic horizon within which Plato thought the philosopher-king, in order to reintroduce moderation into the visionary excesses born of the modern philosophic supposition, running from Kant to Nietzsche, that the philosopher can and should double as a legislator who seeks to realize truth in the polis.[14]

No attentive reader of Badiou would deny the proximity, even excessive proximity, between this return to Plato and his own. Badiou too, after all, seeks to find in Plato a counterpoint both to Heideggerian historicism and to neo-Kantian ethics.[15] Badiou too is a careful student of Nietzsche's overturning of Platonism, redeploying Heidegger's argument about the incompleteness of that overturning as the silent point of reference for his polemic against Gilles Deleuze.[16] Badiou too has affirmed a manifestly political approach to the problem of address within philosophic rhetoric, emphasizing a sharp distinction, if not between esoteric and exoteric writing, then at least between the disciple and the public.[17] Badiou too, as we've noted, appreciates the sense in which the foreclosure of Platonism is a symptom that seizes and holds together otherwise opposed schools of modern political philosophy (especially that of the last century).[18] And, perhaps most importantly, Badiou too has counseled caution toward the figure of the philosopher-king, emphasizing restraint, reserve, and moderation as the antidote to the temptation, internal to philosophy, for philosophy to realize its truths through lawgiving.[19]

On this point, however, the resemblance would seem to end. In his critique of Plato's *Laws*, Badiou fixes on book 10 as the site where Plato succumbs to the temptation to realize truth through law: here where Plato uses the tyrannical prescriptions of criminal law to ban the Sophist from the polis, Badiou argues, Plato abandons philosophy itself, converting its aporetic rigor into a force of terror.[20] Strauss, by contrast, will consider this same book as the very inauguration of the inquiries that define classical political philosophy (and by extension, given Strauss's approach to the quarrel of the ancients and the moderns, political philosophy as such).[21] Because it is only in book 10 of the *Laws* that Plato "directly faces" the problem of the gods, Strauss argues, book 10 must be considered "the most philosophic, the only philosophic part of the *Laws*."[22] For Badiou, the Stranger who appears in the *Laws* in place of Socrates represents the absolute betrayal of Socrates: the Stranger, Badiou writes, is "the generic representative of the Polis, who once again pronounces against Socrates and in favor of the implacable fixity of criminal laws."[23] For Strauss, on the other hand, the Stranger marks the recapitulation and confirmation of Socrates's highest teachings: the fact that someone other than Socrates could teach political philosophy outside of Athens, the birthplace of political philosophy, is proof positive that the teachings of political philosophy can survive Socrates and are transferable across traditions (or what today we would call cultures).[24] And for Strauss, of course, the law against impiety the Stranger devises in the *Laws* does not betray Socrates; it defines impiety in a way that would have been more favorable to Socrates than was Athens's own law against impiety.[25]

No reading of Plato, it would seem, could have less in common with Badiou's. But to the precise extent that Badiou's reading of book 10 of Plato's *Laws* is on the mark, we will be off the mark to separate his reading of Plato from Strauss's, and above all from Strauss's reading of book 10 of the *Laws*—in all of its theologico-political piety, its hermeneutic attention to silence and speech, and its neoconservatism. Fidelity to Badiou's teaching about philosophy's relation to its own immanent disaster, in fact, requires the very opposite: a recognition that Strauss's Stranger, this Stranger with whom Badiou's Stranger is least at home, belongs essentially and irreducibly to the same Platonism Badiou wishes to reopen, as the exemplary figure of the disaster in and through which philosophy estranges itself from its essence, perhaps even as the mask that philosophy wears when it insists that disaster is no disaster at all. Strauss's "zetetic" Platonism, his emphasis on the essentially questioning character of Platonism, is not then simply the polar opposite of Badiou's "re-opening of the Plato question" (although, especially on the point of the syntagma "political philosophy," it is precisely this, with Strauss affirming the possibility of what Badiou rejects).[26] It is also its *uninvited rhyme* and *uncanny double*. Much more than Deleuze or Jacques Rancière, who after all provide Badiou with the consoling figures of a clear-cut and deeply held opposition to Platonism, and against whom Badiou has not failed to engage in open polemics, it is perhaps Strauss's affirmation of Platonism, about which Badiou and his disciples have kept noticeably silent, that provides Badiou's return to Plato with its most intimate and volatile *koinè*.

3

To put a name to this koinè, it will not suffice to traffic in the horse-trading of a compare-and-contrast analysis, or work like a detective in the archives of intellectual history.[27] We instead need to return to the text of the *Laws*, so as to outline in that text the operation of a philosophical apparatus that remains active but unthought in each thinker's renewal of Platonism. To begin comprehending the relations and nonrelations that join and disjoin these respective Platonisms, it will be necessary to consider a deceptively simple question: how precisely does the *Laws* pose law as a problem for philosophy? As our point of departure into this inquiry, we shall take the curious passage that appears in the mathematically exact middle of book 4 of the *Laws*. Here the Athenian Stranger distinguishes true polities from cities (such as aristocracies or democracies) that have achieved victory over themselves, and where it is consequently necessary for a despot to administer the enslaved, defeated faction. To truly name any given city, the Stranger continues, "One must use the name of the god who truly rules as despot over those who possess intellect."[28] When pressed by his interlocutors to explain this surprising assertion, the Stranger asks permission to respond by telling a myth about "the time of Cronos," when there existed "a most prosperous government and settlement [οἴκησις], which is imitated by the best of the arrangements now existing."[29] Permission granted, the Stranger continues:

> Tradition tells us how blissful was the life of men in that age, furnished with everything in abundance, and of spontaneous growth. And the cause thereof is said to have been this: Cronos understood that, as we

have explained, human nature is not at all capable of regulating the human things, when it possesses autocratic authority over everything, without becoming filled with hubris and injustice. So, thinking about these things, he then appointed as kings and rulers for our cities, not human beings, but beings of a race that was nobler and more divine, namely, daemons. He acted just as we now do in the case of sheep and herds of tame animals: we do not set oxen as rulers over oxen, or goats over goats; instead, we exercise despotic dominion over them, because our species is better than theirs. In like manner the god, out of friendship for humanity, set over us at that time the nobler race of daemons, who supervised us in a way that provided much ease both for them and for us. They provided peace and awe and good laws and justice without stint. Thus they made it so that the races of men were without civil strife and happy.

What this present argument is saying, making use of the truth, is that there can be no rest from evils and toils for those cities in which some mortal rules rather than a god. The argument thinks that we should imitate by every advice the way of life that is said to have existed under Cronos; in public life and in private life—in the arrangement of our households and our cities—we should obey whatever within us partakes of immortality, giving the name "law" to the distribution ordained by intelligence [*tēn toû noû dianomēn eponomazontas nomon*]. But if an individual man or an oligarchy or a democracy, possessed of a soul which strives after pleasures and lusts and seeks to surfeit itself therewith, having no continence and being the victim of a plague that is endless and insatiate of evil—if such an one shall rule over a State or an individual by trampling on the laws, then there is (as I said just now) no means of salvation.[30]

That these passages contain Plato's definition of law seems clear—or so we are told, at least, by historians of jurisprudence, who routinely cite these lines in the course of their commentaries on Plato, as well as by Strauss, who interprets these passages as nothing less than Plato's definitive response to the question of the best regime.[31] Upon closer examination, however, the confidence of these commentators seems misplaced. Even Strauss's "theologico-political" reading of these passages, so much more careful than those historians whose haste he strove continually to chasten, passes over a fundamental "perplexity" that stirs within them.[32] When the Stranger says that law (nomos) should be understood as a name for the dispensation (dianomēn) of thought (noû),[33] he engages in what the translator R. G. Bury would call a "double word-play: νοῦς [*nous*] = νόμος [*nomos*], and διανομάς [*dianomas*] = δαίμονας [*daimonas*]. Laws, being the 'dispensations of reason,' take the place of the 'daemons' of the age of Cronos: the divine element in man (το δαιμόνιαν [*to daimonian*]), which claims obedience, is reason (νοῦς [*nous*])."[34] As with other translations associated with the Greek term *nomos*, this wordplay (others have called it a "pun" and even an "anagram") has been obscured and abstracted by its translation into Latin.[35] After 1484, when Marsilius Ficinus rendered the Greek dianomēn with the Latin *dispensationem*, many English translators began translating dianomēn as "dispensation," resulting in a rendering of the *Laws* that seemed to allow law to be defined as "the dispensation of intellect."[36] This translation, which Strauss accepts and deploys, certainly avoids the defects of some of the more brutal alternatives for dianomēn (such as *edict*).[37] It also has qualities of its own: by rendering dianomēn with one of the two Latin equivalents of the Greek *oikonomia*, Ficinus remains faithful to the way that Plato's *Laws* seems to think the polis on the model of the *oikos*.[38] Even so, the Ficinian rendering ends up obscuring a key dynamic in the untranslatable term it seeks to illuminate. Dianomēn, in Plato's wordplay, touches not only nomos (its root, *nemein*, designates precisely the distribution, division, apportionment, or allocation that both Schmitt and Heidegger would connect, in their postwar writings, with nomos[39]), but also the *dianoia* to which Plato attached so much importance in the *Republic* (and which is the essence of philosophical thought as distinct from the prephilosophical convention, the age of Cronos, which is not necessarily the same as a religious age[40]). And although in the *Laws*, as in the *Republic*, dianoia must be understood in relation to nous,[41] the *Laws* gives both terms a very unusual declension. As Heidegger has observed, nous in the *Laws*, in contrast to the rest of Plato's corpus, is thought within the horizon of *poesis* (production), and thence too (given Heidegger's understanding of poesis) to techne.[42] What holds for nous holds as well for the terms to which it is contiguous in Plato's wordplay. "To use Plato's own terms and wordplay more precisely," as Jean-François Pradeau emphasizes in his commentary on this passage, is to draw out precisely this technicity: "the law (*nomos*)," Pradeau therefore translates, "is *the instrument* of the intellect (*nous*)."[43] There would thus seem to be a subtle shade to the Stranger's wordplay that is left in silence when dianomēn is rendered with *dispensation*. The Stranger manages to stretch dianomēn so that it allows for a harmonious ensemble to be made out of a series of otherwise ranked and opposed concepts. In the Stranger's mouth, dianomēn touches prephilosophical as well as philosophical governance (where governance is figured, in each case, on the model of the management of the household by a *despotes*). It pertains as much to human as to animal populations (where both sorts of population are figured as livestock to be shepherded by nobler races). Perhaps above all, it is thought in a mode that deploys rather than bans the power of poesis (where poesis signifies as production, and thus too as techne and enframing). Given the variety of otherwise opposed concepts that are in play in the Stranger's utterance—prephilosophy and philosophy, prelaw and law, knowledge and power, population and governance, thought and instrument—it might not be far off the mark to hypertranslate his coupling of nous and nomos into unapologetically contemporary terms, as an unavowed precursor for one of the most basic and contested concepts of contemporary thought: *dispositif*.[44] On this read, it would be as errant to reduce (as does Badiou) the concept of law in the *Laws* to "criminal prescriptions," "tyrannical commandments," or a "law of death" as it would be to suppose a relation of simple "natural inferiority" (as does Strauss) between nous and nomos.[45] Law, in the *Laws*, instead would be a name for a philosophic apparatus, a machine that conjoins nous and nomos, a device that, in a manner we have yet to fully comprehend, makes one "see and speak."[46]

4

Understood as a discourse on a dispositif, the Stranger's words on law give rise to a new and different perplexity. The apparatus of which he speaks would seem to be defined by a precise if unusual operation. Dianomēn is a place in the Stranger's utterance about law where each one of the other names in his formulation shades into and joins with each of the others, in one and the same movement by which philosophic thought disjoins itself from the prephilosophic thought it at once imitates, rearranges, and displaces. Interpreted strictly within the hermeneutic horizon proper to the *Laws*, this wordplay is not at all an anomaly. As Johann Huizinga showed in his 1944 work *Homo Ludens*, and as Michel Foucault noted in his 1982–83 lectures on Plato, the discourse on serious play saturates Plato's *Laws*.[47] The *Laws*, as Huizinga points out, is a dialogue that speaks of education (*paideia*) as the guidance of children (*paides*) through play (*paidia*).[48] It considers education and play (and not, contra Schmitt, external war [*polemos*]) to be the "supremely serious" problem for lawgiving thought (which sort of thought the *Laws*, in turn, repeatedly calls "the sober play [*paidia*] of old men").[49]

It famously construes man (*anthropon*) as the "plaything" (*paignion*) of the gods.[50] The Stranger's wordplay on nous, dianomēn, and nomos is not then a deviation from the otherwise serious thought that takes place in the *Laws*; to the contrary, by putting a name to the play that allows nous to participate in the very nomos it also orders, this wordplay in fact provides the very paradigm according to which the *Laws* thinks law.[51] In book 7 of the *Laws*, the Stranger pauses to reflect upon the dialogue in which he and his interlocutors have been participating since dawn. Their own dialogue, the Stranger acknowledges, is not only itself akin to a form of tragic poetry; it is also, he asserts, the very "paradigm" (*paradeigma*) for the sort of discourse that ought to govern the guardians' education of the young instead of tragic poetry.[52] This self-reference, which precedes the Stranger's reference to himself and his fellow lawmakers as "makers of a tragedy," provides the interpretive key that alone can allow for a precise understanding of the form of the Stranger's words on the relation of nous and nomos. Read as a part of a paradigm for the "true law" (*nomos alēthēs*) the Stranger later would claim to produce, the very permutation of letters that appears there on the page—where nous, dianomēn, and nomos at once depart from the very root, *nem-*, they also share—now comes to light as an exemplification of the very harmony that the interlocutors of the *Laws* elsewhere, in their discussions of law, seem merely to approximate.[53] In their close concordance with one another, the very communication between the words nous, nomos, and dianomēn reveals itself there—in the letters that appear visibly on the surface of the page itself—as the sensible expression of the Idea, otherwise only purely intelligible, that thought, law, and space could coexist in agreement with one another in an undivided political community where human laws imitate divine laws.[54] Recalling that the Greek word for truth (*alētheia*) is formed from privative prefix *a-* (un- or dis-) and the root *lēthē* (forgetting), the Stranger's wordplay even would appear to function as a sort of pedagogical reminder to the reader of the *Laws*, a mnemonic device that causes the reader to remember that the name nomos points less to the divisive music of tragic poetry than to the silent harmonics of nous, to "the play [*le jeu*] of a thought that permits itself to found the law on an infinitely superior Good."[55] But this would be a most paradoxical sort of recollection, for it would startle the reader into remembering a Oneness that was never forgotten in the first place, that appears for the first time only in Platonic reminiscence. If, as the Stranger argues, nomos may be understood as a name for the dianomēn of nous, it would then be because the name nomos is itself already a distribution (a dianomēn) of the name nous, because the name nous itself already participates in the name nomos—because, in short, to write the name nomos is also, at least in part, to write the name nous. Understood in this way, nomos alēthēs would be a name for that nomos which arrives at its truth in a daring and surprising way—in a manner authorized neither by prephilosophic convention nor by etymology, but simply and only by measuring itself with reference to the Idea of the indivisible, to the unprecedented One as such.

There is, in this serious play, no hint of an internal thought that can take effect only insofar as it inscribes its blueprints upon the passive blank slate of external space. The relation between nous and nomos in Plato's *Laws* cannot then be interpreted, in modern terms, as a relation between mind and matter, much less between the two discrete substances of *res cogitans* and *res extensa*. In fact, in the place where dianomēn joins nous to nomos there would appear to be no relation at all. We seem to find nothing more, and nothing less, than a peculiar sort of community (or *koinonia*), a subtle but nevertheless definite participation of thought within a law that is already itself constitutively spatial, an intimate proximity of names that, in its approximation of the paradigm of indivisibility rendered visible by the Good, itself exemplifies the sort of intimate proximity that would exist in the best possible political community. On this read, the Stranger's wordplay would communicate a most serious teaching indeed: the indivisibility it exemplifies—which extends to include not only nous, dianomēn, and nomos, but also nemein, the concrete distribution of lots and land—would be so thorough and so complete that the cobelonging that defines its very form would already imperceptibly begin making or producing (in the mode of a poesis) a novel form of community. It would allow us to see and speak, for the first time, of the *politeia*, this peculiar new unity that comes into being when and where philosophy discovers in itself an apparatus that enables it, in turn, to immunize the human community against the contagious disease of civil strife, of stasis, of unending internal division and divisiveness.[56]

5

However poetic it may be, the philosophic apparatus of law in the *Laws* cannot be comprehended with recourse to the poem alone. So identical is mathematics to lawgiving in the *Laws* that, as Pradeau will put it in his commentary on the *Laws*, "to legislate is to count."[57] To read the *Laws* on its own terms is consequently to trace its mathematical reasoning; but the more one traces the mathematical reasoning of the *Laws*, the more one realizes that its philosophic apparatus depends for its intelligibility upon operations that allow for mathematics but that are not themselves mathematical in character. There are, after all, constitutive limits upon the sorts of problems that can become intelligible in and for the mode of thought Plato calls dianoia.[58] The apparatus of the law the Stranger sets up in the *Laws* depends for its intelligibility upon one operation in particular: an ungeometrical use of space, a use of space that is specifically political or, more to the point, a use of a very specific political space, the colony (*apoikia*).[59] At the end of book 3, Klinias suddenly reveals that he has been commissioned to settle a new colony and to draw up laws for that colony.[60] This premise will remain the occasion of the *Laws* throughout the rest of the dialogue; it will silently shape the order of all of the questions and responses that subsequently will take place in the text. As such, the space of the colony will have an indispensable function within the philosophic apparatus of law set forth in the *Laws*. It will give the gathered interlocutors the opportunity and indeed the duty to formulate only those laws which philosophy asks of them, as distinct from those laws which the necessities of an existing oikos would demand of them. The premise of the colony, in other words, will allow the interlocutors' philosophizing no longer to be governed by an existing arrangement of the sensible (with its prephilosophical and therefore unphilosophical distribution of labor, agriculture, reproduction, education, and so forth), but now to govern that arrangement. Only in a new apoikia—as distinct from an existing oikos—will it be possible for the order of the intelligible to come to govern and arrange the order of the sensible. The interlocutors of the *Laws* understand this: they grasp that the very possibility of their philosophic discourse is predicated on a divine accident, and for the chance to write the nomoi of an apoikia—for their emancipation, in other words, from the need to rewrite the nomoi of an existing oikos, with the stasis that rewriting would inevitably entail—they thank and praise God.

What this praise conceals is a perplexity that is neither theological nor mathematical in character. Without the clearing produced by colonization, the Stranger would not have been able to reconcile the arithmetic and geometrical orders in his account of the best possible number of lots. He would have been forced to begin counting in medias res, which inevitably would have entailed the recollection of past wrongs, a trace of stasis.[61] In the *Laws*, the apparatus of law depends upon a truly philosophical count—a distribution of land, lots, and life that not only begins but also ends with One. But where exactly is it—in the midst of what already existing nomos or oikos—that one can begin counting from one? If every already existing political and legal order already entails a prephilosophical count, such that any introduction of a philosophical count necessarily will entail a divisive recounting (not only in the mode of nomos, in the form of lots, debts, etc., but also in the mode of nous, in the form of bad memories, grief and grievances related to stasis, etc.), how exactly is it that a philosophical count will be able to come into being at all? But for the possibility of a perfectly empty clearing—an equivalent, we might say, for the zero that Greek mathematics famously lacked—how else could the apparatus of law set itself up in conformity with the requirements of a truly philosophic nous?[62] It's precisely this perplexity—this paradoxical lack of nothing, of a count that could begin with emptiness—that demands or requires the operation of colonization as the prior condition for the philosophic apparatus of law in the *Laws*. It is this same problem that colonization solves more dianoetically than does numerically based amnesty: although both amnesty and the colony do indeed clear the way for the emergence of a philosophic apparatus of law, the colony performs this function more completely than does amnesty. The clearing of the colony provides an empty space that is much more radical, much more fully emptied of division, than is the enforced oblivion produced by amnesty's internally divided oath, its "promise to remember to forget."[63]

The space of the colony is, accordingly, not merely one among problems for the *Laws*. It's the implicit spatiality that lets Plato's *Laws* count, and that as such enables law to become thinkable in and for the philosophic apparatus the *Laws* sets up. At once the innermost limit of the arithmetic and geometric orders, the *topos noetos* that ordains the most dianoetic polis, and the condition for the best possible join between the arithmetic and geometric orders, the space of the colony is the indispensable condition for the philosophic apparatus of law that emerges in the *Laws*. It is the reason the lawgivers begin legislating at all (in the strict sense that the purpose of the last seven books of the *Laws* is to provide legislation for the new colony) and it is the empty space on which alone the lawgivers' harmonious common can become intelligible at all. But if the colony is therefore the paradigmatic nomos for the mode of thought inaugurated in the *Laws*, it is equally that clearing operation that nous requires for itself if the order of the intelligible is to give order, shape, and form to the order of the sensible, rather than the other way around. Colonization is indispensable for nous, that is to say, if nous is to be able to produce a nomos without also becoming nonidentical with itself in the process (for a nous that was produced by a nomos would be, for Plato, no nous at all), and if nomos is to remain self-identical with itself in this apparatus as well (for colonization alone allows the philosopher to produce an apparatus of law free from the fear that his prescriptions will produce recounting within the community and thus too the very stasis against which law is supposed to immunize the community).

In *The Apology*, Plato's first work, Socrates speaks almost as though he were a stranger to Athens.[64] In the *Laws*, Plato's last work, a Stranger speaks in a setting outside Athens almost as though he were Socrates. From the only Platonic dialogue in which Socrates does not appear, the *Laws* would seem to offer a teaching that is perfectly befitting of the Stranger who here seems to appear in Socrates's place: philosophy can solve the war within the home only by presupposing a home away from home (which is literally what a colony, or ap-oikia, is in the *Laws*). Between the nous of philosophy and the nomos of the colony there would appear to be, in short, a relation not simply of hierarchy but also of cobelonging: the colony will have been that nomos that allows thinking itself—nous—to set itself up as a self-founding force, and that, for this reason, is inscribed essentially, if silently, each and every time nous appears in its selfsame autonomy.

Nothing here, of course, should imply that colonization allows the philosopher to escape from grounded practical matters into the clouds of theory. Colonization in the *Laws* is an operation that is at once much more intricate and much less Aristophanean than that. The introduction of the colony into philosophy enables the interlocutors to establish a proper rank—a philosophical rank—between the necessities of household management and the wisdom of philosophic lawgiving. Prior to the harmonious One, prior to the serious play that operates to immunize the community against division and stasis, colonization is that operation internal to the *Laws'* philosophic apparatus which produces the empty space in the absence of which, in turn, that apparatus would not be able to come into its own as philosophy—as a mode of autonomous thought that is capable of governing and arranging, distributing and disposing, the sensible world from the standpoint of the intelligible world. Even, especially, when it is not named as such, the clearing of the colony remains the definitive horizon for the specific mode of nous the *Laws* inaugurates.

6

Contemporary philosophers sometimes seem to presuppose that to be self-conscious of law's effects in and on philosophical thought is to be self-conscious of a very specific juridical form: the mandatory command or tyrannical prescription. But with this presupposition, philosophy demonstrates that it has not yet become fully self-conscious about the mode in which it becomes self-conscious of its own relation to law. From the *Laws* we learn something unexpected about the sort of dispositif that law is. If I should find that I am unable to think politics without first seeing and speaking of an empty space, a clearing or void in which the perfect polity stands a chance of coming into being, then already my voice and gaze dwell within a horizon opened for me by law's philosophic apparatus. The dispositif of the law, at least in Plato's *Laws*, is not then limited to the form of the tyrannical command, the injunction or imperative backed by threats. To seek out the clearing, this space defined by the potential for a home away from home, as though thought's estrangement in an empty space were the prior condition for any thought that truly is thought, is not at all to render inoperative the dispositif of the law. To the contrary, it is already to think in the innermost inside of the law, in the space that philosophy prepares in order for the law to be law, and in the space that law prepares so that philosophy may become philosophy.

The operation of this dispositif is apparent in each of the two reopenings of the Plato question we've outlined. To sharpen the point, it will be useful to recapitulate the teachings on law these respective Platonisms propose to transmit. For Badiou, reopening the Plato question holds out a very definite promise: it is an occasion for philosophy to think anew its relation to the One and thus too to the law, to discover in Plato's aporetic dialogues a way for philosophy to think law without also at the same time participating either in the One or in lawgiving. For Badiou, as we have seen, philosophy ceases to be philosophy as soon as it begins to rely upon criminal prescriptions to enforce its truths upon nonphilosophers. Philosophy can remain philosophy, can avoid its innermost and most intimate disaster, only if it suspends its temptation to use despotic injunctions to declare a permanent end to sophistry. This understanding of philosophy does not, as some commentators seem to have concluded from Badiou's writings on Saint Paul, commit Badiou to simple antinomianism, to a crude antithesis between philosophy and law. It commits him to nothing more, but also nothing less, than a newly aporetic understanding of the relation of philosophy and law. To the extent that philosophy is able to maintain a philosophic relation to its own temptation to issue criminal prescriptions, its own desire to remain self-identical with itself will give rise to an imperative: that philosophers must regard as "*illégal*" (Badiou's quotation marks) any use of law to substantialize or realize Truth.[65] Only by remaining loyal to this paradoxical imperative, this philosophic law against philosophic lawgiving, will philosophy be able to relate to law not as an inner temptation to disaster, but as a proper aporia— in a mode, that is to say, that is not nonphilosophical but now, for the first time, properly philosophical.[66] For Badiou, it would seem, reopening the Plato question would allow us to comprehend the relation between law and philosophy in rigorously philosophical terms: as a nonrelation.[67]

Strauss's return to Plato would seem to circle around an equally intricate set of reflections on law and philosophy. In his well-known writings on the problem of "persecution and the art of writing" that emerge out of his earlier, lesser-known studies of Platonism, Strauss explains why writers who hold heterodox views must communicate their thought "exclusively between the lines."[68] If thinkers did not take care to inscribe their thoughts between the lines, Strauss suggests, they would run the risk that those thoughts would be censored or destroyed, and that philosophic teachings would cease to be transmitted to those few who are capable of them (or, in Strauss's words, those "young men who might become philosophers"). Structuring this hermeneutics, this serious play of speech and silence, is a clear understanding of an irreconcilable gap between philosophy and law.[69] Because law cannot be philosophical—because the nonphilosophical multitude cannot govern itself by thought alone, and stands in need of law's tyrannical commands and threats of force if it is to govern its passions and appetites at all—philosophy cannot fully obey law without also subordinating itself, in the process, to its opposite: nonphilosophy. Between law and philosophy there is not, however, a simple antinomy; there is instead an unstable equilibrium, an opaque force field, in relation to which both law and philosophy each remain constitutively open to the risk of becoming nonidentical with themselves. Just as philosophy that abides by law risks devolving into nonphilosophy, so too law that aspires to philosophy risks throwing into question the tyrannical commands and threats of force that alone allow it to govern nonphilosophers; law that gives full voice to its own self-stultifying aporias is no law at all. For Strauss, albeit in a much different way than for Badiou, the relation between law and philosophy also should be understood as an irreducible nonrelation: as an unbridgeable distance between philosophy's open question ("what is?") and law's definitive declaration ("what is"), and by extension, between Athens and Jerusalem, between reason and revelation.[70] The subtle relations of speech and silence that structure the surfaces of exoteric texts are thus anything but empty forms. There is a content to their form: they are signs of a nonrelation that is no less irreducible and aporetic than is Badiou's philosophic imperative.

7

If we may speak of a koinè that joins Strauss to Badiou, it is not, however, because each thinker finds in Plato the resources to hold open a nonrelation between law and philosophy. It is because each thinker leaves unthought the space that at once enables that nonrelation and collapses it from within. Strauss and Badiou alike underestimate the extent to which the apparatus of law in Plato is not simply a tyrannical command, but also, even primarily, a nomos—a political space.[71] And not just any political space, but a very distinct political space, one whose specifically political character derives, paradoxically, from the absence within it of any polis whatsoever. In short: an impolitical space. The empty space of the colony is not a *res extensa*, an exterior space upon which the philosopher inscribes his interior blueprints. It is that clearing that alone allows philosophic thought to separate itself from the order of the sensible and to set itself up in the *atopia* (or, better, *atopicité*) that, in turn, is the only place where autonomous thinking is really at home with itself; it is that place alone that allows thought to produce laws out of its own autonomy.[72] The blank slate or tabula rasa exemplified by the colony is not then exterior to lawgiving thought; it is the innermost interior and indispensable condition of lawgiving thought. It is the very horizon of thought that allows thought to render itself intelligible to itself as lawgiving thought.

This holds even, especially, where thought cannot name or think the clearing that allows it to see and speak of law; it holds even and especially when thought misrecognizes this clearing as a space exterior to law, a space of nonlaw that would seem to promise to thought an ability to relate to law in the mode of a nonrelation. In Straussian hermeneutics, this misrecognition will take place in a most symptomatic way, through Strauss's excessively literal naming of the blank slate or tabula rasa that appears between the lines in exoteric texts. The space of the colony will provide the horizon and lexicon within which Strauss explains what it means to read writing between the lines. At the opening of his famous 1941 text, Strauss outlines his hermeneutic project, his desire to interpret the blank slate—the surface of the empty page—that is there between the lines, with catachrestic reference to colonization: "This expression [writing between the lines] is clearly metaphoric. Any attempt to express its meaning in unmetaphoric language would lead to the discovery of a terra incognita, a field whose very dimensions are as yet unexplored and which offers ample scope for highly intriguing and even important investigations. One may say without fear of being presently convicted of grave exaggeration that almost the only preparatory work to guide the explorer in this field is buried in the writings of the rhetoricians of antiquity."[73] Strauss's unmetaphoric use of metaphor here may at first appear to be nothing more than play, but read to the letter it has an effect that is far from unserious: a claim that opens with logical paradox—what might it mean to read writing in a space where there is none?—is closed down by rhetorical commonplace (namely, that knowing the unknown is akin to exploring an unexplored land). It is, of course, no accident that Strauss will treat the empty surface of the page as though it could be rendered intelligible as a colonial space (an unknown land that is there to be discovered by a reader who is, in effect, an explorer, a founder of a colony). Quite the opposite: this swerve will have been prescribed for Strauss in advance by the very text in which he claimed to find the best regime in the first place. In Plato's *Laws*, the empty space of the colony is that topos noetos in which alone the best regime may be found each and every time it is possible to find it, up to and including when that empty space is the empty space between the lines of an exoteric text. Strauss's self-conscious metaphorization of the limit to metaphor is, in this sense, the unself-conscious mark within Strauss's thought of a dispositif that Strauss, who thought the relation of law and thought in Plato as dispensation, could not think on its own terms. For Strauss, the poetics of colonization would seem to provide the best, clearest, or perhaps just the most obvious device for seeing and speaking about a mode of thought, philosophy, that seeks to escape the persecutions of law by inscribing its lessons in the empty spaces that appear on the blank page. Loyal Straussians certainly might want to downplay Strauss's playful reference to colonization, as if it were merely an unserious aside. But Strauss's loyalty was not to Strauss but to Plato, and it was a loyalty that was far more excessive then either Strauss or his disciples perhaps are able to admit. In particular, Strauss is excessively loyal, more loyal than he knows or can even manage to know, to that part of the *Laws* that requires the clearing of the colony before thought can be thought as thought. But this same clearing undermines the very hermeneutics it seems to enable, for it collapses from within the nonrelation upon which Straussian hermeneutics at root depends. From the *Laws*, we learn that the clearing in which alone thought is at home is not at all exterior to law, but is to the contrary law's most indispensable condition. The colony, in other words, is not law's antipode; it is the only place where law has a chance to achieve perfection. Strauss deploys the poetics of colonial space in order to name the interpretive horizon inside of which the thoughtful writer may transmit his thought of the best regime in nonrelation with the thoughtless censor who, in turn, seeks to persecute that writer—or, in Platonic terms, where nous may express itself with being ordered by nomos. But precisely this deployment is the best sign that Strauss cannot think the juridicality of the very horizon on which he depends for his interpretations. The empty space that Strauss supposes is exterior to law is itself already a space internal to law, is already the innermost interior and indispensable condition of lawgiving thought. Strauss's return to Plato would thus seem to reopen the Plato question in a manner that exceeds, from within, not only Strauss's own reading of Plato, which circles around a nonrelation between law and philosophy, but also the hermeneutics he proposes to have retrieved from Platonism, which brings that same nonrelation to the surface of the written page now as a problem for reading.

What is true of Strauss's thought in the mode of the poem is true for Badiou's thought in the mode of the matheme. For Badiou, Plato's aporetic thinking can be sustained only insofar as it remains atopic thinking: philosophy's act is nothing more, but also nothing less, than to open an "active void within thought."[74] The "empty gap" that results from this operation allows for the appearance of truths, but only so long as philosophy manages to maintain those truths in nonidentity with the void that provides them with their background.[75] The "ethics of philosophy," as Badiou calls it, is to avoid the temptation to transform this empty gap into a spacing where Truth appears not as a void, but as being.[76] To the extent philosophy caves in to this temptation, it succumbs to its own internal inverse: terror. Philosophy becomes a force of terror when it no longer limits itself to the work of poking a hole in sense or declaring the void inside of the domain of what is, but instead gives truth a presence in a specific place and assigns a specific sacred name, in the process annihilating the void itself and destroying the very possibility of declaring what is not.[77]

On this point, it must be said, there is between Strauss and Badiou no koinè whatsoever. There is only diagnosis. Badiou's ethics of philosophy explains, with great clarity, what precisely is terrible in Strauss's localization of philosophy and law, reason and revelation, in Athens and Jerusalem. This localization of Truth has produced a sacralization of the West, the terror and dogmatism of which require no additional elaboration here.[78] Especially because Strauss privileges a close and sustained reading of Plato's *Laws*, the very text in opposition to which Badiou develops the ethics of philosophy in the first place, Strauss's Platonism is the very paradigm of disaster in the Badiouian sense of the word; it is, in other words, the very best example of philosophy at its worst.[79]

That same exemplarity, however, also points to something else: the sense in which Badiou's own ethics disjoins itself in its most intimate and essential region. The paradox of Badiou's operational void, which strives to maintain the empty place of Truth and so to guard against any disaster, is not that it is disloyal to Plato; it is that it is also excessively loyal to Plato, above all to the Platonic text in which Badiou locates the disaster of Platonism itself.[80] On the terms of Plato's *Laws*, the clearing of an empty space in sense, and the setting up of thought in the operational void that results, is not at all a renunciation of lawgiving thought; it is, to the contrary, the paradigmatic form of lawgiving thought. In the *Laws*, the empty space is not a step back from the ecstasy of place; it is the ecstatic place par excellence. The apoikia of the *Laws*, in fact, is nothing so much as a place of *ek-stasis*, a place that immunizes politics against stasis by placing itself outside of stasis.

To be sure, Badiou's recourse to the "exceptionally severe" laws of mathematics certainly does allow him to displace the unmathematical use of the One that Jacob Klein found at the core of Platonic politics.[81] It is certainly therefore possible to generate a reading of Badiou as the thinker who cancels out the apoikia, thinking it through to completion: by thinking the void that Plato could not think, and by opposing the One that Plato did think, Badiou puts himself in a position to rethink the place and function of the colony in the philosophic apparatus Plato establishes in the *Laws*.[82] But even this reading would need to confront the possibility, immanent to the very procedures of Badiou's ethics of philosophy, that Badiou does not so much cancel out the apoikia as sublate it, iterating its empty space now in a higher form, indeed as the very hallmark of philosophic thought itself.[83] Understood purely from the perspective of its deployment, after all, Badiou's operational void produces the same philosophic autonomy that the colony produces in Plato's *Laws*: the operational void, like the empty space of the colony, allows philosophy to separate the intelligible from the sensible, and to establish the rank of the intelligible over the sensible. It is perhaps no surprise, then, that the space of the colony should reappear so consistently in Badiou's descriptions of philosophy itself. "The philosopher is always a stranger," Badiou argues; the philosopher's thought constitutively exceeds any "home for truth," which is defined by nothing so much as its emptiness, its exteriority to any home, such that thinking can only "take place abroad," in a "foreign" country, such that the hallmark of any true philosophic commitment is its "internal foreignness."[84] It's as though the ethics of philosophy were reducible to a most familiar imperative: that philosophy will have been philosophy only if it first dwells in the topos noetos of the ap-oikia, this empty space, this home away from home.

The ethics of philosophy too, the ethics of philosophy above all, would thus seem to circle around an aporia. This aporia, however, consists not of a nonrelation between law and philosophy, but of a relation of excessive identity, a relation in which philosophy is so completely interior to the empty space of the ap-oikia, and consequently too so completely in thrall to its own autonomy, that the very notion of empty space has become for it, precisely, an imperative. "The event is in excess of all law"—this philosopheme, so central to Badiou's oeuvre, would appear to be capable of thinking everything except the event of law itself, everything except the genesis of law in and from an empty space that reappears, in Badiou's thought, as the imperative of all imperatives, the nonlaw governing any and all philosophic relations to law, as the dead center of the very thinking of thinking undertaken by the thinker of the event. The truth of the void, on the terms of Plato's *Laws*, is that the void is not a void. It is an impolitical space that lawgiving thought must occupy if thought is at all to become able to issue laws in and from its own autonomy. The open void in which Badiou finds the possibility of restraining philosophy from caving in to disaster is, in other words, precisely that space that alone enables the criminal prescriptions that are, for Badiou, the hallmark of disaster itself. Badiou's thought, it would seem, must therefore expose itself to disaster in the very same place, and by virtue of the very same ethical imperative, that allows it the possibility of restraining itself from disaster. In principle, of course, a void that is inconsistent with itself should not be inconsistent with Badiou's Platonism, which emphasizes the necessity of inconsistency in the void.[85] But the inconsistency internal to the colony of the *Laws*—to this atopic space that is the paradigm not only for lawgiving thought but also for the complete absence of lawgiving thought—points to a very different problem: a disjunctive synthesis of law and thought that is as central to Badiou's Platonism as it is unthinkable on the terms of that Platonism.

Notes

I thank Nicole Starrett, Klaus Mladek, George Edmondson, and two anonymous reviewers for their comments on an earlier draft of this essay.

1 See, variously, Badiou, *Manifesto for Philosophy*, 65, 98–100, 120–22. See also Badiou, *Conditions*, 229; Badiou, *Deleuze*, 100–101; Badiou, *Handbook of Inaesthetics*, 38; Badiou, *Briefings on Existence*, 101, 159; Badiou, *Infinite Thought*, 31–37.

2 Badiou, *Manifesto for Philosophy*, 120. Compare Kenneth Reinhard, "Introduction," in Badiou, *Plato's Republic*, viii–ix. Badiou also mentions Stalinist Marxism as one of the six major schools of anti-Platonism of the last century. What Badiou is less clear about, his occasional asides notwithstanding, is the way that anti-Platonism also conditioned the emergence of neoliberalism at the moment of its very birth. Not only Ludwig von Mises (writing in 1944) and Friedrich Hayek (also in 1944), but also Karl Popper (writing in 1945) and Alexander Rüstow (writing in 1949) denounced Plato in particular and by name as the thinker par excellence of state planning and therefore too, in one of the signature slippages of neoliberal thought, totalitarianism. For the neoliberal thought that originated in the Colloque Walter Lippmann of 1938 (convoked by Rüstow) and Mont Pèlerin in 1947 (organized by Hayek, and attended by Mises and Popper), the decentralized and localized modes of savoir faire enabled by the free market not only provide for a less ignorant knowledge of things and goods than that presumed by "modern philosopher-kings" like Stalin and Hitler; these same modes also make for better decision making than that which takes place in command economies, and thence too better politics as well (so long as by *politics* we mean a special sort of biopolitics, i.e., continual enhancements in living standards and in quality of life). "Violent opposition to Platonism" thus binds together not only bitterly opposed schools of philosophy (analytic and continental) but also bitterly opposed schools of political economy (command and neoliberal).

3 Badiou, *Manifesto for Philosophy*, 28, 115; Badiou, *Infinite Thought*, 33–34.

4 Badiou, *Manifesto for Philosophy*, 119; Badiou, *Infinite Thought*, 37–39, 42.

5 See, variously, Badiou, *Manifesto for Philosophy*, 103; Badiou, *Conditions*, 103, 210; Badiou, *Second Manifesto for Philosophy*, 56, 124–25. Badiou, *Briefings on Existence*, 159; Badiou, *The Communist Hypothesis*, 229n1.

6 Of the fifty or so essays collected in Ramond, *Alain Badiou*; Hallward, *Think Again*; and Riera, *Alain Badiou*, only two, one by Jacques Rancière and the other by Claude Imbert, both dating to 1999, devote sustained critical attention to Badiou's Platonism. Since then, Martin Puchner and A. J. Bartlett have published Badiouian rereadings of Plato (Puchner, *The Drama of Ideas*, 185–92;

Bartlett, *Badiou and Plato*). But one searches in vain for a Platonic rereading of Badiou. This situation may change with the publication and English translation of Badiou's "hypertranslation" of Plato's *Republic*, which he developed in the three seminars he devoted to Plato during the years 2007–10 under the rubric "Pour aujourd'hui: Platon!" See Badiou, *The Communist Hypothesis*, 229–30n1; Badiou, *Plato's Republic*.

7 For his seminars, Badiou, *Manifesto for Philosophy*, 152n5.

8 Badiou, *Manifesto for Philosophy*, 122, 134; Badiou, *Conditions*, 155, 158.

9 Badiou, *The Communist Hypothesis*, 229–30.

10 On Heidegger, see Strauss, "An Introduction to Heideggerian Existentialism," in *The Rebirth of Classical Political Rationalism*, 27–46. On neo-Kantianism, see Strauss, "Preface to the English Translation," 15, 18–28. Strauss also, of course, wanted to generate a response within political philosophy to the blithe confidence of social scientific positivism, which Strauss understood to be founded on the basis of the distinction between facts and values. See Strauss, "What Is Political Philosophy?," in *What Is Political Philosophy?*, 18. Compare Strauss, *Natural Right and History*, 35–80.

11 Strauss, *Philosophy and Law*, 37–38. See also Strauss, "Introduction to Heideggerian Existentialism," 41; Strauss, "Preface to the English Translation," 12.

12 Strauss, *Philosophy and Law*, 95–100. See also Strauss, "Persecution and the Art of Writing," in *Persecution and the Art of Writing*, 24; Strauss, "Exoteric Teaching," in *The Rebirth of Classical Political Rationalism*, 63–64; Strauss, "On a Forgotten Kind of Writing," in *What Is Political Philosophy?*, 221–32.

13 Strauss, *The City and Man*, 50–138. For Strauss, modern political philosophers are literally footnotes to Plato. See, on this point, Ferrari, "Strauss's Plato," 48.

14 On moderation, see Strauss, "Liberal Education and Responsibility," in *Liberalism Ancient and Modern*, 24. For a summary of Strauss's reading of Plato, see Esposito, "Introduzione," xxxii–xxxiii. Strauss's critique of the visionary excesses of modern philosophy must be understood alongside his critique of the figure of the prophet in Islamic Aristotelianism: if modern philosophers seek to realize the truth through law, medieval Falasifa understood the truth already to have been realized by the revelations of the prophet. See Strauss, *Philosophy and Law*, 75, 128.

15 On Heidegger and historicism, see Badiou, *Manifesto for Philosophy*, 113–16. On neo-Kantian moralism, see Badiou, *Ethics*.

16 On Nietzsche's overturning of Plato, see Badiou, *Manifesto for Philosophy*, 98–101. On Deleuze's incomplete overturning of Platonism, see Badiou, *Deleuze*, 26–27, 100–101; Badiou, *Logics of Worlds*, 385. Although this is not the place to sort out the truth and error of Badiou's writings on Deleuze, it should be noted that Deleuze—like Badiou, only in the mode of affirmation rather than redress—understood Plato himself to have established the conditions for anti-Platonism. See Deleuze, *The Logic of Sense*, 256.

17 On transmission, discipleship, and universal address, see Badiou, *Conditions*,

27–28, 45, but compare Badiou, *Infinite Thought*, 29, 38; Badiou, *Deleuze*, 96; Badiou and Žižek, *Philosophy in the Present*, 25.

18 Badiou, *Conditions*, 229. To formulate the Plato symptom, Badiou even goes so far as to retranslate Heidegger's 1942 dictum on translation—"Tell me what you think of translation, and I will tell you who you are"—replacing *translation* with *Plato*: "Tell me what you think of Plato, and I will tell you who you are" (Badiou, *Deleuze*, 100). It's as though the name *Plato* were not simply a metonym for translation but more fundamentally an antonym to translation, a name for that which exceeds translation, for that impossible real which remains untranslatable for philosophy, and which as such incessantly calls forth translations in philosophy—as if the entire history of philosophy itself were nothing more than, and necessarily so, a single series of mistranslations of Plato.

19 Badiou, *Manifesto for Philosophy*, 129–30, 135, 144. Badiou, *Conditions*, 89, 127, 166–71; Badiou, *Ethics*, 71, 84–85; Badiou, *Second Manifesto for Philosophy*, 71–72.

20 Badiou, *Manifesto for Philosophy*, 134; Badiou, *Conditions*, 155, 158.

21 Strauss, "What Is Political Philosophy?," 34. In the *Laws*, in contrast to the *Republic*, Plato produces a city in deed and not simply in speech. As such, Strauss characterizes the *Laws* as Plato's "only political work proper," his "most political work," and his "political work *par excellence*." See Strauss, "Plato," 78, cf. 67–68, 72; Strauss, "What Is Political Philosophy?," 29; Strauss, *The Argument and Action of Plato's Laws*, 1.

22 Strauss, *The Argument and Action of Plato's Laws*, 129. Book 10 of the *Laws*, Strauss had earlier written, is Plato's "theological statement *par excellence*." See Strauss, "How Fārābi Read Plato's *Laws*," in *What Is Political Philosophy?*, 134. By this Strauss does not mean that book 10 affirms the theological as a paradigm for politics, only that it raises the question of the theological within politics. See Strauss, *Philosophy and Law*, 76. Strauss does not then fully disagree with Giorgio Agamben's argument that the proof of the existence of the gods in book 10 of the *Laws* is "ironic." See, on this point, Agamben, *The Sacrament of Language*, 28–29.

23 Badiou, *Manifesto for Philosophy*, 122.

24 Strauss, "On Classical Political Philosophy," in *What Is Political Philosophy?*, 84.

25 Strauss, *The Argument and Action of Plato's Laws*, 2, 91, 127, 156. Daniel Tanguay, it should be noted, has suggested that Strauss's own position on the "theological-political problem"—this problem that, in 1924–25, caused Strauss's return to Plato in the first place—is embodied by the Athenian Stranger who manages the dialogue of the *Laws*. See Tanguay, *Leo Strauss*, 233n36. Not dissimilar is the position held by Hans-Georg Gadamer, who argues that the Stranger is the figure in whom "more than anyone Plato has most obviously hidden himself" (Gadamer, *Dialogue and Dialectic*, 71).

26 On "zetetics," see Strauss, *On Tyranny*, 196.

27 All the same, a small gesture in this direction will not be out of order. In his diagnosis of Lacan's anti-Platonism, Badiou locates the error of Lacan's reading

of Plato in Lacan's "strange and restated conviction that Plato concealed his thought more than he presented it" (Badiou, *Conditions*, 245). This reading of Plato, which according to Lacan was shared by his "master" Alexandre Kojève, is of course the reading produced by Strauss under the rubric of the esoteric. That Lacan could have received Strauss through Kojève is less improbable than the reader might suppose. In 1936, the very same year that Strauss noted his plan to coauthor a book with Kojève on Hobbes and Hegel, Kojève undertook preparations to coauthor a book on Freud and Hegel with Lacan. See, on this point, Strauss, *The Political Philosophy of Hobbes*, 58n1; Roudinesco, *Jacques Lacan*, 104–5. Although neither book ever appeared, it at least should be clear that Kojève was in a position to transmit teachings, even to mediate, between these two thinkers during the most formative periods of their intellectual production. Badiou's diagnosis of Lacan's strange reading of Plato, in any event, perhaps amounts to his most explicit critique of Strauss as well.

28 Plato, *Laws*, 713a.

29 Plato, *Laws*, 713b.

30 Plato, *Laws*, 713c–714b.

31 For commentaries on Plato, see, for example, Cairns, *Legal Philosophy from Plato to Hegel*, 35; Friedrich, *The Philosophy of Law in Historical Perspective*, 18–19; Kelley, *A Short History of Western Legal Theory*, 19, 22, 25; Letwin, *On the History of the Idea of Law*, 16. "The best regime is that in which a god or demon rules as in the age of Kronos, the golden age. The nearest imitation of divine rule is the rule of laws" (Strauss, "Plato," 83). Strauss is even more direct in his later book on Plato's *Laws*. What the Athenian seeks here, he argues, is "the highest possible ground of law: rule of law is rule of god" (Strauss, *The Argument and Action of Plato's Laws*, 58).

32 *Perplexity* is the term that Hannah Arendt used to describe these passages in 1951, when she located in them the hermeneutic key for comprehending the relation of law and the Good under conditions of secularization. Arendt, *The Origins of Totalitarianism* (1978), 299.

33 Plato, *Laws*, 714a.

34 See Plato, *Plato IX: Laws*, 286–87n1. See also Pradeau, *Plato and the City*, 142 (calling this passage a "wordplay").

35 Schmitt, *The* Nomos *of the Earth in the International Law of* Jus Publicum Europæum, 75, 342. "Pun": Voegelin, *Plato*, 239n8. "Anagram": Bernadete, *Plato's "Laws,"* 134.

36 On *dispensationem*, Plato, *Omnia diuini Platonis opera*, 454.

37 Strauss, *The Argument and Action of Plato's Laws*, 58, 60–61, 63–64. As a metonym for "dispensation," Strauss sometimes uses "disposition" (2, 58).

38 Aristotle, *Politics*, 1261a. Here a somewhat digressive note is in order. Beginning with Aristotle, Platonic political philosophy has been criticized for confusing the oikos with the polis, the political space of the home with that of the city. This criticism was renewed by Hannah Arendt, and has reappeared in Giorgio

Agamben's study of oikonomia (see Arendt, *Between Past and Future* [1961], 106; Agamben, *The Kingdom and the Glory*, 21, 31, 49–50). Perhaps, however, the problem with Platonism is not so much the collapse of the polis into the oikos, as the classical Aristotelian complaint would have it. What Plato's *Laws* would seem to show is that the oikos cannot on its own terms resolve the stasis it itself sets into motion, the stasis that would unbind it from within and preclude it from remaining an oikos at all. The polis, and later the state, certainly is one of the dispositifs that political philosophy deploys "to prevent this unbinding" (as Badiou has put it in *Being and Event*, 104–11). But it is not the only such dispositif, or even the most definitive one. From the *Laws* one learns that to prevent the stasis it itself inevitably entails, the oikos needs to extend beyond and outside of itself, needs to become a colony, an ap-oikia. The ap-oikia is not then incidental to the oikos. It is the immanently transcendent place where the oikos seeks its perfection. Plato doesn't resolve division in the city, in other words, simply by treating the polis as an oikos—by metaphorizing the city on the model of the Oneness of the despotic family. He solves it also, and perhaps above all, by displacing stasis into a space that is neither that of the oikos nor that of the polis. From this perspective, the problem is not the overextension of the oikos onto the polis. It is the nonidentity of the oikos with itself, its inability to deal with divisions within the home except by extending the home beyond itself, into a home away from home, an iterated home that proposes to resolve the divisions internal to the home by reproducing a model of the home in a space outside of the home. If political philosophy is to think the relation between the polis and the oikos, it will need to think a space that is neither the polis nor the oikos, that is the condition of possibility for its own autonomy as philosophy, and yet that is not itself present within its philosophic lexicon: the ap-oikia. What's unthinkable both for Strauss's Platonism and for Badiou's Platonism is not only the nonidentity of the oikos with itself, but that philosophizing itself should be identical with an activity that is not itself philosophical: the settlement of an as yet unsettled space, of a political space that strictly speaking is not yet a political space at all, even as it remains indispensable for any and all thought of the polis—the impolitical space of a colony.

39 Schmitt, *The* Nomos *of the Earth in the International Law of* Jus Publicum Europæum, 70, 326–27, 345; Heidegger, "Letter on Humanism," 238. For Heidegger, "*nomos* is not law [*Gesetz*] but more originally the destiny secured in and by the dispensation [allocation or allotment] of Being [der Schickung des Seins geborgene Zuweisung]."

40 Agamben, *The Sacrament of Language*, 16–17.

41 Badiou, *Conditions*, 42, 101, 243.

42 Heidegger, *On Time and Being*, 46, 50; Heidegger, "Letter on Humanism," 194.

43 Pradeau, *Plato and the City*, 142, emphasis added.

44 See, variously, Foucault, *The History of Sexuality*, 75–132 ("Le dispositif de sexualité"); Deleuze, "What Is a *Dispositif?*," 159–68; Agamben, "What Is an

Apparatus?," 1–24; Esposito, "The *Dispositif* of the Person," 17–30. "Play," it is worth mentioning, is a subtle but decisive element in Foucault's thinking on the question of the dispositif. Compare Foucault, *The History of Sexuality*, 81–91 (a subsection originally titled "Enjeu" but translated as "Objective"); Badiou, *The Adventure of French Philosophy*, 95. Badiou's use of the term, meanwhile, begins with the very first page of his very first book. See Badiou, *The Concept of Model*, 5. He continues to use the term in *Manifesto for Philosophy* as a name for the mode of philosophy (or, elsewhere, "thought") that is set up in and through Platonism; and, of course, he uses the term freely and consistently in his various assessments of his contemporaries. See Badiou, *Conditions*, 64, see also 171, 307. See also, on this point, Louise Burchell, "Translator's Preface," in Badiou, *Philosophy and Event*, x–xix.

45 Badiou, *Manifesto for Philosophy*, 122, 130–31, 144; Badiou, *Conditions*, 155; Strauss, *Argument and Action*, 137, cf. 87.

46 Deleuze, "What Is a *Dispositif?*," 160.

47 Foucault, *The Government of Self and Others*, 254. Compare Strauss, *The Argument and Action of Plato's Laws*, 105; Huizinga, *Homo Ludens*, 18–19, 27, 37, 159–60, 162, 211–12. See also Jouët-Pastré, *Le jeu et le sérieux dans les Lois de Platon*, 31–37. For Jacques Derrida, meanwhile, Plato merely plays at taking play seriously. See, on this point, Derrida, *Dissemination*, 156–58.

48 Plato, *Laws*, 643d. "Education" here of course is closer to "culture" understood as "formation," as in the German *Bildung* or the Latin *humanitas*. On the latter point, see Heidegger, "Letter on Humanism," 201.

49 Plato, *Laws*, 685a–b, 769a, 803d.

50 Plato, *Laws*, 803c.

51 And, by extension, Platonic political philosophy more generally. As Gilles Deleuze wrote in 1967, Platonic political philosophy acquires its very capacity to reflect upon law only through two forms of "play." "Humor and irony," Deleuze argues, "are the essential forms through which we apprehend the law. . . . Irony is the play [le jeu] of a thought that permits itself to found the law on an infinitely superior Good; humor, the play [le jeu] of that thought which permits itself to sanction the law with reference to an infinitely more just Best." See Deleuze, *Masochism*, 81–82, translation modified.

52 Plato, *Laws*, 811d.

53 Plato, *Laws*, 817b. On anagrams and the permutation of letters in Plato's works, see Derrida, *Dissemination*, 158–59.

54 On this read, in other words, book 4 of the *Laws* would extend and intensify the allegory of reading that governs the turn to the "city in speech" in book 2 of *The Republic* (368d–369a, 402b). It also should be noted that, in the reading we are developing here, Plato's apparatus of law comes into view only and precisely at the vanishing point between two declensions of the political that often are considered distinct: the theologico-political and the biopolitical. If it's the case, as Peter Sloterdijk asserts, that reflections on politics since Plato have always

implicitly unfolded as reflections on the best way to breed and care for flocks of human livestock, then even and especially the rule of Cronos—this divine despotism that, precisely through its withdrawal, provides the wise lawmaker with the model of the best regime—amounts to little more than a blueprint for the breeding and caretaking of man by man (or, in Sloterdijk's memorable phrase, for making "rules for the maintenance of the human zoo"). From this perspective, there is little to no difference between the theologico-politics of the *Laws* and its biopolitics: the best political regime has always already been best because it is also the best biopolitical regimen. See Sloterdijk, "*Rules for the Human Zoo*," 25, 27.

55 Deleuze, *Masochism*, 82.

56 On stasis, see Loraux, *The Divided City*; Agamben, *Stasis*. In contrast to Loraux (who thinks stasis with reference to the distinction between oikos and polis) and Agamben (who thinks stasis as a zone of indistinction between oikos and polis), this essay thinks stasis as the dynamic by which the oikos exceeds itself in the apoikia (see note 38 above).

57 Pradeau, *Plato and the City*, 159. Badiou's own concept of law is loyal to this conception. For Badiou, law is that which ensures the "count-for-one" of that which is presented in the situation. See Badiou, *Being and Event*, 52–53, 93–101.

58 In Badiou's lexicon, dianoetic thought is only the first "pincer of Truth." The second and more fundamental is the "operational void of Truth." Compare Badiou, *Being and Event*, 34; Badiou, *Manifesto for Philosophy*, 130. See also Badiou, *Briefings on Existence*, 87.

59 I explore this in more detail elsewhere. See Sitze, "*Nous* and *Nomos* in Plato's *Laws*," 36–70.

60 Plato, *Laws*, 702c2.

61 Plato, *Laws*, 736c5–737b10.

62 On zero, see Badiou, *Number and Numbers*, 8.

63 See, on this point, Loraux, *The Divided City*, 143–69.

64 Plato, *The Apology of Socrates*, 17c–d.

65 Badiou, "Le (re)tour de la philosophie *elle-même*," in *Conditions*, 72.

66 Badiou, *Conditions*, 167, 170–71. See also the definition of justice and communism ("what is nonlaw may function as law") in Badiou, *Theory of the Subject*, 159.

67 On nonrelation and philosophy, see Badiou and Žižek, *Philosophy in the Present*, 11, 14–15.

68 It should be underlined that Strauss's 1941 "Persecution and the Art of Writing" was not his first study of esoteric writing. This took place in his 1935 *Philosophie und Gesetz*, a study of medieval Jewish and Islamic philosophers that unfolded with close and special attention to Platonism.

69 See, on this point, Esposito, "Introduzione," xix.

70 Strauss, *Natural Right and History*, 91, cf. 121, 123; Strauss, "Jerusalem and Athens," in *Jewish Philosophy and the Crisis of Modernity*, 377–80, 396, 402–4; Strauss, "Progress or Return?," in *The Rebirth of Classical Political Rationalism*, 269–70.

71 On this concept, see Galli, *Political Spaces and Global War*.

72 The term *atopicité* derives from Luc Brisson and Jean-François Pradeau, who use it to characterize the mode of thought that allows the interlocutors in the *Laws* to set up their colony. See Brisson and Pradeau, *Les Lois de Platon*, 55.

73 Strauss, "Persecution and the Art of Writing," 24.

74 Badiou, *Manifesto for Philosophy*, 141.

75 Badiou, *Manifesto for Philosophy*, 143.

76 Badiou, *Manifesto for Philosophy*, 129, 134, 144.

77 Badiou, *Conditions*, 127, 158.

78 See, on this point, Norton, *Leo Strauss and the Politics of American Empire*, 201–20; Xenos, *Cloaked in Virtue*, 125–44.

79 Badiou, *Manifesto for Philosophy*, 134.

80 It should be noted, in fact, that even as Badiou names Plato's *Laws* as the text in which Plato succumbs to disaster, Badiou does not, and perhaps cannot, locate in Plato's *Laws* one of the conditions that he requires in order for a disaster to be a disaster, namely, the "ecstasy of place." The only ecstasy of place he names in Plato he finds not in the *Laws* but in the *Republic*, the "Myth of Er." See Badiou, *Manifesto for Philosophy*, 129; Badiou, *Conditions*, 157.

81 Klein, *Greek Mathematical Thought and the Origin of Algebra*, 90–98. It is worth noting that Heidegger's 1924–25 course at Marburg (published under the title *Plato's Sophist*) was, according to Strauss, attended by Klein "regularly," which may explain some of the points of correspondence between Klein's thinking on this point and Heidegger's (e.g., Heidegger, *Plato's Sophist*, 81). See Strauss, *Jewish Philosophy and the Crisis of Modernity*, 462, cf. 450, 458.

82 Badiou, *Briefings on Existence*, 39, 61, 125.

83 On sublation and/as iteration, see Badiou, *The Rational Kernel of the Hegelian Dialectic*, 53–57, esp. 55.

84 Badiou, *Conditions*, 156; Badiou and Žižek, *Philosophy in the Present*, 23–24.

85 Badiou, *Briefings on Existence*, 116–17, 159.

CHAPTER 7

The Royal Remains:

The People's Two Bodies and

the Endgames of Sovereignty

Eric L. Santner

I

In what is perhaps his most dreamlike prose text, "A Country Doctor," Franz Kafka describes in graphic detail the wound on the side of a young boy, the patient a district physician has been called to attend to in the middle of a snowy night:

> On his right side, near the hip, there is an open wound the size of a palmprint. Many shades of pink, dark in its depths and growing lighter at the edges, tender and grainy, with unevenly pooling blood, open at the surface like a mine. Thus from a distance. Close up, further complications are apparent. Who can look at that without giving a low whistle? Worms, as thick and as long as my little finger, rose-pink themselves and also blood-spattered, firmly attached to the inside of the wound, with little white heads, with many little legs, writhe up toward the light.[1]

The text is unusual for Kafka in its proximity to the sort of expressionist prose he was known to dislike, but it still very much bears the distinctive signature of the author. Here, as in so many other texts, the main character, the provincial doctor named in the title, is faced by a call he cannot fully respond to, a mandate or summons to work—call it a "charge" or "ex-citation" (from *excitare*, to call out or summon)—that turns out to be impossible to discharge. Kafka indicates in the text that there might be large, historical reasons for this impossibility, among them the preponderance of a false conception of medical knowledge and capacities in a secular world. The problem seems to be in part that in such a world spiritual needs now register largely as bodily, somatic disturbances: "Always asking the doctor to do the impossible. They have lost their old faith; the pastor sits at home, plucking his vestments into shreds, one after the other; but the doctor is supposed to accomplish everything with his tender, surgical hands."[2] Here a sacerdotal investiture crisis—the priest literally shreds his vestments—resonates as bodily symptom that induces, in its turn, an excess of demand with respect to the medical arts, one that generates its own investiture crisis: the doctor's inability to fulfill, to satisfy the normative pressures, of his office.[3] The immediate proximity of these remarks to the characterization of the boy as being "blinded by the *life in his wound*" (my emphasis) suggests that one can only begin to grasp the meaning of this palpitating life substance and the crisis it materializes against the background of this collapse of the spiritual into the corporeal, of transcendence into an immanence that can no longer be mastered by the available sciences of immanence.

As Slavoj Žižek has noted, just such a correlation of a surplus of flesh with a crisis of investiture had already been staged by Richard Wagner in his opera *Parsifal*. There Amfortas's inability to administer his office as Grail King—Titurel, the king's father, harasses his son with the admonishing question, "Mein Sohn Amfortas, bist du am Amt?"—takes on the carnal form of an endlessly bleeding wound afflicting the king.[4] Hans Jürgen Syberberg's great dramaturgical innovation in his film adaptation of the opera was to separate the wound from the king's body, to present it as an autonomous bit of surplus flesh unable to find its proper bodily container. To put it in the form of a wordplay that works only in German (and, perhaps, especially in Swiss German), we might say, *Was in der (Eid-)Genossenschaft genossen wird, geht darüber hinaus, was in einer Körperschaft verfasst werden kann*. It is, I would suggest, just such an excess of *jouissance* or *Geniessen* that keeps Kafka's characters in a kind of perpetual motion that in another short fragment he characterized as the uncannily animated or undead dimension of an oath or *Eid*, the mysterious validity of which survives the death of the figure that had previously embodied the *Verfasstheit*, the constitution and composure of the body politic: "They were given the choice to become kings or messengers. Just like children they all chose to be messengers. For this reason there are only messengers; they race through the world and, because there are no kings, they call out to one another proclamations that have become meaningless. They would happily put an end to their miserable life but because of their oath of office they don't dare."[5]

In this context, one will recall that the dream that Freud himself saw as the inaugural dream of psychoanalysis—the dream in which the paradoxical stuff or raw material of the symptom makes a dramatic appearance—is itself a kind of parable of a country doctor overwhelmed by the demands of his office. Much as in the case of Kafka's provincial physician, the famous dream of Irma's injection stages the insufficiency of the sciences of immanence— including, first and foremost, medicine—for the treatment of hysterical symptoms. It thus marks for Freud the very birth of psychoanalysis, its emergence, precisely, as the science that is called on the scene by the hysteric's body, one that manifests a strange excess of life that both belongs and does not belong to the body in question. At one point in this dream that for the most part circulates around Freud's concern that he might have missed some sort of purely physiological cause of Irma's suffering—and so that he himself failed to be a proper man of science, failed to satisfy the normative pressures of his office—Freud looks into his patient's mouth; what he encounters there places Irma in a kind of kinship relation with the boy in Kafka's story as well as with Wagner's Grail King: "She then opened her mouth properly and on the right I found a big white patch; at another place I saw extensive whitish grey scabs upon some remarkable curly structures which were evidently modeled on the turbinal bones of the nose."[6] In the dream Freud essentially places himself in an impossible situation, one in which he can only lose. If Irma is physically sick, then he has failed as a physician; if it is, rather, her hysterical symptoms that persist in spite of Freud's treatment, then he has failed as the inventor of a new science and therapy of psychopathology. The key to the dream will ultimately lie in Freud's discovery—indeed, we might call this the inaugural, self-reflexive finding of psychoanalysis—of the ways in which his own mind has gotten (dis)organized around the fantasy of being found, of being judged to be wanting in the face of the normative pressures of an office or symbolic mandate.

Some ten years later, Freud would encounter the case of yet another figure whose life came to be informed by the threat of being rendered formless, *informe*, under the pressures of a crisis of investiture precisely as a judge. I am referring, of course, to the case of Daniel Paul Schreber, whose psychotic breakdown was precipitated by his nomination as *Senatspräsident* of the Sachsen Supreme Court. Schreber seems to have experienced this crisis as the meltdown of his official, institutional identity into the rotting flesh of a strange new creature, a delusional metamorphosis that led to his eight-year-long institutionalization. Freud based his case study of Schreber on the latter's efforts to account for the meaning behind the madness of his metamorphosis in his now famous *Memoirs of My Nervous Illness*. Schreber felt himself called by divine forces to become a *Luder* and to cultivate a new sort of religious practice we might characterize as *Ludertum*. (In German, the word *Luder* can mean wretch, in the sense of a lost and pathetic creature, but can also signify a cunning swindler or scoundrel; a whore, tart, or slut; and finally, the dead, rotting flesh of an animal, especially in the sense of carrion used as bait in hunting. The French translation of Schreber's *Memoirs* renders this word as *Charogne*, which was also, of course, the title of one of Baudelaire's most famous poems from the *Fleurs du mal*.) Schreber's inability to fulfill the office of his secular *Beruf* engendered a remainder of flesh that formed the kernel of his messianic *Berufung* to restore order to a world in which a state of exception had become the norm, at least in his "own private Germany."[7]

To return to Freud's Irma dream: in his own rather apocalyptic commentary on this primal scene of psychoanalysis—and indeed, citing the dream visions and interpretations of the Book of Daniel—Jacques Lacan, who the following year would dedicate an entire seminar to Daniel Paul Schreber's metamorphosis into a Luder, writes the following:

> There's a horrendous discovery here, that of the flesh one never sees, the foundation of things, the other side of the head, of the face, the secretory glands *par excellence*, the flesh from which everything exudes, at the very heart of the mystery, the flesh in as much as it is suffering, is formless, in as much as its form in itself is something which provokes anxiety. Spectre of anxiety, identification of anxiety, the final revelation of *you are this*— *You are this, which is so far from you, this which is the ultimate formlessness*. Freud comes upon a revelation of the type, *Mene, Tekel, Peres* at the height of his need to see, to know, which was until then expressed in the dialogue of the *ego* with the object.[8]

Lacan returns to the prophetic writing on the wall when he comments on the conclusion of the Irma dream. First Freud: "Not long before, when she was feeling unwell, my friend Otto had given her an injection of a preparation of propyl, propyls . . . propionic acid . . . trimethylamin (and I saw before me the formula for this printed in heavy type). . . . Injections of that sort ought not to be made so thoughtlessly. . . . And probably the syringe had not been clean." Although this is perhaps going a bit too far, I do quite like the detail that the formula for trimethylamin is printed in "heavy type"—is, as Freud puts it, *fettgedruckt*—in which I can't help but hear a slight emphasis on *Fett* qua surplus of flesh. In his own interpretation of the dream, Freud himself notes that trimethylamin was a substance—curiously, in the dream he refers to it as a body or *Körper*, though not explicitly as a fat one—with a possible link to the chemistry of sexual processes: "Thus this substance [*dieser Körper*] led me to sexuality, the factor to which I attributed the greatest importance in the origin of the nervous disorders which it was my aim to cure."[9] But as we know, this would be a cure that would intervene into the peculiar chemistry of the libido not by way of injections but rather by way of speech (after having experimented with hypnotism and even the laying on of hands). The language of the religions of revelation—religions based on the word and its transmission, a transmission that necessarily exceeds comprehension, or to use the famous formulation that Gershom Scholem coined to characterize the nature of revelation in Kafka's universe: a transmission that remains valid in excess of a graspable meaning—all this allows Lacan to locate the symptom and its cure in the field of the signifier, in the discourse of the Other:

> The dream, which culminated a first time, when the *ego* was there, with the horrific image I mentioned, culminates a second time at the end with a formula, with its *Mene, Tekel, Upharsin* aspect, on the wall, beyond what we cannot but identify as speech, universal rumor. . . . Like my oracle, the formula gives no reply whatsoever to anything. But the very manner in which it is spelt out, its enigmatic, hermetic nature, is in fact the answer to the question of the meaning of the dream. One can model it closely on the Islamic formula—*There is no other God but God*. There is no other word, no other solution to your problem, than the word.[10]

The point Lacan is making here is that we are libidinal beings, that we desire in a human rather than animal sense, because our enjoyment is entwined with the signifier, with titles and entitlements, with the various offices with which we come to be invested in the world, offices we are, in turn, called to occupy—*zu besetzen*. The strange surplus flesh that Freud came to call the libido and that constitutes the stuff of our erotic investments in the world is born from the fact that our being is compelled to unfold within a matrix of signifying representations, a field never quite made to the measure of the animal that we also are. It is this very lack of measure, this lack of fit, that opens the wound correlative to our passions and that accounts for the peculiar stuff of which dreams—and nightmares—are made. What accounts for our capacities to experience sublimity and abjection—and the peculiar oscillation between the two extremes—is that we are always contending with a bit of surplus flesh that can never be fully figured out. Some part of the discourse of the Other into which we are inscribed is always, we might say, fettgedruckt.

3

I would like to propose that the urgency of the engagement with the dimension of the flesh that calls psychoanalysis into being, that converted Freud from being a man of medicine into what Merleau-Ponty characterized as the only true philosopher of the flesh, has a precise historical index and one located not so much in the history of the natural sciences but rather in the history of what Foucault referred to as *governmentality*. (Indeed, I propose that we hear this word as a complex wordplay: a shift in mentality, in the way embodied subjects are minded, must be correlated with a shift in the nature of governance and *Herrschaft*, of the elaboration of *potestas* and *auctoritas* in the space of political life.) My argument is, basically, that this visceral yet somehow virtual dimension of the flesh that begins to haunt everyday life in modernity needs to be grasped as what I refer to as the royal remains, the residues of the substance of the king's sublime body that has, in the age of popular sovereignty, entered into the life of the people without ever fully being able to find its proper locus or fully binding *Verfassung*.

It was precisely in response to the pressures generated by this new dispensation that Michel Foucault felt compelled to reject the classical concepts of political theory—above all that of sovereignty—in favor of a new ensemble of concepts and modes of inquiry that would be more responsive, more attuned to the locations and dynamics of political power and authority in modernity. As he put it in a very concise passage in *Discipline and Punish*: "The body of the king, with *its strange material and physical presence*, with the *force* that he himself deploys or transmits to some few others, is at the opposite extreme of *this new physics of power* . . . : a physics of a relational and multiple power, which has its maximum intensity *not in the person of the king, but in the bodies that can be individualized by these relations*."[11] To take the example of Daniel Paul Schreber, we can certainly say that his body was individualized, rendered into a case, indeed into a kind of paradigmatic case, by this new physics of power. I would, however, insist that insofar as the agents of the new physics of power—and here one should include not only Schreber's famous father but also his psychiatrists—imagined themselves to be addressing the care and discipline of living bodies and the biological life and health of populations rather than ministering to the strange materiality of the flesh in its now horizontally dispersed locations, they did not and could not fully grasp the nature of their tasks. Given the messianic place he saw himself as occupying, Schreber might have said about these agents of the new biopolitics: they know not what they do. But this is also true, I think, for the great theorist of biopolitics; Foucault himself did not fully grasp that his new theory of power was responding to the metamorphosis of what Ernst Kantorowicz had so richly elaborated as the political theology of the king's two bodies in medieval and early modern Europe, a metamorphosis that would compel the people to have to figure out what to do with the carnal dimension—with the flesh—of their sovereignty, with the stuff of a second, sublime body. The task was, we might say, to figure out how to figure these royal remains that now intruded so forcefully into the life of the people.

Against this background it makes sense that in the same seminar in which he comments on the inaugural dream of psychoanalysis, Lacan will have further recourse to the uncanny materiality of flesh and the crisis of its figuration. The context of these reflections is a commentary not on the Schreber case—that will come, as I have noted, the following year for Lacan—but rather on Edgar Allan Poe's story "The Facts in the Case of M. Valdemar." The first-person narrator tells of his recent preoccupation with mesmerism and his curiosity about the fact that no one had ever seemed to have investigated the boundary between life and death by means of this technique, that "no person had as yet been mesmerized *in articulo mortis*."[12] The narrator proposes to a terminally ill acquaintance, a certain M. Ernest Valdemar, to allow him to attempt the experiment with him. The prospects appeared good, for Valdemar had already shown himself to be susceptible to mesmerism. His advanced state of tubercular dissolution—it is referred to in the story as phthisis, meaning literally to waste away—furthermore made it possible to predict the time of his demise. When the time of death finally arrives, the narrator is called on the scene and brings Valdemar into a mesmeric trance that miraculously preserves a kind of animation beyond the point of death. The story reaches a climax at the moment when Valdemar answers the narrator's question whether he was asleep with the following words: "'Yes;—

no—I *have been* sleeping—and now—now—*I am dead*'" (281). The narrator's attempt to describe the voice uttering these words—he refers to the utterance as a distinct "syllabification"—is worth quoting at length:

> There was no longer the faintest sign of vitality in M. Valdemar; and concluding him to be dead, we were consigning him to the charge of the nurses, when a strong vibratory motion was observable in the tongue. This continued for perhaps a minute. At the expiration of this period, there issued from the distended and motionless jaws a voice—such as it would be madness in me to attempt describing. There are, indeed, two or three epithets which might be considered as applicable to it in part; I might say, for example, that the sound was harsh, and broken and hollow. But the hideous whole is indescribable, for the simple reason that no similar sounds have ever jarred upon the ear of humanity. There were two particulars, nevertheless, which I thought then, and still think, might fairly be stated as characteristic of the intonation—as well adapted to convey some idea of its unearthly peculiarity. In the first place, the voice seemed to reach our ears—at least mine—from a vast distance, or from some deep cavern within the earth. In the second place, it impressed me (I fear, indeed, that it will be impossible to make myself comprehended) as gelatinous or glutinous matters impress the sense of touch. (280–81)

The narrator then relates that Valdemar had remained in this state of what we might call mesmeric undeadness for a period of seven months. At that point he and the attending physicians decide that they will attempt to break the trance, to free Valdemar from his somatic purgatory, in a word, to awaken him to his own death. As for what follows, the narrator writes, "it is quite impossible that any human being could have been prepared": "As I rapidly made the mesmeric passes, amid ejaculations of 'dead! dead!' absolutely *bursting* from the tongue and not from the lips of the sufferer, his whole frame at once—within the space of a single minute, or even less, shrunk—crumbled—absolutely *rotted* away beneath my hands. Upon the bed, before that whole company, there lay a nearly liquid mass of loathsome—of detestable putridity" (283).

It is worth underlining that Lacan offers this commentary in conjunction with remarks on kingship and its demise, that he links the case of Valdemar to the decline of Oedipus Rex, that is, to *Oedipus at Colonus*, the tragedy of the *entsetzlich* dissolution of the once-great king who now finds himself reduced, as Lacan puts it, to "the scum of the earth, the refuse, the residue, a thing empty of any plausible appearance."[13] What we are faced with here is, I am arguing, not the body in its utter vulnerability, not the precarious biological life we share with the animal and vegetable kingdoms, but rather the enigmatic substance of sovereignty at the historical moment at which it is uncoupled from its primary locus, the body of the king, and, so to speak, takes on a life of its own within the life of the people. We might say that the capacity to be *eingesetzt* and to be *entsetzt* belongs to every body, distinguishes the *Leibhaftigkeit* of every citizen-subject.

4

The French Revolution is, of course, universally seen to mark the period of transition from kings to people as the bearer of the principle of sovereignty. It makes sense, then, to begin a discussion of the modern reorganization of the physiology of the body politic and its impact on the arts—and my focus now turns to the visual arts, in particular—with a discussion of one of the most famous paintings to emerge out of the crucible of that historical turning point, and indeed one that itself appears to be dedicated to this very project of a reconfiguration of the flesh in the wake of the king's—or better: the King's—demise. My guide in this discussion will be T. J. Clark, who himself begins his critical history of visual modernism with a seemingly exorbitant claim about the status of the painting in question, Jacques-Louis David's *Death of Marat*, in the history of modern art (I hope that it will become clear in the course of these reflections why and how this painting can serve as a kind of allegory for my project as a whole). In his *Farewell to an Idea: Episodes from a History of Modernism*, Clark writes the following: "My candidate for the beginning of modernism—which at least has the merit of being obviously far-fetched—is 25 Vendémiaire Year 2 (16 October 1793, as it came to be known). That was the day a hastily completed painting by Jacques-Louis David, of Marat, the martyred hero of the revolution—*Marat á son dernier soupir*, David called it early on—was released into the public realm."[14]

Rather than trying to rehearse the full complexity of Clark's stunning argument, I focus on what for me provides the real key to his claim about the singular status of the *Death of Marat* in his broadly conceived history of modernism. Concerning David's own uncertain grasp of the stakes of his painting and the staging of its initial viewing, Clark writes that David at the very least "knew that picturing Marat was a political matter, part of a process of making [the Revolution] a Jacobin property. . . . He believed that a new world was under construction. No doubt he saw in the cult of Marat the first forms of a liturgy and ritual in which the truths of the revolution itself would be made flesh—People, Nation, Virtue, Reason, Liberty" (29).[15] The problem, however, was that such conversions, still possible within the context of the political theology of kingship (and the forms of picture making it sponsored), did not and perhaps could not succeed under revolutionary and postrevolutionary conditions. "Marat could not be made to embody the revolution because no one agreed about what the revolution was, least of all about whether Marat was its Jesus or its Lucifer. David's picture—this is what makes it inaugural of modernism—tries to ingest this disagreement, and make it part of a new cult object" (38). But this answer too is insufficient. For it is not simply a matter of a provisional disagreement as to the meaning of events, but rather of an impasse affecting the possibility of converting events—and these events in particular—into representative images and bodies that would convincingly incarnate their truths. The problem is that the events in question put under pressure the entire apparatus of representation in all its complex and intersecting meanings. And it is this impasse that, as Clark puts it, forms the gate through which contingency comes to invade painting.

What, as Clark puts it, "changed the circumstances of picturing for good" (46) was, precisely, the entrance of the people onto the stage of power formerly occupied by the monarch: "That is to say, [the revolution] tried to put one kind of sovereign body in place of another. And the body had somehow to be represented without its either congealing into a new monarch or splitting into an array of vital functions, with only instrumental reason to bind them together" (47). Contingency, Clark concludes, "is just a way of describing the fact that putting the People in place of the King cannot ultimately be done. The forms of the social outrun their various incarnations" (47). This means that there is a great deal more at stake here than a provisional disagreement as to the meaning of events. It is rather a question of a fundamental impasse affecting the concept and procedures of representation. The task was to put forth a body that would, as it were, incarnate the now empty place of the king, the figure that had traditionally been charged with corporeally representing the subject for all other subjects of the realm. The task would be, in a word, to incarnate in some ostensibly new way the excarnated principle of sovereignty: "Marat . . . had to be made to stand for the People. By now the enormity of the task should be clear: not just that Marat was such a disputed object, pulled to and fro by the play of factions (though this indeed is part of the problem), but that at a deeper level any body was inadequate to what had now to be done. Or any technique of representation. That representation was henceforth a technique was exactly the truth that had not to be recognized" (47).

The real tour de force of Clark's reading of the *Death of Marat* consists in his account of the ways in which David's painting ends up succeeding at bringing this fundamental impasse to a commanding painterly presence, one that evokes, precisely, what I have characterized as the spectral yet visceral dimension of the flesh no longer figured and contained by means of the royal physiology—by the king's two bodies. For Clark, the locus of the flesh is not exactly where we might assume it to be, that is, in Marat's wounded body, but rather in the large, empty upper half of David's canvas or, at the very least, where the one seems to extend or metamorphose into the other. As Clark puts it, David's treatment of the body "seems to make Marat much the same substance—*the same abstract material*—as the empty space above him. The wound is as abstract as the flesh" (36, emphasis added). The flesh that can no longer be figured in the body of the king becomes, in a word, the abstract material out of which the painting is largely made. The empty upper half of the painting stands in for a missing and, indeed, impossible representation of the people: "It embodies the concept's absence, so to speak. It happens upon representation as technique. It sets its seal on Marat's unsuitability for the work of incarnation" (47). The scumbled surface forming the upper half of the painting thus no longer functions as a simple absence but rather as a positive, even oppressive presence, "something abstract and unmotivated, which occupies a different conceptual space from the bodies below it. This produces, I think, a kind of representational deadlock, which is the true source of the *Marat*'s continuing hold on us" (48). This is, Clark continues, the "endless, meaningless objectivity produced by paint not quite finding its object, symbolic or otherwise, and therefore making do with its own procedures" (48).

Clark goes on to link this apparent failure to a kind of shame that will forever haunt modernism; we might even say that the abstract material out of which the upper half of the painting is made is just the ectoplasmic substance of this haunting: "In a sense . . . I too am saying that the upper half is a display of technique. But display is too neutral a word: for the point I am making, ultimately, is that technique in modernism is a kind of shame: something that asserts itself as the truth of picturing, but always against picturing's best and most desperate efforts" (48). In David, this shame emerges precisely at the point and in the space where "'People' ought to appear, as a kind of aura or halo" (48). What appears at the missing place of the new sovereign body is rather a kind of dream work made painterly flesh in the pure activity of painting; the empty upper half of the image forms not so much a vacancy as the site of an excess of pressure, a signifying stress that opens onto a vision of painting as pure drive: "And yet the single most extraordinary feature of the picture . . . is its whole upper half being empty. Or rather (here is what is unprecedented), not being empty, exactly, not being a satisfactory representation of nothing or nothing much—of an absence in which whatever the subject is has become present—but something more like a representation of painting, of painting as pure activity. Painting as material, therefore. Aimless. In the end detached from any one representational task. Bodily. Generating (monotonous) orders out of itself, or maybe out of ingrained habit. A kind of automatic writing" (45). My own sense is that the shame at issue here pertains not simply or even foremost to painting's failure to reach its object, to what Clark here characterizes as a distinctively modernist stuckness in technique, artifice, mediation, self-reflexivity, and so on—a shame, ultimately, of painting's nominalism, its moving within a frictionless universe untethered from lived life and the things that make it matter; it pertains, rather, to an almost defiling contact with the flesh that one had torn free from the king's sublime physiology and claimed for the people. Among other things, David's painting shows us just how difficult it would be to redeem, to make good on this claim. To put it in the form of a paradox, we might also say that the history of European art from this point on will in some sense be dedicated to the task of figuring out abstraction, this eventful opening onto the nonfigurative understood as the abstract materiality of once representative figures and bodies. Put somewhat differently, the normative pressures proper to painting—the pressures pushing toward what would be recognizable as excellence in painting—was mutating in response to a radical transformation of the political and social form of the normative pressures informing lives more generally.

5

In this context, I'd like to recall the two moments of extreme intensity achieved in Freud's famous dream of Irma's injection, both of which Lacan characterized as a kind of prophetic (and perhaps, in some sense, automatic) writing on the wall. The first was reached in the image of the inflamed tissues of Irma's throat, the second in the letters of a formula that Freud sees in the dream, one he associates with the chemistry of human sexuality. These two elements are, in a way, also present in David's painting: the first in the form of Marat's wounds (and sickly, puffy skin more generally), the second in the pieces of paper filled with writing that stand in a kind of visual symmetry with respect to Marat's martyred, Christlike body. Clark, for his part, places considerable emphasis on these bits of writing, seeing them as more than a means for the idealization of Marat as exemplary friend of the people. For Clark, these bits of writing are the place where, to use a Lacanian locution, the signifier falls into the pictorial space whose meanings it is meant to authorize and becomes an object among other objects, one that juts forward beyond the picture plane and toward the spectator with a peculiar insistence. Rather than sealing the meaning of the image, these discursive bits function instead as a thing-like surplus of script that, as it were, objects to any claim as to the legibility of the historical situation. Apropos of the words just out of sight in Marat's letter and presumed to be "de la patrie," Clark asks, "But is there a final phrase at all? Of course there looks to be something; but it is so scrappy and vestigial, an extra few words where there really is no room left for anything, that the reader continually double-takes, as if reluctant to accept that writing, of all things, can decline to this state of utter visual elusiveness. Surely if I look again—and look hard enough—the truth will out. For spatially, this is the picture's starting point. *It is closeness incarnate*" (40, emphasis added). Clark adds that these bits of painted writing "become the figure of the picture's whole imagining of the world and the new shape it is taking. . . . The boundaries between the discursive and the visual are giving way, under some pressure the painter cannot quite put his finger on, though he gets close" (42).[16] (We should recall here, once again, that the bit of writing in Freud's Irma dream was fettgedruckt, thereby linking it to what Freud first spotted in Irma's throat as a stain of inflamed flesh that has no business being there.)

But as Clark has so persuasively argued, it is in the swirling, vertiginous void that fills the picture's upper half that this pressure finds its proper place—its nonresting place—in the visual field. The spectral materiality of the flesh that forms at the impossible jointure of body and letter, soma and signifier, enjoyment and entitlement—a dimension that can neither be fully imagined nor, finally, be spelled out in a formula—finds its inaugural modern figuration in that dense, agitated, painterly writing on the wall. Clark is right, then, to see in the painting the opening onto a new aesthetic dimension and one that has a very precise historical index. What makes modernism is that its basic materials are compelled to engage with and, as it were, model the dimension of the flesh that is exacerbated to an unbearable degree by the representational deadlock situated at the transition from royal to popular sovereignty. What, in historical experience, can no longer be elevated, sublimated, by way of codified practices of picture making to the dignity of moral allegory, introduced into a realm of institutionally—and, ultimately, transcendentally—authorized meanings, now achieves its sublimity in a purely immanent fashion, that is, in the various ways in which the vicissitudes of this abstract yet inflamed materiality itself becomes the subject matter of the arts.

I would like to emphasize here the difference between the flesh qua partial object, on the one hand, and parts of the body functioning (or not functioning) in harmony within a discrete organism, on the other. To put it in rather oversimplified art historical terms, what Clark describes apropos of the *Death of Marat* demonstrates that the dissolution of the image of Leviathan that forms the famous frontispiece of Hobbes's book on sovereignty—and of the form of sovereignty represented by that image—does not simply yield a multitude, a swarming, unruly mass of body parts (in this case, individuals) adrift and uncoupled from any form or organization. The mass that is unleashed by way of the excarnation of the sovereign, the dissolution of his sublime body, is one that now, so to speak, metastasizes within each individual, one that can indeed crowd out the self from within. To put it another way, what Freud discovered was that individual psychology and the theory of the libido are always, at a profound level, a theory of masses in the multiple meanings of that word.

6

The editors of a volume of essays on the "republican body" have put the problem I have been elaborating here quite succinctly: "With democracy the concept of the nation replaced the monarch and sovereignty was dispersed from the king's body to all bodies. *Suddenly every body bore political weight. . . .* With the old sartorial and behavioral codes gone, bodies were less legible, and a person's place in the nation was unclear."[17] My own argument has, of course, been less about the transformation of social codes than about the agitations of the flesh brought about by this shift, the nature of the matter that accounts for the new political weight of every citizen. I have argued that biopolitics, psychoanalysis, and a variety of modern and modernist aesthetic practices have all struggled with this dimension, with the materiality of this uncanny mass or matter each in different fashion, each with its own degree of comprehension and incomprehension as to the issue at issue in what now issues forth from the bodies of its creaturely citizens.

The ambiguity and ambivalence that attaches to this issue is, perhaps, best captured by the German word that Freud favored when he spoke of the excitations or stimuli that circulate in the social and psychic spheres: *Reiz*. One thinks, for example, of Freud's notion of the *Reizschütz* that, in his view, functions as a kind of callus on the ego-skin and that protects the mind from becoming overwhelmed by stimulus, by *Reizüberflutung*. The danger, we might say, is that the spaces of modern life have become too *reizvoll*, too full of something that threatens psychic life with an overproximity that turns what is charming into the stuff of anxiety and repulsion. And in his *Three Essays on the Theory of Sexuality*, Freud characterizes the drive as "the psychical representation of an endosomatic, continuously flowing source of stimulation, as contrasted with a 'stimulus,' which is set up by *single* excitations coming from *without*."[18] In my reading, one would have to replace the term *innersomatisch* or "endosomatic" with a formulation that would capture the fact that the soma at issue is at some level extraindividual, that the excitations at issue belong to the larger normative framework of the bodies that come to matter within them. So the next time someone characterizes you or something you have achieved as reizvoll, you now know that this is not entirely a compliment: it might ultimately mean that your flesh is showing or, perhaps better, some bit of flesh is showing on and through you as something that sticks out, that doesn't quite fit into or fully belong to your body no matter how much you might try to get it to fit or into shape.

Epilogue

Because the project from which these remarks have been taken was at some level really an attempt to lay the groundwork for a reading of Rainier Maria Rilke's great novel *The Notebooks of Malte Laurids Brigge* (the last quarter of the book is an extended reading of the novel), I'd like to end my essay by, as it were, giving Rilke the last word.

Rilke's novel—one of the first great urban novels in German—tells the story of a now-impoverished twenty-eight-year-old Danish aristocrat who is struggling to become a writer; he does so in large part by exposing himself to the Reizüberflutung of the streets of Paris. What can't fail to strike the reader of this novel, which is composed of seventy-one discrete notebook entries of varying length and complexity, is the proliferation of passages describing bodies that seem unable to contain their insides, somatic pressures and protuberances that push against the boundaries of veins, organs, and skin, internal masses that expand and crowd out the self from within just as the urban masses crowd in upon Rilke's protagonist from without. The bodies at issue in these passages—and *die Masse* that issues forth from them—are taken from various thematic complexes in the novel: bodies encountered on the streets of Paris; bodies recalled from Malte's childhood in various Danish manor houses or *Herrenhäusern* (including his own body); bodies recalled from literature and history, among them those of a series of late medieval and early modern sovereigns. When asked by his Polish translator about the links between some of these thematic complexes, especially those between these suffering sovereigns, Malte's childhood memories, and his contemporary experiences in Paris, Rilke responded that in the novel, "there can be no question of specifying and detaching [*zu präzisieren und zu verselbstständigen*] the manifold evocations. The reader should not be in communication with their historical or imaginary reality, but through them with Malte's experience: who is himself involved with them only as, on the street, one might let a passer-by, might let a neighbor, say, impress one. The connection," Rilke continues, "lies in the circumstance that the particular characters conjured up *register the same vibration-rate of vital intensity* [*Schwingungszahl der Lebensintensität*] *that vibrates in Malte's own nature.*"[19]

Among these evocations one finds, for example, the description of the tormented body of King Charles VI of France who suffered some forty bouts of madness; the state of this royal flesh recalls Kafka's description of the wound on the side of the young patient in "The Country Doctor":

It was in those days when strangers with blackened faces would from time to time attack him in his bed in order to tear from him the shirt which had rotted into his ulcers, and which for a long time now he had considered part of himself. It was dark in the room, and they ripped off the foul rags from under his rigid arms. One of them brought a light, and only then did they discover the purulent sore on his chest where the iron amulet had sunk in, because every night he pressed it to him with all the strength of his ardor; now it lay deep in his flesh, horribly precious, in a pearly border of pus, like some miracle-working bone in the hollow of a reliquary. Hardened men had been chosen for the job, but they weren't immune from nausea when the worms, disturbed, stood up and reached toward them from the Flemish fustian and, falling out of the folds, began to creep up their sleeves.[20]

It is crucial that Malte introduces the figure of the mad king while considering his own descent—his own deposition or *Ent-Setzen*—to the place of *die Fortgeworfenen*, the figures he encounters on the streets of Paris whose only distinction is to lack every distinction or status, whose only entitlement is that of enjoying their bare life, a life often described with reference to their excessive and agitated flesh. The *Lebensintensität* that is vibrating along the same frequencies in the suffering sovereigns evoked in the novel, in Malte's own body, and in those of the outcasts of Paris, is one located not in the biological body but rather in the virtual yet uncannily carnal dimension of sovereignty, in the flesh that has migrated from the body of the king into the life of the people and whose sublimity or greatness—whose *Grösse*—now pushes against the skin of every citizen. It thus makes sense that at the very moment that Malte seeks a cure for the pressures—the internal and external Reizüberflutung that is beginning to drive him mad—among the psychiatrists of the Salpêtrière, he is forced to recall an earlier encounter with this dimension, one that clearly surpasses the capacities of the country doctor from his childhood, one in which the figure of the sovereign master or Herr was already caught up in a kind of chronic state of exception or perhaps better, Entsetzen:

> And then, as I listened to the warm, flaccid babbling on the other side of the door: then, for the first time in many, many years, it was there again. What had filled me with my first, deep horror, when I was a child and lay in bed with fever: the Big Thing. That's what I had always called it, when they all stood around my bed and felt my pulse and asked me what had frightened me: the Big Thing. And when they sent for the doctor and he came and tried to comfort me, I would just beg him to make the Big Thing go away. . . . But he was like all the others. He couldn't take it away, though I was so small then and it would have been so easy to help me. And now it was there again. (61)

Malte goes on to describe in detail the return of this somatic sublime dimension of embodiment:

> Now it was there. Now it was growing out of me like a tumor, like a second head, and was a part of me, although it certainly couldn't belong

to me, because it was so big. It was there like a large dead animal which, while it was alive, used to be my hand or my arm. And my blood flowed through me and through it, as through one and the same body. And my heart had to beat harder to pump blood into the Big Thing: there was barely enough blood. And the blood entered the Big Thing unwillingly and came back sick and tainted. But the Big Thing swelled and grew over my face like a warm bluish boil, and grew over my mouth, and already my last eye was hidden by its shadow. (61–62)

The question with which Rilke leaves us is whether we are up to the challenges posed by this dimension, *diese neue Grösse*, that presents a surplus of immanence that cannot be mastered by the available sciences of immanence, a surplus that seems to call less for new and better science or medicine than for new concepts of politics, community, citizenship, and subjectivity.

Notes

This chapter brings together various parts of my book *The Royal Remains: The People's Two Bodies and the Endgames of Sovereignty* (Chicago: University of Chicago Press, 2011).

1 Kafka, "A Country Doctor."
2 Kafka, "A Country Doctor."
3 This exposure to an excess of demand is figured at the end of the story as the doctor's nakedness and sense of irremediable loss, betrayal, and errancy: "Naked, exposed to the frost of this unhappiest of ages, with an earthly carriage, unearthly horses. I, an old man, wander aimlessly around. My fur coat is hanging at the back of the carriage, but I cannot reach it, and not one of this agile rabble of patients lifts a finger. Betrayed! Betrayed! A false ringing of the night bell once answered—it can never be made good again" (Kafka, "A Country Doctor," 65).
4 See Žižek, *The Sublime Object of Ideology*.
5 Kafka, *Beim Bau der chinesischen Mauer*, 235–36.
6 Freud, *The Interpretation of Dreams*, 139–40.
7 I am referring to my study of the case, Santner, *My Own Private Germany*.
8 Lacan, *The Ego in Freud's Theory and in the Technique of Psychoanalysis*, 154–55. The reference to the Book of Daniel is relevant not only because it is itself a book of dreams, prophetic signs, and interpretations, but also because it links such matters to the fate of kings and questions of sovereignty. Before giving King Belshazzar his interpretation of the enigmatic writing on the wall, Daniel—the name means *God is my judge*—recalls the fate of Nebuchadnezzar in terms that prefigure Shakespeare's series of "sad stories of kings," perhaps most centrally,

that of King Lear: "But when his heart was lifted up and his spirit was hardened so that he dealt proudly, he was deposed from his kingly throne, and his glory was taken from him; he was driven from among men, and his mind was made like that of a beast, and his dwelling was with the wild asses; he was fed grass like an ox, and his body was wet with the dew of heaven until he knew that the Most High God rules the kingdom of men, and sets over it whomever he will" (Daniel 5:20–21). Daniel then provides his prophetic interpretation of the enigmatic signifiers that had appeared to Belshazzar: "This is the interpretation of the matter: MENE, God has numbered the days of your kingdom and brought it to an end; TEKEL, you have been weighed in the balances and found wanting; PERES, your kingdom is divided and given to the Medes and Persians" (Daniel 5:26–28).

9 Freud, *The Interpretation of Dreams*, 140.

10 Lacan, *The Ego in Freud's Theory*, 158.

11 Foucault, *Discipline and Punish*, 208, emphasis added.

12 Poe, "The Facts in the Case of M. Valdemar." Subsequent references appear in the text.

13 Lacan, *The Ego in Freud's Theory*, 232.

14 Clark, *Farewell to an Idea*, 15. Subsequent references appear in the text.

15 In an earlier formulation, Clark refers to this process as that of making Marat a *totem* (26). Here one should no doubt recall Freud's hypothesis of the emergence of totemism out of the murder of the primal father and the incorporation of his powers by way of the ritual repetition of the totem meal—the symbolic enjoyment of his sublime flesh.

16 The *assignat* visible in the image adds an additional twist to the "signifying stress" elaborated by Clark. It introduces the problem of the "backing" of paper money—by gold, land, some piece of the real—at this crucial historical juncture (see 48–50), the capacity, that is, of paper currency to float free of value.

17 Melzer and Norberg, *From the Royal to the Republican Body*, 10–11, emphasis added.

18 Freud, *Three Essays on the Theory of Sexuality*, 168.

19 Letter of November 10, 1925, in Rilke, *Letters*, 371, emphasis added.

20 Rilke, *The Notebooks of Malte Laurids Brigge*, 215. Subsequent references appear in the text.

CHAPTER 8

Arendt:

Thinking Cohabitation and

the Dispersion of Sovereignty

Judith Butler

I would like to consider Hannah Arendt's reflection on thinking and responsibility, but I want to suggest that one place to start is not her essays on these topics—although I refer to them later—but her controversial publication in 1963 of *Eichmann in Jerusalem*, originally a series that she wrote for the *New Yorker* magazine. Although an accomplished philosopher, she decided to go to Jerusalem to report on the trial of the recently captured Adolph Eichmann, who was responsible for formulating and implementing the final solution in Nazi Germany. So Arendt is writing as a reporter, one who interviewed several people involved with the trial. Her report was controversial since she was not pleased with the proceedings of the Israeli court, calling it a public spectacle rather than the exercise of the rule of law. At the same time, in this text, Arendt begins to formulate many of the most important philosophical questions that preoccupied her in the subsequent years: what is thinking, what is judgment, and even what is action? But even more fundamentally, perhaps, who am I, and who are we?

Although Arendt agreed with the final verdict of the trial, namely, that Eichmann should be condemned to death for his crimes, she quarreled with the reasoning put forward at the trial. She thought the trial needed to focus on the acts that he committed, acts that included the making of a genocidal policy. She did not think that the history of anti-Semitism or even the specificity of anti-Semitism in Germany could be tried. She objected to Eichmann's treatment as a scapegoat; she criticized some of the ways that Israel used the trial to establish and legitimate its own legal authority and national aspirations. She thought the trials failed to understand the man and his deeds. The man was either made to stand for all of Nazism and for every Nazi, or he was considered the ultimately pathological individual. It seemed not to matter to the prosecutors that these two interpretations were basically in conflict. She thought that the trial necessitated a critique of the idea of collective guilt, but also a broader reflection on the historically specific challenges of moral responsibility under dictatorship. Indeed, that for which she faulted Eichmann was his failure to be critical of positive law, that is, a failure to take distance from the requirements that Nazi law and policy imposed upon him; in other words, she faults him for his obedience, his lack of critical distance, or his failure to think. But more than this, she faults him for failing to realize that thinking implicates the subject in a sociality or plurality that cannot be divided or destroyed through genocidal aims. In her view, no thinking being can plot or commit genocide. Of course, they can have such thoughts, and formulate and implement genocidal policy, as Eichmann clearly did, but such calculations cannot rightly be called thinking, in her view. How, we might ask, does thinking implicate each thinking *I* as part of a *we* such that to destroy some part of the plurality of human life is to destroy not only one's self, understood as linked essentially to that plurality, but to destroy the very conditions of thinking itself? Many questions abound: is thinking to be understood as a psychological process or, indeed, something that can be properly described, or is thinking in Arendt's sense always an exercise of judgment of some kind, and so implicated in a normative practice? If the *I* who thinks is part of a *we* and if the *I* who thinks is committed to sustaining that *we*, how do we understand the relation between *I* and *we* and what specific implications does thinking imply for the norms that govern politics and, especially, the critical relation to positive law?

It is a book of uneven tone, and sometimes she seems to break out into quarrel with the man himself. For the most part, she reports on the trial and the man in the third person, but there are moments in which she addresses him directly, or engages in irate free indirect discourse. One such moment occurred when Eichmann claimed that in implementing the final solution, he was acting from obedience, and that he had derived this particular moral precept from his reading of Kant.

We can imagine how doubly scandalous such a moment was for Arendt. It was surely bad enough that he formulated and executed orders for the final solution, but to say, as he did, that his whole life was lived according to Kantian precepts, including his obedience to Nazi authority, was too much. He invoked duty in an effort to explain his own version of Kantianism. Arendt writes, "This was outrageous, on the face of it, and also incomprehensible, since Kant's moral philosophy is so closely bound up with man's faculty of judgment, which rules out blind obedience."[1] Eichmann contradicts himself as he explains his Kantian commitments. On the one hand, he clarifies, "I meant by my remark about Kant that the principle of my will must always be such that it can become the principle of general laws" (121). And yet he also acknowledges that once he was charged with the task of carrying out the final solution, he ceased to live by Kantian principles. Arendt relays his self-description: "He no longer 'was master of his own deeds,' and . . . he 'was unable to change anything'" (136). When in the midst of his muddled explanation, Eichmann reformulates the categorical imperative such that one ought to act in such a way that the Führer would approve, or would himself so act, Arendt offers a swift rejoinder, as if she were delivering a direct vocal challenge to him: "Kant, to be sure, had never intended to say anything of the sort; on the contrary, to him every man was a legislator the moment he started to act; by using his 'practical reason' man found the principles that could and should be the principles of law" (121).

Arendt made this distinction between practical reason and obedience in *Eichmann in Jerusalem* in 1963 and seven years later she began her influential set of lectures on Kant's political philosophy at the New School for Social Research in New York City. In a way, we can understand much of Arendt's later work, including her work on willing, judgment, and responsibility, as an extended debate with Eichmann on the proper reading of Kant, an avid effort to reclaim Kant from his Nazi interpretation and to mobilize the resources of his text precisely against the conceptions of obedience that uncritically supported a criminal legal code and fascist regime.

In the end, she has three main complaints against the decision: "the problem of impaired justice in the court of the victors; a valid definition of a crime against humanity; and a clear recognition of the new criminal who commits this crime" (274). I'd like to suggest that it is interesting, maybe even odd, that Arendt thinks that the court failed to understand the person, the criminal, since she is everywhere reminding us that deeds are criminals, not persons, and not peoples. But this last becomes important when she considers the legal convention that the doer of the misdeed must have a clear intention to conduct the misdeed. Can it be said that Eichmann had intentions? If he had no conception of a misdeed, can he be said to have intentionally committed one? It seems one cannot seek recourse to his intention or, indeed, to any psychological feature of this person, not only because the intentional fallacy is right, but because now there are persons who implement mass death without explicit intentions. In other words, it is now possible that some persons have become, historically, instruments of implementation and that they have lost the capacity for what she calls thinking. In a way, the problem is for her both historical and philosophical: how did it come to be that persons are now formed in such a way that thinking, understood as the normative exercise of judgment, is no longer possible for or by them? She rejects the psychological explanation: he is neither perverted nor sadistic, in her view, but simply acted according to a brutal law that had become normal and normalized. What was his crime, finally, according to Arendt? He failed to think; he failed to judge; indeed, he failed to make use of practical reason in the precise sense that Kant described and prescribed. In effect, Eichmann failed to be Kantian, even as he claimed he was.

Toward the end of this highly charged text, there is a curious set of passages in which Arendt addresses Eichmann in the second person and gives voice to a final verdict that the judges in Jerusalem would have done, had they agreed to make visible or manifest "the justice done in Jerusalem." She writes, "You . . . said your role in the Final Solution was an accident and that almost anybody could have taken your place, so that potentially almost all Germans are equally guilty. What you meant to say was that where all, or almost all, are guilty, nobody is." Then she makes her rejoinder, making use of the plural *we* to wage the counterargument: "This is indeed a common conclusion, but one we are not willing to grant you." Later, she adds, "Even if eighty million Germans had done as you did, this would not have been an excuse for you" (255).

She begins the paragraph right before the voicing of the verdict by making the point that where it is not possible to establish intentions, it still must be possible to understand that a crime has been done. She refuses the option of vengeance, maintaining, "We refuse, and consider as barbaric, the propositions 'that a great crime offends nature, so that the very earth cries out for vengeance; that evil violates a natural harmony which only retribution can restore; that a wronged collectivity owes a duty to the moral order to punish the criminal'" (254).[2]

What seems clear, then, is that when the established conventions regarding intention cannot be used, and when vengeance is barbaric and inadmissible, on what grounds does one then sentence Eichmann? One expects perhaps that the verdict that she herself will voice will be the one she would have liked to see, but that conclusion is not unequivocally supported by what comes next. She makes the claim that "these long forgotten propositions" that belong to vengeance, retribution, and natural moral orders were, in fact, both the reason he was brought to trial and the "supreme justification for the death penalty." It would seem that these are precisely the justifications she rejects, although she adds "and yet" these were the reasons, and then adds her own sentence: "Because he had been implicated and had played a central role in an enterprise whose open purpose was to eliminate certain 'races' from the surface of the earth, he had to be eliminated" (277). She then continues, citing the age-old jurisprudential maxim that "justice must not only be done, but must be seen to be done," faults the Jerusalem courts for failing to make apparent (and to bring into the domain of appearance) the justice of their actions. At this point, it seems clear that she thought their actions, including the meting out of the death penalty, were just, but that they had failed to give good public reasons for that conclusion. Right before launching into her own voicing of the verdict, she writes that the "justice" of their actions "would have emerged to be seen by all if the judges had dared to address their defendant in something like the following terms" (254). The direct address that follows is obviously one intended as courageous, compensating for the nondaring of the Jerusalem judges. But is she actually disagreeing with them? Or is she supplying a rationale that they should have used? It is difficult to understand, since she could simply be presenting their rationale in a more courageous way and disagreeing with that rationale (after all, it is the long-forgotten propositions of vengeance that led them, in her view, to their final verdict). But this voicing may be a way to participate in that final judgment and to accept the contemporary form that such long-forgotten propositions now take. It would be odd, if not impossible, for Arendt to champion barbarism, and she has explicitly rejected it. And yet if she is voicing what the judges should have said, and referring also to the justice of their decision, perhaps she is also simply making apparent a rationale with which she disagrees. What seems more likely is that she starts off trying to reenact what they did mean only to begin voicing what they should have meant. She does end this direct address with "you must hang"—an archaic formulation of the death penalty, to be sure, and one that some might consider barbaric indeed. So let us follow this passage and see what can possibly be meant by this outbreak into direct address when Arendt sentences Eichmann to death again.

She makes her final judgment: "There still remains the fact that you have carried out, and therefore actively supported, a policy of mass murder" (279). Eichmann's final crime, though, the one for which he must hang, has to do with the fact that he, addressed as "you and your superiors," took as their own right the decision with whom to share the earth. He thought, and he represented those who thought, that they could determine that they did not need to "share the earth" with the Jewish people, and insofar as they decided that they did not need to share the earth with any specific population, no one, no member of the human race, as she puts it, "[could] be expected to share the earth with you." And it was for this crime, the crime of not sharing, that she concludes, "This is the reason, and the only reason, you must hang" (279).

A voice is conjectured by Arendt that is not her own (and so partially disowned), but so also are there identifiable features of her own voice, and that doubling is there for us to see. So where is Arendt in this voice? Does the voice still carry something of Arendt's view, or is this a voicing of the view with which she disagrees? Is she giving voice to the rationale she opposes, or has she begun, perhaps in spite of herself, to elaborate the rationale she supports? It is surely consistent with her view to claim that nothing more than misfortune made him into a criminal. The reference to him as a "willing instrument in the organization of mass murder" is one way of claiming, as Arendt has, that obedience to the law is tantamount to a support of the genocidal aim of the Nazi law, and this establishes his guilt. Although the conjectured voice explains why people want him dead, Arendt has made a less emotive argument elsewhere: genocide is unacceptable because it constitutes an attack on the plurality of humanity itself. Perhaps giving voice to what the more courageous judges would have said is actually giving voice to what a more emotional Hannah Arendt would have loved to say.

The voice actually interrupts itself at one point, suggesting that both views emanate from this voiced figure of the judge. The language of wanting seems to decide the penultimate line. In the final accusation the conjectured judge underscores Eichmann's wanting not to share the earth "with the Jewish people and the people of a number of other nations," and concludes that the members of the human race do not want to share the earth with him. But then a certain principle emerges within dashes, suggesting that the decision is based not on desire alone, but a principle, even a norm, that ought to be invoked in order to decide cases of genocide: "—as though you and your superiors had any right to determine who should and should not inhabit the world—" (255–56).

The philosophical and political point of her voiced rejoinder to Eichmann (and to the judges) is that one must make clear that there is no right to choose with whom to cohabit the earth or world. Cohabitation with others we never choose is, in effect, an abiding characteristic of the human condition. To exercise a right to decide with whom to cohabit on this earth is to engage a genocidal policy, and it is on the basis of this implementation of genocide that the death penalty is apparently justified. We do not receive in these pages a justification for why that penalty is appropriate rather than some others, although we do know that the appropriateness of the death penalty was debated at the time. Perhaps we are being asked to remember that murder is not the same as genocide, and that the death penalty is not the same as murder. If that is the case, and if Arendt had fully displayed the principles of her reasoning, it may be that implicitly at work in the decision to sentence Eichmann to death is a moral typology of modes of death dealing that would justify the death penalty (state-induced killing under certain legal conditions) and would reject any death dealing that is genocidal.[3] But this justification we do not receive. It is implicit, if it is anywhere, and the voice that makes visible the version of justice that took place in Jerusalem seems to lag at this very moment.

Interestingly, this conjectured voice of the judge speaks in the *we*. Since she is the one who apparently knows what the judges should have said, she speaks in her own voice; and yet, in speaking as a plural subject, a *we*, she also seems to disappear as a singular author. Can we finally separate these two strands, or are they in some ways implicated in one another, suggesting that judgment is not simply an individual act, but an implicit or explicit recognition of plurality itself?

One might reasonably expect the judge to be a figure of sovereignty, and though Arendt clearly enacts the sovereign voice, she does so only against a background of an irreducible vacillation: is she an *I* or is she a *we*? Indeed, this vacillation seems to function as a condition of judgment, one that imposes a certain limit on the sovereignty effect of the utterance itself. If it is in the name of plurality that she speaks, are we to presume that the voice in which she speaks is, in fact, a plural one? We know from Arendt's writings on federalism and on Palestine (which are internally linked discussions, given her support for a federal authority in that region) that her version of democratic politics favors plurality over sovereignty. What seems to be enacted rhetorically within these pages is a splitting up of sovereignty itself, the exposure of the vacillation that is its condition, and the federating of its constituent parts.

When Arendt tries to explain the plurality in whose name (and voice) she speaks, she provides something other than principles to unify this plurality;

she clearly objects to any effort to divide this plurality, although it is, by definition, internally divided. It is one thing to seek to repudiate some part of this plurality, to bar admission of some part into the plurality of the human. And it is another to consolidate or abstract from this internally divided plurality in the name of a single and defining principle. Arendt wants it both ways. Moreover, another conundrum appears since there are, for instance, at least two forms of plurality that she invokes. One belongs to what she calls the self, and another belongs to a broader sociality, one that she associates with the political sphere.[4]

This conundrum is bound up with another since she herself established the domain of thinking as distinct from the domain of plurality. Indeed, thinking, like other solitary and even private activities (distinct from actions), takes place between me and myself or in dialogue with one other. This poses a problem, of course, because not only was Eichmann described as unable to think, as "stupid" (letter to Jaspers), but that failure to think was an essential precondition and part of his crime.[5] If he were thinking, he would not have committed such a crime, since something in thinking, understood normatively, would have precluded the commission of genocide. If, indeed, Arendt argues that thinking commits us in advance to the preservation of plurality, then there has to be a connection between thinking and plurality. So how do we negotiate this apparent paradox?

To speak of the plurality of the self may at first seem like a misnomer, since it may appear that the self may have a single relation to itself, and so be redoubled or dual in some way, but in what way is the self also plural, if it is? Arendt defines responsibility as the act of thinking, and further defines thinking as an exercise of a plural self. Thinking, she tells us, is the process through which we maintain company with ourselves. Thinking is a silent intercourse with ourselves or, rather, with each person and himself or herself (if binary gender holds). We are, in her view, necessarily internally divided, and must remain so, if we are to think at all. She writes, for instance, in "Some Questions of Moral Philosophy," that "even in the singularity or duality of thinking processes, plurality is somehow present in a germinal form insofar as I can think only by splitting up into two, although I am one."[6] Does she mean to suggest that the plurality in germinal form exceeds the dyad? Somewhere it seems a crowd of others is lurking behind or beneath this relation I have to myself. For the most part, she continues to refer to the self who thinks as necessarily redoubled and dyadic; it seems like a social relation and even carries the echo of those relations: "This two-in-one, looked upon from the standpoint of human plurality, is like the last trace of company—even when being *one* by oneself, I am or can become two—which becomes so very important only because we discover plurality where we would least expect it" (106). If the "two-in-one" is like the trace of company, a simile is devised to explain a certain resemblance between duality and the plurality that belongs to a greater sociality. If it were the last trace of company, then there would have been company before, and this present dyad is in some way the outcrop of that prior terrain. "Like the last trace of company" suggests perhaps that departed company actually leaves no trace or that there never really was some prior company. But perhaps the "like" is also the trace of this disappearing sociality, one that we no longer know how or whether to name. It would appear that I am populated precisely when I feel myself most deserted, and that my capacity to hold conversations with myself in some way recalls, or calls upon, those conversations with others that precede my reflexive address.

Arendt seeks to redescribe conscience as a relation of oneself to oneself. "Conflicts of conscience," she writes, "are actually nothing but deliberations between me and myself; they are not resolved through feeling but through thinking. . . . Conscience means no more than this being at peace with myself which is the *sine qua non* of thinking" (108). In a way, her views on these matters follow from the Kantian proposition that the *I* has the capacity to assert its equivalence to itself, the famous equation of the first critique that asserts self-identity as a precondition of thought: "I am I." Curiously, this principle of identity cannot be asserted without redoubling the self at issue, as Hegel pointed out quite clearly in his *Logic*. For Hegel, the *I* that would assert itself as identical must first differentiate itself from itself, thus calling into question the simple identity. What at first appears to be a tautology emerges as a movement of thought. For Arendt, this internal division has to be actively constituted, which means that it is also always at risk of being deconstituted. In her essay "Thinking and Moral Considerations," also in the volume *Responsibility and Judgment*, Arendt explains a kind of internal division that is different from living as a being in the midst of other beings, a plurality that would be proper to our sociality and political life. She writes, "This curious thing that I am needs no plurality in order to establish difference; it carries the difference within itself when it says, 'I am I.' So long as I am conscious, that is, conscious of myself, I am inevitably two-in-one" (184).

Here it would seem that the *I* has the capacity to constitute its own difference from itself, and must constitute that difference, if it is to assume responsibility. It needs no plurality, which means that its self-constituting activity seems to be unconditioned by any preceding sociality. This self-sufficiency will prove important for Arendt's theory of responsibility and, indeed, for her account of judgment. But for now, let us note that a certain equivocation arises here about whether plurality is germinal in thinking (which could be true even as plurality is not necessary for thinking), and a notion of thinking that commits us in advance to social and political plurality.

For Arendt, this capacity for self-division in the self is the very precondition of responsibility. It is a split, but not a splitting off—and the difference is crucial. I would suggest that one way to understand Arendt's point here is that the split is the sign of conscience, but the splitting off is the end of conscience. If the dialogic relation to the self is broken, that constitutes the failure of responsibility. If we ask according to what norms or what criteria we decide whether or not a specific act is right, the answer, according to Arendt, has to do with whether or not we can continue to live with ourselves, to keep company with ourselves, after having committed such an act. Of course, this remark can be read as trying to offer a phenomenological description of a psychological condition. Indeed, we can perform acts that make us want to cut ties with ourselves, to break up with ourselves, to disown and banish the self who committed such a deed. Indeed, we quit speaking to the one who used to be our self and we no longer recognize that one as having anything to do with us. This breakup with the self banishes oneself or, rather, some part-self, to a location to which all lines of communication are stopped. That self receives no more money or tuition, no more care, no place in the will, and whatever we might mean by "the remaining self" disavows and repudiates that self whose apparent misdeed was the cause of this rather stark divorce. Note that this form of disavowal or disownment is not the same as self-recrimination or superegoic self-beratement. In those latter instances, a dialogue is still happening, even though one self judges the other, and the other does not have much to say for itself. Although this scenario is described as an internal dialogue or, indeed, an internal exile, it takes on all the features of a social relation and, in Arendt's description, it is very clearly a question of linguistic address. So is the phenomenological description of the psychological condition sufficient for understanding the reconceptualization of conscience at work? Or are we being asked to see conscience as an implicitly social relation? We seem not to be able to move quickly to such a conclusion, since Arendt distinguishes this solitary and silent dialogue—as well as the rupture in the dialogue—as happening for and within the domain of the self alone. And yet it seems we must ask, is this solitary self as contained and as self-sufficient as her theorization at this moment would imply?

Could there be a distinction between the plurality proper to the self and the plurality proper to sociality? For the moment, let us remember the context in which she is pursuing this question: those who refused to obey the Nazi laws thought that only through disobedience could they continue to live with themselves. They maintained this plurality of the self, whereas those who ceased to think, who followed the rules and became unreflectively obedient, could do so only by severing ties with themselves and so forfeiting the act of thinking itself.[7]

But is this right? Did Eichmann lose the dyadic structure of thinking, or did he never have it? Did his acts make him disown himself, or was there a prevalent cultural disposition to disowning the self that made his acts possible? Was self-disowning in some sense obligatory under these conditions? The question is probably unanswerable, since it presumes that we know what it might be to own a self and that such self-possession is even possible. Neither can we adjudicate the issue psychologically, and Arendt has already told us that she is not interested in a psychological interpretation of his condition. Instead, she offers a certain philosophical anthropology to explain him, one that presumes that personhood requires an inaudible and invisible dialogue that happens within the self, and so one that would have no verification of the existence of such a dialogue in the realm of appearance (and yet it would seem that the realm of audible and visible dialogue leaves its trace precisely here in the inner dialogue that is not unlike the last trace of company). To have thought would have meant to have been in dialogue with himself and so to have maintained his own proper duality. If, however, in having composed genocidal policy, he also failed to think, then thinking must be related to this plurality of the human, this differentiated many to which he belongs, but which he seeks to destroy. Hence, to maintain a dialogue with himself must in some way imply maintaining a dialogic relation to that plurality. And thinking must require both, and implicate us in both.

Perhaps part of the conundrum here has to do with remaining restricted to a numerical understanding of plurality. Perhaps what is most important is the relationship to oneself that is established through a mode of address, one that is essentially linked to addressing and being addressed by others.[8]

In relation to the dialogue with the self, one might be tempted to speak as if there are two selves, something tantamount to a distribution of sovereignty. But it is probably more appropriate to consider that the self is rethought as a dialogic relation, constantly splitting up into parts. This means that there are not two selves, but rather a redoubling in relationality without which there is no thinking and, indeed, no personhood. In fact, I would suggest that the dialogue that thinking is has a performative and allocutory dimension. To think is not necessarily to think about oneself, but rather, to think with oneself (invoking oneself as company, and so using the plural *we*) and to sustain a dialogue with oneself (maintaining a mode of address and addressibility). To act as an individual is to enter into concerted action without fully sacrificing one's singularity and to act in such a way that dialogue with oneself can be continued; in other words, the maxim according to which I live is that any action I take should support rather than destroy my capacity to keep company with myself (should support the receptivity and audibility of that internal dialogue). To the extent that thought is dialogic, it is a linguistic exercise, and this proves important to my capacity to continue to make myself as one who can and does keep company with myself. Although dialogue would imply being addressed by others (or myself as an other) and so require receptivity, in "Some Questions of Moral Philosophy," Arendt casts the dialogic encounter within the self as an active and performative dimension of self-making: "In this process of thought in which I actualize the specifically human difference of speech, I explicitly constitute myself a person, and I shall remain one to the extent that I am capable of such constitution ever again and anew" (95). For Arendt, those who fail to relate to themselves, to constitute themselves, as one does in thinking and judging, fail to actualize as persons. There is a certain kind of speech that is necessary for this actualization of the person to take place; interestingly, it is a silent speech, solitary, but not for that reason a soliloquy. Someone is addressing someone else, and this structure of address provides the rhetorical and linguistic condition of thinking. According to Arendt's reading of Eichmann, he failed to call upon himself. To be called upon, someone must be home. And Arendt concluded that with Eichmann, no one was at home. In fact, Arendt in her reflections on evil in relation to Eichmann makes this quite stunning remark: "In rootless evil there is no person left whom one could ever forgive" (95). Indeed, she had no forgiveness for Eichmann, and was willing, within her own discursively manufactured tribunal, to sentence him to death. And we have to conclude that this is in part because there was no person left there, in her view, that his actions had destroyed the preconditions of his own personhood. Does this mean that to put a nonperson to death is nothing more than a kind of redundancy? We might justifiably pause here and wonder about Arendt's view, whether it is finally acceptable, whether she has actually offered sufficient reasons to accept the death penalty at all.

Interestingly, the dialogic preconditions of conscience presume that there is a call, and that someone is there to receive the call. But in Arendt's formulation, I constitute myself, which means that I bring that someone into being, which means that my call is, strictly speaking, an illocutionary speech act. He failed to call himself up, and so acted irresponsibly, and yet Arendt produces the textual occasion when she pays him a call, addressing him directly, bringing into relief, we might say, the addressability of this subject who failed to address himself. If Eichmann is beyond reach, Arendt's direct address is finally without recipient, unless of course we accept that she is actually addressing us, "the world" that functions as the de facto jurors in the trial.

But does Arendt indirectly constitute Eichmann as a potential interlocutor by addressing him directly? And would this act not be in tension with her conclusion that "no one is home"? In effect, she places him within the sphere of interlocution and, hence, a person of some kind. At the moment that she addresses him, some disposition of language binds them both together; she is part of a human plurality with him, indeed, with the likes of him. And yet the effect of her address to him is to exclude him from that very domain of plurality. The death sentence is one of the paradigmatic instances of the perlocutionary performative, a speech act that under certain conditions can lead to the result that it bespeaks. In this way, the final sentences of that epilogue (sentences in both senses) figure an operation of discourse as action.

Here we can see that a certain equivocation has entered the scene between thinking and acting. Arendt thinks, and she theorizes thinking, but in the Eichmann book, that thinking takes the form of judgment, and judgment is a kind of action. It emerges as the performative action of judging Eichmann himself at the end of that text. When she explicitly theorizes thinking, she notes that it involves keeping company with oneself, but also notes that it involves constituting that self, time and again. And yet Arendt explicitly distinguishes between thought and action, suggesting that even as thought involves this internal capacity to keep company with oneself, action involves keeping company (acting in concert) with others, that generalized plurality that Eichmann sought to destroy, a plurality voiced as the *we* in whose name Arendt condemns him to death. Arendt makes this distinction explicitly, but it is not one that can be consistently maintained throughout her work. This is how she states the distinction when she tries to make it firm: "The main distinction, politically, between Thought and Action lies in that I am only with my own self or the self of another when I am thinking, whereas I am in the company of the many the moment I start to act." She continues, "Power for human beings who are not omnipotent can only reside in one of the many forms of human plurality, whereas every mode of human singularity is impotent by definition" (106). If we take this typology seriously, then we think by ourselves or in dyadic relations, in actual dialogues between this self and another. But only when we are engaged with the many, a plurality that exceeds dyadic relations, do we become capable of action, understood as the exercise of power. I am wondering whether this is true and whether it is, actually, thinkable. After all, the *I* is said to constitute itself through language, and that is already a performative act, and so a version of action. Arendt judges Eichmann, and that seems, at least on the surface, to be a dyadic relation, indeed no less dyadic for being imaginary and strange. Both forms of thinking have assumed linguistic form and, in both instances, the language does not merely describe a reality, but brings one into being (self-constitution is illocutionary; judging is perlocutionary). In this sense, the language is a kind of action, if not a constituting or performative one. And hasn't she already told us that plurality is germinal in thinking? Would that not immediately imply that action is germinal in thought? Can we even have thought that is not in some way related to action or, put more boldly, already incipient action in some mode or another?

Although it sometimes seems that she is separating two different modes of plurality, the one that is the self and the one that is the self with others, does she succeed? She has already told us that solitary thinking carries the trace of social company. There is, I believe, a stronger claim to be made here. One becomes capable of having a dialogue with oneself only on the condition that one has already been engaged in dialogue with others. More specifically, one becomes capable of responding to others only on the condition that one has been first addressed, constituted by others, as one who might be prompted to respond to that interpellation with self-reflection or, indeed, thinking. One is impinged upon by another's voice, through primary interpellations, and this is the beginning of a certain kind of splitting up of the self into forms of nonunity—one might even consider this as a kind of federating effect of primary interpellations. Only as someone brought into language through others do I become someone who can respond to their call, and who can interiorize that dialogic encounter as part of my own thinking. Their voice and the voice of my response are not precisely separated, since I draw upon that other's voice to have a voice at all. It is not a dialogue between fully discrete beings, but a form of enmeshment that becomes the condition of my own individuation. And since there is no single other whose address calls me into language, we have to think of the voice by which I am interpellated as implicitly, if not explicitly, plural or social. When this happens, the dialogue that I am is not finally separable from the plurality that makes me possible. Although the dialogue that I am is not fully reducible to that plurality, there is a necessary overlap, or chiasm, between the two spheres. Is there not a social formation of thinking in Arendt's sense, even if the normative form that thinking takes is radically solitary? And is solitariness not also, in some sense, a social relation?

Eichmann seems to have known neither solitariness nor plurality. So when Arendt addresses him, she figures him as one who ought to have become capable of both. Since he is not quite a person in her view, and she faults him for this, we can reasonably ask, to whom is Arendt addressing herself when, at the end of *Eichmann in Jerusalem*, she sentences Eichmann to death? He is not there to hear her and neither really are the judges. But the judges may well read her, become part of her audience, just as we are. So though her death sentence is directed to him, it is shown to her readers, delivered to us, and that suggests that Arendt, as writer, has moved outside the dyadic encounter with Eichmann to an address to the many, the plural *we* whom she defends and to whom she addresses her remarks. In effect, she displays her death sentence of Eichmann to us, speaks in our name, but does not exactly perform or facilitate the performance of the death sentence. If anything, her way of formulating and justifying the death sentence constitutes a critique of the Israeli courts, positing herself as the judge of the judges, showing us all, the many, what good judgment might finally look like. The voice she delivers at the end articulates good judgment, but also shows us that the voice, the manner of address, even the severing of this criminal from the domain of the living, is what philosophically grounded legal judgment has to be. Of course, Arendt has told us that in bad conscience, we break up with ourselves, cut off all ties, refuse to keep company with ourselves. But does something of this same solitary dialogue take place in relation to the judgments of others? Clearly, Arendt is breaking up with Eichmann in the sense that she has explicitly said that he no longer belongs among the living, that he has given up his claim to personhood, and that his efforts to eliminate the Jewish people constitute an effort to destroy the plurality that constitutes a differentiated humankind. As a result, he deserves to be destroyed instead.

So this is a curious conclusion, since to accept Arendt's death sentence for Eichmann, we would have to know whether she is entitled to break up with him in this way. Is she right to circumscribe that human plurality that deserves to live and to say who it is who deserves to die? Is it the case that because he sought to deny and destroy the plurality of the human through his genocidal policies that he has disqualified himself from continuing to live in that plurality?

Let us backtrack for a moment: if there is a relation between breaking up with oneself and breaking off all relations with another, is that not because the soundless internal dialogue is already linked with the social dialogue that takes place within appearance? Arendt speaks to Eichmann in her text, figures him as not only listening to her words but also dying as a result of her words. The act of banishment, even the death sentence, is still an address, which suggests that the one to whom such words are uttered qualifies as a recipient of speech. The fact that he is not there, in the text, suggests that maybe he is no longer part of the human dialogue that constitutes human plurality. But maybe we have to consider that the judgment of oneself (in bad conscience) is inextricably linked to the address of another and to another. She herself crosses the *I* and the *we* through this unattributed voice, the voicing of plurality itself. And this suggests, once again, that we may not be able to sustain a rigid distinction between the plurality of the self and the plurality of the sociopolitical domain. She performs the crossing of the two, and it may be that without that performance, she cannot make the judgments she considers responsible.

Perhaps Arendt demonstrates to us this important crossing between the *I* and the *we* in matters of judgment. Every human has already to be a *we*, a plurality, a thinking being, in order to be part of the *we* who makes and remakes the world. The one is not simply a precondition of the other; but the two pluralities cross when thinking becomes action, which it does in language, and when it asserts its rights, even when there is no legal basis for doing so, even when that assertion threatens to destroy the legal code that exists. Of course, this conclusion leaves some critics nervous, since it would seem that Arendt appeals finally neither to existing law nor to abstract principle, but to judgment itself. And that seems to presuppose the sovereignty of the one who judges, independent of law and independent of precedent. She wanted Eichmann to have judged in that way, to have transcended his historical circumstances and called them wrong; and she found herself making such an independent judgment as well.

It seems to me that Arendt does something interesting and disturbing by invoking the voice of the judge to condemn Eichmann to death after he has already been so condemned. On the one hand, she summons and produces a figure of sovereign authority outside of all law; on the other hand, she performatively introduces a norm that might distinguish just from unjust law on radically egalitarian grounds. It may well be, for the reasons that both she and Benjamin in "A Critique of Violence" suggest, that we must oppose law, act against it, even engage in provisional anarchism when law becomes unjust. But there is no reason to think that the only way to oppose or suspend law is through recourse to an extralegal sovereignty. That brings Arendt closer to Schmitt than I would like, and it goes against the radical egalitarian consequences of her theory of social plurality.

What would happen if, instead of turning to the sovereign voice as the way to oppose legal violence, she were to have rethought the social, that field of plurality, not only as a site of belonging, but as a site of struggle? In other words, does the chiasmic relation between the *I* and the *we* also expose a fault at the heart of sovereignty, a noncoincidence that makes the voice vacillate between modes, that keeps the ground more slippery than sovereignty? This apparent recourse to sovereignty at the heart of judgment seems to be in tension with the social ontology she has laid out for us. Indeed, it may be that plurality disrupts sovereignty time and again, federating its remains, dispersing sovereignty into federal forms. If to think or, at least, to think well involves thinking in such a way that we seek to preserve the heterogeneity of human life, then when we are thinking, we are thinking heterogeneity. But here we are compelled to note that this heterogeneity is only thought within an anthropocentric horizon. After all, the life that is worth preserving, even when considered exclusively human, is connected to nonhuman life in essential ways; this follows from the idea of the human animal. Thus, if we are thinking well, and our thinking commits us to the preservation of life in some form, then the life to be preserved has bodily form. In turn, this means that the life of the body—its hunger, its need for shelter and protection from violence—would become a major issue of politics.

This produces a problem for the Arendt of *The Human Condition* who consequentially and mistakenly separated the sphere of the public from the sphere of the private. In the sphere of the private we find the question of needs, the reproduction of the material conditions of life, the problem of transience, of reproduction and death alike—everything that pertains to precarious life. The possibility of whole populations being annihilated either through genocidal policies or systemic negligence follows not only from the fact that there are those who believe they can decide among whom they will inhabit the earth, but because such thinking presupposes a disavowal of an irreducible fact of politics: the vulnerability to destruction by others follows from all modes of political and social interdependency, and constitutes a demand on all political forms.

A different social ontology would have to start from this shared condition of precarity in order to refute those normative operations, pervasively racist, that decide in advance who counts as human and who does not. The point is not to rehabilitate humanism, but to accept not only human animality but shared precarity. Perhaps this feature of our lives can become the basis for the rights to protection against genocide, whether deliberate or negligent. After all, even though our interdependency constitutes us as more than thinking beings, indeed as social and embodied, vulnerable and passionate, our thinking gets nowhere without the presupposition of that very interdependency. Indeed, our thinking relies on a bodily life that can never fully be sequestered in any private sphere—indeed, for thinking to become political, there must be a body that, even in Arendt's own term, "appears." Arendt clearly thought that thinking might bind us to others, and so give us a way to think the social bond to which we are committed when we think. My sense is that our commitments emerge as well by virtue of other kinds of proximities, living up against the neighbor, with others we never knew, and never chose.

Notes

1 Arendt, *Eichmann in Jerusalem*, 120–21. Subsequent references to this edition appear in the text.
2 Here Arendt quotes Rogat, *The Eichmann Trial and the Rule of Law*.
3 See Talal Asad's notion of "death dealing" in *On Suicide Bombing*.
4 The social in her view designates a sphere of conformity and nondifferentiation, but sociality, as I use it here, affirms precisely a heterogeneous conception of social interrelations. See Arendt, *The Human Condition*; and Arendt, *Origins of Totalitarianism*.
5 See Avital Ronell on Eichmann's "stupidity" in *Stupidity*.
6 Arendt, "Some Questions of Moral Philosophy," in *Responsibility and Judgment*, 106. Subsequent references to this edition appear in the text.

7 Arendt links thinking with being able to give an account, even with remembering, and then remarks, once again referencing Eichmann, "The greatest evildoers are those who don't remember because they have never given thought to the matter, and, without remembrance, nothing can hold them back" (compare Benjamin's "Conversations with Brecht" for a dispute over the value of remembrance).

8 Note Arendt's similarity to Bakhtin on the notion of addressability.

CHAPTER 9

Beyond the State of Exception:

Hegel on Freedom, Law, and Decision

Andrew Norris

In this essay I argue that the central issues raised by recent discussions of the state of exception are best explored in the context of Hegelian dialectics. The essay proceeds in three stages. In the first, I argue that there is a deep ambiguity in the idea of the state of exception regarding the kind of category or concept that is in question. Specifically, it is unclear whether the idea of the state of exception is a practical or a logical one. Is it simply a historical fact that every (known, or politically or philosophically significant) system of rules relies upon or generates exceptions that cannot be captured by those rules? Or is this an a priori truth about rules as such? I argue that the majority of the extensive work being done in this area by philosophers and literary critics is incompatible with the former, as almost no one working in this area has anything to say about the relative success of actual institutions and practices that might avoid gaps in law and legitimation; instead, they devote their energies to the consideration of conceptual conflict. In a discussion of two examples of this tendency, William Rasch and Giorgio Agamben, I argue that there are good reasons to be skeptical that the *Ausnahmezustand* and the sovereignty with which it is associated are best understood as problems in logic that happen to express themselves in politics. I then turn to the consideration of Hegel, who clearly influences Agamben's analysis, but whose own understanding of the logical issues surrounding the exception is quite different from his. The consideration of Hegel's work in this context is complicated by the fact that, on many readings, there is simply no place in it for the logical problem of the exception to emerge. I argue that these readings are mistaken, and that Hegel offers us one of the best accounts of why the exception appears to be the problem that it does, and what the true significance of that problem might be. In the third and final section I discuss

Hegel's own treatment of sovereignty and argue that, initial appearances notwithstanding, it is significantly different from and superior to that propounded by Schmitt or Agamben.

That idea of the state of exception as an essentially ambiguous one is already apparent in Carl Schmitt's 1922 *Political Theology*, the text with which this concept is most closely associated. Schmitt famously provides a reciprocal definition of sovereignty and the Ausnahmezustand in which each is a *Grenzbegriff* or "borderline concept."[1] For Schmitt, the state of exception is not a concept defined by preexisting, stable criteria—it is not recognized by the sovereign, but rather produced, in a performative fashion, by the sovereign's decision.[2] The decision concerns nothing but the exception, and the exception is nothing but the object of the decision.[3] The liminal quality of each is most obvious in the sense that the exception marks the limit of the legal order, a limit that is neither within nor without that order. No law or rule can justify, interpret, or apply itself, and when a community can no longer agree on a natural mode of interpretation and application of the law, the highest political authority must dictate one. "What characterizes an exception is principally unlimited authority, which means the suspension of the entire existing order. In such a situation it is clear that the state remains, whereas law recedes. Because the exception is different from anarchy and chaos [*Chaos*], order in the juristic sense still prevails even if it is not a legal kind."[4] The need for exceptions and decisions on them is a hard truth that Schmitt argues liberalism has consistently denied and avoided. But it cannot be avoided forever.[5] Why this is so is not entirely clear, however. Is it simply a historical fact that no given community's sense of what is legitimate and appropriate can be sustained forever, given the economic, military, and social instabilities and developments each must confront over time? Or is this an a priori truth about rules as such? Is every rule derived from and based upon the exception such that the explicit emergence of the exception is not just the inevitable unraveling of the rule but an integral part of its very functioning?[6] Posing these questions reveals a second, deeper ambiguity in the idea of the state of exception that undergirds its explicitly liminal nature, an ambiguity concerning the kind of category that the exception is. Is it an essentially practical one, or a logical one?

If the state of exception is a practical matter, sovereign decisions of the sort celebrated by Schmitt might well be required only very infrequently, and only under extreme circumstances that are in principle identifiable and largely avoidable (plague, civil war, natural disasters, constitutional crises, and so on).[7] The central question on this account would not be that of investigating the abstract relation between rule and exception, but that of determining the conditions that most readily lend themselves to avoiding such crises. Here it is striking that Western capitalist liberal republics have a relatively good track record in this area. Whatever their deficiencies—and there is no denying that they have a great deal—they do offer at least a large percentage of their citizenry a relatively stable legal and political order (if a tumultuous economic one). And they do so without, as Schmitt argues they must, resorting to a nondiscursive, supreme centralized sovereign authority.[8] Though they have encouraged a huge set of extralegal administrative bodies in which largely unregulated decisions are made, even in the aggregate these bodies and these decisions hardly amount to a Schmittian sovereign. If the rule of law does not extend to the disposed and those who are the objects of the society's most virulent discrimination, this is less the result of a failing in the law as such than it is a failing either in those who administer it or in the policies to which they commit themselves (such as, in the American case, empire).

However, if *law* in Schmitt's discussion is taken to mean any rule at all, the state of exception becomes an essentially logical problem, one that inevitably emerges as rules are applied and interpreted over time.[9] Here the problem has nothing to do with historical change and the specific difficulties of holding together a political community's understanding of the legitimate and the normal, but rather the internal reliance of the rule upon the decision and the exception. The structure of the decision of a private agent is the same as that of a sovereign. Of course, one might put these two positions together and argue that the internal, logical limitations of rules as such are put under greater pressure when the rules are political laws subject to the vicissitudes of history and internal and external conflict. But the two positions remain nonetheless distinct. One way to bring this out is to observe that those who embrace what I have referred to as the logical reading of the Schmittian exception are committed to the strict inevitability of the emergence of the Ausnahmezustand, and, for this reason, are in a rather weak position from which to criticize the excesses of either the Bush-Cheney administration or the current administration.

Whatever Schmitt's own views on this matter, it is safe to say that the majority of people working on the state of exception today are not inclined to adopt the former, practical approach to it. Instead, they tend to see the state of exception as a philosophical, logical matter. This is reflected in the fact that most people working in this area focus less on the relative success of actual institutions and practices that might avoid gaps in law and legitimation and more on the analysis of conceptual conflict.[10] A good example of this would be William Rasch, who, in his volume *Sovereignty and Its Discontents*, defends a conception of "the political" as "the ineliminable antagonism [that] serves as the condition of possibility for the limited and channeled struggles of both domestic and international politics."[11] On Rasch's account, such struggle demands and revolves around sovereign decisions regarding who is and is not a member of a given group and what commitments define that membership. And the attempt to suppress and eliminate this conflict and this decision can only result in the return of the repressed: "When one excludes the political, one has to guard the borders vigilantly against those willful intruders who deviate from God's will" and the order of peace, a defense that inevitably assumes a violent form.[12] No doubt, at points Rasch argues that the assertion of "the primacy of the political . . . merely registers a pragmatic insight, namely, that assuming incommensurable conflict as an ineradicable feature of social life leads to more benign human institutions than the impossible attempt to instantiate the shimmering City of God."[13] But this is belied by his claims concerning the inevitability of the return of the repressed. It is not surprising, then, that the emphasis of the analysis in Rasch—as in similar studies of the political—is placed heavily upon the logical claim.

Rasch defends and explicitly embraces the logical necessity of Schmitt's sovereign decision in appealing to Bertrand Russell's well-known paradox of the village barber who shaves all and only those men in the village who do not shave themselves. The paradox here is that if the barber does not shave himself, he does not fulfill the first condition, that of shaving all of the men in the village; while if he does shave himself, he does not fulfill the second, that of shaving all those men in the village who do not shave themselves. Rasch argues that this exemplifies the logical limitations of the rational perception of order, as it shows that "for the law of the excluded middle to operate, it must *be* the excluded middle, neither true nor false." The decision for logic is itself a logically ungrounded decision and hence, correctly understood, supports the decisionist critique of logic.[14] As Rasch puts it,

> In a word, the barber is sovereign, for the paradox [that Russell identifies] is the neat trick of sovereign self-exemption, which makes a neat

asymmetry out of an impossible symmetry. The sudden emergence of this figure—the figure of the sovereign—at first seems arbitrary and mysterious. When personified as an individual, an institution, or a general will, sovereignty appears as if it *precedes* the law, giving the law its force. Yet, the sovereign is simply the name given to a logical effect. Rather than prior or opposed to the law, the sovereign is the law's shadow, its included and excluded double. In the set we call "Sicilian village," law is universal. All are equal before the law. Whoever applies the law is also subject to the law. But the law itself is not subject to the law.[15]

This looks compelling on first blush. But on reflection it becomes evident that, in his eagerness to provide a logical basis for Schmitt's model of sovereignty, Rasch has overlooked the empirical assumptions built into his analysis. For the barber's paradox assumes that there is a barber who shaves all and only the villagers who do not shave themselves. But, as logicians after Russell have noted, there may be no such barber, and if there is, it may be a woman.[16]

A somewhat different tack is taken by Giorgio Agamben, without a doubt the central figure in the current debate concerning the state of exception.[17] In the first volume of his *Homo Sacer*, Agamben makes explicit his commitment to the logical reading of the exception in his discussion of the relation between exceptions, examples, and rules. Agamben argues that "exception and example are correlative concepts that are *ultimately indistinguishable*."[18] As the one is an inclusive ex-clusion—*eine Aus-nahme*—so is the other "an *exclusive inclusion*." "The example," he writes, "is truly a paradigm in the etymological sense: it is what is 'shown beside,' and a class can contain everything except its own paradigm. . . . What the example shows is its belonging to a class, but for this very reason the example steps out of its class in the very moment in which it exhibits and delimits it. . . . If one now asks how the rule applies to the example, the answer is not easy, since the rule applies to the example only as a normal case and obviously not as an example."[19] Agamben has described the logic in question here as an "analogical logic" that cannot be separated from its context and the objects that bear it.[20] This analogical logic, however, retains the necessity and universality of the logic it replaces. Every example and every exception as such "suspend" and at the same time "expose their belonging" to the class they exemplify or from which they are ex-cepted.[21] The problem of the exception is, on this account, hardly a political or legal matter; for the problem appears every time one claims that something is presented as being an example of a rule—or an exception to a rule. The exceptional status of the example (as something taken outside the class in order to demonstrate that class) is a necessary feature of classes as such, be they classes of the product of artistic genius or classes of rules. As Agamben puts it, "In every logical system, just as in every social system, the relation between outside and inside, strangeness and intimacy, is this complicated." In every case, "belonging to a class can be shown only by an example."[22] Examples precede classes just as, for Schmitt, decisions precede norms. This has problematic implications for Agamben's own analysis, in particular his central claim that "today it is not the city but rather the camp that is the fundamental biopolitical paradigm of the West."[23] For the clear implication of this analysis is that in claiming a paradigmatic or exemplary status for the camps, Agamben is and can only be making an unregulated decision that cannot be justified to his readers in a nonauthoritarian manner. Since the example precedes and defines the rule, Agamben cannot appeal to an independent rule or standard to justify his claim that the camps are exemplary of anything. The determination that the camp is representative of the rule is one that is made and not in any substantive sense recognized.

Given this, it is perhaps unsurprising that Agamben's own justifications for the logical reading of the state of exception are neither extensive nor terribly convincing. To argue, as Agamben does, that "the rule applies to the example only as a normal case and obviously not as an example" essentializes the categories of the normal case and the example or exception. If we take a group of things that are subsumed under the same rule—say, three species of a particular bird genus—have we really treated one of these species as an example and (for this reason) not as a normal case when we present it as an example of the genus, or as an exception to the standards of the genus?[24] Some may object that such a taxonomical example is too trivial to be useful here or is otherwise inappropriate. But recall that Agamben claims that there is an isomorphism between the exception and the example or paradigm and that "in *every* logical system, just as in every social system, the relation between outside and inside, strangeness and intimacy, is this complicated." Moreover, problems remain even if one sets aside questions of species and genus and takes up what surely is Agamben's real interest, the question of paradigmatic language.[25] In the chapter "What Is a Paradigm" of his book *The Signature of All Things*, Agamben repeats almost word for word the claim cited above concerning the difficulty of applying the rule to the example. Immediately before doing so, he writes, "What is essential here is the suspension of reference and normal use. If, in order to explain the rule that defines the class of performatives, the linguist utters the example 'I swear,' it is clear that this syntagma is not to be understood as the uttering of a real oath. To be capable of acting as an example, the syntagma must be suspended from its normal function, and nevertheless it is precisely by virtue of this nonfunctioning and suspension that it can show how the syntagma works and can allow the rule to be stated."[26]

To evaluate this argument, let us consider a pair of philosophers attending the criminal trial of one of their colleagues. When the first witness is sworn in, the first turns to the second and says quietly, "You were asking what J. L. Austin meant by 'performative.' Well, that oath there is an example of it: the fellow swearing to tell the truth, the whole truth, and nothing but the truth doesn't *report on* or *describe* a performance or act; it *is* the performance." Now, I imagine that Agamben might reply that citing even an immediately present performance like this is not "normal use." Normal use would then be the actual use of the phrase—"the uttering of a real oath," as Agamben puts it—and not a quoting of it or comment upon it. But if Agamben were to take this line, he would be effectively equating not just examples and exceptions but examples, exceptions, and a whole slew of criticisms, praises, and queries. Statements such as the following are completely unremarkable: "Did you really say, 'I swear he did it'?" or, "How dare you say to her, 'You're an old fool'?" or, "I wouldn't exactly call what he's doing 'self-assertion'—it looks more like a cry for help." In none of these cases is the speaker taking the word or phrase she cites as an example of or an exception to a rule, and each of them is perfectly normal.

Agamben's general position might be more compelling if we took examples the identification of which requires a large degree of judgment. Think, for instance, of excellent student essays. Here there is a rule that determines the class, but it is a rule that not all observers or participants will agree upon, as it requires training and sensitivity to apply.[27] Hence students regularly complain that grading in humanities courses is subjective and for that reason unfair. The philosopher of science Paul Feyerabend embraced this skepticism when he gave all of his students at Berkeley the same grade—first, I believe, a C, and then, after the Berkeley administration complained, an A. But even if one shares our students' skepticism regarding the rules used in the grading of their papers, it seems misleading at best to say that anything like this is true of rules as such. To claim otherwise would effectively mean denying any distinction between cases involving the rote application of rules and cases

involving discretion or fine judgment. This is not to deny that rule application may require judgment, only to insist that these broad categories are not
completely meaningless.[28]

If Rasch's and Agamben's approaches to the exception are as problematic as
I have argued, it hardly follows that we are any better off turning to Hegel.
Hegel's claim to speak from the perspective of Absolute Spirit—a culmina-
tion of intellectual and moral life in which there are supposedly no more
mysteries left and our duties are plain to see—is not one that appears open
to anything like a decision on the exception. Nonetheless, I shall argue that
the passage through rather than around the decision is one that Hegel feels
we moderns must make, for both political and philosophical reasons. I shall
further argue that Hegel's position on this matter provides a helpful contrast
to the currently fashionable views of Schmitt. Where Hegel anticipates the
critique of romanticism laid out in Schmitt's *Political Romanticism*, he is clear
that the moment of the "sovereign decision" is a moment in a larger process,
and not, as Schmitt would have it, an ever-present abysmal ground of political life that might, by virtue of its status as ground, legitimately if not legally
swallow all it supports. What for Schmitt remains a decision, albeit one that
ought to be made by the sovereign of a hierarchically organized political
unity, is in Hegel a moment of the free will. Hegel thus promises both to
allow us to integrate irony into a meaningful, coherent life, and to address
the dangers of Schmitt's decisionism without ignoring Schmitt's insight that
no system of rules can apply or ground itself.

As Schmitt notes, what he describes as occasionalism is termed *irony* by
Hegel: the conception of freedom and subjectivity that allows for and even
demands the emergence of the exception is one that celebrates the ironic
detachment of the free individual.[29] Hegel's depiction of this is, on the face
of it, unremittingly negative. Irony is an evil radicalization of the modern,
Kantian conception of the free will. As such it seems an unlikely suspect
to play a central role in the articulation of any modern political life worth
affirming.[30] But, on Hegel's account, such a role is just what it does and
must play in the *Philosophy of Right*'s account of the limitations of the critical philosophy of Kant and Fichte, and hence the necessity of Hegel's own
contributions to political thought. This is clearest in Hegel's discussion of
irony and evil in §§138–41 of the *Philosophy of Right*. These sections are the
central hinge of the book in that they depict both the transition from *Mo-*

ralität to *Sittlichkeit* and the transition from the historical unfolding of the free will in the previous half of the book to the outline of the structure of a rational modern society in the second. Hegel argues that morality as Kant and Fichte conceive of it is too subjective, and fails to accord sufficient ethical significance to the community and the roles it assigns us or makes available to us. Ultimately, Hegel's predecessors are painted as being too Cartesian, too willing to jettison tradition and the wider culture in the hope that the isolated individual can alone develop an adequate morality. But unlike the more conservative of today's communitarians, Hegel's presentation of his alternative conception of Sittlichkeit or ethical life is meant to be a further development of Kantian morality, one that that morality itself calls forth in a process of immanent critique. Hegel makes no appeal to external authority, or contingent, given norms; instead, he claims to present the autonomous, internally driven unfolding of the will, from its initial objectivization of itself in private property to its adequate realization in a complex, articulated modern state that incorporates nuclear families, promulgated legal codes, a capitalistic economy, corporate mediations between the individual and the state, and a constitutional monarchy with a version of the traditional branches of government as conceived since Cicero. This process is one of immanent critique in the sense that it is driven by negation, a fact that comes more prominently into view in the later stages of the process, and in particular in the transitions from one stage to another. Each stage reveals its limitations in the form of internal contradictions that can only be resolved by rising to a higher and more fully articulated form of the free will.

The crucial juncture in this internally driven unfolding of the will is the transition from Kantian morality to Hegelian ethical life. Irony plays a central role in this transition, just as crime does in the transition from *Abstrakte Recht* to *Moralität*, as a negation of a negation. Crime makes morality possible in that the criminal who violates the contractual conditions of abstract right can only be judged from a perspective that respects but nonetheless transcends that right—in Schmitt's terms, one that has a "juristic element" but nonetheless defies "general codification" in the system of right. The judge who merely takes an eye for an eye (and thus engages in a "fair exchange") is no judge at all.[31] To punish rationally, and hence preserve the principle of abstract right, requires a mode of judgment that is not yet developed in that sphere, and that comes into its own only in the next section on morality. Essentially the same is and must be the case with irony, which is the truth of morality as crime is the truth of right, and which signals the need for ethical life as crime signals the need for morality. This means that ethical life can be understood only as the sublation or *Aufhebung* of irony, which is to say, its negation and fulfillment. On Hegelian grounds, then, it is impossible to simply dismiss irony as childish or self-indulgent or evil. But at the same time, it is difficult to see how irony might play the large and productive role Hegel assigns to it. Hegel presents irony as dissolving everything it touches into the arbitrary whim of the subject. All rules lose their validity, and each judgment becomes a manifestation of the individual's sovereign power to decide on the exception. Once this is done, how could anything as substantial and systematically articulated as ethical life ever emerge? The challenge here is much greater than in the case of crime, which operates in a normative world that still lacks, as it were, the depth of a third dimension, a depth supplied by moral judgment. This is not the case with irony, as Hegel himself signals: with the discussion of irony, the development of the free will charted by the first half of *The Philosophy of Right* ends, and the depiction of the social world adequate to that will begins. The dialectical unfolding of the free will ends, then, with the mystery of an exception avant le lettre.[32]

In order to engage with these issues in a helpful way, one needs to appreciate the extent to which Hegel is profoundly concerned with our subjective embrace of the objective truth of modern political life. *The Philosophy of Right* is, among the canonical works of modern political thought, rivaled only by those of Rousseau in the centrality of its concern with alienation and reconciliation. Hegel writes for a world that supposes the spiritual universe to be *"god-forsaken. . . .* According to this atheism of the ethical world, truth lies outside it, and at the same time, since reason is nevertheless also supposed to be present in it, truth is nothing but a problem." While Hegel presents this as a philosophical radicalization of Kant's excessive caution, it also expresses an alienation found more widely in the general culture.[33] As he puts it in the *Encyclopedia,* "The sickness of our time, which has arrived at the point of despair, is the assumption that our cognition is only subjective."[34] In both critical philosophy and the modern age more generally, the fact that truth is simultaneously included and excluded from the world produces a demand that "every thinker . . . take his own initiative, though not in search of the philosopher's stone," which all assume they already have, albeit in a disfigured form (*EL* §22; *PR,* 14). Rather, a sincere decision and assertion of self is demanded: the "self-styled philosophy" of the romanticism that pervades the modern world "has expressly stated that truth itself cannot be known, but that truth consists in what wells up from each individual's heart" (*PR,*

15). This produces a world in which "the arbitrary will of the subject" determines what will count as right and true (*PR* §140R). Modernity, in short, experiences itself as being more or less, as Schmitt's teacher Weber describes it a hundred years later in "Science as a Vocation," a "godless" (*gottfremden*) time in which life "knows only of an unceasing struggle of . . . gods" (*jener Götter*), a struggle that ends only with a manly decision to commit oneself to one's personal demon (*Dämon*) and that demon's values.[35]

The paradox in Weber's formulation is matched in Hegel, where his readers are pictured as being alienated from reality in an essentially unreal way. Their experience of alienation, that is, is a false experience of the world, one Hegel intends to correct. But since the world from which they are alienated is the world of their social and spiritual activity, this alienation is objective as well as subjective. Social alienation can be dismissed as nonactual, as the "superficial outer rind" or "brightly colored covering in which consciousness first resides" only insofar as it does not inhibit the will's realization in the forms of social life outlined in the *Philosophy of Right* (*EL* §6; *PR*, 21). But to the extent that alienation does hold us back from finding ourselves in the family, in civil society, and in the state, that alienation is, if not actual, then something like a rupture within actuality. This way of putting the matter will strike some as being far too paradoxical to be true to Hegel's insistence that the rational is actual and the actual rational (*PR*, 20). In his study of Hegel's "project of reconciliation," Michael Hardimon, for instance, presents what I think most would see as a claim more in keeping with Hegel's intentions: according to Hardimon, Hegel, unlike Marx, does not see the problem of alienation as an objective one, a feature of reality that must be contested and overthrown. Citizens "are *subjectively* alienated because they feel estranged from its arrangements. . . . But their subjective alienation is *pure* (unaccompanied by objective alienation) because, contrary to appearances, the world they inhabit is in fact a home."[36] But a page after writing this, Hardimon notes, "People who are subjectively alienated are not at home in the social world; for . . . being at home in the social world includes an essentially subjective element, and not being at home in the world *is* to be alienated."[37] We are not at home at home, then. As Hardimon does not acknowledge the contradiction here, he does not see that Hegel, like Nietzsche or Pindar, is engaged in the uncanny task of helping us to become what we are.

"The state," Hegel argues, "is the actuality of concrete freedom. But *concrete freedom* requires that personal individuality [*Einzelheit*] and its particular interests . . . should, on the one hand, *pass over* of their own accord into the interest of the universal, and on the other, knowingly and willingly acknowledge this universal interest even as their substantial spirit, and actively pursue it as their ultimate end. The effect of this is that the universal does not attain validity or fulfillment without the interest, knowledge, and volition of the particular [and its] conscious awareness" (PR §260). If *Sittlichkeit* is a matter of the community's customs or *Sitten*, these are not followed simply because an external authority says they must be, but because the subject affirms them. The importance of the "conscious awareness" of this subjective affirmation is indicated by the fact that Hegel makes the cure of alienation one of his central tasks. In contrast, he quite pointedly does not find it necessary to address every existent but unreal failing. In English, to realize something is both to make it real and to understand it. Both of these are required by Hegel's notion of actualization. As Hegel puts it in the preface, "The truth concerning right, ethics, and the state is at any rate as old as its exposition and promulgation in public laws and in public morality and religion. . . . What it needs is to be comprehended as well." The rational matter needs to be given an appropriately rational form; the *Begriff* must be grasped, *begreifen*. It is this comprehension that makes possible "*reconciliation with actuality*" (PR, 22). The other side of the unreality of our alienation from the world is the world's failure to be what it really is, rational. Failing to see what we are, we fail to be what we are. The *Philosophy of Right* and the logic that stands behind and gains political expression in it will correct this. It is not, I think, misleading to describe this work as therapeutic.[38]

There is a variety of ways in which we might be alienated from the modern world. We might be repelled by the conflict and selfishness characteristic of the—for Hegel—relatively new forms of civil society. More specifically, we might conclude that the prevalence of poverty—and Hegel's inability to recommend a solution to it—is evidence that civil society is irrational and destructive. More specifically still, we might take the existence of the rabble or *Pöbel* that on Hegel's own account characterizes the marginalized, superfluous poor who see the social world as making promises of rights and dignities that it systematically denies as evidence that that world is dehumanizing, and hence no proper home for humans. But the main danger Hegel sees is that we will reject modern political society because we do not recognize it as a place in which we can be free. "The fetter of some abstraction" forged by Hobbes, Kant, or Fichte might lead us to believe that our freedom is opposed to the duties and commitments of that society, and that true freedom is found in the abstract decisions of the isolated subject. The result is nihilism, be it Jacobi's or Weber's, according to which the denatured self is fulfilled only in the act of decision itself. The logical extreme to which modern moral consciousness is drawn is evil in the form of irony: the "last and most abstruse form of evil, whereby evil is perverted into good and good into evil and the consciousness, knowing it has the power to accomplish this reversal, consequently knows itself as absolute, is the greatest extreme of subjectivity from the point of view of morality. It is the form to which evil has advanced in our time—thanks to philosophy" (PR §140R). Pure choice takes the form of irony, as only irony displays the simultaneous emptiness and quasi-divine power of the decision. A just decision, say, would reveal me as just, but, as such, as bound by the tenets of justice. Only an empty, ironic choice allows for the assertion of the ultimate mastery of the self, unbound by any commitment or any defining characteristic. As Hegel puts it, for the ironist, "It is not the thing which is excellent, it is I who am excellent and master of both thing and law" (PR §140R).

In Hegel's discussion in both the *Lectures on Aesthetics* and the *Philosophy of Right* it is clear enough that Friedrich Schlegel's romanticism epitomizes for Hegel the sickness he seeks to ward off and correct.[39] Schlegel is the fulfillment of a process begun in Fichte's philosophy of subjectivity, whereby the abstract, simple, and formal *I* becomes the absolute principle and foundation of all knowledge and all philosophy. Subjectivity is the absolute self-certainty (*Gewißheit*) that Hegel identifies with conscience (*Gewissen*) (PR §136), the "abstract self-determination and pure certainty of oneself alone" that is the "judging power" (PR §138). In Fichte this subjectivity takes center stage, and the *I* or *ego* (*Ich*) becomes

> lord and master of everything, and in no sphere of morals, laws, things human and divine, profane or sacred, is there anything that would not have to first have been laid down by the *ego*, and that therefore could not equally well be destroyed by it. Consequently everything genuinely and independently real becomes only a show [*Schein*], not true and genuine on its own account or through itself, but a mere appearance due to the ego in whose power and caprice and at whose free disposal it remains. To admit or cancel it depends wholly on the pleasure of the *ego*, already absolute in itself simply as *ego*.[40]

Because the subject of Fichte's philosophy decides not just what is the case but by what means and according to what standards such judgments are to be made, everything is what it is by virtue of its decisions.[41]

Fichte himself, however, only systematizes a conception of abstract subjectivity that is uncovered well before him; and in the *Philosophy of Right* Hegel identifies such subjectivity with a far less easily vilified figure than the Schlegel Fichte makes possible: Socrates. Immediately before beginning his discussion of evil in PR §139, Hegel discusses the "subjectivity, as abstract self-determination and pure certainty of self alone [that] evaporates into itself all determinate aspects of right, duty, and existence, inasmuch as it is the power of judgment which determines solely from within itself what is good" (PR §138). This is obviously the basis upon which evil is, as Hegel claims in §139, "necessary." Hence it is confusing when Hegel refers to Socrates in both the Remark and the Addition to §138. This is made all the more confusing as Socrates is presented as doing something that may be appropriate for others as well. Where Fichte's (and, before him, Kant's) formalism is simply a limitation of an incomplete idealism, one with disastrous consequences that Fichte himself did not anticipate, Socrates is presented as a potential model for us. That is, Fichte was a step on a road we have taken. Socrates looks like a potential way forward.

> The self-consciousness which has managed to attain this absolute reflection into itself knows itself . . . as a consciousness which cannot and should not be compromised by any present and given determination. In the shapes which it more commonly assumes in history (as the case of Socrates, the Stoics, etc.), the tendency to look *inwards* into the self to know and determine from within the self what is right and good appears in epochs when what is recognized as right and good in actuality and custom is unable to satisfy the better will. . . . This will no longer finds itself in the duties recognized in this world and must seek to recover in ideal inwardness alone that harmony which it has lost in actuality. (PR §138R)

It is tempting to assume that the hypothetical nature of this remark eliminates any problem. We do not live in dark times, but in a world that is actually rational—at least if we see it as such. Socrates however did not share our moral luck. But this only exacerbates the difficulty: how does Socrates avoid becoming (as evil as) Schlegel if his world is even more impoverished than Schlegel's?[42] It is tempting to answer that Socrates is simply a better person than Schlegel. But making any such appeal to contingent (*zufällig*) differences between the two men would mean accepting that Hegel's argument is not about the logic of a particular conception of freedom as it arises in the realization of the idea of right. And this in turn would make hash of the central claim of the *Philosophy of Right* to be an immanent development of the free will: if evil does not follow from the abstract self-certainty of the moral consciousness as crime follows from the assertion of abstract right, the *Philosophy of Right* runs out of gas just as it approaches the gates of the Hegelian state, leaving us stranded more or less where we started. Hence we must find another ground upon which Hegel might distinguish Socrates from Schlegel, while at the same time noting as he does their essential similarity.

In an essay on this topic, Robert Williams provides some help here. Williams notes that a great deal hinges on the correct interpretation of Socratic irony. With Schlegel we begin the turn away from Xenophon to Plato as the privileged source of our understanding of Socrates; and the reason for this is Xenophon's inability to understand Socrates's irony—in Schlegel's view, "the only involuntary and yet completely deliberate dissimulation." In this paradoxical mix of the voluntary and the involuntary "everything should be playful and serious, guilelessly open and deeply hidden. . . . It originates in the union of *savoir vivre* and scientific spirit, in the conjunction of a perfectly instinctive and a perfectly conscious philosophy. It contains and arouses a feeling of indissoluble antagonism between the absolute and the relative, between the impossibility and the necessity of complete communication."[43] Schlegel argues that his own irony and Socrates's are the same. As we have seen, this is a claim that Hegel must contest. Williams sees him doing so by distinguishing between destructive and constructive irony. This is right—the question is, how does Socrates manage to make this distinction? The central line of Williams's discussion is that he does so by virtue of his commitment to "substantial interests."[44] *Pace* Schlegel and Kierkegaard, Socrates's irony is more or less as Gregory Vlastos has described it: a mask that in announcing itself to be a mask reveals the positive commitments it playfully conceals, such as Socrates's care for his friends and interlocutors, and his pursuit of the good, which Williams argues is only comprehensible given some knowledge of the good.[45] All of this is in stark contrast to Schlegel's destructive and unsubstantial irony, which "results in a substanceless subject" and "can dissolve any substantive content and regard it as null and void. . . . Hegel believes irony is directed at everything, including substantive interests."[46]

There is, no doubt, some evidence for this. Immediately after the passage cited above from the *Lectures on Aesthetics*, for instance, Hegel proclaims that "genuine earnestness enters only by means of substantial interest, something of intrinsic worth [*in sich selbst gehaltvolle*] like truth, ethical life, etc."[47] But Hegel's commitment to the intrinsic, substantial content of ethical life is not a commitment to the substantial as opposed to the subjective; indeed, as we have already seen, "the universal [ethical life] does not attain validity or fulfillment without the interest, knowledge, and volition of the particular [and its] conscious awareness." The same is also true in Hegel's aesthetics and his logic.[48] Hence the contrast cannot be drawn quite as starkly as Williams suggests. Indeed, Hegel suggests that the contrasting terms themselves are the product of the subject's mediation—not its limitation. As he puts it in PR §138, "The subjectivity, as abstract self-determination and pure certainty of itself alone *evaporates* into itself all *determinate* aspects of right, duty, and existence, inasmuch as it is the power of *judgment* which determines solely from within itself what is good in relation to a given content, and at the same time the power to which the good, which is at first only an Idea [*vorgestellt*] and an obligation, owes its *actuality*." And in the Addition he emphasizes that "everything which we recognize as right and duty can be shown by thought to be null and void," and says of Socrates, "He evaporated the existing world." This implies both that Socrates practices something like destructive irony, and that his relation to "substantive interest" is much more ambivalent than Williams makes it out to be. Williams's interpretation leaves unexplained how it was that Socrates was able to develop and maintain his commitment to the substantive interests that supposedly distinguish him from the Sophists. Williams is quite right to say that Hegel sees Socrates's conception of the good as overly abstract.[49] But the question remains, how did Socrates manage to develop even an abstract conception of the good, given that his was an evaporating subjectivity in which the Greek world and its substantive interests dissolved?

The answer lies in Socrates's relation to the Sophists. Williams comes close to articulating this, particularly when he writes that Socratic irony "is a determinate negation directed against the Sophists."[50] But this is not quite right: Socratic irony is not "a determinate negation directed *against* the Sophists"; it is "a determinate negation *of* the Sophists." The difference is hardly trivial. As the determinate negation of the Sophists, Socrates was the negation of the negation, not the reassertion of what was initially negated. What does this mean? Williams writes that "the sophistic view is that knowledge is impossible" while "Socrates assumes that once the debris of confused and misleading ideas (such as sophism) is cleared away, knowledge and virtue will be attainable in principle." And he confidently asserts that

Socrates was no Sophist.[51] But as the determinate negation of the Sophists Socrates was very much a Sophist. Indeed, as Plato already hints, he was nothing else.[52] His truth is the truth of sophistry, which, pace Williams, is hardly "debris" for Hegel. Williams refers to the *Lectures on the History of Philosophy*, but only to the section on Socrates. Hence his recollection is perhaps rusty of Hegel's glowing description of the Sophists as the students of Anaxagoras, the agents of the Idea who brought *Bildung* to Greece, and who in dissolving (*Auflösung*) the false, nonspeculative ideas of common sense introduced philosophy to the Greeks.[53]

Socrates is not a defender of the status quo in opposition to the Sophists. As Hegel puts it in the *Encyclopedia Logic*, "Socrates fought the Sophists on all fronts; but he did not do so by setting authority and tradition against their abstract argumentation, but rather by exhibiting the untenability of grounds dialectically, and by vindicating . . . the concept of willing" (*EL* §121A). Rather than a vague or abstract version of maligned substantive interests, we have the undoing of sophistry via sophistry. The two are simply two moments in the progress of the Idea, and that progress is always a negative one—one might say, a skeptical one. "Socrates directed his dialectic first against ordinary consciousness in general, and then, more particularly, against the Sophists" (*EL* §81A). Against ordinary consciousness first, because that was the step taken by Anaxagoras and the Sophists, the step that made Socrates possible. Hegel identifies the essence of sophistry as "making one sided and abstract determinations valid in their isolation . . . in accord with the individual's interest of the moment and his particular situation"; "the decision as to what grounds are to count as valid falls to the subject"—a nihilism that obviously anticipates that which Hegel attributes to Schlegel (*EL* §§81A, 121A). Hegel associates this with a particular reading of Protagoras's dictum, man is the measure: "in this . . . as in all their [maxims] lurks an ambiguity, since the term 'Man' may denote Spirit in all its depth and truth, or in the aspect of mere caprice and private interest."[54] Williams says repeatedly that Socrates opposes the principle that man is the measure.[55] But Hegel says that he opposes only the false interpretation of the principle: "Protagoras' assertion is in its real meaning a great truth. . . . The same statement is brought forward in Socrates and Plato, but with the further modification that here man, in that he is thinking and gives himself a universal content, is the measure. Thus here the great proposition is enunciated on which, from this time forward, everything turns."[56] The correct interpretation is in fact Hegel's own doctrine, as laid out in the *Encyclopedia* and the

Philosophy of Right. The state is the actualization of the will, the concept by which we have seen Socrates "vindicated"; and "the will is a particular way of thinking" (PR §4A).

It is the collapse of the false interpretation of Protagoras's dictum that demonstrates the necessity of the true interpretation. This collapse transpired in both a political and philosophical setting. In his discussion of the Sophists in the *Lectures on the History of Philosophy* Hegel writes, "The end of the state is the universal [*Allgemeine*]," and a half page later he writes, "Thought seeks universal [allgemeine] principles."[57] The polis as a discursive community realized itself in the teaching of the Sophists; but that teaching undermined the common world even as it realized it. As Thucydides shows, as the Peloponnesian war progressed, the false reading of Protagoras's dictum took hold of the city, and "private ambition and private profit led to policies which were bad both for the Athenians and their allies."[58] It is in this corrupt city, and in conversation with the Sophist Gorgias, that Socrates claims that he is "one of the very few among the Athenians, not to say the only one, engaged in the true political art."[59] This art looks forward to an assertion of self as public or universality. As Hegel puts it in the 1817–18 *Lectures on Natural Right and Political Science*, "My genuine conscience is universal conscience."[60] Universality is the truth of the abstraction of the subjectivity of the Sophists, and of Schlegel. Socrates does not reprimand his interlocutors for pursuing their own interest; instead he teaches them that they do not know what that is—nor, in the end, who they really are. It is the desire to assert themselves as the measure that drives them on. Instead of clearing away sophistic debris, Socrates radicalizes this sophistic project and transforms it into its other.

But what would it mean to will the self as universal or general as opposed to abstract? To put the question somewhat differently, if the autonomous self is one that passes through the moment of abstraction, how can it ever become concrete again? Hegel's answer is found in his account of the will. Hegel describes the will as "particularity reflected back into itself and so brought back to universality, i.e., it is individuality" (PR §7). Such formulations are dense and extremely abstract, and they open themselves up to a number of interpretations. One way of approaching this problem is to focus on Hegel's later discussion of the way one can purify one's impulses, give them the form of reason, and make them one's own (PR §19). This is a process in which I become what I am by making myself at home in the world—making my world *my* world, making it one in which I can recognize myself. I do this by taking up (some of) the impulses and relationships that characterize that world as contingent facts and making them things that I choose. This requires me to step back from the things themselves and to ask if I really want them, if they really satisfactorily express who I am. In doing this I apply universal categories to the particular impulses and relationships my history has left me with—categories that are not simply my own invention, but social products.[61] Instead of simply feeling what I do for, say, the people with whom I have close relations, I reflect upon those people and relations in general terms. In realizing that what I feel is best characterized under the general rubric of love, for example, that feeling is deepened—it becomes self-conscious, itself an object of my esteem (as opposed to the person for whom I feel this love). This in turn adds worth and stability to my relationship. When times are hard, and my feelings of love appear to have been replaced by ones of, say, anger and impatience, I do not lose track of the general truth of our relationship as a loving one. I am no longer a prey to my passing feelings—here anger and impatience. But none of this means that I am not an individual who feels specific, individual feelings for another individual. Quite the opposite: I can be such an individual, rather than a Humean bundle of impulses and sensations, only by virtue of passing through these three moments of the will and making some feelings or impulses structural features of my world, or who I am.

This is a dangerous transition, as it may easily happen that I choose to remain abstracted from all concrete relations, and to make this abstraction itself a way of life. This is Hegel's diagnosis of the Terror of the French Revolution: "Only in destroying something does this negative will possess the feeling of itself as existent. Of course it imagines that it is willing some positive state of affairs, such as universal equality or universal religious life, but in fact it does not will that this shall be positively actualized, and for this reason: such actuality leads at once to some sort of order, to a particularization of organizations and individuals alike, while it is precisely out of the annihilation of particularity and objective characterization that the self-consciousness of this negative freedom proceeds" (PR §5R).[62] The difficulty of the transition through and out of this moment of "negative will" has led some to infer that Hegel himself does not in the end think it possible. Slavoj Žižek, for instance, argues in the second and central chapter of *The Ticklish Subject: The Absent Center of Political Ontology* that the only alternative to this "fury of destruction" is the return to particularity as such. On this account, Schmitt as decisionist is the true heir of Hegel, rather than those who claim to be following Hegel in asserting the satisfactory resolution of this dilemma in the ultimate recognition of a concrete universal that somehow magically unifies the demands of universality (I am nothing) and individuality (as this nothing I recognize that I am these things, that I now choose and hence willingly embrace).[63] And no doubt it is true that if all that were going on was the turning off and on of one's feelings and commitments, it is difficult to see why one should choose to turn back on the particular feelings and commitments with which one began. One might well choose any set of relations rather than remain in the psychotic loneliness of utter nonrelation; but one's reasonable horror of such a state would not lend any special advantage to the particular set of relations that had initially been set aside.

An analysis such as Žižek's, however, takes the moment of abstraction profoundly out of context, and leaves unexplained why one abstracts oneself from one's relations to begin with. One simply refuses particularity and then accepts it again—or not. On Hegel's account, in contrast, one initially refuses pure particularity on Rousseauian grounds: the utter contingency of particularity as experienced in contingent impulses is not a sphere in which one can affirm oneself as a free individual.[64] Hence one seeks a mediated mode of universality that will allow one to affirm oneself as willing the particular (these people, these relations) at least in part on conceptual or universal grounds. In these relations the subject is able to experience camaraderie in the form of friendship, or desire in the form of love. Precisely such a mode of abstraction and commitment is enacted in the *Philosophy of Right* itself, which asks the reader to set aside her immediate political commitments in favor of a commitment to the universal free will, a commitment that shall ultimately take as its object the manifold institutions and modes of life that both characterize modernity and make possible the (concrete) free will. As Hegel puts it, *"The free will . . . wills the free will"* (PR §27); but this is, of necessity, a mediated willing in which the free will wills the institutions that make it possible and sustain it.[65]

If Socrates fails to make such a commitment, and tarries in ironic abstraction, it is not because he, like Schlegel, finds freedom in abstraction as opposed to the passage through universality to individuality, but because there is as yet no such set of institutions and forms of life adequate to his will that he might affirm. As is well known, in his discussion of the Greek political work of art in *The Philosophy of History* lectures, Hegel relates the Socratic moment of moral reflection to the rise and collapse of democracy in Athens, and argues that the appearance of subjective freedom with the Sophists and Socrates "plunged the Greek world into ruin, for the polity

[*Verfassung*] which that world embodied was not calculated for this side of humanity—did not recognize this phase; since it had not made its appearance when that polity began to exist. Of the Greeks in the first and most genuine [*wahrhaften*] form of their Freedom, we may assert that they had no conscience."[66] This is often taken as suggesting that the Greeks somehow lacked the interiority of moderns—that they did not and (for some bizarre and wholly unexplained reason) could not question their customs, and ask themselves what was really right and wrong. Hegel's fondness for Sophocles's *Antigone* alone should be enough to indicate that this is not his view. Hegel's point is rather that they could not do this in any but a "*destructive*" fashion, as their polity was not yet equal to such questioning.[67] The Greeks had no conscience because their political constitution or *Verfassung* was not adequate to the demands of subjectivity, and hence did not allow for the mediation of subjective reflection.

Irony hence works quite differently in the modern world than it did in the ancient. For moderns, irony, if not properly disciplined, becomes a rejection of a world that one might well make one's own. Ironists like Schlegel or Jean-Luc Nancy see their irony as a way to ensure their freedom.[68] Hegel is often taken as reacting to this with reactionary fury, as if to say, "Don't think so much about yourself, you petty egoist, think about something important, think about the state!" While his language of "evil" no doubt encourages such an interpretation, it is nonetheless profoundly wrong to attribute this response to Hegel. Hegel's point is that this sort of irony is a failure on its own terms. Hegel's consideration of irony in the context of the questions of freedom and self-assertion is meant to draw out the way that irony is an attempt to assert the self as free. But the self that is thus asserted is too closely bound up with the event of its self-assertion to allow the ironist to recognize himself in his deed. Hence even the boldest self-assertion will only leave the ironist unsatisfied, like someone flipping through the channels on TV late at night. Hegel doesn't deny that this can seem to promise real satisfaction— one need only think of the lord in the dialectic of lordship and bondage to see that one might well choose a form of life that fails to satisfy one's own will and its need to recognize itself in its worldly deeds. Nor does Hegel attempt to get the ironist to pull back to the realm of "substantial values"; he urges him instead to recognize that he has already embraced nihilism, and that the only way forward is to radicalize the self-assertion this involves, to tread "the path of despair [*Verzweiflung*]"—or, as Hegel also says, the "path of doubt [*Zweifel*]."[69]

These lines are of course from the *Phenomenology*, where Hegel lays out the approach of that book. He continues, "For what happens on [this path] is not what is ordinarily understood when the word 'doubt' is used: shilly-shallying about this or that presumed truth, followed by a return to the truth again, after the doubt has been appropriately dispelled—so that at the end of the process the matter is taken to be what it was in the first place." Instead, the "thoroughgoing skepticism" he calls for is one in which one has "the *resolve*, in Science, not to give oneself over to the thoughts of others, upon mere authority, but to examine everything for oneself and to follow only one's own conviction, or better still, to produce everything oneself, and to accept only as one's own deed what is true."[70] If political autonomy is to be justified scientifically, it will require a science that is our own; anything else could only end in an appeal to authority that denies the very autonomy it attempts to justify. In the terms of contemporary politics, this means that, if authoritarianism thrives on the ironic detachment of the populace, the proper response is not to bemoan that irony, but to take it seriously, and to push it into its other. If people seek freedom in fleeing from politics while at the same time embracing it, it is the desire for freedom that must be embraced and encouraged. This is profoundly counterintuitive, as the modernity in which everything solid melts into air seems best opposed by clinging to substantive moral commitments, such as the moral values many claim to defend. But these values are, from the Hegelian perspective, archaic. For moderns, morality is not so much a matter of substance but of form: the form of autonomous willing. Subjective reflection is an absolutely essential moment in this willing, but as part of a process. Evil is the result not of the turn to the subject, but of forgetting that subjectivity seeks a concrete home in which it might recognize itself, rather than a set of objects it can affirm and discard according to its whims and fancies. That the return to the world adequate to the will is not a mere return to archaic substance is revealed in the fact that these institutions are not valued for their alleged inherent value, but because they make possible the realization of our autonomy. Irony, and the subjective decision it celebrates, is the central and most difficult stumbling block on the way to that realization in both in the *Philosophy of Right* and contemporary America. But it is necessary, and passable, for all that.

On the level of the state as a whole this conclusion may not be immediately obvious, as Hegel at times seems to embrace positions that sound much closer to those of Schmitt in the 1920s than one would expect after working though his account of evil and subjective reflection. This is particularly true in Hegel's discussion of *Die Souveränität gegen außen* (PR §§321–29), where the monarch is linked to the necessity of war and to the ability of a soldier who gives his life on the battlefield to attain the status of the universal class that otherwise is limited to the members of the enlightened bureaucracy.[71] The main difficulty here concerns Hegel's treatment of sovereignty. In general, Hegel describes sovereignty as being made up of three moments: the monarch, the legislature, and the executive. Sovereignty is constituted by ideality (PR §278, §278R), and Hegel refers us to PR §7's discussion of the "abstract concept of the will" as "self-relating negativity" (as addressed above) to understand this relation between part and whole. But in "a situation of exigency," which Hegel contrasts with one of peace, "the organism [the state] of which these particular spheres are members fuses into a single concept of sovereignty, and the monarch as it were becomes the sovereign of which it is usually only a moment" (PR §278R). Hence the monarch is the sovereign to which Hegel refers when he argues that, at such times, "the sovereign is entrusted with the salvation of the state at the sacrifice of those particular authorities whose powers are valid at other times, and it is then that that ideality [of the sovereign] comes into its proper actuality [*Wirklichkeit*]" (PR §278R, §323). Using language that plainly evokes his earlier discussion of subjectivity, irony, and evil, Hegel argues that the crown is "the moment of ultimate decision as self-determination" (PR §275), "the moment of individuality" (*Einzelheit*), and the *I* that results from the internal dialectic between the universal and the particular, as opposed to a natural identity that is simply contrasted to a negating alternative located in an external realm (PR §275A). Sovereignty as found in the monarch is "the will's abstract and to that extent ungrounded self-determination in which finality of decision is rooted" (PR §279); and in alternate versions of the lecture notes that make up the main body of the *Philosophy of Right*, this same monarch is described in terms later used by George W. Bush: "It is a turning in the history of the world, that man locate infinity in themselves; that is done especially by the Christian religion, according to which human and divine nature is the same. In the state the monarch is such a maker of decisions."[72]

All of this sounds terribly like the Schmitt of *Political Theology* and *The Concept of the Political*. But Hegel's arguments in favor of the monarch's exclusive right to assume sovereign power à la Schmitt are hardly consistent with the main tenets of his political and legal theory. If, as in Plato, there is an isomorphism between the individuality of the person and the individuality of the state, this in itself does not legitimate the former standing in for the latter. The only grounds upon which this might be validated is the ideality of the state; and this is one in which *"each of these powers* is itself the totality of the constitution" (*PR* §272, emphasis added). If Hegel nonetheless claims a special privilege for the monarch here, this can only be, as above, on the grounds that in a "moment of exigency" the "ideality [of the sovereign] comes into its proper actuality," an actuality that somehow favors the monarch over the other two moments of the constitution. But the *Philosophy of Right* as a whole is devoted to the explication of the actuality of the state. (Recall Hegel's remark in the preface: "Nothing is actual except the Idea.") It is absurd to suggest that the state becomes somehow more actual in a state of emergency. If the monarch, as the supposed concrete moment of individuality (as opposed to the moments of particularity and universality) has a priority over the legislature and the executive, it enjoys this in peace as well as war.[73] And Hegel is quite plain that this is not the case. This has led some to claim that the older Hegel opportunistically altered his political-philosophic position in order to ingratiate himself with the Prussian authorities. Most influentially, K. H. Ilting has advanced this interpretation and argued that Hegel's turn to the monarch represents a "betrayal" of Hegel's own principles.[74] Schnädelbach, too, argues that a comparison between the *Philosophy of Right* and the notes to these lectures that were delivered before the 1819 Karlsbad decrees shows that Hegel made substantive changes that invite the charge of political opportunism in his teaching regarding the monarch.[75] Given that Hegel already held similar views about the privileged position of the hereditary monarch in his Jena *Realphilosophie*, this may not be quite fair. Nonetheless, it is clear that Hegel's strong claims for the priority of the monarch are not justified by his claims about the ideality of the state.[76] Once one acknowledges this, it is no surprise to find Hegel regularly writing disparagingly of the talents of the average sovereign monarch (e.g., *PR* §281A), and in *PR* §280A taking back many of his bolder claims. Defending the institution of monarchy from the suggestion that it makes the welfare of the state overly reliant upon chance—the good fortune to have a monarch who is worthy of his or her position—Hegel says that such fears exaggerate the role of the monarch's particular character: "In a completely organized state, it is only a question of the culminating point of formal decision, and one needs for a monarch only someone who can say 'yes' and dot the 'i.' . . . In a well-organized monarchy, the objective aspect belongs to the law alone, and the monarch's part is merely to set to the law the subjective 'I will.'"[77] Hence though Hegel grants that "there may be circumstances in which it is [the monarch's] private character alone which has prominence," he insists that "in that event the state is either not fully developed, or it is badly constructed" (PR §280A).[78] Though the monarch may (be said to) be the abstract self of the will and the "subjective certainty" of itself that makes the state a real unit (*ein wirkliches Eins*), its "empty, last deciding" is sharply distinguished from the "objective decision" for which the ministers or counselors are responsible. "In this way the element of the capricious is limited."[79] In short, when Hegel criticizes Hobbes in the lectures of the history of philosophy for granting the sovereign a godlike authority in which the sovereign's will replaces law, he might well have been speaking of Schmitt.[80]

This is borne out by Hegel's suggestion in PR §279R that in ancient times "oracles, the entrails of sacrificial animals, and the flight of birds" fulfilled the role that is today played by the monarch's sovereign decision. What is significant here is the manner in which divination worked. In the second book of the *Odyssey*, for instance, when Telemachos is trying to get rid of his mother's suitors, Zeus sends two eagles who fly along together then turn on one another and tear at each other before finally flying away. This is accurately read as a portent of coming disaster by Halitherses, who is said to be far beyond the men of his generation in understanding the meaning of birds and reading their portents, and falsely denied by one of the suitors. It is important to note here that the portent does not itself make a decision, but signals that a decisive act is coming: the purging of the suitors. If this is analogous to the monarch's "final decision," one has to conclude that Hegel misspoke when he described it as such, as the comparison suggests that the monarch only encourages the acceptance of the decisions of the counsel by giving them his stamp of approval. When we consider that in the ancient world when people did reach a decision in defiance of portents it led to disaster, Hegel is best read as signaling an anxiety that the sovereign remain passive and ceremonial. In this light, it is significant that Hegel in PR §279R compares ancient oracles to Socrates's *Dämon*: as Socrates reports in the *Apology*, his Dämon (unlike that of Weber) never says "yes," only "no."[81] If the monarch is sovereign, he does not, as such, decide.

On neither the level of the subject nor that of the state does Hegel suggest that norms will somehow apply themselves. If we are to follow Schmitt so far as to acknowledge that "real life" inevitably "breaks through the crust of a mechanism that has become torpid by repetition," this life will be addressed not by an "absolute," "self-supporting" decision, but by a will that, as "active thought," moves through particularity, through universality, to individuality.[82] To move through particularity entails a confrontation with the exception, but makes that confrontation part of a larger process in which what is sought for is a set of universal concepts that will allow us to become the individuals that we are. As in Schmitt, universality is not affirmed in its own light, but only once we have stepped outside it. But that step is not a step back to mere particularity—the decision of the sovereign leader—but a step forward, into an individuality that retains the mark of the universal. Rather than a choice between rule and exception, we have a dialectic of assertion, abstraction, and realization. No doubt, this logic is not one that produces deductive arguments in favor of a specific form of individuality in any case. But there will be a range of criteria (as laid out in the *Philosophy of Right* but not, say, *Political Theology*) that allows for the elimination of some possibilities and the reasonable evaluation of others. Hegel is under no illusion that we shall necessarily appreciate the validity of the ethical, political, and legal relations he lays out in the *Philosophy of Right*. Indeed, he writes the book precisely because most of us, most of the time, fail to do so. And the account he lays out is not a deduction (in the sense of the "Understanding") from indubitable premises, but one that requires our interpretation and affirmation. Hegel's text does not compel us in this sense. But perhaps the greatest failure of the decisionist view lies in the assumption that the only alternative to discretion is compulsion. The Hegelian account of autonomy, and hence of the will, is meant to point us toward another alternative. No doubt, Hegel himself does not go far beyond this. The fact that his own discussion of the necessary role of Socratic, skeptical subjectivity in the dialectic of modern politics is as cryptic as it is—the fact that it requires the level of interpretive work we have given it here—itself demonstrates that Hegel himself does not, in the end, provide all of the resources we need to understand it. He does, however, provide the framework within which we might begin to do so.[83]

Notes

An earlier version of this chapter appeared as "Willing and Deciding: Hegel on Irony, Evil, and the Sovereign Exception," *Diacritics* 37, nos. 2–3 (2007): 135–56.

1 When the sovereign decides on the exception, he "decides whether there is an extreme emergency as well as what must be done to eliminate it. Although he stands outside the normally valid legal system, he nevertheless belongs to it, for it is he who must decide whether the constitution needs to be suspended in its entirety." Schmitt, *Political Theology*, 5, 7; I silently modify the translation throughout when accuracy demands. German references are from *Politische Theologie*.

2 The Schmittian sovereign is he who decides on the exception; this decision must be made by a single person because there is no common sense among members of the community as to when the constitution needs to be suspended in its entirety. Hence Schmitt does not write, "We are sovereign when we agree to decide upon the exception."

3 "It is precisely the exception that makes relevant the subject of sovereignty, that is, the whole question of sovereignty." Schmitt, *Political Theology*, 6.

4 Schmitt, *Politische Theologie*, 12: "Besteht im juristischen Sinne immer noch eine Ordnung, wenn auch keine Rechtsordnung."

5 Schmitt does not just argue that the political in the form of the sovereign decision must reemerge, but that it should do so. Politics in the sense of the individual's existential commitment to a hierarchical ordering of the community in which the voice of the political *Einheit* has the authority to dispose of the individual's life is, for Schmitt, a positive good that forestalls a nihilistic collapse of meaning. Or so I argue in Norris, "Carl Schmitt on Friends, Enemies and the Political."

6 As Schmitt puts it, "The sovereign decision is the absolute beginning, and the beginning . . . is nothing else than a sovereign decision." Schmitt, *Über die drei Arten des rechtswissenschaftlichen Denkens*, 23–24. Or, in Agamben's terms, "The exception does not subtract itself from the rule; rather, the rule, suspending itself, gives rise to the exception and, maintaining itself in relation to the exception, first constitutes itself as a rule. . . . The sovereign decision on the exception is the originary juridico-political structure on the basis of which what is included in the juridical order and what is excluded from it acquire their meaning." Agamben, *Homo Sacer*, 18, 19.

7 By "largely avoidable" I do not mean to suggest that we might yet live on a candy mountain in which such things cease altogether to plague us, but simply that, for us, today, they are exceptional events in the sense that they are unusual, and not day-to-day events such as adultery, theft, and trucking and bartering.

8 It will be pointed out that the Bush-Cheney administration hardly fit this rosy scenario. I assume here that one reason the actions of this administration were as reprehensible as they were is that they were not necessary. If one feels that

Guantánamo, secret prisons, forced extradition, the violent compromises of the U.S. Constitution and so on were necessary, it is hard to see what grounds one would have for complaint. I press this point in Norris, "Sovereignty, Exception, and Norm." The same would obviously apply to the Obama administration's deeply unfortunate embrace of many of its predecessor's antiterrorist measures.

9 Schmitt may point to this conception of the exception when he rigorously distinguishes the exception from a mere "construct applied to any emergency decree or every state of siege." Schmitt, *Political Theology*, 5.

10 A clear contrast here would be Bruce Ackerman's excellent book, *Before the Next Attack*, which attacks Schmitt's *Political Theology* as "melodramatic" and takes care to give criteria of what is and is not an "existential threat" to the nation. Ackerman argues that states of emergency need to be addressed by an executive branch that is much more responsive to and limited by the other branches of government than the executive branch in the United States currently is. He proposes that the executive be given the ability to declare a state of emergency, but that this declaration must be ratified by the Congress at regular intervals, and each time by a supermajority with an increasing percentage of the vote. Ackerman, *Before the Next Attack*, 56, 21, and 171.

11 Rasch, *Sovereignty and Its Discontents*, 6.

12 Rasch, *Sovereignty and Its Discontents*, 15.

13 Rasch, *Sovereignty and Its Discontents*, 17.

14 Rasch, *Sovereignty and Its Discontents*, 92.

15 Rasch, *Sovereignty and Its Discontents*, 90. Given this appeal to the logical, it is somewhat ironic that Rasch is fiercely critical of Agamben for making "structural" arguments that, appearances notwithstanding, are "historical only in the most apocalyptic sense," relying as they do on the hope that "the logical paradox of sovereignty [can] be overcome by the installation of a new ontology" (95, 93).

16 See, e.g., Read, *Thinking about Logic*, 149.

17 My discussion of Agamben here follows that in Norris, "The Exemplary Exception"; I discuss the echoes of Hegel in Agamben's account of the paradigm and the example at 276 and 282.

18 Agamben, *Homo Sacer*, 21, emphasis added.

19 Agamben, *Homo Sacer*, 22.

20 Agamben, *The Signature of All Things*, 18 and 7. On page 19 of the same book, however, Agamben argues that what he is discussing "is not logic but analogy."

21 Compare Agamben, *The Signature of All Things*, 31.

22 Agamben, *Homo Sacer*, 22.

23 Agamben, *Homo Sacer*, 181.

24 Or consider an even more straightforward example. I could be an example of a political philosopher interested in both "analytic" and "continental" modes of philosophy. As an example, am I somehow distinguished from other such professors? Or do they, in the comparison, likewise become examples?

25 Agamben, *Homo Sacer*, 21.

26 Agamben, *The Signature of All Things*, 24.

27 Compare Agamben's discussion of the members of an order following the example of their founder in Agamben, *The Signature of All Things*, 21–22. In such cases it seems perfectly fair to speak of "a form of knowledge that is neither inductive nor deductive but analogical. It moves from singularity to singularity." Agamben, *The Signature of All Things*, 31.

28 Denying this is a mistake I myself once made. Norris, "Introduction," 9.

29 Schmitt cites Hegel in his own attack upon romantic irony as a flight from the decision. Schmitt, *Political Romanticism*, 70–72.

30 Throughout this essay I use the term *modern* rather loosely. Hegel is concerned with modern Europeans, and there is no reason to believe that he would see his argument as applying to, say, Amazonian tribes or the miserable inhabitants of "failed states" such as Afghanistan.

31 Hegel, *Philosophy of Right*, §§101–2. All citations from the *Philosophy of Right* come from *Elements of the Philosophy of Right*, edited by Allen Wood and translated by H. B. Nisbet and from the Suhrkamp *Werke*. Subsequent references to this edition appear in the text as PR.

32 No wonder then that, as Herbert Schnädelbach observes, "Dieser übergang ist immer wieder als einer der schwächsten und unplausibelsten der ganzen [*Philosophy of Right*] kritisiert worden." Schnädelbach, *Hegels praktische Philosophie*, 244.

33 In the *Logic* Hegel describes Kant's appeal to a distinction between what can be thought and what can be known as a solution to the antinomies as being "like attributing to someone a correct perception, with the rider that nevertheless he is incapable of perceiving what is true but only what is false." Hegel, Introduction to *Science of Logic*, 46; cited in Forster, *Hegel and Skepticism*, 177.

34 Hegel, *The Encyclopedia Logic*, §22. That Hegel seeks to confront this "sickness of his time" as such is signaled in the fact that he lectures on these matters repeatedly for huge numbers of students, most of whom would not themselves become professional philosophers. See Pinkard, *Hegel*, 456. Subsequent references to the *Encyclopedia* appear in the text as EL.

35 Weber, "Science as a Vocation," 153, 152, and 156; Weber, "Wissenschaft als Beruf," 610, 608, 613. On Schmitt's exposure and response to Weber, see William Scheuerman, *Between the Norm and the Exception*, 251n7.

36 Hardimon, *Hegel's Social Philosophy*, 133.

37 Hardimon, *Hegel's Social Philosophy*, 134.

38 It is not only that, of course. As Terry Pinkard emphasizes in his recent biography, Hegel was a reformist liberal with a long-standing interest in the French Revolution and the Napoleonic reforms. And the *Philosophy of Right* of course outlines institutions that were not found in the Prussia of Hegel's own day. But the emphasis of the *Philosophy of Right* is not on proposing changes, but on reconciling us to what is (actual), and thereby making it—our lives, us—what it really is. For a related account of the role of the therapeutic in Hegel, see Pippin, "The Absence of Aesthetics in Hegel's Aesthetics."

39 Many will protest that Hegel's characterization of Schlegel is hardly fair or accurate. This need not concern us here, as the issue here is the status of irony and the subjective decision in Hegel, and not Schlegel's own views.

40 Hegel, *Lectures on Aesthetics*, 64–65.

41 This is somewhat misleading. Fichte does argue that what kind of philosopher one is is itself the expression of an existentialist decision that cannot be guided by reason; but he sees this decision as itself the expression of one's true character. See Fichte, "[First] Introduction," 18. But, as with Schlegel, the point here is not the accuracy of Hegel's reading of Fichte, but his own position.

42 See Hegel's contrast between ancient Athens and modern Europe in his *Lectures on the History of Philosophy*, vol. 1, 365. On the deficiencies of this text, to which one working on this topic must nonetheless refer, see Beiser's introduction to *The Cambridge Companion to Hegel*, xxxi–xxxii.

43 Schlegel, "Critical Fragment 108," 13.

44 Williams, "Hegel on Socrates and Irony," 70, 74, 76, 79, 80.

45 See Vlastos, "Socratic Irony," in *Socrates*. For an excellent critique of Vlastos's reading, see chapter 3 of Nehamas, *The Art of Living*. The central text on the subject is of course Kierkegaard, *The Concept of Irony*. Considering the depth of Kierkegaard's antipathy to Hegel, this early work is extraordinarily Hegelian in tone and content.

46 Williams, "Hegel on Socrates and Irony," 73, 72.

47 Hegel, *Lectures on Aesthetics*, 65; Hegel, *Werke, Vorlesungen über die Ästhetik* I, 94.

48 In the *Aesthetics* Hegel argues that the experience of the beautiful art object is one in which the demands of the object and of the subject are brought into harmony with one another. The distorted perspective of "unfree" or "finite intelligence" presents us with a false dilemma in which we must choose between the freedom of the subject and that of the object. From this perspective, that of the Understanding, the cognitive freedom of the subject is hopelessly compromised by the given quality of the apparently independent object; the subject's freedom is found only in the imposition of its will upon the object, and hence the denial of the object's freedom in its reduction to an object of use. But for Hegel, "in both these relations, both sides are finite and one-sided, and their freedom is a purely supposititious freedom." In contrast, in aesthetic experience the object is considered in its "subjective unity and life" as "an end in itself," while the subject in his "liberal contemplation" of the object escapes both the cognitive subordination to the given and the practical reduction to unrealized intention. "His relation to the fulfillment of his subjective intentions is no longer the finite one of the mere 'ought'; he has gone beyond it and what now confronts him is the perfectly realized Concept and end." Hegel, *Lectures on Aesthetics*, 112–14. For an excellent and clear account of the necessary role of the subject in the presuppositionless science of Hegel's logic, see Houlgate, *The Opening of Hegel's Logic*.

49 Williams, "Hegel on Socrates and Irony," 79.

50 Williams, "Hegel on Socrates and Irony," 80.

51 Williams, "Hegel on Socrates and Irony," 77, 78.

52 At Plato, *The Sophist*, 268a–d, the Stranger describes what is plainly meant to be Socrates as "the real and genuine Sophist."

53 Hegel, *Lectures on the History of Philosophy*, 354.

54 Hegel, *The Philosophy of History*, 269.

55 Williams, "Hegel on Socrates and Irony," 68, 82.

56 Hegel, *The Philosophy of History*, 373–74.

57 Hegel, *The Philosophy of History*, 356.

58 Thucydides, *History of the Peloponnesian War*, 163.

59 Plato, *Gorgias*, 521d. The claim here is much stronger than that found in Xenophon, where Socrates suggests that he knows how to rule (as opposed to actually ruling) and that he prepares others for politics. Compare Xenophon, *Conversations of Socrates*, 162, 98.

60 Hegel, *Lectures on Natural Right and Political Science*, §66. Compare Hegel, *Vorlesungen über die Geschichte der Philosophie*, 405. And compare Pierre Hadot on the force of Socratic dialectic: "Caring for ourselves and questioning ourselves occur only when our individuality is transcended and we rise to the level of universality, which is represented by what the two interlocutors have in common." Hadot, *What Is Ancient Philosophy?*, 28–29. Hadot does not recognize that Hegel shares his estimation of Socratic dialectic and attributes the standard view laid out by Williams to Hegel at 37.

61 Robert Pippin rightly argues that a central strand of this process involves the recognition of our sociality, the nature of which we distort if we "see social practices, conventions, and the like as results of simultaneously held individual commitments, as if the content of such commitments could be understood apart from, independently of, the expectations, possible reactions, oppositions, and so forth within a community of subjects." Pippin, "Responses to Conway, Mooney, and Rorty," 360–61 and passim. This is not exactly a turn from the self to society, but a recognition that the self is a social self.

62 This critique does not support the liberal alternative, as it also undercuts the sort of negative conceptions of liberty championed by liberals like Isaiah Berlin and by (quite different) liberals like Friedrich Hayek.

63 Žižek, *The Ticklish Subject*, 113, 114.

64 As Rousseau puts it in *The Social Contract*, "man acquires with civil society, moral freedom, which alone makes man the master of himself; for to be governed by appetite alone is slavery, while obedience to a law one prescribes to oneself is freedom" (65).

65 Alan Patten correctly argues that, for Hegel, freedom is "*recursive*: the determinations that give content to freedom turn out to be the ones the agents must pursue if they are to be in a position to deliberate and pursue the ends and determinations that give content to freedom." Patten, *Hegel's Idea of Freedom*, 100. For further critique of Žižek's reading of Hegel, see Dews, "The Tremor of Reflection: Slavoj Žižek's Lacanian Dialectics," in *The Limits of Disenchantment*.

66 Hegel, *The Philosophy of History*, 253.

67 Hegel, *The Philosophy of History*, 252.

68 I discuss the role of irony in Nancy's political thought in Norris, "Jean-Luc Nancy and the Myth of the Common." I discuss his ironist reading of Hegel in Nancy, *Hegel*, in Norris, "Beyond the Fury of Destruction." The celebration of irony is, of course, a central theme in contemporary modern society. Contemporary political culture requires a level of sophistication that often appears as the ability to ironically if not cynically engage and disengage with one's fiercely held commitments: on one day the commitment to return integrity to politics in general or the White House in particular is everything, on the next a demand for consistency and an attack on public hypocrisy is dismissed as petty, legalistic, and naive. Our political culture is a part of our more general culture—and by "our culture" I mean American culture, the culture of Hollywood movies, television, pop music, and so on that is obviously hegemonic in more and more parts of the world. Here in its home in the States at least this culture is a profoundly ironic one, and ironic in a sense that fits well with Hegel's claims: our endless regurgitation of the past—*Happy Days*, *Planet of the Apes*, *Charlie's Angels*, *Starsky and Hutch*—demonstrates our culture's collective embrace of the truth of that past and its meaning for us, while the smirking irony in which it increasingly comes clothed demonstrates our recognition of its essential falsity, its utter lack of meaning. Politically this finds a good match in the fact that in our time, "homeland" is a site of pervasive homelessness and compromised citizenship.

69 Hegel, *The Phenomenology of Spirit*, 49; Hegel, *Phänomenologie des Geistes*, 72.

70 Hegel, *The Phenomenology of Spirit*, 49–50.

71 Compare the discussion of sacrifice and sovereignty in PR 324R and Hegel, *Natural Law*, 93: "the individual proves his unity with the people unmistakably through the danger of death alone."

72 Hegel, *Die Philosophie des Rechts*, 272–73. As Bush put it in a defense of his embattled secretary of defense, "I'm the decider, and I decide what's best." George W. Bush, quoted in "Bush Names New Budget Chief; More Changes Coming but Rumsfeld Will Stay in Job, President Says," *Washington Post*, April 19, 2006.

73 Hegel sometimes writes as if this is indeed the case. At PR §273, for instance, Hegel argues, "We begin with the power of the crown, i.e. with the moment of individuality, *since* this includes the state's three moments as a totality in itself" (emphasis added). The legislature is the moment of universality, the executive is the moment of particularity, and the crown is the moment of individuality (PR §275). Of these three, individuality is privileged, as it alone contains the other moments: "Universality [and] particularity . . . are only abstractions; what is concrete and true is the universality which has the particular as its opposite, but the particular which by its reflection into itself has been equalized with the universal. This unity is individuality" (PR, 7R). Compare EL I, §163: "Jedes Moment des Begriffs ist selbst der ganze Begriff (§160), aber die Einzelheit,

das Subjekt, ist der als Totalität *gesetzte* Begriff." This obviously contradicts the claim, quoted above, that each moment contains the other two. Moreover, imagine if a state had only the "concrete" moment of the monarch, and lacked the supposed "abstractions" that surround it in the *Philosophy of Right*. In this light Peter Steinberger is quite right to argue that Hegel's language of the dominance of one moment is not in keeping with his own thinking: "For Hegel, the state is in some sense an entity of sovereignty; but as the state is, so to speak, a monad, only *it* in its entirety can be sovereign. Of course, sovereignty may *actively* manifest itself in one or another of its members; hence, we can say that decisions come directly from this or that institution. But to say that the monarch or the majority is sovereign over against the rest of the state is to ignore the state's fundamental unity." Steinberger, *Logic and Politics*, 214.

74 Ilting, "The Structure of Hegel's *Philosophy of Right*," 105–6. For a history of this approach to the text, see Riedel's introduction to *Materialien zu Hegels Rechtsphilosophie*; for critical evaluations, see Siep, "Vernuftrecht und Rechtsgeschichte"; and Pinkard, *Hegel*, 457, and chapters 10–12.

75 Schnädelbach, *Hegels praktische Philosophie*, 170–71. On the Karlsbad decrees and the censorship and political climate in which Hegel finished the *Philosophy of Right*, see Pinkard, *Hegel*, chapter 10.

76 Axel Honneth argues that Hegel's commitment to the hereditary monarch in the *Realphilosophie* represents a retreat from a political to a metaphysical understanding of the state. Honneth, *The Struggle for Recognition*, 60.

77 From this Shlomo Avineri concludes that the sovereign is "a mere symbol of the unity of the state" and that it is "both essential—without him the 'i's go undotted—but also ultimately trivial." Avineri, *Hegel's Theory of the Modern State*, 188. Likewise, Allen Wood rightly concludes from PR §280A and §279A and other student lecture notes that "the state's policies are *not* at the mercy of the individual judgment of the sovereign prince." Wood, *Hegel's Ethical Thought*, 282n5.

78 Hegel argues in PR §279A that the monarch is "bound by the concrete decisions of his ministers" and that he "may" not act capriciously. This "may" is repeated in PR §280A, and in each case one wonders how Hegel's *dürfen* improves upon the Kantian *sollen* he consistently castigates. (In PR §280A Hegel also writes that "the throne *must be* such that the significant thing in his holder is not his particular makeup.") Hegel repeats tirelessly that it is not the job of a philosopher to offer empty ideals or "oughts." Is a state that is not "completely organized" one that is not fully real? Here it is helpful to recall PR §214R: "Reason itself requires us to recognize that contingency, contradiction, and show have a sphere and right of their own, restricted though it be, and it is irrational to strive to resolve and rectify contradictions within that sphere."

79 Hegel, *Die Philosophie des Rechts*, 274, 164. Compare PR §278A, where Hegel clearly distinguishes sovereignty as he understands it from a despotic state where a particular will, be it that of the monarch or the people, "counts as law or rather takes the place of law." This is consistent with Hegel's discussion

of the limits of legal norms in his discussion "Right as Law" (PR §§211–14), where he acknowledges that no law can apply itself to a particular case: "In this sphere, the concept merely lays down a general limit, within which vacillation is allowed. This vacillation must be terminated, however, in the interest of getting something done, and for this reason there is a place within that limit for contingent and arbitrary decisions [willkürliche Entscheidung]" (PR §214). Hegel hardly sees this as leading to a suspension of law as such, à la Schmitt. In PR §214R he admits, "Reason cannot determine, nor can the concept provide a principle whose application could decide whether justice requires for an offense (i) a corporal punishment of forty lashes or thirty-nine. . . . And yet an offense is done if there is one lash too many." The implication that justice is present but indeterminable does not cause Hegel the worry that it does Schmitt and Hobbes, that someone must make it present by declaring it to be correct, and that it is only present in being so determined. The borders are vague but real, and the judge's decision, which "pertains to abstract subjectivity, to formal self-certainty [formellen Gewißheit]," must stay "within a certain limit."

80 Hegel, Vorlesungen über die Geschichte der Philosophie, 226.

81 Hegel is likely following Xenophon here; Xenophon, "Socrates' Defense," depicts Socrates himself making this comparison, to his own advantage. Xenophon, Conversations of Socrates, 43–44; compare Hegel, The Phenomenology of Spirit, 431.

82 Schmitt, Political Theology, 12; Schmitt, Politische Theologie, 19.

83 While space does not permit an adequate discussion of the matter, I would suggest that we turn to figures such as Stanley Cavell, who give a more detailed account of the role of individual subjectivity in the therapeutic "road of doubt" that allows modern citizens the opportunity to become what they are in a world that, despite its often hopeless appearance, offers them that possibility in a way that previous societies did not. If the pairing of Cavell and Hegel seems odd, one might recall (1) Cavell's remark that one of the sources for the phrase "the truth of skepticism" (a phrase that names the central teaching of The Claim of Reason) is "Hegel's use of 'the truth of x' where x is a concept he has just sublated, denied at one level but preserved at another," and (2) his comment that he can find no better term than Aufhebung for Wittgenstein's mode of criticism, his "most original contribution [to] philosophy." Cavell, "Reply to Four Chapters," 289; and Cavell, "Aesthetic Problems of Modern Philosophy," 85.

CHAPTER 10

Humans and (Other) Animals in a Biopolitical Frame

Cary Wolfe

Michel Foucault argues in *The History of Sexuality* that "for millennia, man remained what he was for Aristotle: a living animal with the additional capacity for a political existence; modern man is an animal whose politics places his existence as a living being in question."[1] Moreover, as Foucault famously defines biopolitics, it "is the power to make live. Sovereignty took life and let live. And now we have the emergence of a power that I would call the power of regularization, and it, in contrast, consists in making live and letting die."[2] Foucault develops this line of investigation later in his career. In the lectures collected in *"Society Must Be Defended,"* for example, he argues that a "new mechanism of power" arose in the seventeenth and eighteenth centuries, one that had "very specific procedures" and "new instruments." This new type of power, he argues, is "absolutely incompatible with relations of sovereignty," and it is based on "a closely meshed grid of material coercions rather than the physical existence of a sovereign."[3] Foucault thus allows us to see, as Roberto Esposito points out, that for biopolitics the fundamental mechanism concerns not sovereignty and law but rather "something that precedes it because it pertains to its 'primary material.'"[4]

Even more importantly for our purposes, Foucault argues that this shift from sovereignty to biopower involves a new concept of the subject, one who is endowed with fundamental interests that cannot be limited to or contained by the simple legal category of the person. But a trade-off is involved here. If the subject addressed by biopolitics constitutes a new political resource, it also requires a new sort of political technology if it is to be fully controlled and exploited. The biosubject, you might say, is far more multidimensional and robust than the thin subject of laws and rights; that is both its promise and its challenge as a new object of political power.

As Foucault characterizes it, the subject theorized during this period by English empiricist philosophy is something new, defined not so much by freedom or the struggle of soul versus body, but rather as a subject "of individual choices which are both irreducible and non-transferable."[5] Those choices and the ability to make them derive, he argues, not from reason but from the capacity to feel (and the desire to avoid) pain, which is "in itself a reason for the choice beyond which you cannot go." It is a reason beyond reason, you might say, "a sort of irreducible that does not refer to any judgment, reasoning, or calculation."[6] And this means, he argues, that "the subject of right and the subject of interest are not governed by the same logic."[7] In opposition to what Foucault calls *homo juridicus* (or *homo legalis*)—the subject of law, rights, and sovereignty—we find in this new subject, *homo oeconomicus*, "an essentially and unconditionally irreducible element against any possible government," a "zone that is definitively inaccessible to any government action," "an atom of freedom."[8] The subject of interest thus "overflows" the subject of right, "surrounds" him and, indeed, is the "permanent condition" of his possibility.[9]

This "displacement," as Maurizio Lazzarato characterizes it, of the problem of sovereignty doesn't neglect it but merely points out that "the grounding force will not be found on the side of power, since power is 'blind and weak'" (as Foucault puts it)—hence, its growing need, in an increasingly complex and differentiated field of operation, for the various techniques of management, surveillance, and so on that it deploys.[10] What we are dealing with here is not a withdrawal of sovereignty and the law, but rather, as Esposito writes, how the pivot of real political power gradually shifts from the domain of legal codes and sanctions to "the immanent level of rules and norms that are addressed instead to bodies."[11] Politics, law, and economics now function primarily not in a top-down but in a bottom-up fashion, and become operators for the effective management of the health, well-being, and increase of the population, conceived now as an object of biological intervention. Norms are thus addressed neither to individual rights holders nor, in Esposito's words, to "their confluence in a people defined as the collective subject of a nation, but rather to the living being in the specificity of its constitution."[12] But that very "specificity," precisely because of its own complexity, which increases all the more as new regimes of knowledge are brought to bear upon it, contains new challenges, new aleatory elements that must be managed and directed.

As Lazzarato argues, three important points follow from this: first, "biopolitics is the form of government taken by a *new dynamic of forces* that, in conjunction, express power relations that the classical world could not have known"; second, "the fundamental political problem of modernity is not that of a *single* source of sovereign power, but that of a *multitude of forces*. . . . If power, in keeping with this description, is constituted from below, then we need an ascending analysis of the constitution of power *dispositifs*"; and third, "Biopower coordinates and targets a power that does not properly belong to it, that comes from the 'outside.' *Biopower is always born of something other than itself.*"[13]

Here, then—with Foucault's emphasis on bodies before the law—we find a potentially creative, aleatory element that inheres in the very gambit of biopower, one not wholly subject to the thanatological drift of a biopolitics subordinated to the paradigm of sovereignty. Quite the contrary, those bodies are enfolded via biopower in struggle and resistance, and because those forces of resistance are thereby produced in specifically articulated forms, through particular dispositifs, there is a chance—and this marks in no small part Foucault's debt to Nietzsche (as both Esposito and Deleuze point out)—for life to burst through power's systematic operation in ways that are more and more difficult to anticipate.[14] Power/knowledge complexifies the political resource called the body, the better to control it at ever more micrological levels, but complexity increases risk. Thus, as Lazzarato notes, Foucault actually "interprets the introduction of 'life into history' constructively because it presents the opportunity to propose a new ontology, one that begins with the body and its potential, over and against the prevailing Western tradition of understanding the political subject as above all a subject of law."[15] Indeed, Lazzarato argues, one of Foucault's key insights is that without factoring "freedom" and the "resistance of forces" into the equation as constitutive, "the *dispositifs* of modern power remain incomprehensible."[16]

But as Esposito rightly observes, all of this leaves us with "a decisive question: if life is stronger than the power that besieges it, if its resistance doesn't allow it to bow to the pressure of power, then how do we account for the outcome obtained in modernity of the mass production of death?" In short, "Why does biopolitics continually threaten to be reversed into thanatopolitics?"[17] For Esposito, Foucault leaves hanging "the question of the relation of modernity with its 'pre,' but also that of the relation with its 'post.' What was twentieth-century totalitarianism with respect to the society that preceded it? Was it a limit, a tear, a surplus in which the mechanism of biopower broke free . . . or, on the contrary, was it society's sole and natural outcome?"[18]

Are the Nazi death camps, to use Agamben's words, not "a historical fact and an anomaly belonging to the past," but rather "the hidden matrix and *nomos* of the political space in which we are still living"?[19] If the latter, then Foucault would be forced to join Agamben in seeing genocide as the underlying paradigm and constitutive tendency of modernity.[20] But such a position, as Esposito points out, is at odds not only with Foucault's strong sense of historical distinctions and disjunctions, but also with the sense of life's inevitable expression of itself through resistance that Lazzarato's reading underscores. And so, for Esposito, Foucault's analysis of biopower ends at an impasse, caught between an essentially affirmative view of the biopolitical and a thanatological one.

For Esposito, it is this impasse that the paradigm of immunization (one also explored by Jacques Derrida, Donna Haraway, and Niklas Luhmann, among others) helps us to avoid. In his view, Foucault is unable to develop the full implications of his insight in the lectures of 1976 that "the very fact that you let more die will allow you to live more"; he is unable to see that the affirmative and thanatological dimensions of biopolitics—either "a politics *of* life or a politics *over* life," as Esposito puts it—are joined in a single mechanism.[21] "This is where Foucault seeks out the black box of biopolitics," Esposito writes; "in the liminal space where death is not solely the archaic figure against which life defines itself . . . but rather one of its inner folds, a mode—or tonality—of its own preservation."[22] Like Derrida's *pharmakon,* it is "a gentle power that draws death into contact with life and exposes life to the test of death."[23] The immunitary mechanism thus "saves, insures, and preserves the organism, either individual or collective, to which it pertains, but it does not do so directly, immediately, or frontally."[24]

For Esposito, articulating the immunological mechanism with greater precision also allows us to make headway on the question of the specifically modern character of biopolitics. It is certainly the case that the exercise of biopower may be traced to the ancient world—in the availability of slave bodies to their masters, or in the politics of health and hygiene in ancient Rome. But what distinguishes these from modern biopolitics is that such practices were oriented toward a "collective, public, communal" objective.[25] "Tracing it back to its etymological roots," Esposito writes, "*immunitas* is revealed as the negative or lacking [*privata*] form of *communitas*. If *communitas* is that relation, which in binding its members to an obligation of reciprocal donation, jeopardizes individual identity, *immunitas* is the condition of dispensation from such an obligation and therefore the defense against the expropriating features of *communitas*."[26] Such a paradigm can be traced to Hobbes, he argues, in light of whose concept of sovereignty the actual underlying function of what we call "the individual" becomes clear.[27] In reality, it is "the immunitary ideologeme through which modern sovereignty implements the protection of life"—not of the individual, not even of the body, but of life itself.[28] Ideologically speaking, the discourse of the person or the individual doesn't undo the split between the bodily, the animal or corporeal, on the one hand, and the rational element on the other, but rather serves as a means for the latter to subjugate the former.[29] Here, at the nexus of the person or the individual and the immunitary mechanism, the biopolitical takes a specifically modern turn, as the person becomes the access point, as it were, to life's management and protection.

Here, however, in the face of the massive thanatological drift of modern biopolitics associated above all with Agamben's work, we need to complicate considerably this relationship between immunitary protection, the body, the animal, and the person, and we need to remember the fundamental ambivalence of Foucault's notion of biopower, an ambivalence underscored, as we saw earlier, by Lazzarato. For at the very historical moment when the scale and efficiency of factory farming have never been more nightmarish—it has been compared, by Derrida and by others, to the genocide of the Jews by the Nazis (a term whose biopolitical resonance is clear enough in light of Agamben's work)—some animals are receiving unprecedented levels of care, so much so that the pet care industry in the United States grew in total expenditures from $17 billion in 1994 to nearly $36 billion in 2005 to $45.5 billion in 2009.[30] The late 1990s saw the birth of the famous Missyplicity Project, dedicated to cloning companion animals for those who can afford it, and short of that (as any owner of a companion animal will testify) the range and quality of veterinary care available today, much of it highly specialized and expensive (dental cleaning requiring general anesthesia, ultrasounds, CAT scans, EKGs, chemotherapy for veterinary oncology, and much else besides—the capacity to "make live," in Foucault's words), far outstrips what was either available or marketable even a generation ago.[31] And this has led in turn to another growth industry unheard of until relatively recently: pet health care insurance, estimated in 2010 to be a $271 million business and on track to balloon to $500 million by 2012.[32]

What all this adds up to, of course, is a historically remarkable shrinkage in the gap between human beings and their animal companions regarding quality of life in areas such as food quality, health care, and other goods and services.[33] Clearly, then, many animals flourish not in spite of the fact that they are animals but because they are animals—or even more precisely, perhaps, because they are felt to be members of our families and our communities, regardless of their species. And yet, at the very same moment, billions of animals in factory farms, many of whom are very near to or indeed exceed cats and dogs and other companion animals in the capacities we take to be relevant to standing (the ability to experience pain and suffering, anticipatory dread, emotional bonds and complex social interactions, and so on), have as horrible a life as one could imagine, also because they are animals. Clearly, then, the question here is not simply of the animal as the abjected other of the human *tout court*, but rather something like a distinction between *bios* and *zoe* that obtains within the domain of domesticated animals itself.

We find here an additional insight that thickens Derrida's well-known observation that the designation "*the* animal" is therefore an "asininity" because it effaces the vast diversity of nonhuman life under a single definite article. Indeed, we might say, paraphrasing Esposito, that "*the* Animal" is an "ideologeme" that masks what Rosi Braidotti, following Deleuze, calls the "transversal" relations in which animals, and our relations with them, are caught under biopolitical life.[34] From this vantage, it makes little or no sense to lump together in the same category the chimpanzee who endures biomedical research, the dog who lives in your home and receives chemotherapy twice a week, and the pig who languishes in the factory farm. Nor does it even make sense to assume that such groupings proceed along species lines, strictly speaking. As Braidotti puts it, "In the universe that I inhabit as a post-industrial subject of so-called advanced capitalism, there is more familiarity, i.e. more to share in the way of embodied and embedded locations, between female humans and the cloned sheep Dolly, or oncomouse and other genetically engineered members of the former animal kingdom, than with humanistic ideals of the uniqueness of my species."[35]

This new differentiation of the biopolitical field is what Esposito is after at the end of *Bios*, where he insists that a turn away from the thanatological and autoimmunitary logic of biopolitics can only take place if life as such— not just human (versus animal) life, not just Aryan (versus Jewish) life, not just Christian (versus Islamic) life—becomes the subject of immunitary protection. Esposito writes, "We can say that the subject, be it a subject of knowledge, will, or action as modern philosophy commonly understands it, is never separated from the living roots from which it originates in the form of a splitting between the somatic and psychic levels in which the first is never decided [*risolve*] in favor of the second. . . . This means that between man and animal—but also, in a sense, between the animal and the vegetal and between the vegetal and the natural object—the transition is rather more fluid than was imagined."[36] And what this means, in turn, is that "there is a modality of *bios* than cannot be inscribed within the borders of the conscious subject, and therefore is not attributable to the form of the individual or of the person."[37]

To put it another way, if Agamben's contribution is to articulate powerfully how the "anthropological machine" cannot function without producing this remainder called "animal," which is at the same time the retroactively posited origin that must be excluded by the political project of "man," then Esposito's advance is to recognize that the animal is not something that need be always already abjected. But if one of the great contributions of biopolitical thought is to show how it is impossible to talk about race without talking about species—this fact, after all, is at the core of the biopolitical confrontation with the Nazi camps—what must now be added (and what is already at work in Derrida's critique of the idea of "*the* animal" in the singular) is that race and species must, in turn, give way to their own deconstruction in favor of a more highly differentiated thinking of life in relation to biopower, if the immunitary is not to turn more or less automatically into the autoimmunitary. Or in Esposito's words, "The most complete normative model is indeed what already prefigures the movement of its own deconstruction in favor of another that follows from it."[38]

But where Esposito is wrong, I think, is in his insistence on "the principle of unlimited equivalence for every single form of life."[39] The problem, of course (or one of the problems), is that if all forms of life are taken to be equal, then it can only be because they, as the living, all equally embody and express a positive, substantive principle of Life not contained in any one of them. Thus, as Eugene Thacker puts it, "The contradiction is clear: Life is that which renders intelligible the living, but which in itself cannot be thought, has no existence, is not itself living."[40] As Thacker points out, later philosophers such as Kant "would recast this dilemma in terms of an antinomy: every assertion about life as inherently ordered, organized, or purposeful is always undermined by the assertion itself and its irrevocable object of thought."[41] But of course, such a Kantian solution is precisely what is unavailable to Esposito, given his reliance on Simondon and Deleuze in the final pages of *Bios* and its framing of an affirmative biopolitics.

To put this slightly otherwise—updating the Kantian position via Derrida—what Esposito is unable to articulate is that what "binds him to his own biological matrix" is nothing living, but neither is it Life. Rather, as Martin Hägglund has argued, it is the trace structure and "spacing" that is "the condition for anything that is subject to succession, whether animate or inanimate, ideal or material."[42] Such a structure (or more precisely, system) is, strictly speaking, dead; it is a *machinalité* (to use Derrida's term).[43] Far from metaphysical, however, such a system is perfectly compatible with a materialist and naturalistic account of how life evolves out of nonliving matter, how even the most sophisticated forms of intentionality or sensibility arise out of the inorganic sytematicity of repetition and recursivity, retention and protention.[44] What Henry Staten calls the "strong naturalist view" holds that life may emerge from matter organized in particular ways but rejects the idea that "life is somehow hidden in matter and just waiting to manifest itself." Life is thus one possible outcome of materiality, but it is certainly not a normal or expected one—indeed, it is highly improbable, not the rule but the exception.[45] In this way, the arche-materiality of the structure of succession, of what Derrida calls "living-on," allows, as Hägglund puts it, "for a conceptual distinction between life and matter that takes into account the Darwinian explanation of how the living evolved out of the non-living, while asserting a distinguishing characteristic of life that does not make any concessions to vitalism."[46]

I return to the importance of this point for the question of "biologistic continuism" below, but for now I want to note a separate but related problem in Esposito's thinking about life: the slippage in and around the term *species*, which appears to be symptomatic of Esposito's desire to hold this problem of vitalism at bay without falling back into the lexicon of the person as the locus of the norm. Esposito argues that the specific place where the immunitary logic operates in biopolitics is "at the juncture between the spheres of the individual and the species. When Foucault identifies the object of biopower as the population . . . he is referring to the only element that groups all individuals together into the same species: namely, the fact that they have a body. Biopolitics addresses itself to this body—an individual one because it belongs to each person, and at the same time a general one because it relates to an entire genus."[47] But if the entire point of an affirmative biopolitics for Esposito is to realize the force of "life, singular and impersonal," that "cannot but resist whatever power, or knowledge, is arranged to divide it," that thus produces "new knowledge and new power as a function of its own quantitative and qualitative expansion," then it is not clear how the call of an affirmative biopolitics can be "for a new alliance between the life of the individual and the life of the *species*," since such "life" forces clearly don't stop at the water's edge of species and are instead operative at—and in fact, beneath—the level of "flesh."[48] To put it another way, *species* here cannot do any heavy lifting for Esposito, for the very same reasons that "the body" cannot be cordoned off from the "flesh"—indeed, life, if anything, radicalizes the logic of the flesh, the being in common of embodied beings that cannot be limited to *Homo sapiens*, either philosophically or pragmatically. To put it another way, Esposito may be right that the body is the immunitary site upon which biopolitics seizes control over life, but the cordoning off of the body within the domain of species simply reinstates the very autoimmunitary, thanatological movement that his affirmative biopolitics wants to resist.[49] What is needed here, then, is a third way, one that can think life and norm together, without falling back on either the lexicon of the person or, at the other extreme, the radically dedifferentiating discourse of life, which is unworkable both philosophically and pragmatically.

So the problem is not Esposito's insistence—quite correct, in my view—that "what we call the subject, or person, is nothing but the result, always provisory, of a process of individuation, or subjectification, quite irreducible to the individual and his masks," nor is it his core argument that for an affirmative biopolitics, "there can be nothing but a clear distancing from the hierarchical and exclusionary apparatus of the category of the person, in any of its declensions, theological, juridical, or philosophical."[50] It is rather that the only alternative that Esposito seems to be able to imagine to this indexing of biopolitical norms is simply its other extreme, a sort of neo-vitalism that ends up radically dedifferentiating the field of the living into a molecular wash of singularities that all equally manifest life. And so, as Thacker notes, "The concept of life—and whether such a concept is possible—places philosophy in a hovering, wavering space between an onto-theology and an onto-biology."[51]

Be that as it may, Esposito's position, pragmatically speaking, fares no better. First, it replays all of the quandaries around biocentrism brought to light during the 1970s and 1980s in North America during the heyday of the deep ecology movement—debates that Esposito (or for that matter his fellow Italian political philosophers) would have little reason, perhaps, to know about. As Tim Luke notes, if all forms of life are given equal value, then we face questions such as the following: "Will we allow anthrax or cholera microbes to attain self-realization in wiping out sheep herds or human kinder-gartens? Will we continue to deny salmonella or botulism micro-organisms their equal rights when we process the dead carcasses of animals and plants that we eat?"[52] In the face of such challenges, all that Esposito can offer is ret-rofitting Spinoza's concept of natural right to make "the norm the principle of unlimited equivalence for every single form of life."[53] As Esposito char-acterizes it, "the juridical order as a whole is the product of this plurality of norms and the provisional result of their mutual equilibrium," and for this reason no "normative criterion upon which exclusionary measures" could be based is possible.[54] But such a position—and its key markers in the fore-going quotation are "plurality" and "equilibrium"—is in essence no different from deep ecology's guiding principles of biocentrism (or, in a slightly more refined version that Esposito would be forced to reject, biodiversity). There are perhaps those who would respond to Luke's foregoing questions in the affirmative—who would argue that, yes, all forms of life should be equally allowed to take their course, even if it means a massive die-off of the species *Homo sapiens*. But biopolitically speaking, that hardly solves the problem, of course, because when we ask what the demographic distribution of such an event would likely be, we realize that the brunt would surely be absorbed by largely black and brown poor populations to the south of Europe and North America, while those in the "rich North Atlantic democracies" (to use Richard Rorty's no-nonsense phrase) who could afford to protect themselves would surely do so.[55]

A further problem with equating the norm with "the principle of unlim-ited equivalence" of life pure and simple is underscored by the prominent contemporary development of synthetic biology. As one article puts it, "post-genomic biology—biology 2.0, if you like—has finally killed the idea of vital-ism."[56] In fact, the explosion of new developments in the field has depended in no small part on two factors: more and more widely accessible computing power of considerable magnitude and, more importantly, the rapidly falling costs of DNA sequencing. For example, the human genome sequenced by the International Human Genome Sequencing Consortium took thirteen years and cost $3 billion; now, using the latest technology, the same work can be done in eight days at a cost of about $10,000—a figure that is sure to be even lower as you read these words. And projections were that by 2013 the same work would take about fifteen minutes and cost about $1,000.[57] When, with much media fanfare, Craig Ventner and Hamilton Smith reported on May 20, 2010, in *Science* magazine that they had created a living creature with no ancestor from scratch using off-the-shelf laboratory chemicals—a bacterium of the family *M. genitalium*—it seemed perverse to some, and analogies with Mary Shelley's *Frankenstein* were ready at hand.[58] And it perhaps seemed even more perverse when Ventner and his team added some DNA designed from scratch to watermark the organism with a cipher that contains the URL of a website and three quotations.[59] As many scientists point out, however, for all of its pathbreaking possibilities, synthetic biology is quite continuous with the enfolding of life and technology that reaches back hundreds, if not thousands, of years.[60]

Precisely here, it seems to me, it is worth remembering the sort of point made by Derrida in his discussion of cloning in *Rogues*. As he observes, those who oppose cloning object to it in the name of "the *nonrepetitive* unicity of the human person," the "incalculable element" of "a unique, irreplaceable, free, and thus nonprogrammable living being."[61] But what is overlooked here, he argues, is that

> so-called identificatory repetition, the duplication, that one claims to re-
> ject with horrified indignation, is already, and fortunately, present and at
> work everywhere it is a question of reproduction and of heritage, in cul-
> ture, knowledge, language, education, and so on, whose very conditions,
> whose production and reproduction, are assured by this duplication. . . .
> This is yet another way of ignoring what history, whether individual or
> not, owes to culture, society, education, and the symbolic, to the incalcu-
> lable and the aleatory—so many dimensions that are irreducible, even for
> "identical" twins, to this supposedly simple, genetic naturalness. What is
> the consequence of all of this? That, in the end, this so-called ethical or
> humanist axiomatic actually shares with the axiomatic it claims to oppose
> a certain geneticism or biologism, indeed a deep zoologism, a fundamen-
> tal but unacknowledged reductionism.[62]

Derrida's commentary here—and the example of synthetic biology in general—enables us to see how the biopolitical frame makes possible the thinking of a more nuanced and differentiated set of ethical and political relations
with regard to forms of life, but only if we do not succumb to the sort of
neo-vitalism that, at the end of *Bios*, seems to leave us with a stark choice:
either life and an affirmative biocentrism on the one hand, or, on the other,
the autoimmune disorder that is bound to eventuate if the continuum of
life is broken.

What begins to dawn on us at this point, then, is the full complexity of the confrontation with "biologistic continuism" as articulated by Derrida, which assumes its most challenging and illuminating form in his reading of Heidegger.[63] Heidegger was right, Derrida argues, to reject the idea of "some homogeneous continuity between what calls *itself* man and what *he* calls the animal," and he was also right to insist that the fundamental questions here are not biological but, if you like, phenomenological if not indeed ontological (though Derrida's caveat of "what calls *itself* man" would eventually challenge that last characterization).[64] And Heidegger was also right, as Dominick LaCapra observes, in his "departure from Husserl's attempt to center philosophy on the intentional consciousness of the meaning-generating, radically constructivist ego or subject," and his increasing emphasis on understanding "human being in relation to Being and not vice versa," a project in which "the dignity of the human being is enhanced if it is seen within a larger relational network that is not unproblematically centered on human freedom or human interests."[65] What Heidegger was wrong about, Derrida argues, was his insistence that whatever is at stake here—phenomenologically, ontologically, ethically—corresponds to a difference in kind, an absolute limit, between "*the* human" and "*the* animal" (which is precisely why Derrida calls it a dogma).[66] Derrida's position, on the other hand, consists "not in effacing the limit" between different forms of life "but in multiplying its figures, in complicating, thickening, delinearizing, folding, and dividing the line precisely by making it increase and multiply."[67] And here the problems with the headlong rush toward life that we find late in Esposito's *Bios* come fully into view: that the vast differences between the orangutan, the wasp, and the kudzu plant—Derrida even calls them "abysses," but they are abysses that, unlike Heidegger, apply within the animal kingdom—fall out because those differences are all reduced to the same kind of difference.[68]

Not one line, then, but many. But not "no line" either, and a further way of delinearizing it is to realize that the material processes—some organic, some not—that give rise to different ways of responding to the world for different living beings are radically asynchronous, moving at different speeds, from the glacial pace of evolutionary adaptations and mutations to the fast dynamics of learning and communication that, through neurophysiological plasticity, literally rewire biological wetware. In this light, it is clear, as Matthew Calarco puts it, that "the presubjective conditions that give rise to human subjectivity" cannot be restricted to humans alone. Instead, the more fundamental issue is the "complex networks of relations, affects, and becomings into which both human beings and animals are thrown. As such, posthumanism is confronted with the necessity of returning to first philosophy with the task of creating a nonanthropocentric ontology of life-death."[69] This does not mean that whoever is the addressee here—human or nonhuman—is defined by the transcendence of the biological; the point is rather that everything that is relevant here applies in ways that have nothing to do with species designation and, moreover, operates in a way that is not wholly reducible to the facticity of biological existence, either human or animal. Paradoxically, then, the rejection of biologistic continuism in fact makes possible a more robust naturalistic account of the processes that give rise to that which cannot be reduced to the biological alone—or even, more radically still, to the organic per se. For as Derrida notes in a late interview, "Beginning with *Of Grammatology,* the elaboration of a new concept of the trace had to be extended to the entire field of the living, or rather to the life/death relation," and it is by virtue of the trace and its technicity that both humans and (at least some) animals are "thrown."[70]

We are now in a better position to fully grasp the biopolitical point of Derrida's observation in the "Eating Well" interview that "the power to ask questions," which, "in the end, is how Heidegger defines the *Dasein,*" may be seen as anterior—before—the question of the subject, of the *who* for whom and to whom we are responsible, but only to give way to "another possibility," a more fundamental one that "overwhelms the question itself, reinscribes it in the experience of an 'affirmation,' of a 'yes' or of an 'en-gage' . . . that 'yes, yes' that answers before even being able to formulate a question, that is responsible without autonomy, before and in view of all possible autonomy of the who-subject."[71] "Not only is the obligation not lessened in this situation," Derrida continues, "but, on the contrary, it finds in it its only possibility, which is neither subjective nor human. Which doesn't mean that it is inhuman or without subject, but that it is out of this dislocated *affirmation* . . . that something like the subject, man, or whoever it might be can take shape."[72] *Whoever it might be.* Why "without autonomy"? Because this originary "yes," as Martin Hägglund puts it, "answers to the trace structure of time that is the condition for life in general."[73] That is to say, it answers to the fact that the other is just as constitutively other to itself as I am to myself, just as constitutively prosthetic, brought into being by a technicity and spacing that is radically neither self nor other, radically nonliving. This means, in turn, that "every finite other is absolutely other, not because it is absolutely in itself," as Hägglund writes, "but on the contrary because it can never be in itself."[74]

Of course, there are many, many forms of life—plant life, bacterial life, and much else—that fall outside the parameters I have been describing, at least as far as we know at the moment: indeed, the overwhelming majority of life forms on earth. But my foregrounding of the *who* here is meant to remind us that while it is no doubt worthwhile to continually rethink the relations between different forms of life, whatever they may be, and, beyond that, to understand as fully as possible the complex ways in which they are enmeshed and networked with the inorganic world (as Jane Bennett, Bruno Latour, and others have explored), the questions of ethics, law, justice, and hospitality pose a specific kind of challenge: namely, that in a "parliament of things" (Latour) or a "political ecology of things" (Bennett) some of those things are also whos and not just whats—even as any who becomes one only by virtue of also being, prosthetically, a what.[75] Is there not a qualitative difference between the chimpanzee used in biomedical research, the flea on her skin, and the cage she lives in—and a difference that matters more (one might even say, in Derridean tones, "infinitely" more) to the chimpanzee than to the flea or the cage?[76] I think there is.

This is not to reinstate what is obviously an untenable opposition between persons and things; indeed, the prosthetic logic of the who and the what that I have been pursuing argues precisely the opposite. But it is to put our finger on a specific challenge entailed by thickening and deepening, rather than flattening, our description of the worlds and networks we share, and their qualitative dimensions—a challenge that returns us, but at a different angle of approach, to the question of biocentrism that we discussed earlier. The problem is summed up well by philosopher Levi Bryant, who writes that the issue is "asking how the domain of value might be extended *beyond* the human, without humans being at the center, or all questions of value pertaining to nonhumans being questions about the *relationship* of humans to nonhumans. In other words, the litmus test . . . revolves around whether that domain of value would continue to be a domain of value *even if* humans cease to exist. That seems to be a pretty tall order or very difficult to think." "No case could here be made," he continues, "that there's something of *intrinsic* value in nonhumans such as animals or the planets. Rather, we would be committed to the thesis that there are only *relative* values of some sort or another. . . . The planet, for example, would only take on value-predicates in relation to humans. Were humans to not exist, the planet would neither be valueless or valuable. It would just *be*."[77]

But as I have been arguing, a third possibility exists, which is that questions of value indeed necessarily depend upon a "to whom it matters," but that "to whom" need not be—indeed, as we have already seen, cannot only be—human, either in the sense of excluding by definition nonhuman animals, or in the sense of a human who is not always already radically other to itself, prosthetically constituted by the ahuman and indeed inorganic. Bryant is right, in other words, that were there no "to whom," "the planet would neither be valueless or valuable. It would just *be*." But he is wrong to assume that this hinges on whether humans alone exist.

From this vantage—to put it slightly otherwise—the problem with the recourse to life as the ethical sine qua non is that it bespeaks the desire for a nonperspectival ethics, ethics imagined fundamentally as a noncontingent view from nowhere, a view which—for that very reason—can declare all forms of life of equal value. And here, we can bring to light what is particularly problematic about Esposito's recourse to Spinozan natural right as the background against which he seeks to ground norms in a naturalistic basis.[78] As Esposito puts it, we find in the norm "the principle of unlimited equivalence for every single form of life"; and (following Spinoza), "the juridical order as a whole is the product of this plurality of norms and provisional result of their mutual equilibrium."[79] But the question, of course, is this: from what vantage would it be judged that the equilibrium invoked by Esposito is achieved? Spinoza's answer, as we know, was God: each particular thing "is determined by another particular thing to exist in a certain way, yet the force by which each one perseveres in existing follows from the eternal necessity of the nature of God."[80] But of course, as Niklas Luhmann would be the first to remind us, what *God* names here is the desire for the impossible, or at the very least (to put it a little more charitably), the premodern: an observer who can be both self-referential, contingent, socially constructed and historically specific, and universal and transhistorical at the same time. In other words, what is wanted here is an escape from responsibility for the inescapable fact that all norms are exclusionary simply because they are contingent (as Rorty would put it), selective and self-referential (Luhmann), or, for Derrida, performative and conditional.

That is to say, there is no "god's eye view"; there are only "limited points of view." But the fact that any norm is unavoidably perspectival doesn't dictate either relativism, solipsism, or autoimmunitary closure. Quite the contrary—and it would take another entire essay to fully develop this point—because of its constitutive self-referential blindness (Luhmann), its constitutively performative and conditional character (Derrida), such a limited perspective constitutes the opening to the other and to the outside, to the necessity of other observations (Luhmann), and even to futurity or the "to come" of justice itself (Derrida). Indeed, for these very reasons, the equilibrium Esposito invokes is to be not desired but avoided. If there are, as Hägglund writes, "potentially an endless number of others to consider, and one cannot take any responsibility without excluding some others in favor of certain others," then "what makes it *possible* to be responsible is thus what at the same time makes it *impossible* for any responsibility to be fully responsible."[81] And for the very same reasons, an ethics of pure equilibrium without decision, without discrimination—without, in short, selection, discrimination, and perspective—would be, paradoxically, unethical. It's not that we shouldn't strive to be fully responsible; it's simply that to do so is necessarily to do so selectively and partially, thus conditionally, which in turn will unavoidably call forth the need in the future to be more fully responsible than we have already been.

Notes

An earlier version of this chapter appeared in my book *Before the Law: Humans and Other Animals in a Biopolitical Frame* (Chicago: University of Chicago Press, 2012).

1 Cited by Esposito, *Bios*, 33.
2 Foucault, *"Society Must Be Defended,"* 247.
3 Foucault, *"Society Must Be Defended,"* 35–36.
4 Esposito, *Bios*, 29.
5 Foucault, *The Birth of Biopolitics*, 271–72.
6 Foucault, *The Birth of Biopolitics*, 272.
7 Foucault, *The Birth of Biopolitics*, 274.
8 Foucault, *The Birth of Biopolitics*, 271.
9 Foucault, *The Birth of Biopolitics*, 274.
10 Lazzarato, "From Biopower to Biopolitics," 104.
11 Esposito, *Bios*, 28.
12 Esposito, *Immunitas*, 136.
13 Lazzarato, "From Biopower to Biopolitics," 101, 103.
14 In Foucault's words, "Where there is power, there is resistance, and yet, or rather consequently, this resistance is never in a position of exteriority in relation to power" (quoted in Esposito, *Bios*, 38). See Deleuze, *Foucault*, 71.

15 Lazzarato, "From Biopower to Biopolitics," 100.

16 Lazzarato, "From Biopower to Biopolitics," 104.

17 Esposito, *Bios*, 39.

18 Esposito, *Bios*, 42.

19 Agamben, *Homo Sacer*, 166.

20 Esposito, *Bios*, 43.

21 Foucault, *"Society Must Be Defended,"* 255; Esposito, *Bios*, 32, emphasis added.

22 Esposito, *Immunitas*, 136.

23 Esposito, *Immunitas*, 127.

24 Esposito, *Bios*, 46.

25 Esposito, *Bios*, 56.

26 Esposito, *Bios*, 50.

27 Esposito, *Bios*, 46; see also Esposito, "The Person and Human Life," 210–11.

28 Esposito, *Bios*, 60–61.

29 Esposito, "The Person and Human Life," 208, 210.

30 Jacques Derrida, *The Animal That Therefore I Am*, 26. Statistics provided by American Pet Products Manufacturer's Association, accessed September 10, 2008, https://www.fetchpetcare.com; and Berkowitz, "Pets Are a Booming Industry."

31 On the Missyplicity Project, see Haraway, *When Species Meet*, 151–53.

32 Berkowitz, "Pets Are a Booming Industry."

33 Berkowitz, "Pets Are a Booming Industry."

34 Braidotti, *Transpositions*, 100.

35 Braidotti, *Transpositions*.

36 Esposito, *Bios*, 180.

37 Esposito, *Bios*, 192.

38 Esposito, *Bios*, 188.

39 This is not by any means only Esposito's problem. Even in Derrida's work, we find a tension or slippage between his careful differentiation of forms of life and the "multiplicity of heterogeneous structures and limits" that obtain among living beings, on the one hand, and a countervailing tendency to speak of "the living in general" on the other (*The Animal That Therefore I Am*, 48).

40 Thacker, *After Life*, 234.

41 Thacker, *After Life*.

42 Hägglund, "The Arche-Materiality of Time," 265.

43 Derrida, *Without Alibi*, 136.

44 Hägglund, "The Arche-Materiality of Time," 272–73. "Far from metaphysical" for the following reason: "The deconstructive notion of the trace is logical rather than ontological. Accordingly, my argument does not assume the form of an unconditional assertion ('being is spacing, hence arche-materiality') but rather the form of a conditional claim ('if your discourse commits you to a notion of succession, then you are committed to a notion of spacing and hence arche-materiality'). The discourse in question can then be ontological, episte-

mological, phenomenological, or scientific—in all these cases the logic of the trace will have expressive power insofar as there is an implicit or explicit commitment to a notion of succession" (270).

45 Staten, quoted in Hägglund, "The Arche-Materiality of Time," 275.

46 Hägglund, "The Arche-Materiality of Time," 275.

47 Esposito, *Immunitas*, 29–30.

48 Esposito, "The Person and Human Life," 218, emphasis added.

49 Esposito, *Immunitas*, 14–16.

50 Esposito, "The Person and Human Life," 217–18.

51 Thacker, *After Life*, 240.

52 Luke, "The Dreams of Deep Ecology," 51.

53 Esposito, *Bios*, 186.

54 Esposito, *Bios*, 187.

55 Rorty, "Postmodern Bourgeois Liberalism," 198. For a discussion of these questions in relation to biocentrism and deep ecology, see Bookchin and Foreman, *Defending the Earth*, 123–27.

56 "Biology 2.0," *Economist*, June 19, 2010, 4.

57 "Biology 2.0."

58 "Genesis Redux," *Economist*, May 22, 2010, 81–82.

59 "Genesis Redux," 82.

60 See Specter, "Annals of Science," 65.

61 Derrida, *Rogues*, 146–47.

62 Derrida, *Rogues*, 147.

63 Derrida, *The Animal That Therefore I Am*, 30.

64 Derrida, *The Animal That Therefore I Am*.

65 LaCapra, *History and Its Limits*, 127.

66 Derrida, *Of Spirit*, 57.

67 Derrida, *The Animal That Therefore I Am*, 29.

68 Derrida, *The Animal That Therefore I Am*, 30–31.

69 Calarco, *Zoographies*, 89–90.

70 Derrida and Roudinesco, *For What Tomorrow?*, 63.

71 Derrida, "'Eating Well,' or the Calculation of the Subject," 100.

72 Derrida, "'Eating Well,' or the Calculation of the Subject."

73 Hägglund, *Radical Atheism*, 96.

74 Hägglund, *Radical Atheism*, 94.

75 Bennett is quite right that "the philosophical project of naming where subjectivity begins and ends is too often bound up with fantasies of a human uniqueness in the eyes of God, of escape from materiality, or of mastery of nature; and even where it is not, it remains an aporetic or quixotic endeavor." It is that aporia that I am trying to address in the foregoing, and in a manner that I think is consonant with Bennett's observation that she is courting "the charge of performative self-contradiction: is it not a human subject who, after all, is articulating this theory of vibrant matter? Yes and no, for I will argue that what looks like a

performative contradiction may well dissipate if one considers revisions in operative notions of matter, life, self, self-interest, will, and agency"—her version, in short, of what I have been articulating here as the prosthetic relation of the who and the what. Bennett, *Vibrant Matter*, ix. Latour's formulation appears in *We Have Never Been Modern*.

76 "Infinitely" here should be taken, of course, not in the sense of "positive infinity" that Derrida criticizes in Levinas but rather in the sense of the "infinite finitude of *différance*" that constitutes the alterity of a *who* who is also always already other to itself, constituted by what it is not (the trace, technicity, and so on; Hägglund, *Radical Atheism*, 95, 94).

77 Bryant, "Questions about the Possibility of Non-correlationist Ethics."

78 Esposito, *Bios*, 187.

79 Esposito, *Bios*, 186.

80 Spinoza, quoted in Esposito, *Bios*, 186.

81 Hägglund, *Radical Atheism*, 94.

CHAPTER II

Thing-Politics and Science

Carsten Strathausen

On the Concept of Things

In 1993, Bruno Latour called for replacing our current "modern Constitution"—defined by the nature-society distinction and the continuing legacy of Cartesian rationalism—with the more egalitarian and less anthropocentric "Parliament of Things." "It is time," Latour concluded, "to speak of democracy again, but of a democracy extended to things themselves."[1] Latour's call did not go unheeded. Other historians of science—such as Lorraine Daston, Peter Galison, and Hans-Jörg Rheinberger—have each made compelling arguments in favor of a relationist and thing-oriented political epistemology.[2] In the words of Latour's collaborator Isabelle Stengers, the left needs to "decenter political theory from the abstract concept of 'humans.'"[3] This sentiment is echoed by prominent political and cultural theorists, who likewise champion thing-power as the most promising way to conceive of a different sociopolitical order beyond the anthropocentric legacy of (neo) liberalism. John Protevi, for example, recognizes contemporary political theory's "turn to a new, nonmechanistic materialism"—a new materialism that William Connolly names "immanent materialism" and Jane Bennett calls "vital materialism."[4]

What unites these new materialisms, according to Diana Coole and Samantha Frost, the editors of an anthology with that title, is their rejection of classical Marxist theory and economic determinism in favor of a more complex—and affect-oriented—notion of biopolitics, coupled with a keen interest in science studies (notably post-Newtonian physics as well as current advances in biotechnology and the life sciences).[5] Thing-politics, in short, embraces a "materialist theory of politics" that takes "the 'stuff' of politics seriously" and acknowledges the "*constitutive* power" of nonhuman things in the political realm.[6]

This essay takes thing-politics at its word. I want to look closely at some key concepts such as affect, life, individual, and, above all, the concept of knowledge itself. My inquiry is guided by the following question: what is the price to pay for "the multimodal methodology" of these new (vitalist, nonmechanistic, immanent) materialisms that currently inform the post-humanities? I am particularly interested in the institutional and epistemological consequences that ensue from "the multitiered ontologies, the complex systems, and the stratified reality" endorsed by thing-politics.[7] This multiplicity of different methodological-ontological frameworks, I argue, gives rise to disciplinary tensions about conceptual meanings and discursive practices. Although these tensions produce new ways of thinking about the present, they also exacerbate or cover up the epistemological paradoxes that define the limit of meaningful interdisciplinary collaboration across the disciplines. Each academic discipline comprises a complex system of discursive practice that creates its own dynamics and follows its own laws of structural development. For that, precisely, is its academic purpose: each discipline, by its very nature, is charged with presenting a substantially different view of how things are: "Disciplines seek to be complete worlds unto themselves; they aspire to explain everything, albeit in their own way."[8] From this perspective, it seems hardly surprising that thing-politics continues to wrestle with the epistemological tensions that arise within and in between the concepts it employs: because these concepts are rooted in different academic disciplines and derive from different methods of inquiry and discursive practices.

My study of thing-politics seeks to acknowledge both the potential collaboration between science and the humanities and the actual conflicts that exist between them. In order to conceptualize this conflictual terrain in terms of thing-politics, we must first and foremost recognize concepts as objects in their own right. Yet precisely because concepts are objects, their (potential) interaction is restricted by the (actual) stratification of their historical-contextual environment, largely defined by the use of language and other human practices. Semantics matter in science no less than in the humanities, because concepts not only cooperate but also compete with one another: they collide or connect, merge or dissipate, depending on the particular circumstances of their encounter. Due in large part to Deleuze's influence in posthumanist discourse, contemporary critics, I argue, tend to disregard the semantic ambiguity within concepts and the epistemological conflicts that frequently arise between them. The concept of biopolitics provides an excellent case in point: "Compressed (and at the same time destabilized) by competing readings and subject to continuous rotations of meaning around its own axis, the concept of biopolitics risks losing its identity and becoming an enigma."[9] The same problem hampers the ongoing debate about human nature in neo-Darwinian theory and evolutionary psychology. Like many other historians of the sciences, Evelyn Fox Keller, for example, laments the "morass of linguistic and conceptual vegetation" that has grown around the nature-nurture debate over centuries past. Keller's deliberate choice of metaphors ("morass," "vegetation," "tangle") renders language itself organic and alive. It is precisely this ongoing, quasi-organic evolution of language, Keller contends, that causes "the slippage of meaning, or polysemy, of our basic vocabulary," and it is this constant slippage of meaning that continues to nourish the terminological and conceptual confusions surrounding the gene myth and the nature-nurture debate.[10]

A similar danger of conceptual incoherence, I believe, threatens contemporary thing-politics and its attempt to rethink the relation between vitalism and materialism—two concepts that are traditionally considered to be mutually exclusive. Marxist materialism, for one, has always remained suspicious of vitalist philosophy (e.g., Nietzsche, Bergson, Heidegger), which it deemed inherently irrational and potentially fascist.[11] According to classical Marxist theory from Marx to Lenin, vitalism mystifies the (scientific) laws of nature and disavows the historical inevitability of revolutionary change. Twentieth-century Frankfurt School Marxists (e.g., Adorno, Eagleton, Jameson) likewise denounced vitalism because it purportedly projects human qualities onto lifeless matter. This anthropomorphization of nature, in their view, mystifies the real process of reification at the heart of capitalism. Vitalism thus reinforces rather than exposes the commodity fetishism that fuels the capitalist mode of production. Adorno's harsh critique of the "thing-cult" of symbolist art and poetry is exemplary in this regard. "The aesthetic weakness of this thing-cult, its obscurantist demeanor and its blending of religion with arts and crafts, reveals the real power of reification, which can no longer be gilded with a lyrical halo and brought back within the sphere of meaning."[12]

Mindful of this critical history, the new materialists are careful to distinguish thing-politics from both Marxist materialism and traditional vitalism alike. Although Jane Bennett, for example, recognizes some important "affinities between Adorno's nonidentity and thing-power," she emphasizes that Adorno "is quick—too quick from the point of view of the vital materialist—to remind the reader that objects are always 'entwined' with human subjectivity."[13] Yet Bennett also distances herself from "vitalism in the traditional sense; I equate affect with materiality, rather than posit a separate force that can enter and animate a physical body."[14]

At the same time, however, thing-politics, much like contemporary chaos and complexity theory, embraces the notion that physical laws of nature are necessary but insufficient to predict how things behave or matter evolves over long periods of time. In recent decades, numerous philosophers and renowned scientists have argued "that the unfolding of the universe is *not sufficiently describable by natural law*."[15] The physicist and Nobel laureate Ilya Prigogine agrees: "We need a 'divine' point of view to retain the idea of determinism. But no human measurement, no theoretical predictions, can give us initial conditions with infinite precision."[16] Prigogine, therefore, stresses "the role of human creativity in science," which is often undervalued by practicing scientists and philosophers alike.[17] "If the world were formed by stable dynamical systems," Prigogine concludes, "it would be radically different from the one we observe around us. It would be a static, predictable world, but we would not be here to make the predictions."[18] More recently, Robert E. Ulanowicz has charged that neither Newtonian nor Darwinian approaches are "sufficient for explaining how real change—in the form of creative advance or emergence—takes place in nature."[19]

To be sure, nobody denies that a theory that contradicts the basic laws of natural science is demonstrably false. Yet scientific falsifiability (as described by Karl Popper, Donald T. Campbell, Gerhard Vollmer, and others) does not amount to objective verification and the predictability of events. On the contrary: the main characteristic of organic life is the emergence of new and unforeseen systemic effects. Although these effects can be explained in principle with the help of mathematical models and statistical analyses, their occurrence in each individual case is unpredictable, as Manuel DeLanda has made clear.[20] No theory, not even Darwinian evolution, is able to determine in advance what exactly is possible (and what not) within the boundaries of natural law. This is precisely why Prigogine, Kauffman, and Ulanowicz all emphasize the importance of—and need for—human creativity for the production of knowledge. There remains ample room for competing explanatory models of human nature in both the humanities and the life sciences today.

In order to study the epistemological effects of the new materialisms, we need to come to terms with the peculiar nature of those living things called humans. In saying this, I do not want to advocate a return to the structuralist Marxism of Louis Althusser, who famously considered the humanist ideology of the subject constitutive of all societies, including communism.[21] But I do believe that we cannot conceptualize social politics without at least some notion of human agency that distinguishes it from that of other "actants."[22] My main argument is that thing-politics in its current form renders this task difficult, if not impossible. If one of the goals of thing-politics is to study the social effects of affect, then we must primarily consider our knowledge and experience of these things and affects. What matters politically is to conceptualize the forces that, on the one hand, take shape in human bodies, while, on the other hand, they take hold of human bodies. For this reason alone, thing-politics entails an irreducible phenomenological dimension.

Another reason why we need to retain some notion of human agency is that epistemology itself becomes unthinkable without it. There is no science without observation, no knowledge without concepts, and neither politics nor history without human beings. Most—if not all—academic disciplines are based on this premise, the negation of which will inevitably increase the intellectual disconnect between the humanities and the sciences. If thing-politics continues to pursue what appears to be an antihuman—as opposed to an antihumanist—discourse, it might inhibit rather than foster interdisciplinary exchange about how to understand the role of affect in contemporary politics. Yet we need more discursive sites of critical engagement, not less. And the most promising site for these engagements, in my view, remains the university in general and the empirical sciences in particular. How better to influence the current discourse on biotechnologies than by actively engaging—through institutional collaboration and intellectual debate—with colleagues in the social and life sciences?

I do not believe that the humanities' critical engagement with the life sciences will shift the—already unbalanced—institutional power dynamics further to the sciences' advantage. Nor do I share the widespread anxiety among humanities scholars about "the colonization of the cultural sphere by a scientific mode of thinking."[23] While I do not want to belittle these concerns, they seem at least partly based on the failure to appreciate the disciplinary and methodological diversity both within contemporary biology (between molecular and evolutionary biology; between research on plants, animals, and humans; between biochemistry, biophysics, bioinformatics, biogenetics, bioengineering, etc.) and in between the natural sciences at large.[24] The history of science demonstrates that there simply is no scientific mode of thinking currently practiced anywhere, because scientific theory and practice remains always bound to—territorialized upon—particular spatiotemporal coordinates. The production of scientific knowledge is always territorialized: it occurs at a particular place at a particular time, which is why science encompasses a multiplicity of diverse and often contradictory theories, methodologies, and procedures.

This disciplinary diversity of science provides ample opportunities for the humanities to actively engage and influence both academic and popular debates on the science of life. Yet the political left keeps "territorializ[ing] itself on the category of resistance," a resistance that all too often "is little more than the denunciation of all possibility of knowledge and truth, as if communicative capitalism was not already implicated in fundamental changes to the conditions of possibility for credibility," as Jodi Dean points out.[25] In my view, the more critical approach to communicative capitalism might be a certain affirmation, if you wish, of scientific practice.[26] An intellectually open engagement with whatever contemporary science has to offer in conceptual terms has nothing to do with "being epistemologically intimidated by the sciences."[27] Yet it has everything to do with what the humanities have always done best, namely, to explore different forms of knowledge and understanding.[28]

With this premise in mind, the remainder of this essay is structured into three more parts. The second section situates thing-politics within the post-reductionist paradigm of contemporary science. I argue for the conceptual irreducibility of humans to things by drawing a distinction between Deleuze's concept of singularity and Foucault's concept of self. For only the latter provides a basis for epistemological research and yields insight into the production of knowledge. In the third section, I examine in greater detail the conceptual tensions surrounding the current debate of biopolitics. I focus in particular on Roberto Esposito's work *Bios*. Although I support his attempt to replace the humanist notion of the individual with the less restrictive concept of individuation, I particularly call attention to the inevitability of human agency in scientific-discursive practices. For it is precisely these practices that enable us humans to recognize and engage the individuation of things in the first place. In the last section, I briefly return to Marx in order to suggest that the new materialisms should retain at least one aspect of old (Marxist) materialism, namely, its pragmatist understanding of human beings as the agents of history.

There is broad consensus among leftist political philosophers about the need for new concepts to help analyze the dynamic structures of global capitalism. Carlo Galli, for example, argues that globalization "organizes new spaces for itself in a new way," which requires a new vocabulary able to analyze and critique the traditional concept of space and its relation to politics.[29] Thing-politics responds to this challenge by reconceptualizing the incessantly shifting spatial configurations of contemporary geopolitics. But how can we map these emergent political spaces in epistemological terms? One possibility would be to return to the *Ideenkonstellation* (constellation of ideas) by which Walter Benjamin sought to conceptualize the *Origin of the German Tragic Play*. Yet Benjamin's vision of ideas as quasi-planetary objects caught in interstellar constellations presupposes a well-ordered and stable Newtonian space whose equilibrium is maintained by the gravitational forces between these objects. The emergent epistemological landscape of today's new materialism, by contrast, seems less determined by the absolute laws of mechanical physics and more akin to the self-regulatory structures of dynamic systems and living organisms.

At the same time, however, I am hesitant to envision this new materialist landscape as a rhizome in Deleuze's sense—in spite of the term's strong biological connotation and Deleuze's explicit reference to plants, fungi, and the brain as rhizomatic structures. Given Deleuze's distaste for metaphorical language, we ought to think of rhizomes as actually living organisms, which implies a homeostatic, self-regulatory mechanism at its core and in charge of maintaining its overall systemic stability. There is no organism without environment, but neither is there an environment without an organism.[30] Deleuze's nonorganic version of vitalism, unlike that of Canguilhem and Foucault, fails to reflect upon this centrist organization of life. In botanical terms, a rhizome denotes a mass of roots that distinguishes certain groups of plants from others. Like all plants, however, rhizomes are subject to the laws of evolution. The concepts evoked by contemporary thing-politics, by contrast, are not rhizomatically organized. On the contrary, they were originally conceived in different sociohistorical contexts and emerged from different disciplinary practices. If anything, one might think of each academic discipline as a rhizome and conclude that the (epistemological) transfer of specific concepts from one discipline to another is no less challenging than the (bioengineered) transfer of specific morphological characteristics from one plant to another. In both cases, the transplanted object needs to take root in its new environment; otherwise, it won't grow. The current medley of concepts in thing-politics is too heterogeneous to effect a rhizomatic structure.

It is important to remember that Deleuze primarily thinks of concepts as independent singularities that create their own space of extension and existence. Although he acknowledges that "every concept has a history" that renders it "both absolute and relative," he nonetheless insists that the "concept speaks the event, not the essence or the thing."[31] The Deleuzian concept, in other words, "is self-referential: it posits itself and its object at the same time it is created."[32] Yet its objects are neither material things nor "the lived," but always "the contour, the configuration, the constellation of an event to come."[33] In epistemological terms, Deleuzian concepts are as autonomous and irreducibly singular as Leibniz's monads: "The concept is obviously knowledge—but knowledge of itself, and what it knows is the pure event, which must not be confused with the state of affairs in which it is embodied."[34] Historians of science, by contrast, insist that this "confusion" between the "pure event" and the actual "state of affairs" is crucial for the production of (scientific) knowledge. Concepts are objects, to be sure, but they are not entirely self-referential. Instead, they remain bound to precisely those material things and "the lived" state of affairs from which (some of) Deleuze's philosophy ultimately cuts them off.

Foucault, too, regarded concepts as historically determined objects of thought that remain inextricably caught up in the actual limits and constraints of the specific discursive practices from which they emerged. His perspective reflects the influence of his teachers—Bachelard, Canguilhem, Althusser—and their epistemological commitment to the historical study of scientific practice.[35] This difference between Foucault and Deleuze—between a historical epistemology that focuses on the relational being of concepts as opposed to a creative ontology that focuses on their singular becoming—is crucial if we want to come to terms with thing-politics, for two reasons.[36] First, the former (Foucauldian) approach enables and requires the kind of historical-epistemological questions the latter (Deleuzian) approach renders more or less meaningless. Deleuze's ontology, according to which relations are external to their terms, literally spells the end of epistemology. Concepts produce knowledge only if conceived in terms of their sociohistorical and political (inter)relations. Conceived as nonrelational singularities in Deleuze's sense, however, concepts are essentially unknowable and hence nonscientific.

In fact, Deleuze distinguishes philosophical from logical concepts precisely because the latter reduces concepts to functions and "makes science the concept par excellence."[37] Deleuze is right, of course: epistemology does privilege science in order to understand how knowledge is produced. As historians of science (from Canguilhem and Bachelard to Hacking, Rheinberger, and Daston) have repeatedly pointed out, concepts are productive precisely because they shape things in both epistemological and ontological terms. They remind us that matter and meaning, thing and thought coemerge as intertwined beings in the world. Yet they also emphasize that these beings remain site specific and historically determined. Concepts are inherently relational objects, not independent singularities.

This leads us to the second reason why we should distinguish between the Foucauldian and the Deleuzian approach toward thing-politics. It concerns the concept of the human, for which Deleuze's antiphenomenological philosophy does not have much use. Since "the enemy is the organism"—"organism" understood as the coagulated "organization of the organs" in living bodies—Deleuze's overall goal is to disarticulate this organization, not to study it.[38] Knowledge, for Deleuze, is not the product of human investigation, but results from the incessant movement of "pure thought" passively registered by humans in/as sensation: "We must try to imagine events of pure thought, radical or transcendental events that determine a space of knowledge for any one era," Deleuze contends.[39] "Contemplating is creating, the mystery of passive creation, sensation."[40] Deleuze, in fact, never made a secret of the vitalist strand in his philosophy ("Everything I've written is vitalistic, at least I hope it is") and he clearly considered Foucault's work, too, as partaking of the vitalist tradition, particularly in regard to the theme of subjectification, which "amounts essentially to inventing new possibilities of life" and new "styles of thought"—"a vitalism rooted in aesthetics."[41]

For all his critique of human subjectivity, however, Foucault never went quite as far as Deleuze in trying to liberate thought from "the critical ontology of ourselves" and "the hermeneutics of the subject."[42] This is not to claim that Foucault, toward the end of his career, endorsed the kind of humanist individualism he had previously critiqued.[43] For regardless of how one interprets Foucault's notion of self—be it in the traditional sense of liberal "individuality," as Nikolas Rose argues, or more along phenomenological lines, as Peter Hallward suggests, or, finally, as a process of "individuation taking place through intensities," as Deleuze and Nealon insist—what matters most for thing-politics is the fact that Foucault, unlike Deleuze, never abandoned the concept of the human subject: "Whereas Deleuze would like to get rid of the relational subject altogether," Hallward concludes, "Foucault wants to *purge* the subject, to eliminate everything that specifies or objectifies the subject."[44] Even in his later lectures, Foucault continued to think through the self, whereas Deleuze always thought beyond it.

The significance of this distinction has become increasingly apparent during the recent affective turn in the humanities, which has spawned a lively debate about whether—or how—to conceptualize the relation between sensation and sense, matter and meaning.[45] Although Brian Massumi laments the fact that "there is no cultural-theoretical vocabulary specific to affect," he quickly adds that such a vocabulary must be part of an "asignifying philosophy" in order to respect the "autonomy of affect" that remains irreducible to human modes of cognition.[46] Regardless of its philosophical merits, Massumi's Deleuzianism—that is, his understanding of affect as a virtual, apersonal, and asignifying force of becoming—has clearly contributed to the increasing disciplinary rift between the humanities and the social sciences. Lawrence Grossberg is not alone in contesting the "leap from a set of ontological concepts to a description of an empirical and affective context."[47] "Affect can let you off the hook," Grossberg worries, because it "appeal[s] back to an ontology that escapes," meaning that "affect has come to serve, now, too often as a 'magical' term."[48]

I share Grossberg's concerns. I, too, believe that unless we recognize affects as "material, physiological things"—things that emerge from neuronal connections, hormonal streams, and changes in blood flow and other physiological traits that sustain living organisms and take hold of human bodies—it will be difficult, if not impossible, to study "the transmission of affect" at the level of everyday life.[49] And yet it is precisely this transmission that matters politically. Why care about affects at all, unless they are "understood as forces in human affairs that can be . . . transformed"?[50] To be sure, politics concerns the affective relations among all things, not only humans. Politics is not just a matter of (cognitive) comprehension and recognition, but also involves (precognitive) apprehension and recognizability, as today's critics rightly point out.[51] Yet the laws of affective social transformations cannot be conceptualized in isolation from the empirical research that helps define these laws. What matters in contemporary politics is neither the virtual dimension of affect nor its stratified actualization, but precisely the dynamic thresholds at which affect materializes and seizes (human) bodies.

One may agree or disagree with Manuel DeLanda's claim that these thresholds belong to the "intensive" and thus constitute a third ontological plane in Deleuze's philosophy distinct from both the "virtual" and the "actual."[52] The crucial point remains that the dynamic laws of intensive transformation need to be studied empirically with the help of scientific inquiry as practiced in different academic disciplines.

Deleuze's ontology of pure becoming preempts epistemology, however, because the infinite space of the virtual disables the conceptual tension between the objectivity of science and the subjectivity of human experience that constitutes knowledge. Modern science exists only because of this tension, as Erwin Schrödinger points out: "The material world has only been constructed at the price of taking the self, that is, mind, out of it, removing it; mind is not part of it."[53] Put differently, the rationalist notion of scientific objectivity presupposes—and can only operate in conjunction with—the humanist separation of lifeless things from human subjectivity. "What a paradox!" Edmund Husserl exclaimed in his famous lecture on the crisis in European sciences in 1932: "Nothing could cripple the peculiar force of the rapidly growing and, in their own accomplishments, unassailable exact sciences or the belief in their truth. And yet, as soon as one took into account that they are the accomplishments of the consciousness of knowing subjects, their self-evidence and clarity were transformed into incomprehensible absurdity."[54] The entire discourse of Western philosophy, Boris Groys has cogently argued, ultimately comes down to this: "*Logos* is paradox," or, in Niklas Luhmann's terms: "The *form* of rationality itself under modernity is paradoxical."[55] Analytical philosophers call this phenomenon norm circularity or the principle of relativity. As Willard van Ornam Quine explains, "What makes sense is to say not what the objects of a theory are, absolutely speaking, but how one theory of objects is interpretable or reinterpretable in another."[56] Insofar as classical science refuses to acknowledge its constitutive relativist nature, it remains a profoundly metaphysical enterprise, as Canguilhem, Lyotard, and many others have argued.[57] Yet once we acknowledge the first-person / third-person distinction as the very foundation of scientific knowledge (as in cybernetics, biology, and system theory), the process of thinking immediately gets entangled in paradox and logical contradictions, as outlined above.

Logical paradox, however, does not spell the end of knowledge, nor does it condemn us to complete ignorance about the world we live in. On the contrary: paradox enables knowledge; it is the sine qua non of scientific inquiry and epistemological investigation into the paradoxical nature of things. Knowledge and meaning emerge precisely through "the de-paradoxification of the fundamental and constitutive paradox that underlies all ordered structures" because "*universalization* can be achieved only through *specification*."[58] Paraphrasing Luhmann and Wolfe, we might say that science, like any other complex-dynamic system, works "only *because* it is such a reduction of complexity."[59] The production of knowledge is predicated on the chiasmic relation of blindness and insight, between operational closure and environmental permeability. The claim that the real is a (scientific) construction is true only and precisely because (scientific) constructions are themselves determined by the infinite complexity of the real. This paradox literally informs the being of humans and their relation to the material world. "Things," Lorraine Daston clarifies, "knit together matter and meaning."[60] As she explains elsewhere: "Things are both socially constructed *and* real. That is, they depend crucially on the cultural resources at and in a given context . . . *and* they capture some aspect of the world; they work. But they are neither historically inevitable nor metaphysically true. Rather they are contingent to a certain place and yet valid for certain purposes."[61] In any given situation, humans experience things both exactly as they are in and of themselves and as something actively constructed by us and for us. Scientific knowledge—originally conceived by Galileo, Kepler, Descartes, Bacon, and so on as the objective mathematization of nature—is never just an abstract method of representation, but always remains rooted in life and the living. Not only is knowledge based on human practice; it is itself a human practice that constitutes "a form of life."[62]

Although some tough-minded realists continue to struggle with the methodological and epistemic consequences ensuing from the paradoxical nature of Western rationality, most scientific disciplines have accepted and productively integrated this dilemma into their discursive practices. Daston aptly points out that most scientists today "take it for granted that things are simultaneously material and meaningful."[63] They hardly have a choice in the matter, given the century-old history of philosophical reflection and scientific evidence demonstrating the chiasmic intertwinement of epistemological and ontological questions.[64] Ever since Einstein's and Heisenberg's revolutionary discoveries of relativity and quantum physics some one hundred years ago, post-Newtonian physics was forced to recognize the behavioral unpredictability of nonlinear systems. The original conundrum in quantum physics was that the scientist's observation of particles interacts with—and thus changes—the (state of) things observed. Heisenberg repeatedly remarked upon the insufficiency of classical logic to explain quantum physics: "The mathematical scheme of quantum theory can be interpreted as an extension or modification of classical logic," in particular the "law 'tertium non datur.'"[65]

A key distinction between classical physics and quantum physics thus concerns the replacement of absolute laws with statistical laws of probability. In Heisenberg's words, a probability function "does not in itself represent a course of events in the course of time. It represents a tendency for events and our knowledge of events. The probability function can be connected with reality only if one essential condition is fulfilled: a new measurement is made to determine a certain property of the system. Only then does the probability function allow us to calculate the probable result of the new measurement."[66] Anticipating what cybernetics and (general) system theory would later formulate in terms of autopoiesis and second-order observation, Heisenberg recognized that only a second measurement is able to supplement the limited information obtained by means of the first. Obviously, this amounts to an infinite regress of ever more observations—none of which, however, is able to reveal what exactly "happens to the system between the initial observation and the next measurement."[67]

Quantum physics, much like the nonlinear dynamics of complex systems explored by mathematicians since the 1970s, required scientists to shift focus "from objects to relationships, from quantity to quality, from substance to pattern."[68] Post-Newtonian physics, in other words, amounts to a fundamental reconceptualization of the natural laws of science. These laws can no longer be stated in absolute, determinist terms, but instead are based on statistical data that predict probabilities rather than certainties. Today's physics analyzes dynamic potentials, not static facts.[69] The same holds true for the various "knowledges produced by the new biology." Based on the molecular, cellular, and holistic study of individual organisms and whole populations, the laws currently developed by the life sciences are "probabilistic rather than deterministic" in nature.[70]

Population genetics provides a case in point. As Evelyn Fox Keller points out, genetics can only answer "statistical question[s] about the relative contributions of variations in genetics and in the environment to our differences from each other."[71] These statistics, however, are only "of limited use in trying to tease out the influence of genotype on phenotype."[72] In other words, geneticists' statistical information about the distribution of trait differences among a given (i.e., arbitrarily defined) population does not answer the question about the power of genes to determine the unique development of a single organism. Contrary to popular belief, genes are not, strictly speaking, agents, because they do not act in and of themselves. Rather, genes are activated in and through their specific environment, and the result of their activation can only be measured statistically in terms of probability, but not actually in terms of the specific traits of a unique individual.

Before moving on to the next section, let me briefly emphasize that none of the above amounts to some postmodern cult of fashionable nonsense or scientific irrationalism.[73] Instead, the demise of the traditional concept of objectivity is based on developments in numerous scientific fields, including mathematics, physics, and the life sciences, all of which acknowledge the importance of postreductionist ways of thinking. Neither Heisenberg nor Schrödinger, neither Husserl nor Luhmann ever denied the existence of material reality, nor did they reduce scientific knowledge to just one among many arbitrary constructions of how the world is. To say that matter and meaning are inextricably intertwined is not the same as saying that matter and meaning are identical and literally amount to the same thing. On the contrary, the crucial point is to avoid this unproductive short circuit between the epistemological and the ontological realm. If we allow both realms to collapse into one and the same thing, we effectively undermine the production of new knowledge, because we reify the dynamic interplay between matter and meaning on which all scientific inquiry is based. Instead, epistemology remains—and ought to remain—in a state "of perpetual crisis," as Hans-Jörg Rheinberger points out.[74] The very production of scientific knowledge depends upon this crisis, for there is no knowledge independent of the problems it encounters: "As long as epistemic objects and their concepts remain blurred, they generate a productive tension."[75] The goal is precisely not to "confuse ontological questions (about what exists) with epistemological questions (about how we know about it)," but to demonstrate "why these questions have to be answered together."[76]

Defining Life: Individual versus Individuation

This (all too brief) overview may suffice to demonstrate the scientific credentials behind the new materialism of thing-politics.[77] My goal has been to demonstrate that the sciences have, by and large, been able to make sense of—and productively engage with—the logical paradoxes that found the humanist tradition of Western rationalism. On the political side, however, the legacy of this tradition has proven disastrous. The "anthropological machine of humanism" has given rise to a highly normative—and normalizing—understanding of human nature, which in turn has shaped the modern history of liberal-democratic philosophy from Locke and Hobbes to John Rawls and Jürgen Habermas.[78] One of its key concepts is that of the human individual, which is meant to capture the physical-organic integrity—the holistic gestalt—of a living body. In the liberal tradition, life is therefore considered a personal property of the individual, which means that being alive is tantamount to (the being of) individuals. As Judith Butler rightly points out, liberal political philosophy "tends to presuppose already constituted communities, already established subjects" but fails to analyze "how these subjects and communities are constituted" and become recognizable as such in the first place.[79]

Yet the countless humanitarian crises of the twentieth and twenty-first centuries have exposed—and continue to expose—the political impotence of liberal philosophy and its unfaltering belief in the (always already) given identity of individuals, communities, and nation-states. It was precisely this presumed naturalness of liberalist discourse that fueled much of the postmodern critique of traditional humanism, which Sartre famously characterized as "nothing but an ideology of lies, a perfect justification for pillage."[80] Sartre's overall goal, like that of most French intellectuals at the time, was not to destroy but rather "to remake humanism."[81] It is therefore hardly accidental that Louis Althusser qualified his philosophy as a theoretical antihumanism, or that Foucault repeatedly sought to clarify the antihumanist—as opposed to antihuman—tenets of his philosophy. Not only leftist progressives (e.g., Alain Badiou, Jacques Rancière, Slavoj Žižek, Gilles Deleuze), but also conservative thinkers (e.g., Carl Schmitt, Leo Strauss) throughout the twentieth century have argued that liberal human rights discourse is ineffective at best and counterproductive at worst.

Hannah Arendt was among the first to make this claim. Although human rights are meant to protect refugees, migrants, and those who, for whatever reason, are no longer protected by the nation-state, they are, in fact, only applied to those who continue to enjoy state rights anyhow. Human rights, in other words, are the phantasmagorical double—rather than the primordial foundation—of citizen rights. Without the legal-administrative power of nation-states to implement them, human rights are politically meaningless, a concept without a referent. For there is nobody to administer these rights nor anybody to whom these rights are actually being applied. Once reduced to the status of bare life, to use Giorgio Agamben's term, the human being falls outside all—that is, both the sacred and the secular—order of things. Like the rationalist concept of objectivity, the liberal notion of human rights is a metaphysical construct inherited from the Western humanist tradition. As Arendt points out again and again, the human does not exist; only humans do. What humans share, however, "are not attributes of human nature, however we may define it, but qualities of a world constructed by humans."[82]

Today more than ever, the liberal concept of the human individual and its inalienable rights seems out of touch with life as it currently takes shape in molecular research and biotechnological procedures. As numerous studies have pointed out, the increased cooperation among financial investors, corporate industry, and the life sciences has led to an enormous production (and consumption) of sophisticated products, prostheses, and medical procedures that affect and modify the internal regulatory systems of living organisms.[83] And yet, although contemporary biotechnology is meant to serve and protect life—and, above all else, human life—its major effect, paradoxically, consists in undermining our traditional humanist belief in subjectivity, individuality, and the integrity of the human body. For it has become increasingly unclear what exactly constitutes life or human life in the first place. As the life sciences and medical examiners penetrate deeper and deeper into living organisms, they expose the dynamic complexity of self-regulatory mechanisms that question not only the body's ontological status as a unified being—a material thing in the world—but also reveal the precariousness of our epistemological concepts that seek to endow this bodily matter with cognitive meaning.

This means that the (philosophical, scientific, legal) concepts of life, as well as their material referents, are inherently unstable, or, in Butler's words, precarious.[84] Life itself, not just human life, requires its own concept—a concept less entangled with the rationalist anthropomorphism that characterizes the modern liberal understanding of the human subject as a free individual. Nobody has argued this point more convincingly than Roberto Esposito. Esposito's reading of Foucault seeks to unbind today's biopolitics from the history of modern sovereignty precisely in order to replace the static concept of the liberal individual with the more dynamic and process-oriented concept of individuation. What renders Esposito's philosophy important for us today, I think, is not only his detailed historical account of modern biopolitics or his careful negotiation of a middle path in between

Agamben's negative vision of biopolitics (understood as the exploitation of bare life) and Hardt and Negri's affirmative vision (of the multitude as an emergent biopolitical power).[85] Even more crucial, in my view, is Esposito's recognition that an affirmative vision of biopolitics requires the invention of a new conceptual framework that expresses—and protects—the irreducible multiplicity of life's becoming.

According to Esposito, biopolitics—both its concept and its practice—has become "not only the instrument but also the object of a bitter philosophical and political fight over the configuration and destiny of the current age."[86] Much of the confusion, Esposito argues, can be traced back to a conceptual ambiguity in Foucault's remarks on biopolitics. In his first volume of *The History of Sexuality* and his later lecture series from the mid-1970s to the early 1980s, Foucault provides a detailed historical investigation of different modes of governmentality in the modern age. He frequently distinguishes between disciplinary power and biopower as two different approaches—or technologies—for the organization of modern societies. While the first regime seeks to discipline the individual human (body), the second regime tries to engineer the development of entire populations: "Both technologies are obviously technologies of the body, but one is a technology in which the body is individualized as an organism endowed with capacities, while the other is a technology in which bodies are replaced by general biological processes."[87]

According to Esposito, however, Foucault's distinction between biopower and sovereign power "oscillates between a continuist attitude" and one "more inclined to mark differential thresholds."[88] For it remains unclear whether biopolitics produces subjectivity or death, that is, whether it constitutes "a politics of life or a politics over life": "If biopolitics is born with the end of sovereignty . . . , this means that the history of biopolitics is largely modern and in a certain sense postmodern. If instead, as Foucault suggests on other occasions, biopolitics accompanies the sovereign regime, constituting a particular articulation of a specific tonality, then its genesis is more ancient, one that ultimately coincides with that of politics itself, which has always in one way or another been devoted to life."[89] The crucial step in Esposito's argument is to link this ambiguity to a larger conceptual problem at the center of Foucauldian discourse, which concerns "the relation (not only historical, but conceptual and theoretical) between sovereignty and politics."[90] Esposito contends that Foucault essentially conceives the history of modern politics in terms of sovereignty, which leads him to regard disciplinary power and biopower as two consecutive regimes under the overall category of modern sovereignty. Esposito, by contrast, considers biopolitics—not sovereignty—the main concept that informs and structures the history of modern politics. In other words, whereas Foucault proceeds on the basis of a structural-conceptual link between sovereignty and modernity, Esposito replaces this link with that between biopolitics and modernity. For him, biopolitics is inherently modern and comprises different historical versions that range from early social contract theory and disciplinary power all the way to Nazi thanatopolitics and today's concerns about "the preservation of life through reproduction."[91] The overarching paradigm that unites the historically distinct regimes of modern biopolitics, Esposito argues, is their shared reliance upon "immunization [as] a negative [form] of the protection of life."[92]

Immunity, biopolitics, and modernity are thus coconstitutive in Esposito's view. Modern biopolitics has always been immunitarian, because modernity has always sought to discipline the (individual and social) body, first through the "juridification of life," and then, increasingly since the end of the nineteenth century, through the "biologization of law."[93] Regardless of the specific biopolitical regime, however, the immunitary paradigm operative within each has always remained the same, from Hobbes to Hitler: it is the inherently paradoxical attempt to protect life by regulating life, that is, to "shelter life in the same powers [*potenze*] that interdicts its development."[94]

This immunitary paradigm at the heart of modern biopolitics finally reached its structural limit with the rise of German fascism. Unlike any of its precursors, the Nazi regime pushed modern biopolitics over a critical threshold by completely (con)fusing body and politics. Nazi thanatopolitics, Esposito argues, is "actualized biology," because it literalizes the hitherto largely metaphorical tradition of conceiving modern politics in terms of life. "What before had always been a vitalistic metaphor becomes a reality in Nazism."[95] Due to this literalization of our modern biopolitical vocabulary, Nazism "represents the threshold with respect to the past that makes every updating of its lexical apparatus impractical."[96] Esposito especially mentions concepts such as sovereignty, law, and democracy as the "modern political categories that have been shaken and overturned" by twentieth-century biopolitics.[97]

As long as we continue to use these categories, Esposito concludes, political philosophy will remain trapped in the same biopolitical logic from which it seeks to escape. Since modern biopolitics neither emerged nor dissipated with the rise and fall of Nazism, it will persist until we develop a different political vocabulary that reconceptualizes the relation between life and politics along the nonnormative creativity of life's becoming.[98] Any affirmative vision of biopolitics, in other words, requires not only the rejection of the liberal concept of human individuality; it also requires that we leave behind the entire philosophical tradition of thinking individual being as such. Unless biopolitical discourse stops fixating on the (being of) individuals, it will inevitably remain chained to the self-destructive logic of the modern immunitarian paradigm and its paradoxical effort to protect life by destroying life. Instead, we must conceive of life in terms of individuation as opposed to the being of individuals, because the immunitarian paradigm holds no dominion over the infinite potential of life's becoming. Affirmative biopolitics thus "discovers in life its immanent norm, giving to the norm the potentiality [Potenza] of life's becoming."[99] In the final pages of his book and with explicit reference to Canguilhem and Deleuze, Esposito therefore envisions life as a self-regulatory process not only in the biological sense of the term (i.e., homeostasis, autopoiesis), but also in its juridical, normative sense: "The logic of the living," Esposito suggests, "is capable of introducing a powerful semantic in the juridical norm against the immunitary normalization of life."[100]

Although I support Esposito's attempt to reconceptualize modernity's political vocabulary along the lines of individuation, I am not sure—nor does Esposito himself specify—how to conceptualize "the multiplicity of juridical norms" that are said to emerge from this epistemological shift. In my view, this lack of specificity is itself symptomatic: it reminds us, once again, that the concept of individuation—like that of the individual or any other concept—is an (epistemological) object like any other. As such, individuation remains bound to specific discursive practices that seek to define its historical specificity (and not its singularity in Deleuze's sense). Here is how Gilbert Simondon describes these practices: "We cannot have either an immediate or a mediated knowledge of individuation, but only one that is in process parallel to the process with which we are already familiar. We cannot *know individuation* in the common sense of the phrase; we can only individuate, individuate ourselves and in ourselves."[101] In other words, the paradoxical attempt of human beings to obtain knowledge about the process of individuation that constitutes (their own) living presence becomes meaningful only in and through the (scientific) process itself. Like any other concept, individuation cannot be conceived in isolation from its empirical roots in science without losing its epistemological coherence. This is not to deny that "individuality is not a term, if by that we mean a limit: it is a term in a relation."[102] But this relation, Canguilhem insists again and again, is profoundly distorted if conceptualized as an independent entity apart from its constitutive terms and the discursive practices that constitute it. Doing so signals the end of science and epistemology, because both presuppose and require human agency in the pragmatist sense of the term. They are literally unthinkable without it.[103]

Labor

Like the new materialisms today, old (Marxist) materialism rejected the bourgeois humanist notion of subjectivity in favor of a scientific materialist view of nature. According to the early Marx, the fact that mankind continues "to create and posit things" provides empirical proof that we ourselves are also "posited by things, because that is what [we] essentially are by nature."[104] Yet humans, for Marx, are nonetheless particular and somewhat privileged things. More than any other creature on earth, humans constantly intervene and substantially alter the material world surrounding them. Man labors, and this labor, in Marx's view, is "an exclusively human characteristic" that remains irreducible to animal behavior.[105] The human being, for Marx, is a laboring animal that can realize itself as human only in and through the deliberate, goal-oriented action called labor. While the later Marx focused almost exclusively on the analysis of alienated labor in capitalist society, the early Marx ventured to characterize labor in a communist society as "a free expression of life, hence enjoying life." And he added, "My labor would thus confirm the particularity of my individuality, of my individual life."[106] However dialectically intertwined the respective natures of humans and things might be, Marx leaves no doubt that, at the end of the day, things themselves are neither actants nor agents in sociohistorical terms; only humans are.[107]

Notes

1 Latour, *We Have Never Been Modern*, 142.
2 Rheinberger, *An Epistemology of the Concrete*; Daston, preface to *Things That Talk*; Galison, *Image and Logic*.
3 Stengers, "Including Nonhumans in Political Theory," 13.

4 Protevi, *Political Affect*, xii; Connolly, *A World of Becoming*, 71; Bennett, *Vibrant Matter*, 13.

5 Diana Coole and Samantha Frost provide an excellent overview of the basic ontological, epistemological, and posthumanist premises shared by the new materialisms; compare Coole and Frost, "Introducing the New Materialisms," 1–43. According to Protevi, the theoretical influences shaping the new materialisms are based on "advances in a number of fields: dynamical systems modeling, what is commonly called 'complexity theory'; the ontology of Gilles Deleuze and Felix Guattari; the autonomous systems theory proposed by Humberto Maturana and Francisco Varela; developmental systems theory (DST), a new development in biological thought; new research on human emotion; and the situated cognition school in cognitive science" (Protevi, *Political Affect*, xiii–xiv). See also Alaimo and Hekman, "Introduction," 1–19.

6 Braun and Whatmore, "The Stuff of Politics," x, ix, xv.

7 Coole and Frost, "Introducing the New Materialisms," 32.

8 Chandler, "Introduction," 740.

9 Esposito, *Bios*, 15. Braun and Whatmore likewise assert that the current debate on biopolitics is "cast in ahistorical and metaphysical terms" ("The Stuff of Politics," xi).

10 Keller, *The Mirage*, 34.

11 Compare Lukács, *Von Nietzsche zu Hitler*.

12 Adorno, *Notes to Literature*, 40.

13 Bennett, *Vibrant Matter*, 49–51.

14 Bennett, *Vibrant Matter*, xiii. Similarly, the microbiologists Margulis and Sagan argue that "life is less mechanistic than we have been taught to believe; yet, since it disobeys no chemical or physical law, it is not vitalistic" (Margulis and Sagan, *What Is Life?*, 217).

15 Kauffman, "Foreword," ix–xvii.

16 Prigogine, *The End of Certainty*, 38.

17 Prigogine, *The End of Certainty*, 188.

18 Prigogine, *The End of Certainty*, 55.

19 Ulanowicz, *A Third Window*, back cover.

20 Manuel DeLanda rightly emphasizes the difference between explaining the phenomenon of emergence in principle versus predicting what exactly will be the result of such an emergence in reality. DeLanda is a realist, and he vehemently rejects the vitalist philosophy of the late nineteenth and early twentieth centuries. Yet he also understands that emergence still remains "something that is objectively irreducible" and hence unpredictable in its particular effects. DeLanda, *Intensive Science and Virtual Philosophy*, 3.

21 Compare Althusser, *For Marx*.

22 The term was originally coined by Bruno Latour in *The Politics of Nature*. Like Latour, Bennett thinks of nonhuman bodies as "actants rather than objects," because "so-called inanimate things have a life . . . a moment of independence

from and resistance to us and other bodies—a kind of thing-power" (Bennett, "Thing-Power," 45, 53).

23 In 2005, the online journal *Culture Machine* devoted an entire volume to the discussion of the interplay between scientific (complexity) theory and the humanities, with many of the essays expressing more skepticism than support for the idea. As the editorial introduction notes, "the power of the exact sciences to determine in advance what is worthy of questioning and so to mitigate against the risks of the untimely makes theoretical biology a thoroughly ambivalent force" (Cooper, Goffey, and Munster, "Biopolitics, For Now").

24 Compare Köchy, *Biophilosophie*, particularly 18ff. Connolly first addressed this problem a decade ago: "My sense is that in their laudable attempt to ward off one type of reductionism too many cultural theorists fall into another: they lapse into a reductionism that ignores how biology is mixed into thinking and culture and how other aspects of nature are folded into both" (*Neuropolitics*, 3).

25 Nealon, *Foucault beyond Foucault*, 110; Dean, *Democracy and Other Neoliberal Fantasies*, 9.

26 Deleuze and Guattari famously claimed that "those who criticize without creating . . . are the plague of philosophy" and "inspired by resentment" (Deleuze and Guattari, *What Is Philosophy?*, 28ff). Brian Massumi likewise suggests that "techniques of negative critique [must] be used sparingly" in cultural studies in order "to shift to [more] affirmative methods" of investigation (*Parables for the Virtual*, 13). Bennett agrees: "A relentless approach toward demystification works against the possibility of positive formulations," meaning that "we need both critique and positive formulations of alternatives" (*Vibrant Matter*, xv).

27 Biagioli, "Postdisciplinary Liaisons," 825.

28 Lennard Davis makes precisely this point. He proposes to establish what he calls "biocultural studies" in order to examine "the intersection of science, technology, medicine, and culture" (Davis, "Biocultures and Education," 37).

29 Galli, *Political Spaces and Global War*, 105.

30 "Physics is a science of fields, of milieus. But it has been discovered that, in order for there to be an environment, there must be a center. It is the position of a living being, its relation to the experience it lives in as a totality, that gives the milieu meaning as conditions of existence. Only a living being, infra-human, can coordinate a milieu. To explain the center by the environment would thus seem to be a paradox" (Canguilhem, *Knowledge of Life*, 70).

31 Deleuze and Guattari, *What Is Philosophy?*, 17, 21.

32 Deleuze and Guattari, *What Is Philosophy?*, 22.

33 Deleuze and Guattari, *What Is Philosophy?*, 22, 23ff.

34 Deleuze and Guattari, *What Is Philosophy?*, 33.

35 As Ian Hacking points out, "concepts have their being in historical sites" (*Historical Ontology*, 25). Like Canguilhem, Daston, Rheinberger, and others, Hacking considers "epistemological concepts as objects that evolve and mutate" (*Historical Ontology*, 9).

36 Compare Hallward, "The Singular and the Specific."

37 Deleuze and Guattari, *What Is Philosophy?*, 150.

38 Deleuze, *A Thousand Plateaus*, 158. For a more detailed account, see Strathausen, "Epistemological Reflections on Minor Points in Deleuze."

39 Deleuze, *Desert Islands and Other Texts*, 93.

40 Deleuze and Guattari, *What Is Philosophy?*, 212.

41 Deleuze, *Negotiations*, 143, 91.

42 Foucault, cited by Hallward, "The Limits of Individuation," 107. See also Foucault, *The Hermeneutic of the Subject*.

43 For a strong rebuttal of this reading of Foucault, see Nealon, *Foucault beyond Foucault*.

44 Rose, *The Politics of Life Itself*, 130; Hallward, "The Limits of Individuation," 101; Deleuze, *Negotiations*, 93; Nealon, *Foucault beyond Foucault*, 5ff.

45 Clough and Halley, *The Affective Turn*.

46 Massumi, *Parables for the Virtual*, 27, 35.

47 Grossberg, "Affect's Future," 315.

48 Grossberg, "Affect's Future," 315.

49 Brennan, *The Transmission of Affect*, 6.

50 Brennan, *The Transmission of Affect*, 164.

51 See Butler, *Frames of War*, 15; Connolly, "Materiality," 81, 82; and Panagia, *The Political Life of Sensation*. See also Rancière, *The Politics of Aesthetics*.

52 DeLanda, *Intensive Science and Virtual Philosophy*.

53 Schrödinger, *What Is Life?*, 162–63.

54 Husserl, *The Crisis of European Sciences and Transcendental Phenomenology*, 89. Likewise Schrödinger, *What Is Life?*, 162ff.

55 Groys, *The Communist Postscript*, 6ff; Wolfe, *What Is Posthumanism?*; Luhmann, quoted in Wolfe, *What Is Posthumanism?*, 109.

56 Quine, *Ontological Relativity*, 50.

57 "Newtonian space, which was to underlie so many empiricist and relativist professions of faith, is founded on metaphysics" (Canguilhem, *Knowledge of Life*, 118). Lyotard agrees: "Any discourse of general physics is a metaphysical discourse, as we have known since Aristotle and Leibniz" (*The Inhuman*, 5).

58 Compare Wolfe, *What Is Posthumanism?*, 27; Luhmann, quoted in Wolfe, *What Is Posthumanism?*, 114.

59 Wolfe, *What Is Posthumanism?*, 122.

60 Daston, "Speechless," 10.

61 Daston, "Science Studies and the History of Science," 813.

62 Paoloa Marrati and Todd Meyers, "Foreword: Life, as Such," in Canguilhem, *Knowledge of Life*, viii. By contrast, Deleuze and Guattari insist that the "concept is no more a function of the lived than it is a scientific or logical function" (*What Is Philosophy?*, 150).

63 Daston, "Speechless," 17.

64 Apart from contemporary historians of science mentioned above, this tradition also includes Nietzsche, Fleck, Wittgenstein, Husserl, Heisenberg, Wiener, Planck, Bachelard, Canguilhem, Quine, Kuhn, von Förster, Maturana, Varela, Luhmann, Rorty, and many others.

65 Heisenberg, *Physics and Philosophy*, 155.

66 Heisenberg, *Physics and Philosophy*, 19–20.

67 Heisenberg, *Physics and Philosophy*, 21.

68 Capra, *The Web of Life*, 113.

69 As Ilya Prigogine states, "For unstable systems we have to formulate the laws of dynamics at the statistical level. This changes our description of nature in a radical way. In such a formulation, the basic objects of physics are no longer trajectories or wave functions; they are probabilities." Prigogine, *The End of Certainty*, 73ff. Similarly von Bertalanffy, *Problems of Life*, 172; and Schrödinger, *What Is Life?*, 10.

70 Rose, *The Politics of Life Itself*, 51.

71 Keller, *The Mirage*, 32.

72 Keller, *The Mirage*, 39.

73 Compare Stove, *Scientific Irrationalism*; Sokal and Bricmont, *Fashionable Nonsense*.

74 Rheinberger, *An Epistemology of the Concrete*, 21.

75 Rheinberger, *An Epistemology of the Concrete*, 156. In Canguilhem's view, the use of scientific concepts is "at once both inevitable and artificial," because the scientist "strives to grasp a becoming whose meaning is never so clearly revealed to our understanding as when it disconcerts it." Canguilhem, *Knowledge of Life*, 22. Rheinberger calls this tension between matter and meaning "contained excess" (*An Epistemology of the Concrete*, 156), while Heisenberg referred to it as the "deficiency of knowledge" first encountered in quantum physics (*Physics and Philosophy*, 15).

76 Dennett, *Kinds of Minds*, 2.

77 For a more detailed account, see the excellent studies by Manuel DeLanda (*Intensive Science and Virtual Philosophy*) and John Protevi (*Political Physics*), as well as the editors' introductions in *Political Matter* (Braun and Whatmore, "The Stuff of Politics) and *New Materialisms* (Coole and Frost, "Introducing the New Materialisms").

78 Agamben, *The Open*, 29.

79 Butler, *Frames of War*, 31ff.

80 Sartre, preface to *The Wretched of the Earth*, 21.

81 Williams, "Edward Said," 23. Similarly, Neil Badmington argues that the "antihumanist resistance movement" of the mid-twentieth century was precisely that: a critique not of—or directed against—the human per se, but only against a humanist tradition that needed to be overcome "if radical change, the thinking of difference, is to become a possibility" (Badmington, "Introduction," 7).

82 Arendt, *Über die Revolution*, 36 (my translation).

83 Nikolas Rose speaks of "biovalue" and "bioeconomy" as a new economic sphere that seeks to extract "biovalue" from "the vital properties of living processes" (*The Politics of Life Itself*, 32); Kaushik Sunder Rajan coins the term *biocapital* to denote "a form of enterprise inextricable from contemporary capitalism" and based on the "implosion of the economic and [the] epistemic" (*Biocapital*, 3, 283); Eugene Thacker's concept of "biomedia" makes the point that the "biological and the digital domains are no longer rendered ontologically distinct, but instead are seen to inhere in each other" (*Biomedia*, 7).

84 "It can only be that life, conceived as precarious life, is a generalized condition, and that under certain political conditions it becomes radically exacerbated or radically disavowed" (Butler, *Frames of War*, 48).

85 Compare Timothy Campbell, translator's introduction to Esposito, *Bios*, xix–xxxi.

86 Esposito, *Bios*, 14.

87 Foucault, *"Society Must Be Defended,"* 249.

88 Esposito, *Bios*, 9.

89 Esposito, *Bios*, 32, 52.

90 Esposito, *Bios*, 42.

91 Esposito, *Bios*, 147.

92 Esposito, *Bios*, 46.

93 Esposito, *Bios*, 182.

94 Esposito, *Bios*, 56.

95 Esposito, *Bios*, 112.

96 Esposito, *Bios*, 149.

97 Esposito, *Bios*, 11.

98 Esposito, *Bios*, 146.

99 Esposito, *Bios*, 194.

100 Esposito, *Bios*, 191. Timothy Campbell's excellent introduction provides a detailed account of Esposito's overall philosophy and his focus on individuation. According to Campbell, Esposito emphasizes "every living form's interdependence with other living forms," which, in turn, helps to recognize and develop a "multiplicity of norms within the sphere of law" (translator's introduction, xxxviii).

101 Simondon, "The Genesis of the Individual," 317.

102 Canguilhem, *Knowledge of Life*, 49.

103 As Paul Rabinow points out, it appears that "ethnographic studies of laboratory life, like those of Bruno Latour," seek not merely to "[correct] a positivist and idealist understanding of science as a single unified activity . . . , but also [try to dismantle] the very idea of science—a position as far from Canguilhem's as one could imagine" (Rabinow, introduction to *A Vital Rationalist*, 13). Canguilhem's aim, according to Rabinow, "was not to attack science but to show it in action in its specificity and plurality" (13).

104 Marx, quoted in Fetscher, *Der Marxismus*, 94 (my translation).
105 Karl Marx, cited by Stack, *The First Darwinian Left*, 74.
106 Marx, quoted in Fetscher, *Der Marxismus*, 98 (my translation).
107 For a detailed and informed discussion of Marx's and Engel's reception of Darwinism and their understanding of "human nature," see Stack, *The First Darwinian Left*, 64–75.

Ackerman, Bruce. *Before the Next Attack: Preserving Civil Liberties in an Age of Terrorism*. New Haven, CT: Yale University Press, 2006.

Adorno, Theodor. *Minima Moralia: Reflections from Damaged Life*. Translated by E. F. N. Jephcott. London: Verso, 2005.

———. *Notes to Literature*, vol. 1. Edited by Rolf Tiedemann. Translated by Shierry Weber Nicholsen. New York: Columbia University Press, 1991.

Adorno, Theodor, and Walter Benjamin. *The Complete Correspondence, 1928–1940*. Edited by Henri Lonitz. Translated by Nicholas Walker. Cambridge, MA: Harvard University Press, 2001.

Agamben, Giorgio. *The Coming Community*. Translated by Michael Hardt. Minneapolis: University of Minnesota Press, 1993.

———. *Democracy in What State?* New York: Columbia University Press, 2012.

———. "Form-of-Life." In *Radical Thought in Italy: A Potential Politics*, edited by Paolo Virno and Michael Hardt. Minneapolis: University of Minnesota Press, 1996.

———. *Homo Sacer: Sovereign Power and Bare Life*. Translated by Daniel Heller-Roazen. Stanford, CA: Stanford University Press, 1998.

———. *The Kingdom and the Glory: For a Theological Genealogy of Economy and Government*. Translated by Lorenzo Chiesa. Stanford, CA: Stanford University Press, 2011.

———. *The Open: Man and Animal*. Translated by Kevin Attell. Stanford, CA: Stanford University Press, 2003.

———. *The Sacrament of Language: An Archaeology of the Oath*. Translated by Adam Kotsko. Stanford, CA: Stanford University Press, 2010.

———. *The Signature of All Things: On Method*. Translated by Luca D'Isanto and Kevin Attell. New York: Zone, 2009.

———. *Stasis: Civil War as a Political Paradigm*. Translated by Nicholas Heron. Stanford, CA: Stanford University Press, 2015.

———. *The Time That Remains: A Commentary on the Letter to the Romans*. Translated by Patricia Dailey. Stanford, CA: Stanford University Press, 2005.

———. "What Is an Apparatus?" In *What Is an Apparatus and Other Essays*, translated by David Kishik and Stefan Pedatella. Stanford, CA: Stanford University Press, 2009.

Alaimo, Stacy, and Susan Hekman. "Introduction: Emerging Models of Materiality in Feminist Theory." In *Material Feminisms*, edited by Stacy Alaimo and Susan Hekman. Bloomington: Indiana University Press, 2008.

Althusser, Louis. *For Marx*. Translated by Ben Brewster. New York: Vintage, 1970.

Améry, Jean. *At the Mind's Limits*. Translated by Sidney Rosenfeld and Stella P. Rosenfeld. Bloomington: Indiana University Press, 1980.

Anderson, Ben. "Modulating the Excess of Affect: Morale in a State of 'Total War.'" In *The Affect Theory Reader*, edited by Melissa Gregg and Gregory J. Seigworth. Durham, NC: Duke University Press, 2010.

Arecco, Sergio. *Pier Paolo Pasolini / Sergio Arecco*, in *Appendice conversazione con Pier Paolo Pasolini*. Rome: Partisan, 1972.

Arendt, Hannah. *Between Past and Future: Six Exercises in Political Thought*. New York: Viking, 1961. Reprint, New York: Penguin, 2006.

———. *Eichmann in Jerusalem: A Report on the Banality of Evil*. New York: Viking, 1963.

———. "Es gibt nur ein einziges Menschenrecht." *Die Wandlung* 4 (1949): 754.

———. *The Human Condition*. Chicago: University of Chicago Press, 1958.

———. *The Origins of Totalitarianism*. San Diego: Harvest, 1968. Reprint, New York: Harcourt, Brace, Jovanovich, 1978.

———. *Responsibility and Judgment*. Edited by Jerome Kohn. New York: Schocken, 2003.

———. *Über die Revolution*. Munich: Piper, 1974.

Asad, Talal. *On Suicide Bombing*. New York: Columbia University Press, 2007.

Avineri, Shlomo. *Hegel's Theory of the Modern State*. Cambridge: Cambridge University Press, 1972.

Bachmann, Gideon. "Pasolini on de Sade: An Interview during the Filming of *120 Days of Sodom*." *Film Quarterly* 29 (1975–76): 39–45.

Badiou, Alain. *The Adventure of French Philosophy*. Edited and translated by Bruno Bosteels. New York: Verso, 2012.

———. *Being and Event*. Translated by Oliver Feltham. New York: Continuum, 2005.

———. *Briefings on Existence: A Short Treatise on Transitology Ontology*. Edited and translated by Norman Madarasz. Albany: State University of New York Press, 2006.

———. *The Communist Hypothesis*. Translated by David Macey and Steve Corcoran. New York: Verso, 2010.

———. *The Concept of Model: An Introduction to the Materialist Epistemology of Mathematics*. Edited and translated by Zachary Luke Fraser and Tzuchien Tho. Melbourne: re.press, 2007.

———. *Conditions*. Translated by Steven Corcoran. New York: Continuum, 2008.

———. *Deleuze: The Clamor of Being*. Translated by Louise Burchill. Minneapolis: University of Minnesota Press, 1999.

———. "The Democratic Emblem." In *Democracy in What State?*, edited by Giorgio Agamben. New York: Columbia, 2010.

———. *Ethics: An Essay on the Understanding of Evil*. Translated by Peter Hallward. New York: Verso, 2001.

———. *Handbook of Inaesthetics*. Translated by Alberto Toscano. Stanford, CA: Stanford University Press, 2005.

———. *Infinite Thought: Truth and the Return to Philosophy*. Edited and translated by Oliver Feltham and Justin Clemens. New York: Continuum, 2005.

———. *Logics of Worlds*. Translated by Alberto Toscano. New York: Continuum, 2009.

———. *Manifesto for Philosophy*. Translated by Norman Madarasz. Albany: State University of New York Press, 1999.

———. *Number and Numbers*. Translated by Robin Mackay. New York: Polity, 2008.

———. *Philosophy and Event*. Translated by Louise Burchell. Malden, MA: Polity, 2013.

———. *Philosophy for Militants*. Translated by Bruno Bosteels. London: Verso, 2012.

———. *Plato's Republic: A Dialogue in Sixteen Chapters*. Translated by Susan Spitzer. New York: Columbia University Press, 2012.

———. *The Rational Kernel of the Hegelian Dialectic*. Edited and translated by Tzuchien Tho. Melbourne: re.press, 2011.

———. *Second Manifesto for Philosophy*. Translated by Louise Burchill. New York: Polity, 2011.

———. *Theory of the Subject*. Translated by Bruno Bosteels. New York: Continuum, 2009.

Badiou, Alain, and Slavoj Žižek. *Philosophy in the Present*. Edited by Peter Engelmann. Translated by Peter Thomas and Alberto Toscano. New York: Polity, 2009.

Badmington, Neil. "Introduction: Approaching Posthumanism." In *Posthumanism*, edited by Neil Badmington. New York: Palgrave, 2000.

Bartlett, A. J. *Badiou and Plato: An Education by Truths*. Edinburgh: Edinburgh University Press, 2011.

Bataille, Georges. "The Critique of the Foundations of the Hegelian Dialectic." In *Visions of Excess: Selected Writings, 1927–1939*. Minneapolis: University of Minnesota Press, 1985.

Bauer, Bruno. "The Capacity of the Present-Day Jews and Christians to Become Free." *Philosophical Forum* 8 (1978): 135–49.

Beiser, Frederick. Introduction to *The Cambridge Companion to Hegel and Nineteenth-Century Philosophy*, edited by Frederick Beiser. Cambridge: Cambridge University Press, 2008.

Benjamin, Walter. *The Arcades Project*. Edited by Rolf Tiedemann. Translated by Howard Eiland and Kevin McLaughlin. Cambridge, MA: Belknap, 2002.

———. "Capitalism as Religion." In *Selected Writings*, vol. 1, *1913–1926*, edited by Marcus Bullock and Michael W. Jennings. Cambridge, MA: Belknap, 2004.

———. "Conversations with Brecht." In *Understanding Brecht*, translated by Anna Bostock. London: Verso, 1983.

Bennett, Jane. "Thing-Power." In *Political Matter: Technoscience, Democracy, and Public Life*, edited by Bruce Braun and Sarah J. Whatmore. Minneapolis: University of Minnesota Press, 2010.

———. *Vibrant Matter: A Political Ecology of Things*. Durham, NC: Duke University Press, 2010.

Berkowitz, Lana. "Pets Are a Booming Industry." *Houston Chronicle*, February 23, 2010. http://www.chron.com/disp/story.mpl/pets/6881710.html.

Bernadete, Seth. *Plato's "Laws": The Discovery of Being*. Chicago: University of Chicago Press, 2000.

Biagioli, Mario. "Postdisciplinary Liaisons: Science Studies and the Humanities." *Critical Inquiry* 35, no. 4 (2009): 816–33.

Bobbio, Norberto. *Left and Right: The Significance of a Political Distinction*. Translated by Allan Cameron. Chicago: University of Chicago Press, 1996.

Bodei, Remo. *Geometria delle passioni: Paura. speranza. felicità: Filosofia e uso politico*. Milan: Feltrinelli, 1991.

Bodei, Remo, Dario Borso, and Mario Tronti. *Società politica e Stato in Hegel, Marx e Gramsci*. Padova: Cleup, 1977.

Bolaffi, Angelo. *Il crepuscolo della sovranità: Filosofia e politica nella Germania del Novecento*. Rome: Donzelli, 2002.

Bongie, Chris. *Exotic Memories: Literature, Colonialism and the Fin de Siecle*. Stanford, CA: Stanford University Press, 1991.

Bookchin, Murray, and Dave Foreman. *Defending the Earth: A Dialogue between Murray Bookchin and Dave Foreman*. Edited by Steve Chase. Boston: South End, 1991.

Braidotti, Rosi. *Transpositions*. Cambridge: Polity, 2006.

Braun, Bruce. "Biopolitics and the Molecularization of Life." *Cultural Geographies* 14, no. 6 (2007): 6–28.

Braun, Bruce, and Sarah J. Whatmore. "The Stuff of Politics: An Introduction." In *Political Matter: Technoscience, Democracy and Public Life*, edited by Bruce Braun and Sarah J. Whatmore. Minneapolis: University of Minnesota Press, 2010.

Breier, Karl-Heinz. *Hannah Arendt zur Einführung*. Hamburg: Junius, 2001.

Brennan, Teresa. *The Transmission of Affect*. Ithaca, NY: Cornell University Press, 2004.

Brisson, Luc, and Jean-François Pradeau. *Les Lois de Platon*. Paris: Presses Universitaires de France, 2007.

Broch, Hermann. *Politik: Ein Kondensat*. In *Werke*, vol. 9, edited by P. M. Lützeler. Frankfurt: Suhrkamp, 1974–81.

Brown, Steven D., and Ian Tucker. "Eff the Ineffable: Affect, Somatic Management and Mental Health Service Users." In *The Affect Theory Reader*, edited by Melissa Gregg and Gregory J. Seigworth. Durham, NC: Duke University Press, 2010.

Bryant, Levi. "Questions about the Possibility of Non-correlationist Ethics." *Larval Subjects* [blog], January 28, 2010. http://larvalsubjects.wordpress.com/2010 /01/28/questions-about-the-possibility-of-non-correlationist-ethics/.

Butler, Judith. *Frames of War: When Is Life Grievable?* New York: Verso, 2009.

———. "Who Owns Kafka?" *London Review of Books*, March 3, 2011.

Cacciari, Massimo. *Krisis: Saggio sulla crisi del pensiero negativo da Nietzsche a Wittgenstein*. Milano: Feltrinelli, 1976.

———. "Law and Justice: On the Theological and Mystical Dimensions of the Modern Political." In *The Unpolitical: On the Radical Critique of Political Reason*, edited by Alessandro Carrera and translated by Massimo Verdicchio. New York: Fordham University Press, 2009.

———. *Pensiero negativo e razionalizzazione*. Venezia: Marsilio, 1977.

———. *Sull'autonomia del politico*. Milano: Feltrinelli, 1977.

Cairns, Huntington. *Legal Philosophy from Plato to Hegel*. Baltimore, MD: Johns Hopkins University Press, 1949.

Calarco, Matthew. *Zoographies: The Question of the Animal from Heidegger to Derrida*. New York: Columbia University Press, 2008.

Canguilhem, Georges. *Knowledge of Life*. Edited by Paola Marrati and Todd Meyers. Translated by Stefanos Geroulanos and Daniela Ginsburg. New York: Fordham University Press, 2008.

Capra, Fritjof. *The Web of Life: A New Scientific Understanding of Living Systems*. New York: Anchor, 1996.

Caruth, Cathy. *Unclaimed Experience: Trauma, Narrative, and History*. Baltimore, MD: Johns Hopkins University Press, 1996.

Casarino, Cesare. "Oedipus Exploded: Pasolini and the Myth of Modernization." *October* 59 (1992): 27–47.

Cavell, Stanley. "Aesthetic Problems of Modern Philosophy." In *Must We Mean What We Say?* Cambridge: Cambridge University Press, 1969.

———. "Reply to Four Chapters." In *Wittgenstein and Skepticism*, edited by Denis McManus. New York: Routledge, 2004.

Chandler, James. "Introduction: Doctrines, Disciplines, Discourses, Departments." *Critical Inquiry* 35, no. 4 (2009): 729–46.

Cheah, Pheng. "Second Generation Rights as Biopolitical Rights." In *The Meanings of Rights: The Philosophy and Social Theory of Human Rights*, edited by Costas Douzinas and Conor Gearty. Cambridge: Cambridge University Press, 2014.

Ciccarelli, Roberto. *Immanenza: Filosofia, diritto e politica della vita dal XIX al XX secolo*. Bologna: Il Mulino, 2008.

Clark, T. J. *Farewell to an Idea: Episodes from a History of Modernism*. New Haven, CT: Yale University Press, 1999.

Clough, Patricia Ticineto, and Jean Halley, eds. *The Affective Turn: Theorizing the Social*. Durham, NC: Duke University Press, 2007.

Cofrancesco, D. *Destra e sinistra: Per un uso critico di due termini chiave*. Verona: Bertani, 1984.

Colletti, Lucio. *Intervista politico-filosofica: Con un saggio su "Marxismo e dialettica."* Rome: Laterza, 1974.

Colombo, Furio. "We Are All in Danger: The Last Interview with Pier Paolo Pasolini, November 1, 1975." Translated by Pasquale Verdicchio. *Left Curve* 30 (2006).

Connolly, William E. *Neuropolitics: Thinking, Culture, Speed.* Minneapolis: University of Minnesota Press, 2009.

——. *A World of Becoming.* Durham, NC: Duke University Press, 2010.

Consolo, Vincenzo. "The Disappearance of the Fireflies." In *Reading and Writing the Mediterranean: Essays by Vincenzo Consolo*, edited by Norma Bouchard and Massimo Lollini and translated by Norma Bouchard. Toronto: University of Toronto Press, 2006.

Coole, Diana, and Samantha Frost. "Introducing the New Materialisms." In *New Materialisms: Ontology, Agency, and Politics*, edited by Diana Coole and Samantha Frost. Durham, NC: Duke University Press, 2010.

Cooper, Melinda, Andrew Goffey, and Anna Munster. "Biopolitics, for Now." *Culture Machine* 7 (2005). http://www.culturemachine.net/index.php/cm/article/view/24/31.

Copjec, Joan. *Imagine There's No Woman.* Cambridge, MA: MIT Press, 2002.

Daston, Lorraine. Introduction to *Things That Talk: Object Lessons from Art and Science*, edited by Lorraine Daston, 9–24. New York: Zone, 2007.

——. "Science Studies and the History of Science." *Critical Inquiry* 35, no. 4 (2009): 798–815.

——. "Speechless." In *Things That Talk: Object Lessons from Art and Science*, edited by Lorraine Daston. New York: Zone, 2007.

Davis, Lennard. "Biocultures and Education." *Profession* (2009): 36–43.

Dean, Jodi. *Democracy and Other Neoliberal Fantasies: Communicative Capitalism and Left Politics.* Durham, NC: Duke University Press, 2009.

de Benoist, Alain. "End of the Left-Right Dichotomy: The French Case." *Telos* 102 (1995): 73–90.

De Giovanni, Biagio, Roberto Esposito, and Giuseppe Zarone, eds. *Divenire della ragione moderna: Cartesio, Spinoza, Vico.* Naples: Liguori, 1981.

DeLanda, Manuel. *Intensive Science and Virtual Philosophy.* London: Continuum, 2002.

Deleuze, Gilles. *Cinema 1: The Movement-Image.* Translated by Hugh Tomlinson and Barbara Habberjam. Minneapolis: University of Minnesota Press, 1996.

——. *Cinema 2: The Time-Image.* Translated by Hugh Tomlinson and Robert Galeta. Minneapolis: University of Minnesota Press, 1995.

——. *Desert Islands and Other Texts, 1953–1974.* Edited by David Lapoujade. Translated by Michael Taormina. New York: Semiotexte, 2004.

——. *Foucault.* Translated by Sean Hand. Minneapolis: University of Minnesota Press, 1988.

——. "Immanence: A Life." In *Pure Immanence: Essays on a Life.* Translated by Anne Boyman. New York: Zone, 2001.

———. *The Logic of Sense*. Edited by Constantin Boundas. Translated by Mark Lester with Charles Stivale. New York: Columbia University Press, 1990.

———. *Masochism: Coldness and Cruelty*. Translated by Jean McNeil. New York: Zone, 1989.

———. *Negotiations 1972–1990*. Translated by Martin Joughin. New York: Columbia University Press, 1996.

———. "What Is a *Dispositif*?" In *Michel Foucault, Philosopher*. Translated by Timothy Armstrong. New York: Routledge, 1992.

Deleuze, Gilles, and Félix Guattari. *A Thousand Plateaus: Capitalism and Schizophrenia*. Translated by Brian Massumi. Minneapolis: University of Minnesota Press, 1987.

———. *What Is Philosophy?* Translated by Hugh Tomlinson and Graham Burchell. New York: Columbia University Press, 1994.

Deleuze, Gilles, and Claire Parnet. *Dialogues*. Translated by Hugh Tomlinson and Barbara Habberjam. New York: Columbia University Press, 1987.

Dennett, Daniel C. *Kinds of Minds: Toward an Understanding of Consciousness*. New York: Basic Books, 1997.

Derrida, Jacques. *Adieu to Emmanuel Levinas*. Translated by Michel Naas and Pascale-Anne Brault. Stanford, CA: Stanford University Press, 1999.

———. *The Animal That Therefore I Am*. Edited by Marie-Louise Mallet. Translated by David Wills. Stanford, CA: Stanford University Press, 2008.

———. *The Beast and the Sovereign*, vol. 1. Edited by Michel Lisse, Marie-Louise Mallet, and Ginette Michaud. Translated by Geoffrey Bennington. Chicago: University of Chicago Press, 2009.

———. *Dissemination*. Translated by Barbara Johnson. Chicago: University of Chicago Press, 1981.

———. "'Eating Well,' or the Calculation of the Subject: An Interview with Jacques Derrida." Translated by Peter Connor and Avital Ronnell. In *Who Comes after the Subject?*, edited by Eduardo Cadava, Peter Connor, and Jean-Luc Nancy, 96–119. New York: Routledge, 1991.

———. "No Apocalypse, Not Now (Full Speed Ahead, Seven Missiles, Seven Missives)." Translated by Catherine Porter and Philip Lewis. *Diacritics* 14 (1984): 20–31.

———. *Of Spirit: Heidegger and the Question*. Translated by Geoffrey Bennington and Rachel Bowlby. Chicago: University of Chicago Press, 1989.

———. *Rogues: Two Essays on Reason*. Translated by Pascale-Anne Brault and Michael Naas. Stanford, CA: Stanford University Press, 2005.

———. "Violence and Metaphysics." In *Writing and Difference*. Translated by Alan Bass. London: Routledge, 1978.

———. *Without Alibi*. Edited and translated by Peggy Kamuf. Stanford, CA: Stanford University Press, 2002.

Derrida, Jacques, and Elisabeth Roudinesco. *For What Tomorrow? A Dialogue*. Translated by Jeff Fort. Stanford, CA: Stanford University Press, 2004.

Dews, Peter. *The Limits of Disenchantment*. London: Verso, 1995.

Didi-Huberman, Georges. *Images in Spite of All: Four Photographs from Auschwitz.* Translated by Shane Lillis. Chicago: University of Chicago Press, 2008.

———. *Survivance des lucioles.* Paris: Minuit, 2009.

Douzinas, Costas, and Slavoj Žižek. *The Idea of Communism.* London: Verso, 2010.

Duso, Giuseppe, ed. *La politica oltre lo stato: Carl Schmitt.* Venezia: Arsenale, 1981.

———, ed. *Weber: Razionalità e politica.* Venice: Arsenale Cooperativa Editrice, 1980.

Esposito, Roberto. *Bios: Biopolitics and Philosophy.* Translated by Timothy Campbell. Minneapolis: University of Minnesota Press, 2008.

———. *Categorie dell'impolitico.* Bologna: Il Mulino, 1998.

———. "Community, Immunity, Biopolitics." Translated by Michela Russo. *e-misférica* 10, no. 1 (2013).

———. "The *Dispositif* of the Person." Translated by Timothy Campbell. *Law, Culture and the Humanities* 8, no. 1 (2012): 17–30.

———. *Immunitas: The Protection and Negation of Life.* Translated by Zakiya Hanafi. London: Polity, 2011.

———. "Introduzione." In *Gerusalemme e Atene: Studi sul pensiero politico dell'Occidente,* by Leo Strauss. Turin: Einaudi, 1998.

———. "La Politica al Presente," edited by Robert Ciccarelli. In *Impersonale: In dialogo con Roberto Esposito,* edited by Laura Bazzicalupo, 13–37. Milan: Mimesis Edizioni, 2008.

———. *La politica e la storia: Machiavelli e Vico.* Naples: Liguori, 1980.

———. *Ordine e conflitto: Machiavelli e la letteratura politica del Rinascimento italiano.* Naples: Liguori, 1984.

———. "The Person and Human Life." Translated by Diana Garvin and Thomas Kelso. In *Theory after "Theory,"* edited by Jane Elliott and Derek Attridge, 205–20. London: Routledge, 2011.

———. *Third Person.* Translated by Zakiya Hanafi. London: Polity, 2012.

Felman, Shoshana, and Dori Laub. *Testimony: Crises of Witnessing in Literature, Psychoanalysis, and History.* New York: Routledge, 1992.

Ferrari, G. R. F. "Strauss's Plato." *Arion* 5, no. 2 (1997): 36–65.

Fetscher, Irving. *Der Marxismus: Seine Geschichte in Dokumenten.* Munich: Piper, 1983.

Feuer, Lewis S. "The Dream of Benedict de Spinoza." *American Imago* 14, no. 3 (1957): 225–42.

Fichte, Johann. "[First] Introduction." In *Introductions to the Wissenschaftslehrre.* Translated by Daniel Breazeale. Indianapolis, IN: Hackett, 1994.

Forster, Michael. *Hegel and Skepticism.* Cambridge, MA: Harvard University Press, 1989.

Foucault, Michel. "The Art of Telling the Truth." In *Politics, Philosophy, Culture: Interviews and Other Writings, 1977–1984.* Edited by Lawrence Kritzman. Translated by Alan Sheridan et al. New York: Routledge, 1988.

———. *The Birth of Biopolitics: Lectures at the Collège de France, 1978–1979.* Edited by

Michel Senellart. Translated by Graham Burchell. New York: Palgrave Macmillan, 2008.

———. "Che cos'è l'illuminismo? Che cos'è la rivoluzione?" *Il Centauro* 11–12 (1984): 229–36.

———. *Discipline and Punish: The Birth of the Prison*. Translated by Alan Sheridan. New York: Vintage, 1977.

———. "For an Ethic of Discomfort." In *Power*, edited by James D. Faubion. New York: New Press, 1994.

———. "Governmentality." In *Power*, edited by James D. Faubion. New York: New Press, 1994.

———. *The Government of Self and Others: Lectures at the Collège de France, 1982–1983*. Edited by Michel Senellart. Translated by Graham Burchell. New York: Palgrave, 2010.

———. *The Hermeneutic of the Subject*. New York: Palgrave, 2005.

———. *The History of Sexuality*, vol. 1, *An Introduction*. New York: Vintage, 1990.

———. "Illuminismo e critica." In *Illuminismo e critica*, edited by Paolo Napoli. Rome: Donzelli, 1997.

———. *The Politics of Truth*. Edited by Sylvere Lotringer. Translated by Lysa Hochroth and Catherine Porter. Los Angeles: Semiotexte, 2007.

———. *Power/Knowledge: Selected Interviews and Other Writings 1972–1977*. Edited by Colin Gordon. New York: Pantheon, 1980.

———. *Psychiatric Power: Lectures at the Collège de France, 1973–1974*. Edited by Jacques Legrange. Translated by Graham Burchell. New York: Picador, 2006.

———. *"Society Must Be Defended": Lectures at the Collège de France, 1975–1976*. Edited by Mauro Bertani and Alessandro Fontana. Translated by David Macey. New York: Picador, 2003.

———. "So Is It Important to Think?" In *Power*, edited by James D. Faubion. New York: New Press, 1994.

———. "The Subject and Power." *Critical Inquiry* 8 (1982): 777–95.

Fraenkel, Ernst, Gianni Arrigo, and Gaetano Vardaro, eds. *Laboratorio Weimar: Conflitti e diritto del lavoro nella Germania prenazista*. Rome: Ed. Lavoro, 1982.

Freud, Sigmund. *The Interpretation of Dreams*. Translated by James Strachey. New York: Avon, 1965.

———. *Three Essays on the Theory of Sexuality*. In *The Standard Edition of the Complete Psychological Works of Sigmund Freud*, edited and translated by James Strachey, vol. 7, 125–230. London: Hogarth Press, 1955.

Friedrich, Carl. *The Philosophy of Law in Historical Perspective*. Chicago: University of Chicago Press, 1963.

Gadamer, Hans-Georg. *Dialogue and Dialectic: Eight Hermeneutical Studies on Plato*. Translated by P. Christopher Smith. New Haven, CT: Yale University Press, 1980.

Galison, Peter. *Image and Logic: A Material Culture of Microphysics*. Chicago: University of Chicago Press, 1997.

Galli, Carlo. *Contingenza e necessità nella ragione politica moderna*. Rome: Laterza, 2009.

———. *Genealogia della politica: Carl Schmitt e la crisi del pensiero politico moderno*. Bologna: Il Mulino, 2010.

———. *L'umanità multiculturale*. Bologna: Il Mulino, 2008.

———. *Political Spaces and Global War*. Edited by Adam Sitze. Translated by Elisabeth Fay. Minneapolis: University of Minnesota Press, 2010.

Gentili, Dario, ed. *La crisi del politico: Antologia de il Centauro, 1981–1986*. Edited by Bruno Accarino. Naples: Guida, 2007.

Giddens, Anthony. *Beyond Left and Right: The Future of Radical Politics*. Cambridge: Polity, 1994.

Granel, Gérard. "Untameable Singularities: Some Remarks on *Broken Hegemonies*." *Graduate Faculty Philosophy Journal* 19, no. 2 (1997): 215–28.

Grossberg, Lawrence. "Affect's Future: Rediscovering the Virtual in the Actual." In *The Affect Theory Reader*, edited by Melissa Gregg and Gregory J. Seigworth. Durham, NC: Duke University Press, 2010.

Groys, Boris. *The Communist Postscript*. Translated by Thomas Ford. New York: Verso, 2010.

Hacking, Ian. *Historical Ontology*. Cambridge, MA: Harvard University Press, 2002.

Hadot, Pierre. *What Is Ancient Philosophy?* Translated by Michael Chase. Cambridge, MA: Harvard University Press, 2002.

Hägglund, Martin. "The Arche-Materiality of Time: Deconstruction, Evolution and Speculative Materialism." In *Theory after "Theory,"* edited by Jane Elliott and Derek Attridge. London: Routledge, 2011.

———. *Radical Atheism: Derrida and the Time of Life*. Stanford, CA: Stanford University Press, 2008.

Hallward, Peter. "The Limits of Individuation." *Angelaki* 5, no. 2 (2000): 93–111.

———. "The Singular and the Specific." *Radical Philosophy* 99 (2000): 6–18.

———, ed. *Think Again: Alain Badiou and the Future of Philosophy*. New York: Continuum, 2004.

Hamilton, Alastair. *The Appeal of Fascism: A Study of Intellectuals and Fascism, 1919–1945*. London: Blond, 1971.

Haraway, Donna J. *When Species Meet*. Minneapolis: University of Minnesota Press, 2008.

Hardimon, Michael. *Hegel's Social Philosophy: The Project of Reconciliation*. Cambridge: Cambridge University Press, 1994.

Hardt, Michael, and Antonio Negri. *Commonwealth*. Cambridge, MA: Belknap, 2009.

———. *Empire*. Cambridge, MA: Harvard University Press, 2000.

Harth, Erich. "Art and Reductionism." *Journal of Consciousness Studies* 11, nos. 3–4 (2004): 111–16.

Hegel, G. W. F. *Die Philosophie des Rechts: Die Mitschriften Wannenman Heidelberg*

1817–1818 und Homeyer Berlin 1818–1819. Edited by K. Ilting. Stuttgart: Frommann, 1974.

———. *Elements of the Philosophy of Right*. Edited by Allen Wood. Translated by H. B. Nisbet. Cambridge: Cambridge University Press, 1991.

———. *The Encyclopedia Logic*. Translated by T. Geraets, W. Suchting, and H. Harris. Indianapolis: Hackett, 1991.

———. Introduction to *Science of Logic*. Translated by A. V. Miller. New York: Humanities, 1976.

———. *Lectures on Aesthetics*, vol. 1. Translated by T. M. Knox. Oxford: Oxford University Press, 1975.

———. *Lectures on Natural Right and Political Science: The First Philosophy of Right, Heidelberg 1817–1818, with Additions from the Lectures of 1818–1819*. Translated by J. Stewart and P. Hodgson. Berkeley: University of California Press, 1995.

———. *Lectures on the History of Philosophy*, vol. 1. Translated by E. S. Haldane. Lincoln: University of Nebraska Press, 1995.

———. *Natural Law*. Translated by T. M. Knox. Philadelphia: University of Pennsylvania Press, 1975.

———. *Phänomenologie des Geistes*. Frankfurt: Suhrkamp, 1986.

———. *The Phenomenology of Spirit*. Translated by A. V. Miller. New York: Oxford University Press, 1977.

———. *The Philosophy of History*. Translated by J. Sibree. New York: Dover, 1956.

———. *Vorlesungen über die Geschichte der Philosophie*, vol. 3. Frankfurt: Suhrkamp, 1986.

———. *Werke*. Edited by Eva Moldenhauer and Karl Markus Michel. Frankfurt am Main: Suhrkamp, 1970.

Heidegger, Martin. *Being and Time*. Translated by John Macquarrie and Edward Robinson. New York: Harper and Row, 1962.

———. *Four Seminars*. Translated by Andrew Mitchell and Francoise Raffoul. Bloomington: Indiana University Press, 2003.

———. "Letter on Humanism." In *Basic Writings*, edited by David Farrell. San Francisco: Harper and Row, 1976.

———. *Off the Beaten Track*. Edited and translated by Julian Young and Kenneth Haynes. Cambridge: Cambridge University Press, 2002.

———. *On Time and Being*. Translated by Joan Stambaugh. New York: Harper and Row, 1972.

———. *Plato's Sophist*. Translated by Richard Rojcewicz and Andre Schuwer. Bloomington: Indiana University Press, 1997.

Heisenberg, Werner. *Encounters with Einstein*. Princeton, NJ: Princeton University Press, 1983.

———. *Physics and Philosophy: The Revolution in Modern Science*. New York: Harper, 1954.

Hewitt, Andrew. *Political Inversions: Homosexuality, Fascism, and the Modernist Imaginary*. Stanford, CA: Stanford University Press, 1996.

Honneth, Axel. *The Struggle for Recognition: The Moral Grammar of Social Conflicts.* Translated by Joel Anderson. Cambridge, MA: MIT Press, 1995.

Houlgate, Stephen. *The Opening of Hegel's Logic.* West Lafayette, IN: Purdue University Press, 2006.

Huizinga, Johann. *Homo Ludens: A Study of the Play-Element in Culture.* Boston: Beacon, 1950.

Husserl, Edmund. *The Crisis of European Sciences and Transcendental Phenomenology.* Evanston, IL: Northwestern University Press, 1970.

Hynes, Maria. "Rethinking Reductionism." In *Culture Machine* 7 (2005). http://www.culturemachine.net/index.php/cm/article/view/33/41.

Ilting, K.-H. "The Structure of Hegel's *Philosophy of Right*." In *Hegel's Political Philosophy: Problems and Perspectives*, edited by Z. A. Pelczynski. Cambridge: Cambridge University Press, 1971.

Jouët-Pastré, Emanuelle. *Le jeu et le sérieux dans les Lois de Platon.* Sankt Augustin, Germany: Academia, 2006.

Kafka, Franz. *Beim Bau der chinesischen Mauer und andere Schriften aus dem Nachlaß.* Frankfurt am Main: Fischer, 1992.

———. "A Country Doctor." In *Kafka's Selected Stories*, translated by Stanley Corngold. New York: W. W. Norton, 2007.

———. "Poseidon." In *Parables and Paradoxes*, edited by Nahum N. Glatzer. New York: Schocken, 1975.

———. "A Problem for the Father of the Family." In *The Transformation ("Metamorphosis") and Other Stories*, edited and translated by Malcolm Pasley. New York: Penguin, 1992.

Kant, Emmanuel. *Political Writings.* Edited by Hans Reiss. Translated by H. B. Nisbet. Cambridge: Cambridge University Press, 1991.

Kauffman, Stuart. "Foreword: The Open Universe." In *A Third Window: Natural Life beyond Newton and Darwin*, by Robert E. Ulanowicz. West Conshohocken, PA: Templeton Foundation Press, 2009.

Keller, Evelyn Fox. *The Mirage of a Space between Nature and Nurture.* Durham, NC: Duke University Press, 2010.

Kelley, J. M. *A Short History of Western Legal Theory.* Oxford: Oxford University Press, 1992.

Kierkegaard, Søren. *The Concept of Irony, with Continual Reference to Socrates.* Translated by Howard Hong and Edna Hong. Princeton, NJ: Princeton University Press, 1989.

Klein, Jacob. *Greek Mathematical Thought and the Origin of Algebra.* New York: Dover, 1992.

Köchy, Kristian. *Biophilosophie.* Dresden: Junius, 2008.

Kojève, Alexandre. *Outline of a Phenomenology of Right.* Edited and translated by Bryan-Paul Frost and Robert Howse. Lanham, MD: Rowman and Littlefield, 2000.

Koselleck, Reinhart. "Crisis." Translated by Michaela W. Richter. *Journal of the History of Ideas* 67, no. 2 (2006): 357–400.

———. *Critique and Crisis: Enlightenment and the Pathogenesis of Modern Society.* Cambridge, MA: MIT Press, 1988.

———. *Futures Past: On the Semantics of Historical Time.* Translated by Keith Tribe. Cambridge, MA: MIT Press, 1985.

Lacan, Jacques. *The Ego in Freud's Theory and in the Technique of Psychoanalysis, 1954–1955.* Book 2 of *The Seminar of Jacques Lacan.* Translated by Sylvana Tomaselli. New York: W. W. Norton, 1991.

———. *The Other Side of Psychoanalysis, 1969–1970.* Book 17 of *The Seminar of Jacques Lacan.* Translated by Russell Grigg. New York: W. W. Norton, 2007.

LaCapra, Dominick. *History and Its Limits: Human, Animal, Violence.* Ithaca, NY: Cornell University Press, 2009.

Laclau, Ernesto. *On Populist Reason.* London: Verso, 2005.

Langan, Celeste. "Romantic Neutrality: Bullets, Bulletins and *Don Juan.*" Paper presented at the North American Society for the Study of Romanticism, Vancouver, August 19, 2010.

Latour, Bruno. *The Politics of Nature.* Translated by Catherine Porter. Cambridge, MA: Harvard University Press, 2004.

———. *We Have Never Been Modern.* Translated by Catherine Porter. Cambridge, MA: Harvard University Press, 1993.

Lazzarato, Maurizio. "From Biopower to Biopolitics." *Pli* 13 (2002): 99–113.

Lefranc, Georges. *Les gauches en France, 1789–1972.* Paris: Payot, 1973.

Letwin, Shirley Robin. *On the History of the Idea of Law.* Edited by Noel B. Reynolds. Cambridge: Cambridge University Press, 2005.

Levi, Primo. "Stereotypes." In *The Drowned and the Saved,* translated by Raymond Rosenthal. New York: Vintage, 1988.

Levinas, Emmanuel. "Au-delà de l'etat dans l'état." In *Nouvelles lectures talmudiques.* Paris: Editions de Minuit, 2005.

Loraux, Nicole. *The Divided City: On Memory and Forgetting in Ancient Athens.* Translated by Corinne Pache with Jeff Fort. New York: Zone, 2002.

Lotringer, Sylvere, and Christian Marazzi. "The Return of Politics." In *Autonomia: Post-political Politics,* edited by Sylvere Lotringer and Christian Marazzi and translated by Peter Caravetta and John Johnston. Los Angeles: Semiotexte, 2007.

Lukács, Georg. *Von Nietzsche zu Hitler oder Der Irrationalismus und die Deutsche Politik.* Frankfurt: Fischer, 1966.

Luke, Tim. "The Dreams of Deep Ecology." *Telos* 76 (1988): 65–92.

Lyotard, Jean-François. *The Inhuman: Reflections on Time.* Stanford, CA: Stanford University Press, 1992.

———. *The Postmodern Condition: A Report on Knowledge.* Translated by Geoff Bennington and Brian Massumi. Minneapolis: University of Minnesota Press, 1984.

Maggi, Armando. *The Resurrection of the Body: Pier Paolo Pasolini from Saint Paul to Sade*. Chicago: University of Chicago Press, 2009.

Mannheim, Karl. *Conservatism: A Contribution to the Sociology of Knowledge*. London: Routledge and Kegan Paul, 1986.

Margulis, Lynn, and Dorion Sagan. *What Is Life?* Berkeley, CA: University of California Press, 2000.

Marramao, Giacomo. "'Technica sociale,' State e transizione tra socialdemocrazia weimariana e austromarximo." In *Weimar: Lotte sociali e sistema democratico nella Germania degli anni Venti*, edited by Lucio Villari. Bologna: Il Mulino, 1978.

——, ed. *Tecnologia e potere nelle società post-liberali*. Naples: Liguori, 1981.

——. "Teoria della crisi e problema dello Stato." In *Stato e teorie marxiste*, edited by Lelio Basso et al. Milan: Mazzotta, 1977.

Marx, Karl. *Capital*, vol. 1. Translated by Ben Fowkes. New York: Penguin, 1990.

——. "A Contribution to the Critique of Political Economy." In *Later Political Writings*, edited by Terrell Carver. Cambridge: Cambridge University Press, 1996.

——. "Economic and Philosophic Manuscripts of 1844." In *The Marx-Engels Reader*, edited by Robert C. Tucker. New York: W. W. Norton, 1978.

——. "The Eighteenth Brumaire of Louis Bonaparte." In *The Marx-Engels Reader*, edited by Robert C. Tucker. New York: W. W. Norton, 1978.

——. "From the Paris Notebooks." In *Early Political Writings*, edited by Joseph O'Malley. Cambridge: Cambridge University Press, 1994.

——. *Grundrisse: Foundations of the Critique of Political Economy*. Translated by Martin Nicolau. London: Penguin, 1993.

——. "On Feuerbach." In *Early Political Writings*, edited by Joseph O'Malley. Cambridge: Cambridge University Press, 1994.

Marx, Karl, and Friedrich Engels. *Karl Marx, Friedrich Engels Gesamtausgabe*. Berlin: Dietz, 1982.

——. "Manifesto of the Communist Party." In *The Marx-Engels Reader*, edited by Robert C. Tucker. New York: W. W. Norton, 1978. Reprinted in *Later Political Writings*, edited by Terrell Carver. Cambridge: Cambridge University Press, 1996.

Massumi, Brian, ed. *Parables for the Virtual: Movement, Affect, Sensation*. Durham, NC: Duke University Press, 2002.

Meister, Robert. *After Evil: A Politics of Human Rights*. New York: Columbia University Press, 2012.

Melzer, Sara, and Kathryn Norberg, eds. *From the Royal to the Republican Body: Incorporating the Political in Seventeenth- and Eighteenth-Century France*. Berkeley: University of California Press, 1998.

Mill, John Stuart. *Autobiography*. In *The Collected Works*, edited by John M. Robson and Jack Stillinger, vol. 1. Toronto: University of Toronto Press, 1981.

Miller, Jacques-Alain. *Le Neveu de Lacan: Satire*. Paris: Verdier, 2003.

Minkkinen, Panu. "Michel Foucault on Sovereignty and Law." Paper presented at the Eighth Annual Conference of the Association for the Study of Law, Culture and the Humanities, University of Texas at Austin, College of Liberal Arts, March 11–12, 2005.

Moravia, Alberto. "Dall'Oriente a Salò." *Nuovi Argomenti*, January–March 1976, 93–95.

Myer, Ernst. "Discussion: Footnotes on the Philosophy of Biology." *Philosophy of Science* 36 (1949): 197–202.

Nancy, Jean-Luc. *Hegel: The Restlessness of the Negative*. Minneapolis: Minnesota University Press, 2002.

Nealon, Jeffrey T. *Foucault beyond Foucault*. Stanford, CA: Stanford University Press, 2008.

Negri, Antonio. *The Savage Anomaly: The Power of Spinoza's Metaphysics and Politics*. Translated by Michael Hardt. Minneapolis: University of Minnesota Press, 2008.

——. *Spinoza*. Rome: Derive Approdi, 2006.

——. *Subversive Spinoza: Uncontemporary Variations*. Translated by Timothy Murphy. Manchester: Manchester University Press, 2004.

——. *Time for Revolution*. Translated by Matteo Mandarini. New York: Continuum, 2004.

Nehamas, Alexander. *The Art of Living: Socratic Reflections from Plato to Foucault*. Berkeley: University of California Press, 1998.

Nietzsche, Friedrich. *Twilight of the Idols*. In *Twilight of the Idols and The Anti-Christ*, translated by R. J. Hollingdale. New York: Penguin, 2003.

Norris, Andrew. "Beyond the Fury of Destruction: Hegel on Freedom." *Political Theory* 32, no. 3 (2004): 409–18.

——. "Carl Schmitt on Friends, Enemies and the Political." *Telos* 112 (1998): 68–88.

——. "The Exemplary Exception: Philosophical and Political Decisions in Giorgio Agamben's *Homo Sacer*." In *Politics, Metaphysics and Death: Essays on Giorgio Agamben's* Homo Sacer, edited by Andrew Norris. Durham, NC: Duke University Press, 2005.

——. "Introduction: Giorgio Agamben and the Politics of the Living Dead." In *Politics, Metaphysics, and Death: Essays on Giorgio Agamben's* Homo Sacer, edited by Andrew Norris. Durham, NC: Duke University Press, 2005.

——. "Jean-Luc Nancy and the Myth of the Common." *Constellations* 7, no. 2 (2000): 272–95.

——. "Sovereignty, Exception and Norm." *Journal of Law and Society* 34, no. 1 (2007): 31–45.

Norton, Anne. *Leo Strauss and the Politics of American Empire*. New Haven, CT: Yale University Press, 2004.

Panagia, Davide. *The Political Life of Sensation*. Durham, NC: Duke University Press, 2009.

Pasolini, Pier Paolo. "Abiura" [Repudiation]. In *Trilogia della vita*. Milan: Garzanti, 1995.

——. *Ecrits corsairs*. Translated by Philippe Guilhon. Paris: Flammarion, 1976.

——. *Heretical Empiricism*. Edited by Louise K. Barnett. Translated by Ben Lawton and Louise K. Barnett. Washington, DC: New Academia, 2005.

——. *Le nuova gioventù*. Turin: Einaudi, 1975.

——. *Poesie a Casarsa*. Bologna: Libreria Antiquaria Mario Landi, 1942.

——. "La scomparsa delle luciole." In *Scritti corsari: Gli interventi più discussi di un testimone provocatorio*. Milan: Garzanti, 1975.

Patten, Alan. *Hegel's Idea of Freedom*. Oxford: Oxford University Press, 1999.

Pinkard, Terry. *Hegel: A Biography*. Cambridge: Cambridge University Press, 2000.

Pippin, Robert. "The Absence of Aesthetics in Hegel's Aesthetics." In *The Cambridge Companion to Hegel and Nineteenth-Century Philosophy*, edited by Frederick Beiser. Cambridge: Cambridge University Press, 2008.

——. "Responses to Conway, Mooney and Rorty." *Inquiry* 45 (2002): 359–72.

Plato. *Complete Works*. Edited by John M. Cooper. Indianapolis, IN: Hackett, 1997.

——. *Gorgias*. Translated by W. D. Woodhead. In *The Collected Dialogues of Plato*, edited by E. Hamilton and H. Cairns. Princeton, NJ: Princeton University Press, 1961.

——. *Omnia diuini Platonis opera*. Translated by Marsilij Ficini. Basel: Apud Hier. Frobenium et Nic. Episcopium, 1551.

——. *Plato IX: Laws*. Edited by E. Caps, D. T. E. Page, and W. H. D. Rouse. Translated by R. G. Bury. New York: G. P. Putnam's Son, 1926.

Poe, Edgar Allan. "The Facts in the Case of M. Valdemar." In *The Complete Stories and Poems of Edgar Allan Poe*. New York: Doubleday, 1966.

Potter, Tim. "The Italian Election." *International Socialism* 1st series (1976): 7–8.

Pradeau, Jean-François. *Plato and the City: A New Introduction to Plato's Political Thought*. Translated by Janet Lloyd. Exeter, U.K.: University of Exeter Press, 2002.

Prigogine, Ilya. *The End of Certainty: Time, Chaos, and the New Laws of Nature*. New York: Free Press, 1997.

Protevi, John. *Political Affect: Connecting the Social and the Somatic*. Minneapolis: University of Minnesota Press, 2009.

——. *Political Physics: Deleuze, Derrida, and the Body Politic*. London: Bloomsbury, 2001.

Puchner, Martin. *The Drama of Ideas: Platonic Provocations in Theater and Philosophy*. Oxford: Oxford University Press, 2010

Quine, Willard van Ornam. *Ontological Relativity*. New York: Columbia University Press, 1977.

Rabinow, Paul. Introduction to *A Vital Rationalist: Selected Writings from Georges Canguilhem*, edited by François Delaport and translated by Arthur Goldhammer. New York: Zone, 2000.

Rajan, Kaushik Sunder. *Biocapital: The Constitution of Postgenomic Life*. Durham, NC: Duke University Press, 2006.

Ramond, Charles, ed. *Alain Badiou: Penser le multiple*. Paris: L'Harmattan, 2002.

Rancière, Jacques. *Aesthetics and Its Discontents*. Translated by Steven Corcoran. Cambridge: Polity, 2010.

———. *The Aesthetic Unconscious*. Translated by Debra Keates and James Swenson. Cambridge: Polity, 2009.

———. *Disagreement: Politics and Philosophy*. Translated by Julie Rose. Minneapolis: University of Minnesota Press, 1999.

———. *Dissensus: On Politics and Aesthetics*. Edited and translated by Steven Corcoran. New York: Continuum, 2010.

———. *Film Fables*. Translated by Emiliano Battista. Oxford: Berg, 2006.

———. *On the Shores of Politics*. Translated by Liz Heron. London: Verso, 1995.

———. *The Politics of Aesthetics*. New York: Continuum, 2006.

———. "Should Democracy Come? Ethics and Politics in Derrida." In *Derrida and the Time of the Political*, edited by Pheng Chea and Suzanne Guerlac. Durham, NC: Duke University Press, 2009.

Rasch, William. *Sovereignty and Its Discontents: On the Primacy of Conflict and the Structure of the Political*. London: Birkbeck Law, 2004.

Read, Stephen. *Thinking about Logic: An Introduction to the Philosophy of Logic*. Oxford: Oxford University Press, 1995.

Rémond, René. *Les Droites en France*. Paris: Aubier-Montaigne, 1982.

Revelli, Marco. *Le due destre: Le derive politiche del post-fordismo*. Turin: Bollati Boringhieri, 1996.

———. *Sinistra Destra: L'identità smarrita*. Rome: Laterza, 2007.

Rheinberger, Hans-Jörg. *An Epistemology of the Concrete: Twentieth-Century Histories of Life*. Durham, NC: Duke University Press, 2010.

Rhodes, John David. *Stupendous, Miserable City: Pasolini's Rome*. Minneapolis: University of Minnesota Press, 2007.

Ricciardi, Alessia. "Rethinking *Salò* after Abu Ghraib." *Postmodern Culture* 21 (2011).

Riedel, Manfred. Introduction to *Materialien zu Hegels Rechtsphilosophie*, vol. 1, edited by Manfred Riedel. Frankfurt: Suhrkamp, 1975.

Riera, Gabriel, ed. *Alain Badiou: Philosophy and Its Conditions*. Albany: State University of New York Press, 2005.

Righi, Andrea. *Biopolitics and Social Change in Italy from Gramsci to Pasolini to Negri*. New York: Palgrave Macmillan, 2011.

Rilke, Rainer Maria. *Letters: 1910–1925*. Translated by Jane Bannard Greene and M. D. Herter Norton. New York: W. W. Norton, 1972.

———. *The Notebooks of Malte Laurids Brigge*. Translated by Stephen Mitchell. New York: Vintage, 1990.

Rogat, Yosal. *The Eichmann Trial and the Rule of Law*. Santa Barbara, CA: Center for the Study of Democratic Institutions, 1962.

Ronell, Avital. *Stupidity*. Urbana-Champaign: University of Illinois Press, 2003.

Rorty, Richard. "Postmodern Bourgeois Liberalism." In *Objectivity, Relativism and Truth: Philosophical Papers*, vol. 1. Cambridge: Cambridge University Press, 1991.

Rose, Nikolas. *The Politics of Life Itself: Biomedicine, Power and Subjectivity in the Twenty-First Century.* Princeton, NJ: Princeton University Press, 2007.

Roudinesco, Élizabeth. *Jacques Lacan: Outline of a Life, History of a System of Thought.* Translated by Barbara Bray. New York: Columbia University Press, 1997.

Rousseau, Jean-Jacques. *The Social Contract.* Translated by M. Cranston. New York: Penguin, 1968.

Rumble, Patrick Allen, and Bart Testa, eds. *Pier Paolo Pasolini: Contemporary Perspectives.* Toronto: University of Toronto Press, 1994.

Santambrogio, A. *Destra e sinistra: Un'analisi sociologica.* Rome: Laterza, 1998.

Santner, Eric. *My Own Private Germany: Daniel Paul Schreber's Secret History of Modernity.* Princeton, NJ: Princeton University Press, 1996.

Sartre, Jean-Paul. Preface to *The Wretched of the Earth,* by Frantz Fanon. New York: Grove, 1963.

Scheuerman, William. *Between the Norm and the Exception: The Frankfurt School and the Rule of Law.* Cambridge, MA: MIT Press, 1994.

Schlegel, Friedrich. "Critical Fragment 108." In *Philosophical Fragments,* translated by Peter Firchow. Minneapolis: University of Minnesota Press, 1991.

Schmitt, Carl. *The Crisis of Parliamentary Democracy.* Translated by Ellen Kennedy. Cambridge, MA: MIT Press, 1988.

——. *The* Nomos *of the Earth in the International Law of* Jus Publicum Europæum. Translated by G. L. Ulmen. New York: Telos, 2006.

——. *Political Romanticism.* Translated by Guy Oakes. London: MIT Press, 1986.

——. *Political Theology: Four Chapters on the Concept of Sovereignty.* Translated by G. Schwab. Cambridge, MA: MIT Press, 1985.

——. *Politische Theologie,* 7th ed. Berlin: Duncker and Humblot, 1996.

——. *Über die drei Arten des rechtswissenschaftlichen Denkens,* 2nd ed. Berlin: Duncker and Humblot, 1993.

Schnädelbach, Herbert. *Hegels praktische Philosophie: Ein Kommentar der Texte in der Reihenfolge ihrer Entstehung.* Frankfurt: Suhrkamp, 2000.

Schrödinger, Erwin. *What Is Life? With Mind and Matter and Autobiographical Sketches.* Cambridge: Cambridge University Press, 1967.

Schürmann, Reiner. *Broken Hegemonies.* Translated by Reginald Lilly. Bloomington: Indiana University Press, 2003.

——. *Heidegger on Being and Acting: From Principles to Anarchy.* Bloomington: Indiana University Press, 1997.

Sedgwick, Eve Kosofsky. *Touching Feeling: Affect, Pedagogy, Performativity.* Durham, NC: Duke University Press, 2003.

Shelley, Mary Wollstonecraft. *The Last Man.* Edited by Hugh J. Luke Jr. Lincoln: University of Nebraska Press, 2006.

Siciliano, Enzo. *Pasolini.* Translated by John Shepley. New York: Random House, 1982.

Siep, Ludwig. "Vernuftrecht und Rechtsgeschichte: Kontext und Konzept der

Grundlinien im Blick auf die *Vorrede."* In *G.W.F. Hegel, Grundlinien der Philoso-phie des Rechts,* edited by Ludwig Siep. Berlin: Akademie, 1997.

Simondon, Gilbert. "The Genesis of the Individual." In *Incorporations,* edited by Jonathan Crary and Sanford Kwinter. New York: Zone, 1992.

Sitze, Adam. *"Nous* and *Nomos* in Plato's *Laws." theory@buffalo* 14 (2010): 36–70.

Sloterdijk, Peter. *"Rules for the Human Zoo*: A Response to the *Letter on Human-ism."* Translated by Mary Rorty. *Environment and Planning D: Society and Space* 27 (2009): 12–28.

Smock, Ann. *What Is There to Say? Blanchot, Beckett, des Forêts, Melville.* Lincoln: University of Nebraska Press, 2003.

Sokal, Alan, and Jean Bricmont. *Fashionable Nonsense: Postmodern Intellectuals' Abuse of Science.* New York: Picador, 1999.

Specter, Michael. "Annals of Science: A Life of Its Own." *New Yorker,* September 28, 2009.

Spinoza, Baruch. "The Letters." In *Complete Works,* edited by Michael L. Morgan, translated by Samuel Shirley. Indianapolis, IN: Hackett, 2002.

Stack, David. *The First Darwinian Left: Socialism and Darwinism, 1859–1914.* Chel-tenham, U.K.: New Clarion Press, 2003.

Steinberger, Peter. *Logic and Politics: Hegel's Philosophy of Right.* New Haven, CT: Yale University Press, 1988.

Stengers, Isabelle. "Including Nonhumans in Political Theory: Opening Pandora's Box?" In *Political Matter: Technoscience, Democracy, and Public Life,* edited by Bruce Braun and Sarah J. Whatmore. Minneapolis: University of Minnesota Press, 2010.

Sternhell, Zeev. *Neither Right nor Left: Fascist Ideology in France.* Translated by Da-vid Maisel. Princeton, NJ: Princeton University Press, 1986.

Stove, David. *Scientific Irrationalism: Origins of a Postmodern Cult.* New Brunswick, NJ: Transaction, 2001.

Strathausen, Carsten. "Epistemological Reflections on Minor Points in Deleuze." *Theory and Event* 13, no. 4 (2010).

Strauss, Leo. *The Argument and Action of Plato's Laws.* Chicago: University of Chi-cago Press, 1975.

———. *The City and Man.* Chicago: University of Chicago Press, 1978.

———. *Jewish Philosophy and the Crisis of Modernity: Essays and Lectures in Modern Jewish Thought.* Edited by Kenneth Hart Green. Albany: State University of New York Press, 1997.

———. *Liberalism Ancient and Modern.* Chicago: University of Chicago Press, 1995.

———. *Natural Right and History.* Chicago: University of Chicago Press, 1953.

———. *On Tyranny.* Chicago: University of Chicago Press, 2000.

———. *Persecution and the Art of Writing.* Chicago: University of Chicago Press, 1988.

———. *Philosophy and Law: Contributions to the Understanding of Maimonides and His Predecessors.* Translated by Eve Adler. Albany: State University of New York Press, 1995.

———. "Plato." In *History of Political Philosophy*, edited by L. Strauss and J. Cropsey. Chicago: University of Chicago Press, 1987.

———. *The Political Philosophy of Hobbes: Its Genesis and Basis*. Translated by E. M. Sinclair. Chicago: University of Chicago Press, 1952.

———. "Preface to the English Translation." In *Spinoza's Critique of Religion*, translated by E. M. Sinclair. Chicago: University of Chicago Press, 1965.

———. *The Rebirth of Classical Political Rationalism: An Introduction to the Thought of Leo Strauss*. Chicago: University of Chicago Press, 1989.

———. *What Is Political Philosophy? And Other Studies*. Chicago: University of Chicago Press, 1988.

Tanguay, Daniel. *Leo Strauss: An Intellectual Biography*. Translated by Christopher Nadon. New Haven, CT: Yale University Press, 2007.

Thacker, Eugene. *After Life*. Chicago: University of Chicago Press, 2010.

———. *Biomedia*. Minneapolis: University of Minnesota Press, 2004.

Thucydides. *History of the Peloponnesian War*. Translated by Rex Warner. New York: Penguin, 1972.

Ulanowicz, Robert E. *A Third Window: Natural Life beyond Newton and Darwin*. West Conshohocken, PA: Templeton Foundation Press, 2009.

Viano, Maurizio. *A Certain Realism: Making Use of Pasolini's Film Theory and Practice*. Berkeley: University of California Press, 1993.

———. "The Left According to the Ashes of Gramsci." *Social Text* 18 (1987–88): 51–60.

Virno, Paolo. *Multitude: Between Innovation and Negation*. Translated by Isabella Bertoletti, James Cascaito, and Andrea Casson. Los Angeles: Semiotexte, 2008.

———. "Natural-Historical Diagrams: The 'New Global' Movement and the Biological Invariant." In *The Italian Difference: Between Nihilism and Biopolitics*, edited by Lorenzo Chiesa and Alberto Toscano. Melbourne: re.press, 2009.

Vlastos, Gregory. *Socrates: Ironist and Moral Philosopher*. Ithaca, NY: Cornell University Press, 1991.

Voegelin, Eric. *Plato*. Columbia: University of Missouri Press, 2000.

von Bertalanffy, Ludwig. *Problems of Life: An Evaluation of Modern Biological Thought*. New York: John Wiley and Sons, 1952.

Weber, Max. "Science as a Vocation." In *Max Weber: Essays in Sociology*, translated by H. Gerth and C. Mills. New York: Oxford University Press, 1977.

———. "Wissenschaft als Beruf." In *Gesammelte Aufsätze zur Wissenschaftslehre*, edited by J. Winkelmann. Tübingen: J. C. B. Mohr, 1968.

Williams, Patrick. "Edward Said: The Struggle for Humanism." *Indigo* 3 (2010): 20–29.

Williams, Robert. "Hegel on Socrates and Irony." In *Hegel's History of Philosophy: New Interpretations*, edited by D. Duquette. Albany: State University of New York Press, 2003.

Wolfe, Cary. *What Is Posthumanism?* Minneapolis: University of Minnesota Press, 2010.

Wood, Allen. *Hegel's Ethical Thought*. Cambridge: Cambridge University Press, 1990.

Xenophon. *Conversations of Socrates*. Edited and translated by Hugh Tredennick and Robin Waterfield. New York: Penguin, 1990.

Xenos, Nicholas. *Cloaked in Virtue: Unveiling Leo Strauss and the Rhetoric of American Foreign Policy*. New York: Routledge, 2008.

Žižek, Slavoj. *First as Tragedy, Then as Farce*. London: Verso, 2009.

——. *The Sublime Object of Ideology*. London: Verso, 1989.

——. *The Ticklish Subject: The Absent Center of Political Ontology*. London: Verso, 1999.

JUDITH BUTLER is Maxine Elliot Professor in the Department of Comparative Literature and the Program of Critical Theory at the University of California,
Berkeley. She is the author of numerous books, including *The Psychic Life of Power*,
Precarious Life, *Frames of War*, and, most recently, *Notes toward a Performative Theory of Assembly*. Some of her political essays have lately been brought together under
the title *Senses of the Subject*.

GEORGE EDMONDSON is associate professor of English at Dartmouth College.
He is the author of *The Neighboring Text: Chaucer, Boccaccio, Henryson*.

ROBERTO ESPOSITO is professor of philosophy at the Italian Institute for Human Sciences, Naples. He is the author of numerous books, including *Communitas*,
Immunitas, *Bios: Biopolitics and Philosophy*, *Living Thought*, *Third Person*, *Categories
of the Impolitical*, and *Terms of the Political*.

CARLO GALLI is professor of history, culture, and civilization at the University
of Bologna. He is the author of numerous books and essays, including *Political
Spaces and Global War* and *Janus's Gaze: Essays on Carl Schmitt*, and serves as the
editor in chief of the journal *Filosfia Politica*. He has been a member of the Italian
Parliament since 2013.

KLAUS MLADEK is associate professor of German studies and comparative literature at Dartmouth College. He is the editor of *Police Forces: A Cultural History of
an Institution* and the author of *Stages of Justice* (forthcoming).

ALBERTO MOREIRAS is professor of Hispanic studies at Texas A&M University.
He is the author of numerous books and articles, including *The Exhaustion of Difference*, *Línea de Sombra: El no sujeto de lo político*, and *Tercer espacio: Duelo y literature
en América Latina*, the English translations of which are both forthcoming from
Duke University Press. In addition, he serves as coeditor of *Journal of Spanish Cultural Studies* and *Res publica*.

ANDREW NORRIS is associate professor of political science and affiliated professor of philosophy at the University of California, Santa Barbara. He is the author of numerous articles and the editor or coeditor of *Truth and Democracy*, *The Claim to Community: Essays on Stanley Cavell and Political Philosophy*, and *Politics, Metaphysics and Death: Essays on Giorgio Agamben's* Homo Sacer. He is currently at work on a book, *Publicity and Partiality: Stanley Cavell on the Political*.

ERIC L. SANTNER is the Philip and Ida Romberg Distinguished Service Professor in Modern Germanic Studies at the University of Chicago. He is the author or coauthor of numerous books, including *The Psychotheology of Everyday Life*, *On Creaturely Life*, and, most recently, *The Royal Remains: The King's Two Bodies and the Endgames of Sovereignty*.

ADAM SITZE is associate professor of law, jurisprudence, and social thought at Amherst College. He is the author of *The Impossible Machine: A Genealogy of South Africa's Truth and Reconciliation Commission* and the editor of four works of contemporary Italian political theory, including Galli's *Political Spaces and Global War* and *Janus's Gaze: Essays on Carl Schmitt*.

CARSTEN STRATHAUSEN is professor of German and English and holds the Catherine Paine Middlebush Chair in Humanities at the University of Missouri. He is the author of *The Look of Things: Poetry and Vision around 1900*, the editor of *A Leftist Ontology*, and the translator of Boris Groys's *Under Suspicion: A Phenomenology of Media*, for which he also wrote the introduction.

REI TERADA is professor of comparative literature at the University of California, Irvine. She is the author of numerous books and articles, including *Feeling in Theory* and *Looking Away*, and is winner of the René Wellek Prize.

CARY WOLFE is Bruce and Elizabeth Dunlevie Professor of English and director of 3CT: Center for Critical and Cultural Theory at Rice University. He is the author or editor of numerous books, including *Animal Rites: American Culture, the Discourse of Species, and Posthumanist Theory*; *Zoontologies: The Question of the Animal*; *What Is Posthumanism?*; and *Before the Law: Humans and Other Animals in a Biopolitical Frame*.

Habermas, Jürgen, 76, 306

Hacking, Ian, 300, 313n35

Hadot, Pierre, 269n60

Hägglund, Martin, 8, 138–39, 141, 280, 285–86, 288, 289n44

Hallward, Peter, 300–301

Hamlet (Shakespeare), 4

Hanafi, Zakia, 63–99

Haraway, Donna, 276

Hardimon, Michael, 249

Hardt, Michael, 5, 22, 125–26, 131, 133, 138, 308

haunting, 135, 162, 206, 211–12

Hayek, Friedrich, 83, 87, 193n2

Hegel, G. W. F., 8, 22–23, 39–40, 49–50, 71, 106, 129–30, 158, 228, 239–40, 246–60

hegemony, 82, 93–97, 135, 139, 160–61, 270n68

Heidegger, Martin, 22–23, 83–85, 113–15, 122–23, 132–33, 196n39, 284–85, 294

Heisenberg, Werner, 303–5

Hewitt, Andrew, 167n22

History of Sexuality (Foucault), 17n17, 308

Hitler, Adolf, 70, 193n2, 309

Hobbes, Thomas, 11, 15, 68, 74, 89, 104, 106–10, 116, 123–26, 214, 250, 277, 306, 309

Holocaust, the, 162–63, 220–21, 224–26, 230, 237, 275–77

Homo Ludens (Huizinga), 180

Homo Sacer (Agamben), 243

Honneth, Axel, 271n76

Horkheimer, Max, 125

hospitality, 6, 139–42

Huizinga, Johann, 180

Human Condition, The (Arendt), 236–37

humanism: animality and, 1–2, 8, 21, 121–23, 205–6, 237, 273–91; natural history and, 21–24; posthumanism and, 292–93, 295–96; technology and, 27, 35, 64, 79, 90–97, 113, 118, 132–33,

149, 272, 282, 307. *See also* biopolitics; Enlightenment; law, the; politics; subjectivity

human rights. *See* rights talk; subjectivity

Hume, David, 257

Husserl, Edmund, 284, 302, 305

Idea, the, 130, 142n12, 173–200

Ilting, K. H., 262

immanence, 92, 113–17, 119, 247

Immunitas (Esposito), 107, 109, 119

immunitas (term), 8–9, 101, 106–12, 114–15, 117, 122, 276–77, 281, 287–88, 309–10

impersonal, 4–5, 101, 118–23

impolitical, 4, 15, 84, 100–107, 112–13, 159–60

individuation, 115–17, 234, 281, 297, 305–11

Intellighenzia, 103

investiture, 7, 201–19

irony, 8, 247–48, 251, 253–55, 258–60, 264, 270n68

Islam, 89, 91

Italy, 6, 12, 64, 66–67, 82, 89–95, 147, 149–50, 156–57, 161–62

Jacobins, 71, 209–10

Jameson, Fredric, 294

Jaspers, Karl, 227

judgment, 3, 221–23, 225–29, 232–36, 240–48, 254–56

July Revolution, 69

justice, 73, 76, 141, 161–62. *See also* Arendt, Hannah; ethics; law, the

Kafka, Franz, 4, 48–55, 168n31, 201–3, 216, 218n3

Kant, Immanuel, 4, 24–39, 56n13, 68, 74, 107, 113, 160–61, 175, 221–23, 246–48, 250, 252, 279

Kantorowicz, Ernst, 7, 207

Keller, Evelyn Fox, 294, 304

Kierkegaard, Søren, 253